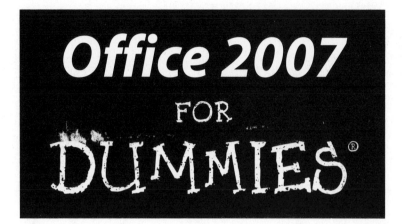

Office 2007 FOR DUMMIES®

by Wallace Wang

BICENTENNIAL
1807
WILEY
2007
BICENTENNIAL

Wiley Publishing, Inc.

Office 2007 For Dummies®

Published by
Wiley Publishing, Inc.
111 River Street
Hoboken, NJ 07030-5774
www.wiley.com

Copyright © 2007 by Wiley Publishing, Inc., Indianapolis, Indiana

Published by Wiley Publishing, Inc., Indianapolis, Indiana

Published simultaneously in Canada

For general information on our other products and services, please contact our Customer Care Department within the U.S. at 800-762-2974, outside the U.S. at 317-572-3993, or fax 317-572-4002.

For technical support, please visit www.wiley.com/techsupport.

Wiley also publishes its books in a variety of electronic formats. Some content that appears in print may not be available in electronic books.

Library of Congress Control Number: 2006934817

ISBN-13: 978-0-470-00923-9

ISBN-10: 0-470-00923-3

Manufactured in the United States of America

10 9 8 7

1B/RV/QU/QX/IN

WILEY

About the Author

The author currently divides his time between writing computer books, writing articles for *CPU Magazine*, performing stand-up comedy, and writing and speaking on a weekly comedy radio show along with fellow comedians Rick Gene, Wes Sample, and Justin Davis. The show airs on 103.7 Free FM in San Diego (`http://1037freefm.com`).

He also spends much of his time trying to keep his various computers running properly using an odd mixture of Windows, Linux, and Mac OS X software. Eventually, he hopes to find the elusive combination of hardware and software that can create the mythical dream of a computer that actually works when you want it to.

Dedication

This book is dedicated to a variety of people, including the following:

All the long-suffering victims forced to learn the arcane features of Microsoft Office, which seem to change with every version, not always for the best. Take heart. You're not stupid — it's the people who write, sell, and encourage the clumsy and complicated computer programs on the market who are the really stupid ones.

All the friendly folks at the Riviera Comedy Club, located at the Riviera Hotel & Casino (www.theriviera.com) in Las Vegas: Steve Schirripa (who appears in HBO's hit show, *The Sopranos*), Don Learned, Bob Zany (www.bobzany.com), Gerry Bednob, Russ Rivas, Bruce Clark, Darrell Joyce, and Kip Addotta.

Additional thanks must also go to Chris (the Zooman) Clobber, Dante, Rick Gene, Wes Sample, Justin Davis, and Leo (the man, the myth, the legend) Fontaine just because they like seeing their names in print for no apparent reason.

Continuing the theme of thanking people who had nothing to do with this book, the author would also like to dedicate this book to LeStat's, the best little coffeehouse in San Diego, for providing a warm, friendly environment to practice stand-up comedy in the safety and comfort of intelligent people who haven't drowned their inhibitions away in alcohol.

Final thanks go to Cassandra (my wife), Jordan (my son), and Bo, Scraps, Tasha, and Nuit (our cats) for making my life more interesting by the minute.

Author's Acknowledgments

Margot Hutchison and Bill Gladstone at Waterside Productions deserve special acknowledgment because if it weren't for their work, I might never have been hired to write this book; and you would be reading some other author's acknowledgments and dedication. These two are the best agents an author could hope for, so they deserve all the 15 percent of the book royalties that they get.

Some other people who deserve thanks include Bob Woerner, acquisitions editor; Jean Rogers, project editor; and Teresa Artman, copy editor; and the rest of the happy gang of editors, managers, and workers who make Wiley Publishing the best publisher to work for because they're the complete opposite of their competition.

Additional thanks go to technical editor Lee Musick for making sure that everything in this book is accurate.

A final note of thanks go to anyone who has actually read the About the Author, Dedication, and Author's Acknowledgments pages because those pages usually contain useless information that nobody except the author and his closest friends even care about. Thanks for reading this — and say a prayer for all the trees that sacrificed their pulp to allow authors (such as myself) the indulgence to print paragraphs such as this.

Publisher's Acknowledgments

We're proud of this book; please send us your comments through our online registration form located at www.dummies.com/register/.

Some of the people who helped bring this book to market include the following:

Acquisitions, Editorial, and Media Development

Associate Project Editor: Jean Rogers

Acquisitions Editor: Bob Woerner

Senior Copy Editor: Teresa Artman

Technical Editor: Lee Musick

Editorial Manager: Kevin Kirschner

Media Development Specialists: Angela Denny, Kate Jenkins, Steven Kudirka, Kit Malone

Media Development Coordinator: Laura Atkinson

Media Project Supervisor: Laura Moss

Media Development Manager: Laura VanWinkle

Media Development Associate Producer: Richard Graves

Editorial Assistant: Amanda Foxworth

Sr. Editorial Assistant: Cherie Case

Cartoons: Rich Tennant (www.the5thwave.com)

Composition

Project Coordinator: Kristie Rees

Layout and Graphics: Jonelle Burns, Lavonne Cook, Denny Hager, Joyce Haughey, Barbara Moore, Barry Offringa, Heather Ryan

Proofreaders: David Faust, Techbooks

Indexer: Techbooks

Anniversary Logo Design: Richard Pacifico

Publishing and Editorial for Technology Dummies

    Richard Swadley, Vice President and Executive Group Publisher

    Andy Cummings, Vice President and Publisher

    Mary Bednarek, Executive Acquisitions Director

    Mary C. Corder, Editorial Director

Publishing for Consumer Dummies

    Diane Graves Steele, Vice President and Publisher

    Joyce Pepple, Acquisitions Director

Composition Services

    Gerry Fahey, Vice President of Production Services

    Debbie Stailey, Director of Composition Services

Contents at a Glance

Introduction *1*

Part I: Getting to Know Microsoft Office 2007.................*7*

Chapter 1: Getting to Know Microsoft Office 2007..9

Chapter 2: Editing Data...29

Chapter 3: Getting Help from Office 2007...43

Part II: Working with Word *51*

Chapter 4: Typing Text in Word..53

Chapter 5: Formatting Text...71

Chapter 6: Designing Your Pages...91

Part III: Playing the Numbers with Excel....................*125*

Chapter 7: The Basics of Spreadsheets: Numbers, Labels, and Formulas.............127

Chapter 8: Playing with Formulas..159

Chapter 9: Charting and Analyzing Data...181

Part IV: Making Presentations with PowerPoint..........*203*

Chapter 10: Creating a PowerPoint Presentation...205

Chapter 11: Adding Color and Pictures to a Presentation......................................221

Chapter 12: Showing Off a Presentation..241

Part V: Getting Organized with Outlook.......................*259*

Chapter 13: Organizing E-Mail with Outlook...261

Chapter 14: Storing Contacts and Organizing Tasks...287

Chapter 15: Scheduling Your Time...301

Part VI: Storing Stuff in Access *309*

Chapter 16: Using a Database...311

Chapter 17: Searching, Sorting, and Querying a Database......................................331

Chapter 18: Creating a Database Report...353

Part VII: The Part of Tens..*368*

Chapter 19: Ten Tips for Using Office 2007...369

Chapter 20: Ten Keystroke Shortcuts for Office 2007..379

Index *387*

Table of Contents

Introduction 1
    Who Should Buy This Book 1
    How This Book Is Organized...1
        Part I: Getting to Know Microsoft Office 2007 2
        Part II: Working with Word 2
        Part III: Playing the Numbers with Excel 2
        Part IV: Making Presentations with PowerPoint.................2
        Part V: Getting Organized with Outlook 3
        Part VI: Storing Stuff in Access 3
        Part VII: The Part of Tens 3
    How to Use This Book 3
        Conventions 4
    Icons Used in This Book...4
    Getting Started 5

Part I: Getting to Know Microsoft Office 2007 7

    Chapter 1: Getting to Know Microsoft Office 2007 9
        Loading an Office 2007 Program 10
        Getting to Know the New User Interface...............................11
            The File menu 12
            Using the Quick Access toolbar 19
            Using the Ribbon 23
        Customizing an Office 2007 Program...................................26
        Exiting Office 2007...27

    Chapter 2: Editing Data 29
        Adding Data by Pointing..29
        Selecting Data 31
            Selecting data with the mouse.......................................31
            Selecting data with the keyboard 33
            Selecting multiple chunks of data
                with the mouse and keyboard..................................34
        Editing Data with the Pop-up Toolbar 34
        Deleting Data..35
        Cutting and Pasting (Moving) Data......................................36
        Copying and Pasting Data 37

Dragging with the Mouse to Cut, Copy, and Paste....................................37
Undo and Redo...38
Sharing Data with Other Office 2007 Programs.............................39
Using the Office Clipboard 40
Viewing and pasting items off the Office Clipboard......................40
Deleting items from the Office Clipboard....................................41

Chapter 3: Getting Help from Office 2007 ....**43**
Browsing the Help Window...43
Searching in the Help Window 45
Making the Help Window Easier to Read 46
Resizing the Help window 46
Enlarging the text in the Help window...47
Keeping the Help window visible at all times 48
Printing the text in the Help window 48
Viewing the Table of Contents 48

Part II: Working with Word..*51*

Chapter 4: Typing Text in Word **53**
Moving the Cursor with the Mouse 53
Moving the Cursor with the Keyboard............................54
Viewing a Document 55
Switching between views 56
Using Full Screen Reading view 57
Using Outline view 58
Navigating through a Document 62
Navigating with the mouse...62
Using the Go To command 63
Finding and Replacing Text..64
Using the Find command...64
Using the Find and Replace command 66
Checking Your Spelling..66
Checking Your Grammar..68
Proofreading Your Document 68
Typing Symbols 69

Chapter 5: Formatting Text **71**
Changing the Font 72
Changing the Font Size 73
Changing the Text Style..74
Changing Colors 75
Changing the color of text...75
Highlighting text 76
Justifying Text Alignment...76

Adjusting Line Spacing 77
Making Lists 78
    Indenting list items...79
    Converting list items back into text.............................79
    Customizing a list 80
    Renumbering numbered lists..80
Using the Ruler 82
    Adjusting left and right paragraph margins.................83
    Defining indentation with the Ruler 84
Showing Formatting Marks 84
Using Format Painter 86
Using Styles..87
Using Templates 88
    Creating a new document from a template..................88
    Creating a document based on an existing document 89
Removing Formatting from Text 89

Chapter 6: Designing Your Pages **91**
Inserting New Pages..91
Adding (And Deleting) a Cover Page 92
Inserting Page Breaks 93
Inserting Headers and Footers 93
    Creating a header (or footer)..93
    Defining which pages to display a header (or footer) 94
    Deleting a header (or footer) 95
Organizing Text in Tables...96
    Creating a table by highlighting rows and columns 96
    Creating a table with the Insert Table dialog box 97
    Creating a table with the mouse..................................98
    Creating a table from existing text 99
Formatting and Coloring a Table......................................102
    Selecting all or part of a table...................................102
    Aligning text in a table cell.......................................103
    Coloring all or part of a table....................................104
    Adding borders 104
    Picking a table style 106
    Resizing columns and rows..107
    Defining cell margins..108
    Defining cell spacing 109
    Splitting (and merging) cells......................................110
Sorting a Table..111
Deleting Tables 112
    Deleting an entire table..112
    Deleting rows and columns...113
    Deleting cells 114
    Deleting cell borders..115

Making Text Look Artistic 115
  Creating drop caps 115
  Creating WordArt...116
Dividing Text into Columns..118
  Editing columns 118
  Removing columns 120
Previewing a Document before Printing..120
  Defining page size and orientation.......................................120
  Using Print Preview 122
  Printing 123

Part III: Playing the Numbers with Excel 125

Chapter 7: The Basics of Spreadsheets: Numbers, Labels, and Formulas 127

Understanding Spreadsheets..127
Storing Stuff in a Spreadsheet 128
  Typing data into a single cell 128
  Typing data in multiple cells 129
  Typing in sequences with AutoFill 130
Formatting Numbers and Labels...131
  Formatting numbers 131
  Formatting cells 134
Navigating a Spreadsheet...138
  Using the mouse to move around in a spreadsheet 138
  Using the keyboard to move around a spreadsheet.............138
  Naming cells 140
Searching a Spreadsheet 142
  Searching for text 142
  Searching for formulas...143
Editing a Spreadsheet...144
  Editing data in a cell..144
  Changing the size of rows and columns with the mouse.............144
  Typing the size of rows and columns 145
  Adding and deleting rows and columns 146
  Adding sheets 146
  Renaming sheets 146
  Rearranging sheets...148
  Deleting a sheet 148
Clearing Data 148
Printing Workbooks...149
  Using Page Layout view 150
  Adding a header (or footer) 151
  Printing gridlines 152
  Defining a print area..152

Inserting (and removing) page breaks 153
Printing row and column headings 155
Defining printing margins 156
Defining paper orientation and size 156
Printing in Excel 158

Chapter 8: Playing with Formulas **159**

Creating a Formula 159
    Organizing formulas with parentheses 162
    Copying formulas 163
Using Functions 164
    Using the AutoSum command 166
    Using recently used functions 167
Editing a Formula 168
Goal Seeking 168
Creating Multiple Scenarios 170
    Creating a scenario 170
    Viewing a scenario 172
    Editing a scenario 173
    Viewing a scenario summary 174
Auditing Your Formulas 175
    Finding where a formula gets its data 176
    Finding which formula(s) a cell can change 176
Data Validation 177

Chapter 9: Charting and Analyzing Data **181**

Understanding the Parts of a Chart 181
Creating a Chart 184
Editing a Chart 185
    Moving a chart on a worksheet 185
    Moving a chart to a new sheet 186
    Resizing a chart 187
Using the Chart Tools 187
    Changing the chart type 188
    Changing the data source 189
    Switching rows and columns 189
    Changing the parts of a chart 190
    Designing the layout of a chart 191
    Deleting a chart 192
Organizing Lists in Pivot Tables 192
    Creating a pivot table 193
    Rearranging labels in a pivot table 196
    Modifying a pivot table 197
    Filtering a pivot table 199
    Summing a pivot table 201

Part IV: Making Presentations with PowerPoint...........203

Chapter 10: Creating a PowerPoint Presentation 205
Defining the Purpose of Your Presentation 205
Creating a PowerPoint Presentation...206
    Designing a presentation with Slide view.......................................208
    Designing a presentation with Outline view 210
Working with Text 213
    Typing text in a text box...213
    Formatting text 214
    Aligning text 215
    Adjusting line spacing...216
    Making numbered and bullet lists..217
    Making columns...218
    Moving and resizing a text box...219
    Rotating a text box 220

Chapter 11: Adding Color and Pictures to a Presentation 221
Applying a Theme 221
Changing the Background...224
    Choosing a solid color background 224
    Choosing a gradient background 226
    Choosing a picture background 228
Adding Graphics to a Slide...229
    Placing picture files on a slide 230
    Placing clip art on a slide 230
    Creating WordArt...232
    Resizing, moving, and deleting graphic images..............................232
    Rotating graphics 233
    Layering objects 234
Adding Movies to a Slide..235
    Adding an animated cartoon to a slide 235
    Adding a movie to a slide 235
Adding Sound to a Slide 237
    Adding an audio file to a presentation 238
    Adding an audio clip to a presentation 239
    Adding a CD audio track to a presentation.....................................239

Chapter 12: Showing Off a Presentation 241
Spell-Checking Your Presentation...241
Adding Visual Transitions...242
    Adding slide transitions 243
    Text transitions..245

Adding Hyperlinks...246
    Creating Web page hyperlinks 246
    Creating hyperlinks to external files 247
    Creating hyperlinks to different slides 247
    Running a program through a hyperlink.........................249
Viewing a Presentation 250
    Creating a custom slide show.....................................251
    Hiding a slide 252
    Organizing with Slide Sorter view 253
    Timing yourself 254
Creating Handouts 256
Packing Presentations to Go...257

Part V: Getting Organized with Outlook 259

Chapter 13: Organizing E-Mail with Outlook 261

Configuring E-Mail Settings 261
    Adding an e-mail account 265
    Deleting an e-mail account 266
    Editing an e-mail account 266
Creating E-Mail..267
    Creating a new e-mail message....................................267
    Replying to an e-mail message.....................................269
    Using a stored e-mail address to create a new e-mail message....270
    Forwarding an e-mail message 271
Attaching Files to Messages..272
    Attaching a file to a message 272
    Attaching Outlook information to another message 273
Formatting E-Mail 274
    Formatting text 274
    Adding signatures to your messages 275
Reading and Organizing E-Mail...279
    Categorizing messages 279
    Retrieving a file attachment from a message.................282
Deleting E-Mail Messages 284

Chapter 14: Storing Contacts and Organizing Tasks 287

Storing Contact Information 287
Searching Contact Information..289
Viewing and Printing Contact Information 290
Categorizing Contact Information..291
    Creating categories 292
    Storing names in categories..293
    Viewing names by categories......................................294

Sharing Contact Information 294
Defining Tasks..295
    Creating a task 296
    Editing a task..297
    Organizing and viewing your tasks 298
    Finishing a task 299
    Deleting a task..299

Chapter 15: Scheduling Your Time 301
Setting Appointments 301
    Making a new appointment 301
    Editing an appointment 304
    Deleting an appointment 305
    Defining a recurring appointment 305
    Editing a recurring appointment 306
Printing Your Schedule...307

Part VI: Storing Stuff in Access 309

Chapter 16: Using a Database 311
Understanding the Basics of a Database........................312
Designing a Database...313
    Creating a database from scratch 314
    Creating a database from a template 316
Editing and Modifying a Database 317
    Naming a field 317
    Adding and deleting a field 317
    Defining the type and size of a field 318
Typing Data into a Database...321
    Using Datasheet view...321
    Using Form view 322
    Creating a form 322
    Viewing and editing data in a form.......................323
    Editing a form..324
Closing and Saving a Database..328
    Closing a database table...328
    Closing a database file 329

Chapter 17: Searching, Sorting, and Querying a Database 331
Searching a Database...332
    Searching for a specific record 332
    Filtering a database...333
Sorting a Database 339

Querying a Database..340
  Creating a simple query...340
  Creating a crosstab query...343
  Creating a query that finds duplicate field data............346
  Creating an unmatched query 348
  Viewing and deleting queries...350

Chapter 18: Creating a Database Report 353

Using the Report Wizard 353
Viewing and Printing a Report...357
Manipulating the Data in a Report.......................................359
  Counting records or values...360
  Sorting a field 361
  Filtering a field 362
Editing a Report...363
  Resizing fields 364
  Deleting fields 365
Deleting a Report 366

Part VII: The Part of Tens................................*367*

Chapter 19: Ten Tips for Using Office 2007 369

Saving Office 2007 Files 369
Password-Protecting Your Files...370
Guarding Against Macro Viruses and Worms....................371
Create Your Own Word Keystroke Shortcuts 372
Zooming In (And Out) to Avoid Eyestrain...........................373
When in Doubt, Right-Click the Mouse...............................374
Freezing Row and Column Headings in Excel.....................374
Displaying Slides Out of Order in PowerPoint...................375
Reduce Spam in Outlook...375
  Setting up Outlook's junk e-mail filter............................375
  Creating a Safe Senders list 377
  Creating a Blocked Senders list 378
Using Pocket Office 378

Chapter 20: Ten Keystroke Shortcuts for Office 2007 379

Protecting Yourself with Undo (Ctrl+Z) and Redo (Ctrl+Y)...379
Cut (Ctrl+X), Copy (Ctrl+C), and Paste (Ctrl+V) 380
  Using the Cut and Paste commands 380
  Using the Copy and Paste commands 381
  Using the Paste command with the Office Clipboard....381
Saving a File (Ctrl+S)..382

Printing a File (Ctrl+P) 382
Checking Your Spelling (F7) 382
Opening a File (Ctrl+O) 383
Creating a New File (Ctrl+N) 384
Finding Text (Ctrl+F) 384
Finding and Replacing Text (Ctrl+H) 385
Closing a Window (Ctrl+W) 386

Index *387*

Introduction

● ●

Microsoft Office 2007 contains loads of new features. Unfortunately, finding — let alone using — these new features can be troublesome. So, with Office 2007, Microsoft added its most important feature ever — making the programs easier to use.

Office 2007's biggest change is its new user interface. If you're familiar with the more traditional pull-down menus and toolbar icons from previous editions of Microsoft Office, you'll soon find that this latest version of Microsoft Office is designed to help you make the most out of Word, Excel, PowerPoint, Access, and Outlook so you can find the features you need and use them right away.

Who Should Buy This Book

This book is targeted toward two distinct groups. First, there are the people already familiar with Microsoft Office who want to bone up on the new ways that Office 2007 works. For these people, this book can serve as a handy reference to finding where Microsoft put various commands in the new Office 2007 user interface.

Then there's a second group of people who may not be familiar with any Microsoft Office program at all. For these people, this book can serve as a guide through word processing (Microsoft Word), number calculations (Microsoft Excel), presentations (Microsoft PowerPoint), database management (Microsoft Access), and managing your personal resources like time, appointments, and e-mail (Microsoft Outlook).

No matter how much (or how little) you may know about Microsoft Office, this book introduces you to the most common features so you can start being productive with Office 2007 right away.

How This Book Is Organized

To help you find what you need, this book is organized into parts where each part covers a different program in Office 2007.

Part I: Getting to Know Microsoft Office 2007

Microsoft Office 2007 may look confusing at first glance, but after you understand how it works, you'll find that it's surprisingly easy to use. This part of the book explains the new Office menus and toolbars while also showing you common commands that you can use in any Office 2007 program. By the time you finish this part of the book, you'll better understand how to use the individual programs that make up the rest of Office 2007.

Part II: Working with Word

Word processing is the most popular use for Office 2007, so this part of the book explains the basics to using Word. Not only does this part of the book explain how to create and save text, but it also covers different ways to alter text, such as using color, changing fonts, adding headers and footers, checking spelling and grammar, and printing your written masterpiece so it looks perfect.

Part III: Playing the Numbers with Excel

If you need to manipulate numbers, you need Microsoft Excel. This part of the book explains the three basic parts of any spreadsheet, how to format data, how to create formulas, and how to create different types of charts to help you visualize what your spreadsheet numbers really mean. Not only will this part of the book give you the lowdown on spreadsheets, but it shows you how Microsoft Excel can make creating, formatting, and displaying spreadsheets simple and easy — and most importantly, useful and fun.

Part IV: Making Presentations with PowerPoint

Throw away your overhead transparencies and clumsy whiteboard and pads of paper. If you need to give a presentation to a large group, you need to know how to create colorful and visually interesting presentations using PowerPoint instead. With PowerPoint, you can organize a presentation into slides that can display text, pictures, and even animation. By mastering

PowerPoint, you can create presentations that grab an audience's attention and emphasize the points you want to make.

Part V: Getting Organized with Outlook

Almost nobody feels like they have enough time to stay organized, so this part of the book explains why and how to use Microsoft Outlook. With Outlook, you can read, sort, and write e-mail, keep track of appointments, store names and addresses of your most important contacts, and even organize your daily to-do tasks. By reading about how to use Outlook in this part of the book, you can see how to turn your computer into a personal assistant to make you more productive.

Part VI: Storing Stuff in Access

If you need to store large amounts of information, such as tracking inventories, organizing customer orders, or tracking prospective customers, you may need to use a database program like Microsoft Access. In this part of the book, you'll see how to use Access to store, retrieve, sort, and print your data in different ways. With Access able to slice and dice your information, you can better analyze your data to understand how your business really works.

Part VII: The Part of Tens

Almost every program offers multiple ways of accomplishing the same task, and Office 2007 is no exception. After you get familiar with using Office, take a peek in this part of the book to read about different types of shortcuts you can use to work with Office even faster than before. This part of the book also offers tips for using Office to make the programs even easier and more useful. By the time you get to this part of the book, you may not be an Office expert, but you'll be much more comfortable using Office — and then you'll feel comfortable exploring and experimenting with different features on your own.

How to Use This Book

Although you can just flip through this book to find the features you need, consider reading Part I of this book to discover how the new menus and toolbar icons of Office 2007 work and how they differ from previous versions of

Microsoft Office. After you understand the basics to the way Office 2007 works, you'll have a much better understanding for how each specific program works.

Conventions

To get the most from this book, you need to understand the following conventions:

- The *mouse pointer* appears as an arrow and serves two purposes. First, you use the mouse pointer to select data (text, numbers, e-mail messages, and so on) to change. Second, you use the mouse pointer to tell Office 2007 which commands you want to use to change the data you selected.

- *Clicking* means moving the mouse pointer over something on the screen (such as a menu command or a button), pressing the left mouse button once, and then letting go. Clicking tells the computer, "See what I'm pointing at? That's what I want to choose right now."

- *Double-clicking* means pointing at something with the mouse pointer and clicking the left mouse button rapidly twice.

- *Dragging* means holding down the left mouse button while moving the mouse. Dragging typically moves something from one location to another, such as moving a word from the top of a paragraph to the bottom.

- *Right-clicking* means moving the mouse pointer over something and clicking the right mouse button once. Right-clicking typically displays a shortcut menu of additional options.

In addition to understanding these terms to describe different mouse actions, you also need to understand different keystroke conventions too. When you see an instruction that reads Ctrl+P, that means to hold down the Ctrl key, press the P key, and then let go of both the Ctrl and P key at the same time.

Icons Used in This Book

Icons highlight important or useful information.

This icon highlights information that can save you time or make it easier for you to do something.

 This icon emphasizes information that can be helpful, although not crucial, when using Office 2007.

Look out! This icon highlights something dangerous that you need to avoid before making a mistake that you might not be able to recover from again.

This icon highlights interesting technical information that you can safely ignore but which might answer some questions for why Office 2007 works a certain way.

Getting Started

The best way to master anything is to jump right in and start fiddling with different commands just to see what they do and how they work. In case you're afraid of breaking your computer or wiping out important data, play around with Office 2007 on a "dummy" document filled with useless information you can afford to lose (like your boss's income tax returns).

Here's your first tip. Any time you do something in Office 2007, you can undo or take back your last command by pressing Ctrl+Z. (Just hold down the Ctrl key, press the Z key, and release both keys at the same time.) There, now that you know about the powerful Undo command, you should have a surging sense of invulnerability when using Office 2007, knowing that at any time you make a mistake, you can turn back time by pressing Ctrl+Z to undo your last command.

If you get nothing else from this book, always remember that the Ctrl+Z command can save you from yourself. See? Mastering Office 2007 is going to be easier than you think.

Part I
Getting to Know Microsoft Office 2007

"The odd thing is he always insists on using the latest version of Office."

In this part . . .

At first glance, Microsoft Office 2007 may seem a complicated beast that gobbles up megabytes of hard drive space and offers enough features to overwhelm even the most battle-hardened veteran of the personal computer wars. But after you get over your initial impression (or fear) of Office, you can understand (and even admire) the elegant madness behind its massive bulk.

Despite the fact that Microsoft Office 2007 contains more commands than any sane person could ever possibly use, it can be conquered. Perhaps the most important part of this book explains the completely redesigned user interface of Microsoft Office 2007. While this user interface may look strange and confusing at first, it's actually much easier to learn than previous incarnations of Microsoft Office. After you get familiar with this new user interface, you'll find yourself being more productive than ever before.

To guide you through the multitude of commands you may need to get your work done, Office provides several ways to get help, one of which (hopefully) will actually provide you with the answers you need.

Besides showing you how to get help within Office, this part of the book also explains how to get the various programs of Office started in the first place. After you start using Office, this part of the book also shows you some of the more common keystroke and menu commands that all Office programs share. That way when you figure out how to use one Office program, you can quickly learn and use any other Office program with a minimum of retraining and hassle, and you can then join the ranks of the many happy people already using Microsoft Office 2007 to get their work done.

Chapter 1

Getting to Know Microsoft Office 2007

In This Chapter

▶ Starting an Office 2007 program

▶ Understanding the Office 2007 user interface

▶ Using the Quick Access toolbar

▶ Customizing an Office 2007 program

▶ Exiting from Office 2007

Microsoft Office 2007 consists of five core programs: Word, Excel, PowerPoint, Access, and Outlook. Each of these core programs specializes in manipulating different data. Word manipulates words, sentences, and paragraphs; Excel manipulates numbers; PowerPoint manipulates text and pictures to create a slide show; Access manipulates data, such as inventories; and Outlook manipulates personal information, such as e-mail addresses and phone numbers.

Although each Office 2007 program specializes in storing and manipulating different types of data, they all work in similar ways. First, you have to enter data into an Office 2007 program by typing on the keyboard or loading data from an existing file. Second, you have to tell Office 2007 how to manipulate your data, such as underlining, enlarging, coloring, or deleting it. Third, you have to save your data as a file.

To help you understand this three-step process of entering, manipulating, and saving data, Office 2007 offers similar commands among all its programs so you can quickly jump from Word to PowerPoint to Excel without having to relearn entirely new commands to use each program. Even better, Office 2007 rearranges its numerous commands so finding the command you need is faster and easier than ever before. (If you think this implies that previous versions of Microsoft Office were clumsy and hard to use, you're right.)

If you're already familiar with computers and previous editions of Microsoft Office, you may want to browse through this chapter just to get acquainted with how Office 2007 rearranges common program commands. If you've never used a computer before or just don't feel comfortable using Microsoft Office, read this chapter first.

Loading an Office 2007 Program

The first step to using Office 2007 is loading the program you want to use. To load any Office 2007 program, follow these steps:

1. **Click the Start button on the Windows taskbar.**

   A pop-up menu appears.

2. **Choose All Programs.**

   Another pop-up menu appears.

3. **Choose Microsoft Office.**

   A list of programs appears on the Start menu, as shown in Figure 1-1.

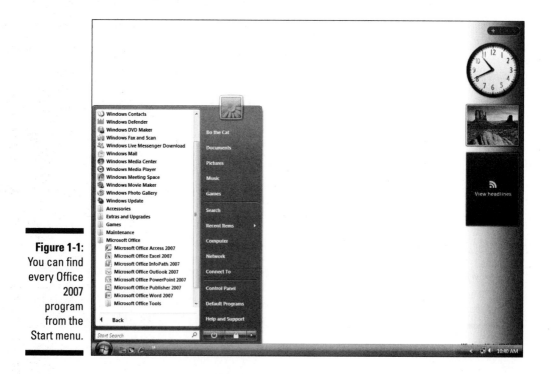

Figure 1-1: You can find every Office 2007 program from the Start menu.

4. **Choose the Office 2007 program you want to use, such as Microsoft Word or Microsoft PowerPoint.**

   Your chosen program appears on the screen.

Getting to Know the New User Interface

Office 2007 offers a new user interface for Word, Excel, PowerPoint, Access, and some parts of Outlook. This new user interface consists of three parts, as shown in Figure 1-2:

- Office Button
- Quick Access toolbar
- Ribbon

Office Button

Quick Access toolbar

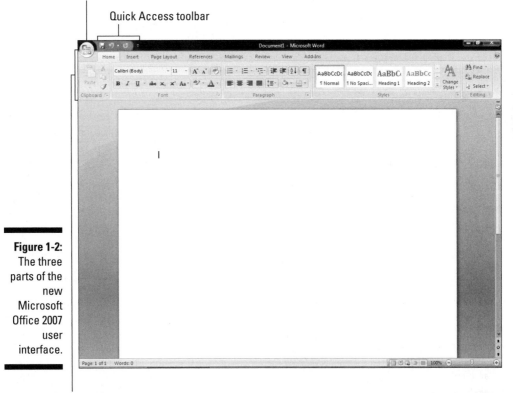

Figure 1-2:
The three parts of the new Microsoft Office 2007 user interface.

Ribbon

The File menu

The File menu contains commands for opening, saving, printing, and closing a file. In Word, a file is called a *document.* In Excel, a file is called a *workbook.* In PowerPoint, a file is called a *presentation.* In Access, a file is called a *database.*

In previous versions of Office, the File menu was clearly labeled File. In Office 2007, the File menu appears when you click the Office Button in the upper-left corner (refer to Figure 1-2).

You can display the File menu by clicking the Office Button or by pressing Alt+F.

Creating a new file

When you first load an Office 2007 program, it automatically creates an empty file for you to use right away. In case you need to create a new file after you've already loaded an Office 2007 program, follow these steps:

1. **Click the Office Button.**

   A drop-down menu appears, as shown in Figure 1-3.

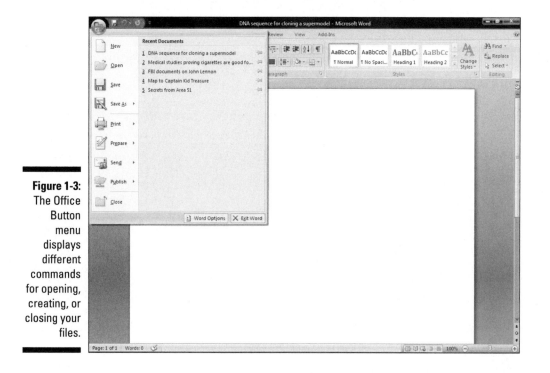

Figure 1-3:
The Office Button menu displays different commands for opening, creating, or closing your files.

2. Choose New.

A New dialog box appears, as shown in Figure 1-4. Depending on which program you're using, the dialog box may read New Document (for Word), New Workbook (for Excel), and so on.

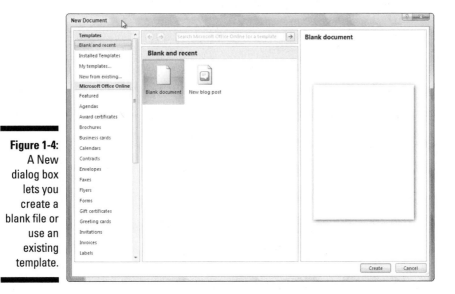

Figure 1-4:
A New dialog box lets you create a blank file or use an existing template.

3. Click Blank (such as Blank Document or Blank Workbook) and then click the Create button.

Depending on which program you're using, you may choose Blank Document for Word or Blank Presentation for PowerPoint. A blank file appears ready for you to start storing data in it.

Creating a new file from a template

Rather than create a blank file, you may find it easier to use a template instead. A *template* contains predefined formatting for creating different types of files easily, such as calendars, newsletters, sales reports, or a corporate slide show presentation. Office 2007 provides three types of templates:

✔ Office 2007 templates installed on your computer

✔ Templates available over the Internet on the Microsoft Web site

✔ Existing files that you create and format yourself

Using an Office 2007 template on your computer

Installing Office 2007 automatically installs dozens of templates for Word, Excel, PowerPoint, and Access. To use one of these templates, follow these steps:

1. **Click the Office Button and choose New.**

   A New window appears (refer to Figure 1-4).

2. **Click Installed Templates.**

   The New window displays all the installed templates on your computer.

3. **Click the template you want to use and then click the Create button.**

   Office 2007 creates a new file based on your chosen template.

Downloading and using a template off Microsoft's Web site

Microsoft provides a huge library of templates that you can download from its Web site. To retrieve these templates, you need to connect to the Internet and then follow these steps:

1. **Click the Office Button and then choose New.**

   A New window appears (refer to Figure 1-4).

2. **Click a category underneath Microsoft Office Online, such as Calendars or Award Certificates.**

   The New window displays all the templates available from the Microsoft Web site, as shown in Figure 1-5.

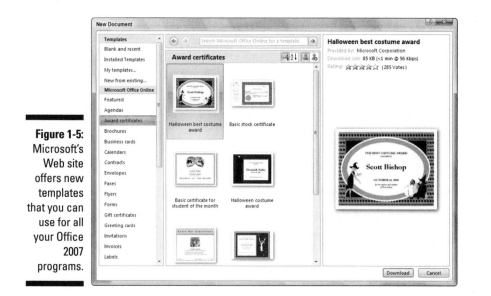

Figure 1-5: Microsoft's Web site offers new templates that you can use for all your Office 2007 programs.

3. **Click the template you want to use and then click the Download button.**

    Office 2007 downloads and creates a new file based on your chosen template.

Opening an existing file

When you load an Office 2007 program, you'll probably want to edit a file that you had created and modified before. To open an existing file, you need to tell Office 2007 the location and name of the file you want to open. Just follow these steps:

1. **Click the Office Button and then choose Open.**

    An Open dialog box appears, as shown in Figure 1-6.

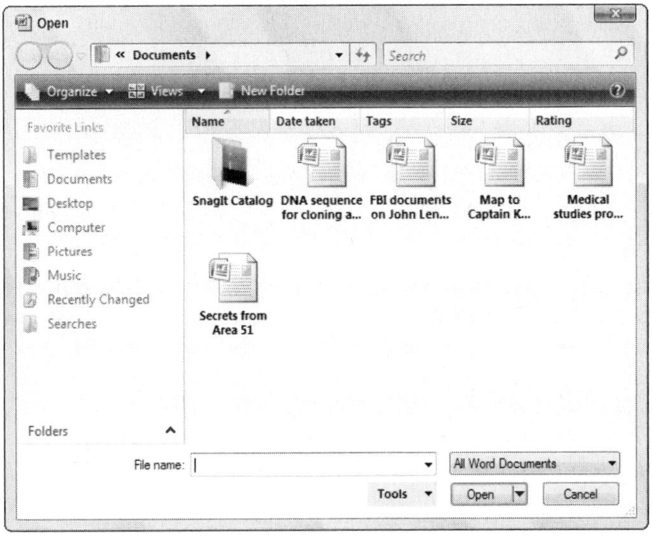

Figure 1-6: The Open dialog box lets you change drives and folders to find the file you want to use.

2. **(Optional) To choose a different drive to look for files, click Computer under the Favorite Links panel (see the left side of Figure 1-6). Then click the drive where you want to load the file, such as the C: drive.**

3. **(Optional) Click a folder and then click Open to search for a file inside a folder. Repeat this step as many times as necessary.**

4. **Click the file you want to open and then click Open.**

    Your chosen file appears ready for editing.

When you click the Open command under Microsoft Word, Excel, PowerPoint, and Access, an additional window appears to the right that contains a list of the last files you opened. If you want to load a file you've recently used, just click that filename to load that file.

Saving files

Saving a file stores all your data on a hard disk or other storage device (such as a Compact Flash card). The first time you save a file, you need to specify three items:

- ✔ The drive and folder to store your file
- ✔ The name of your file
- ✔ The format to save your file

The drive and folder where you store your files is completely arbitrary. However, it's a good idea to store similar files in a folder with a descriptive name, such as *Tax Evasion Information for 2008* or *Extortion Letters to Grandma.* By default, Office 2007 stores all your files in the Documents folder.

The name of your file is also completely arbitrary, but it's also a good idea to give your file a descriptive name such as *Latest Resume to Escape My Dead-End Job* or *Global Trade Presentation for World Domination Meeting on September 9, 2008.*

The format of your file defines how Office 2007 stores your data. The default file format is known as *Office 2007 format,* which simply means that only people with Office 2007 can reliably open and view the contents of that file. If you want to share your files with people who don't use Office 2007, you have to save your files in a different file format.

Saving a file for Office 2007

If you're the only person who needs to view and edit your files, you can save a file in Office 2007 format by following these steps:

1. **Click the Office Button.**

   A drop-down menu appears.

2. **Click Save.**

   If this is the first time you're saving the file, a Save As dialog box appears, as shown at the top of Figure 1-7.

Figure 1-7:
The Save As
dialog box
lets you
choose the
name, file
format, and
a location to
save your
file.

For a quick way to choose the Office Button➪Save command, click the
Save icon that appears to the right of the Office Button or press Ctrl+S.

3. **(Optional) To specify a drive and folder to save your file, click Browse
Folders.**

   This causes the dialog box to expand, as shown in the bottom dialog box
   in Figure 1-7. Now you can click Computer, under Favorite Links, and
   then click a folder. Or, click the New Folder button; when the New Folder
   dialog box appears, type a name for your new folder and then click OK.

4. **Click in the File Name text box and type a descriptive name for your
   file.**

5. **Click Save.**

After you've saved a file, you'll only have to go through Steps 1 and 2 because
you don't have to specify a location and filename to save an existing file.

Saving a file for older versions of Microsoft Office

If you need to share files with people using older versions of Microsoft Office, you need to save your files in a different file format known as *97-2003,* such as *Word 97-2003 Document* or *PowerPoint 97-2003 Presentation.*

This special 97-2003 file format saves Office 2007 files so that previous versions of Microsoft Office 97/2000/XP/2003 can open and edit your files.

When you save files in the 97-2003 format, Microsoft Office 2007 saves your files with a three-letter file extension, like `.doc` or `.xls`. When you save files in the Office 2007 format, Microsoft Office 2007 saves your files with a four or five-letter file extension, such as `.docx` or `.pptx`, as shown in Table 1-1.

Table 1-1	File Extension Names Used by Different Versions of Microsoft Office	
Program	*Microsoft Office 2007 File Extension*	*Microsoft Office 97-2003 File Extension*
Microsoft Word	`.docx`	`.doc`
Microsoft Excel	`.xlsx`	`.xls`
Microsoft PowerPoint	`.pptx`	`.ppt`
Microsoft Access	`.accdb`	`.mdb`

To save your Office 2007 files as a 97-2003 format, follow these steps:

1. **Click the Office Button and then choose Save As.**

   A Save As dialog box appears.

2. **Click in the Save as Type list box.**

   A list of different formats appears, as shown in Figure 1-8.

   When you choose the Save As command in Step 1, you're making a copy of your original file.

3. **Choose the 97-2003 format option, such as Word 97-2003 Format or Excel 97-2003 Format.**

   The Save as Type list box displays a huge list of file formats, such as XML Data or Text. Most programs can accept files stored in the 97-2003 format, but many older programs cannot, so you may have to resort to saving a file in one of these other formats instead.

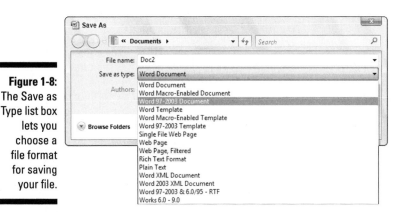

Figure 1-8:
The Save as
Type list box
lets you
choose a
file format
for saving
your file.

4. **(Optional) Click in the File Name text box and type a descriptive name for your file.**

5. **Click Save.**

Closing a file

When you're done editing a file, you need to close it. Closing a file simply removes the file from your screen but keeps your Office 2007 program running so you can edit or open another file. If you haven't saved your file, closing a file will prompt you to save your changes.

To close a file, follow these steps:

1. **Click the Office Button and then choose Close.**

   If you haven't saved your file, a dialog box appears asking whether you want to save your changes.

   For a faster way to choose the Close command, press Ctrl+F4.

2. **Click Yes to save your changes, No to discard any changes, or Cancel to keep your file open.**

   If you click either Yes or No, Office 2007 closes your file.

Using the Quick Access toolbar

The Quick Access toolbar appears to the right of the Office Button (refer to Figure 1-2) near the top of the screen, displaying icons that represent commonly used commands such as Save, Undo, and Redo as shown in Figure 1-9.

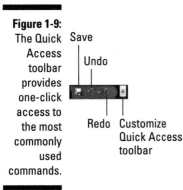

Figure 1-9:
The Quick
Access
toolbar
provides
one-click
access to
the most
commonly
used
commands.

Save

Undo

Redo   Customize
        Quick Access
        toolbar

Using the Quick Access icons

If you click the Save icon in the Quick Access toolbar, Office 2007 saves your current file. If you're saving a new file, a dialog box pops up, asking you to choose a name for your file.

If you click the Print icon in the Quick Access toolbar, Office 2007 immediately prints one copy of your entire file through the default printer. (If you want to specify a different printer to use, the number of copies to print, or specific pages to print, click the Office Button and choose Print instead.)

The Redo icon reverses the last Undo command you chose. For example, if you delete a paragraph, Office 2007 makes that paragraph disappear. Then if you immediately click the Undo icon, the paragraph magically reappears. If you immediately click the Redo icon, the Redo command reverses the Undo command and deletes the paragraph once more.

The Undo icon is unique in that it offers two ways to use it. First, you can click the Undo icon to undo the last action you chose. Second, you can click the downward-pointing arrow that appears to the right of the Undo icon to display a list of one or more of your previous actions, as shown in Figure 1-10.

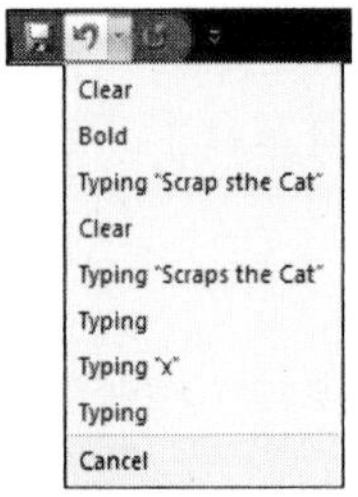

Figure 1-10:
The Undo
icon
displays a
list of
actions you
can undo.

Clear
Bold
Typing "Scrap sthe Cat"
Clear
Typing "Scraps the Cat"
Typing
Typing "x"
Typing
Cancel

The most recent action you chose appears at the top of this list, the second most recent action appears second, and so on. To undo multiple commands, follow these steps:

1. **Click the downward-pointing arrow that appears to the right of the Undo icon in the Quick Access toolbar.**

2. **Move the mouse pointer to highlight one or more actions you want to undo.**

3. **Click the left mouse button.**

   Office 2007 undoes all the multiple actions you selected.

Adding icons

The Quick Access toolbar is designed to put your most commonly used commands where you can always find them. To add other icons to the Quick Access toolbar, follow these steps:

1. **Click the Customize Quick Access Toolbar arrow (refer to Figure 1-9).**

   A pull-down menu appears.

   You can add an icon to the toolbar by just clicking on an icon name, such as Quick Print or New, from the pull-down menu.

2. **Click More Commands.**

   An Options window appears, as shown in Figure 1-11. The panel on the right shows all the current icons on the Quick Access toolbar. The panel on the left shows all the additional icons you can add.

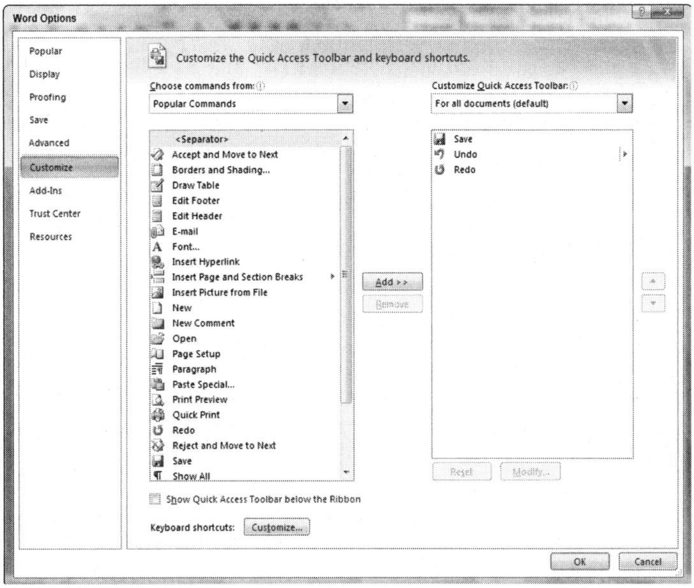

Figure 1-11: The Options window lets you select the icons you want to add to the Quick Access toolbar.

3. **Click in the Choose Commands From list box and choose a menu title, such as File or Page Layout.**

   The left panel displays a list of icons and commands.

4. **Click an icon and then click the Add button.**

5. **(Optional) Repeat Steps 3 and 4 for each additional icon you want to add to the Quick Access toolbar.**

6. **Click OK.**

   Your chosen icon (or icons) now appears on the Quick Access toolbar.

Removing icons

You can remove icons from the Quick Access toolbar at any time. To remove an icon, follow these steps:

1. **Right-click an icon on the Quick Access toolbar.**

   A pull-down menu appears.

2. **Click Remove from Quick Access Toolbar.**

   Office 2007 removes your selected icon from the Quick Access toolbar.

Moving the Quick Access toolbar

The Quick Access toolbar can appear in one of two places:

- ✔ Above the Ribbon (its default location)
- ✔ Below the Ribbon

To move the Quick Access toolbar, follow these steps:

1. **Click the Customize Quick Access Toolbar arrow.**

   A pull-down menu appears.

2. **Choose Place Quick Access Toolbar Below (or Above) the Ribbon.**

   If the Quick Access toolbar currently appears over the Ribbon, you'll see the Place Quick Access Toolbar Below the Ribbon command. If the Quick Access toolbar appears under the Ribbon, you'll see the Place Quick Access Toolbar Above the Ribbon command.

Minimizing the Ribbon

You can tuck the Ribbon out of sight temporarily so it only appears when you click on a tab such as Home or Insert. To hide the Ribbon, follow these steps:

1. **Click the downward-pointing arrow that appears to the right of the Undo icon in the Quick Access toolbar.**

   A pull-down menu appears.

2. **Click Minimize the Ribbon.**

   Office 2007 hides the Ribbon and only displays the tabs. To display the Ribbon again, repeat these two steps.

Using the Ribbon

The Ribbon organizes commands into categories called *contextual tabs.* Each tab displays a different group of commands. For example, the Page Layout tab displays only those commands related to designing a page, and the Insert tab displays only those commands related to inserting items into a file, such as a page break or a picture, as shown in Figure 1-12.

Figure 1-12: Each tab displays a different group of related commands.

Using the Ribbon is a two-step process. First, you must click the tab that contains the command you want. Second, you click the actual command.

Tabs act exactly like traditional pull-down menus. Whereas a pull-down menu simply displays a list of commands, tabs display a list of icons that represent different commands.

Deciphering Ribbon icons

The main idea behind organizing commands within tabs is to avoid overwhelming you with a barrage of different commands. Although most icons include a short text description, you can get additional help deciphering different icons through ScreenTips, which typically displays the following, as shown in Figure 1-13:

🖝 The official name of the command (which is Format Painter in Figure 1-13)

🖝 The equivalent keystroke shortcut you can use to run the command (which is Ctrl+Shift+C in the figure)

🖝 A short explanation of what the command does

Figure 1-13: ScreenTips explain what each command does.

To view the ScreenTip for a command, move the mouse pointer over a command and wait a few seconds for the ScreenTip appear.

Shortcut keystrokes let you choose a command from the keyboard without the hassle of clicking a tab and then clicking the command buried inside that tab. Most shortcut keystrokes consist of two or three keys, such as Ctrl+P or Ctrl+Shift+C.

Using Live Preview

In the past, you might have known what a particular command did, but you would never know how it would affect your file until after you chose that command. Oftentimes, you might choose a command, see how it changed your file, and then undo the change because it may not be what you really wanted.

To avoid this hassle of constant experimentation with different commands, Office 2007 offers a feature called *Live Preview*. Live Preview lets you move the mouse pointer over certain icons displayed in a tab and then immediately see the changes displayed in your current file.

To use Live Preview, follow these steps:

1. **Move the cursor (or click the mouse) on an object (text, picture, table, and so on) that you want to change.**

2. **Move the mouse pointer over any command.**

   Office 2007 shows you how your chosen object will look if you choose the command, as shown in Figure 1-14.

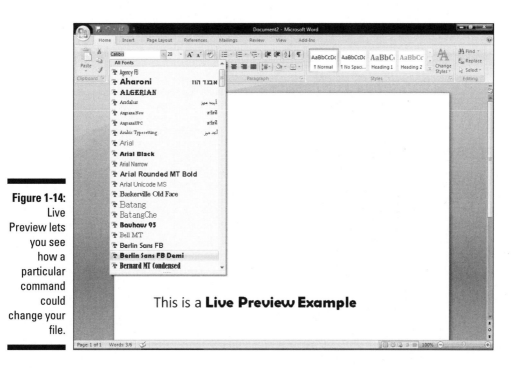

Figure 1-14:
Live
Preview lets
you see
how a
particular
command
could
change your
file.

3. **Click the command to change your object (or move the mouse pointer away from the command so you don't choose that command).**

In Word, Live Preview will not work if you display your document in Draft view.

Giving commands to Office 2007

To give a command to Office 2007, you need to follow these basic steps:

1. Select an item (text, picture, table, and so on) that you want to modify.
2. Click a tab that contains the command you want.
3. Click the command you want to use.

Command icons work in one of three ways, as shown in Figure 1-15:

- ✔ **Clickable icons:** Clicking an icon immediately chooses a command to alter your data. The Bold and Italic icons are examples of icons that you click only once to choose them.
- ✔ **List box icons:** Some icons display a downward-pointing arrow to the right. Clicking these icons displays a list of additional options. The Font and Font Size icons are examples of list box icons.
- ✔ **Gallery icons:** Some icons display a downward-pointing arrow that displays a drop-down list of additional commands, called a *gallery*.

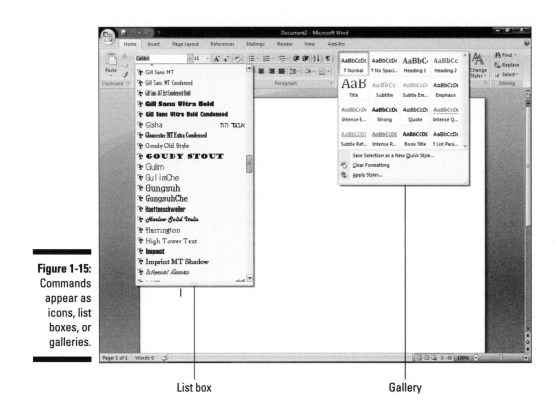

Figure 1-15:
Commands
appear as
icons, list
boxes, or
galleries.

Figure 1-15:
Commands
appear as
icons, list
boxes, or
galleries.

List box   Gallery

Customizing an Office 2007 Program

If you want to modify how a particular Office 2007 program works, you can customize its features. To customize an Office 2007 program, follow these steps:

1. **Load the Office 2007 program you want to customize.**

2. **Click the Office Button.**

   A pull-down menu appears.

3. **Click the Options button in the bottom-right corner, such as Word Options or Excel Options.**

   An Options dialog box appears, as shown in Figure 1-16.

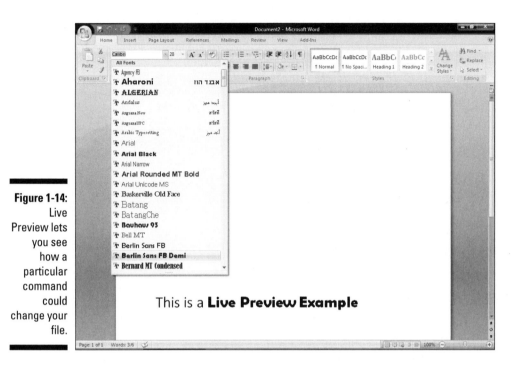

Figure 1-14:
Live
Preview lets
you see
how a
particular
command
could
change your
file.

3. **Click the command to change your object (or move the mouse pointer away from the command so you don't choose that command).**

In Word, Live Preview will not work if you display your document in Draft view.

Giving commands to Office 2007

To give a command to Office 2007, you need to follow these basic steps:

1. Select an item (text, picture, table, and so on) that you want to modify.
2. Click a tab that contains the command you want.
3. Click the command you want to use.

Command icons work in one of three ways, as shown in Figure 1-15:

- ✔ **Clickable icons:** Clicking an icon immediately chooses a command to alter your data. The Bold and Italic icons are examples of icons that you click only once to choose them.

- ✔ **List box icons:** Some icons display a downward-pointing arrow to the right. Clicking these icons displays a list of additional options. The Font and Font Size icons are examples of list box icons.

- ✔ **Gallery icons:** Some icons display a downward-pointing arrow that displays a drop-down list of additional commands, called a *gallery*.

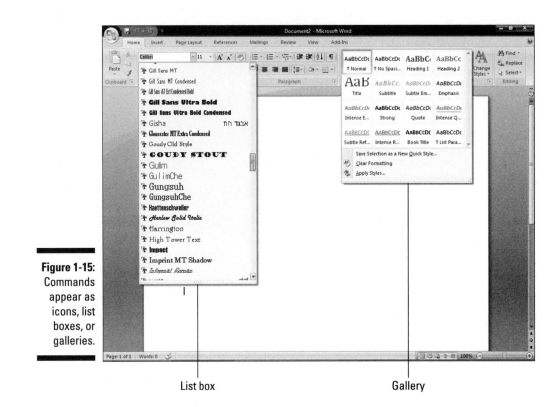

Figure 1-15:
Commands
appear as
icons, list
boxes, or
galleries.

List box   Gallery

Customizing an Office 2007 Program

If you want to modify how a particular Office 2007 program works, you can customize its features. To customize an Office 2007 program, follow these steps:

1. **Load the Office 2007 program you want to customize.**

2. **Click the Office Button.**

   A pull-down menu appears.

3. **Click the Options button in the bottom-right corner, such as Word Options or Excel Options.**

   An Options dialog box appears, as shown in Figure 1-16.

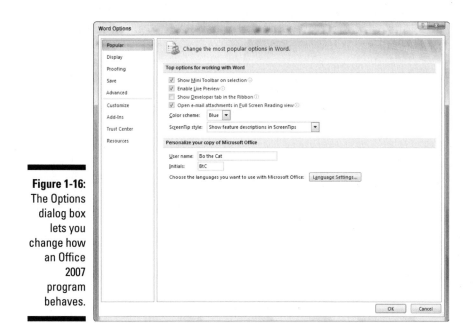

Figure 1-16:
The Options dialog box lets you change how an Office 2007 program behaves.

4. **Click a category, such as Save or Display.**

The Options dialog box displays multiple options for you to customize.

5. **Click OK when you're done choosing different customizing options.**

If you click the Save category in Step 4, you can define a default file format and file location for storing files for each Office 2007 program (Word, Excel, and so on).

Exiting Office 2007

No matter how much you may love using Office 2007, eventually there will come a time when you need to exit an Office 2007 program and do something else with your life. To exit from any Office 2007 program (except Outlook), choose one of the following:

✔ Click the Close box in the upper-right corner of the Office 2007 window.

✔ Click the Office Button and then click the Exit button (refer to Figure 1-3).

✔ Press Alt+F4.

If you try to close an Office 2007 program before saving your file, a dialog box pops up to give you a chance to save your file. If you don't save your file before exiting, you'll lose any changes you made to that file.

To exit Microsoft Outlook, just choose File➪Exit.

Chapter 2

Editing Data

· ·

In This Chapter

▶ Selecting data

▶ Using the pop-up toolbar

▶ Copying, cutting, and pasting

▶ Copying and cutting with the mouse

▶ Sharing data within Office 2007

· ·

*A*lthough you create a file only once, you can edit it many times. *Editing* can add, rearrange, or delete data, such as text, numbers, or pictures. All Office 2007 programs work in similar ways to edit data, so whether you use Word, Excel, PowerPoint, or Access, you'll know the right commands to edit data no matter which program you may be using.

Whenever you edit a file, save your file periodically by clicking the Save icon in the Quick Access toolbar, pressing Ctrl+S, or clicking the Office Button and choosing Save. That way if your computer crashes or the power goes out, you won't lose all the editing changes you made.

Adding Data by Pointing

When you enter data into a file, your data appears wherever the cursor appears on the screen. The cursor appears as a blinking vertical bar, which basically says, "Anything you type now will appear right here!"

Because the cursor won't always magically appear exactly where you want to type data, you must move the cursor using either the mouse or the keyboard. To move the cursor using the mouse, follow these steps:

1. **Move the mouse pointer where you want to move the cursor.**

2. **Click the left mouse button.**

    The cursor appears where you click the mouse pointer.

To move the cursor using the keyboard, you can use one of many cursor movement keys:

✔ **The (up/down/left/right) arrow keys**

✔ **The Home/End keys**

✔ **The Page Up/Page Down keys**

Use the up/down/right/left arrow keys when you want to move the cursor a small distance, such as up one line or right to the next cell in an Excel spreadsheet.

To move the cursor faster, hold down the Ctrl key and then press the arrow keys. If you hold down the Ctrl key, the up-arrow key moves the cursor up one paragraph, the down-arrow key moves the cursor down one paragraph, the left-arrow key moves the cursor left one word, and the right-arrow key moves the cursor right one word.

Pressing the Home key moves the cursor to the beginning of a sentence (or a row in a spreadsheet), and pressing the End key moves the cursor to the end of a sentence (or a row in a spreadsheet).

Pressing the Page Up/Page Down keys moves the cursor up or down one screen at a time.

Using any of the cursor movement keys moves the cursor to a new location. Wherever the cursor appears will be where you can enter new data. Table 2-1 lists ways to move the cursor in each Office 2007 program.

Table 2-1		Moving the Cursor in Office 2007 Programs		
Keystroke	*Word*	*Excel*	*PowerPoint*	*Access*
Home	Beginning of the line	Column A of the current row that cursor appears in; (Ctrl+ Home appears in; moves to cell A1)	Displays first slide; beginning of the line (when text box is selected)	First field of the current record
End	End of the line	NA; (Ctrl+End moves to last cell)	Displays last slide; end of the line (when text box is selected)	Add New Field of current record
Page Up	Half a page up	Up 27 rows	Displays previous slide	Up 25 records
Page Down	Half a page down	Down 27 rows	Displays next slide	Down 25 records

Keystroke	Word	Excel	PowerPoint	Access
Up/Down arrow	Up/down one line	Up/down one row	Next/previous slide; up/down one line (when text box is selected)	Up/down one record
Left/Right arrow	Left/right one character	Left/right one column	Next/previous slide; left/right one character (when text box is selected)	Left/right one field

Selecting Data

To modify data, you must tell Office 2007 what you want to change by selecting it. Then choose a command that changes your data, such as underlining text or deleting a picture.

To select anything in Office 2007, you can use either the mouse or the keyboard. Generally, the mouse is faster but takes some time getting used to coordinating the motion of the mouse with the movement of the mouse pointer on the screen. The keyboard is slower but much simpler to use.

Selecting data with the mouse

The mouse provides two ways to select data. The first way involves pointing and dragging the mouse, as shown in Figure 2-1.

1. **Point the mouse pointer at the beginning or end of the data you want to select.**

2. **Hold down the left mouse button and drag (move) the mouse pointer over the data to select it.**

When you drag the mouse, hold down the left mouse button. If you don't hold down the left mouse button as you move the mouse, you won't select any data when you move the mouse pointer across the screen.

You can also select data by clicking the mouse. To select a picture, such as a chart in Microsoft Excel or a photograph added to a Microsoft Word document, just click the picture to select it. Office 2007 displays rectangles, called *handles,* around the border of any selected picture, as shown in Figure 2-2.

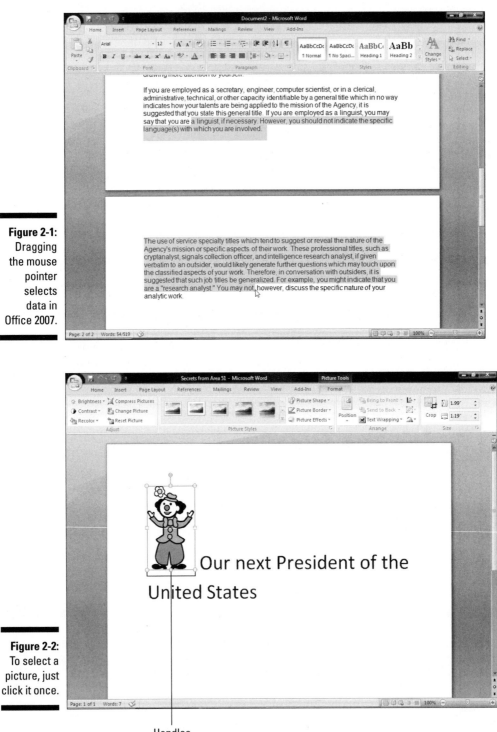

Figure 2-1:
Dragging
the mouse
pointer
selects
data in
Office 2007.

Figure 2-2:
To select a
picture, just
click it once.

Handles

To select text with the mouse, you can click the mouse in one of three ways, as shown in Figure 2-3:

- ✔ **Single-click:** Moves the cursor
- ✔ **Double-click:** Selects the word that you click
- ✔ **Triple-click:** Selects the entire paragraph that contains the word you click

Office 2007 defines a *paragraph* as any chunk of text that begins on a separate line and ends with a Return character (¶), created by pressing the Enter key.

Selecting data with the keyboard

To select data with the keyboard, you need to use the following keys:

- ✔ **The cursor movement keys (up/down/left/right arrow keys, Home/End keys, or Page Up/Page Down keys)**
- ✔ **The Shift key**

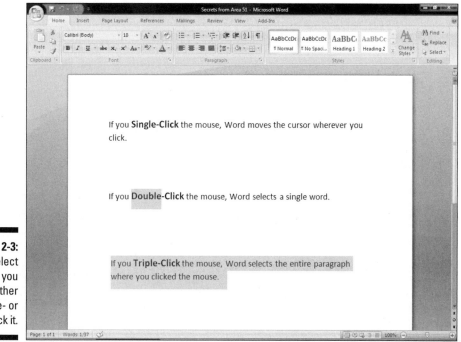

Figure 2-3:
To select text, you can either double- or triple-click it.

The cursor movement keys simply move the cursor. The Shift key acts like the left mouse button and tells Office 2007 what to select. To select data, you have to follow these steps:

1. **Move the cursor to the beginning or end of the data you want to select.**

2. **Hold down the Shift key. (Keep it pressed down.)**

3. **Move the cursor using any of the cursor movement keys, such as the up-arrow key or the End key.**

4. **Release the Shift key.**

You may find it easier to place the cursor with the mouse and then hold down the Shift key while pressing a cursor movement key to select data more precisely than you can by dragging the mouse.

To select all the data in a file, press Ctrl+A.

Selecting multiple chunks of data with the mouse and keyboard

For greater flexibility in selecting data, you can use both the mouse and the keyboard to select multiple chunks of data at the same time. To select two or more chunks of data, follow these steps:

1. **Select a picture or chunk of text using either the keyboard or the mouse.**

2. **Hold down the Ctrl key.**

3. **Select another picture or chunk of test using either the keyboard or the mouse.**

4. **Repeat Step 3 for each additional item you want to select.**

5. **Release the Ctrl key when you're done selecting data.**

Editing Data with the Pop-up Toolbar

As soon as you select data, Office 2007 displays a pop-up toolbar that displays the most commonly used commands (displayed as icons). This pop-up toolbar appears to the upper right of the data you selected as a faint image. The closer you move the mouse towards this pop-up toolbar, the darker and sharper the toolbar appears, as shown in Figure 2-4. The farther you move away from the toolbar, the fainter it appears.

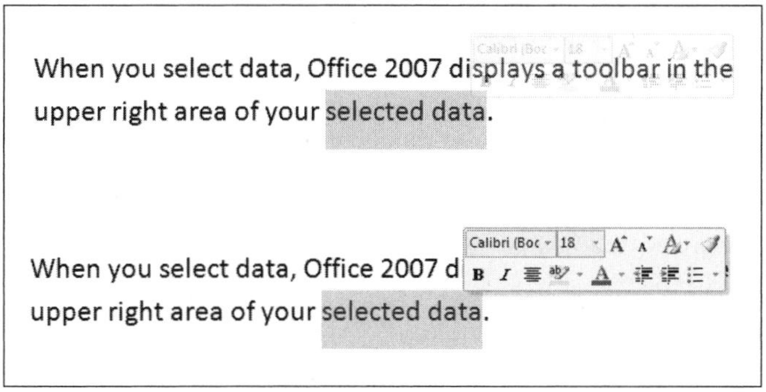

Figure 2-4:
Whenever
you select
data,
Office 2007
displays a
pop-up
toolbar in
the upper-
right area.

When you select data, Office 2007 displays a toolbar in the upper right area of your selected data.

When you select data, Office 2007 d
upper right area of your selected data.

To use this pop-up toolbar, follow these steps:

1. **Select data using the mouse.**

   Selecting data with the keyboard will *not* display the pop-up toolbar.

2. **Move the mouse pointer to the area to the upper right of the selected data.**

   The pop-up toolbar appears.

   The closer you move the mouse to the toolbar, the more visible the toolbar will appear.

3. **Click a command (icon) on the pop-up toolbar.**

Deleting Data

The simplest way to edit a file is to delete your existing data. If you just need to delete a single character, you can use one of two keys:

- ✔ **Backspace:** Deletes the character immediately to the left of the cursor
- ✔ **Delete:** Deletes the character immediately to the right of the cursor

If you need to delete large chunks of text, follow these steps:

1. **Select the data you want to delete using either the keyboard or the mouse. (See the earlier section, "Selecting Data.")**

2. **Press the Delete key.**

   Office 2007 wipes away your data.

Cutting and Pasting (Moving) Data

Moving data in Office 2007 requires a two-step process: cut and paste. When you *cut* data, you delete it but save a copy in a special area of the computer's memory known as the *Clipboard*. When you *paste* data to a new location, you copy the data off the Clipboard and paste it in your file, as shown in Figure 2-5.

To move data, follow these steps:

1. **Select the data you want to move, using the keyboard or mouse as explained in the earlier section, "Selecting Data."**

2. **Choose one of the following:**
   - Click the Cut icon (from the Home tab).
   - Right-click the mouse; when the pop-up menu appears, choose Cut.
   - Press Ctrl+X.

3. **Move the cursor to a new location.**

4. **Choose one of the following:**
   - Click the Paste icon (from the Home tab).
   - Right-click the mouse; when the pop-up menu appears, choose Paste.
   - Press Ctrl+V.

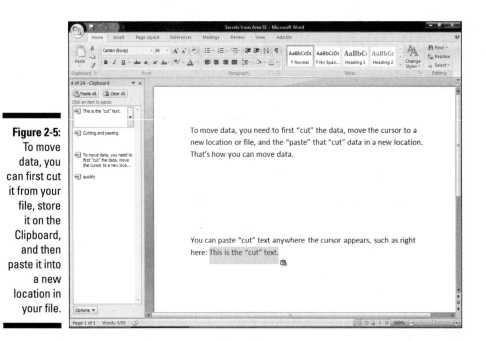

Figure 2-5: To move data, you can first cut it from your file, store it on the Clipboard, and then paste it into a new location in your file.

If you select data in Step 3, you can replace the selected data with the pasted data you selected in Steps 1 and 2.

Copying and Pasting Data

Unlike the Cut command, the Copy command leaves your selected data in its original location but places a second copy of that data somewhere else. To copy and paste data, follow these steps:

1. **Select the data you want to copy, using the keyboard or mouse, as explained in the earlier section, "Selecting Data."**

2. **Choose one of the following:**

   • Click the Copy icon.

   • Right-click the mouse; when the pop-up menu appears, choose Copy.

   • Press Ctrl+C.

3. **Move the cursor to a new location.**

4. **Choose one of the following:**

   • Click the Paste icon.

   • Right-click the mouse; when the pop-up menu appears, choose Paste.

   • Press Ctrl+V.

Dragging with the Mouse to Cut, Copy, and Paste

The mouse can also cut/copy and paste data. To move data with the mouse, follow these steps:

1. **Select the data you want to move using the methods described in the earlier section, "Selecting Data."**

2. **Move the mouse pointer over the highlighted data.**

3. **Hold down the left mouse button and drag (move) the mouse.**

   The mouse pointer displays an arrow and a box while the cursor turns into a dotted vertical line.

   Alternatively, to copy data, hold down the Ctrl key while holding down the left mouse button and dragging (moving) the mouse. The mouse pointer displays an arrow and a box with a plus sign while the cursor turns into a dotted vertical line.

4. **Move the dotted vertical line cursor where you want to place the data you selected in Step 1.**

5. **Release the left mouse button.**

   Your data appears in its new location.

Undo and Redo

To protect you from mistakes, Office 2007 offers a special Undo command, which essentially tells the computer, "Remember that last command I just gave? Pretend I never chose it."

You can use the Undo command any time you edit data and want to reverse your changes. The two ways to choose the Undo command are

- ✔ **Click the Undo icon on the Quick Access toolbar (see Figure 2-6).**
- ✔ **Press Ctrl+Z.**

Figure 2-6:
The Undo and Redo icons appear on the Quick Access toolbar.

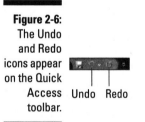

Undo   Redo

Sometimes you may make many changes to your file and suddenly realize that the last five or ten changes you made messed up your data by mistake. To undo multiple commands, follow these steps:

1. **Click the downward-pointing arrow that appears to the right of the Undo icon.**

   A list of your previously chosen commands appears.

2. **Move the mouse pointer to highlight all the commands that you want to undo, as shown in Figure 2-7.**

3. **Click the left mouse button.**

   Office 2007 undoes your chosen commands.

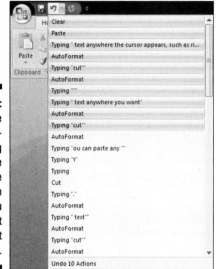

Figure 2-7:
The
downward-
pointing
arrow to the
right of the
Undo icon
lets you
view a list
of your last
commands.

Until you choose the Undo command at least once, the Redo icon appears dimmed. The Redo command lets you reapply the last command you chose to undo. The two ways to choose the Redo command are

✔ **Click the Redo icon (refer to Figure 2-6).**

✔ **Press Ctrl+Y.**

Each time you choose the Redo command, you reverse the effect of the last Undo command. For example, if you use the Undo command four times, you can choose the Redo command only up to four times.

Sharing Data with Other Office 2007 Programs

Cutting, copying, and pasting data may be handy within the same file, but Office 2007 also gives you the ability to cut, copy, and paste data between different programs, such as copying a chart from Excel and pasting it into a PowerPoint presentation.

Using the Office Clipboard

When you cut or copy any data, Windows stores it in a special part of memory called the *Clipboard*. This Windows Clipboard can only hold one item at a time, so Office 2007 comes with its own Clipboard called the *Office Clipboard*, which can store up to 24 items.

Whereas the Windows Clipboard works with any Windows program (such as Microsoft Paint or WordPerfect), the Office Clipboard works only with Office 2007 programs (such as Word, Excel, PowerPoint, Access, and Outlook). To store data on the Office Clipboard, you just need to use the Cut or Copy command, and Office 2007 automatically stores your data on the Office Clipboard.

The two big advantages of the Office Clipboard are

- ✔ **You can store up to 24 items.**

  The Windows Clipboard can store only one item.

- ✔ **You can select what you want to paste from the Clipboard.**

  The Windows Clipboard lets you paste only the last item cut or copied.

Viewing and pasting items off the Office Clipboard

After you use the Cut or Copy command at least once, your data gets stored on the Office Clipboard. You can then view the Office Clipboard and choose which data you want to paste from the Clipboard into your file.

To view the Office Clipboard and paste items from it, follow these steps:

1. **Move the cursor to the spot where you want to paste an item from the Office Clipboard.**

2. **Click the Office Clipboard icon.**

   The Office Clipboard pane appears, as shown in Figure 2-8. The Office Clipboard also displays an icon that shows you the program where the data came from, such as Word or PowerPoint.

3. **Click the item you want to paste.**

   Office 2007 pastes your chosen item into the file where you moved the cursor in Step 1.

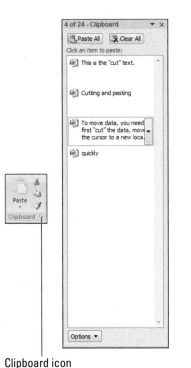

Paste All Clear All

Click an item to paste:

This is the "cut" text.

Cutting and pasting

To move data, you need
first "cut" the data, move
the cursor to a new loca.

quickly

Options ▼

Figure 2-8:
The Office
Clipboard
pane lets
you view the
current
contents of
the Office
Clipboard.

Paste
Clipboard

Clipboard icon

4. Click the Close box of the Office Clipboard window to tuck it out of sight.

If you click the Paste All button, you can paste every item on the Office Clipboard into your file.

Deleting items from the Office Clipboard

You can add up to 24 items to the Office Clipboard. The moment you add a 25th item, Office 2007 deletes the oldest item from the Office Clipboard to make room for the new cut or copied item.

You can also manually delete items from the Office Clipboard as well, by following these steps:

1. Click the Office Clipboard icon (refer to Figure 2-8).

The Office Clipboard appears.

2. Move the mouse pointer over an item on the Office Clipboard.

A downward-pointing arrow appears to the right. A pop-up menu appears, as shown in Figure 2-9.

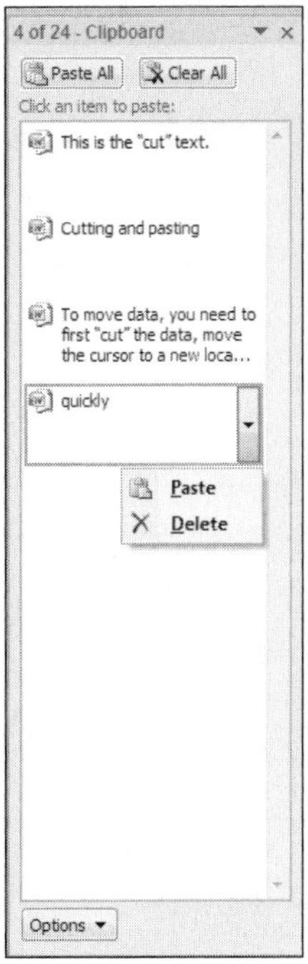

Figure 2-9:
To remove
an item from
the Office
Clipboard,
click the
downward-
pointing
arrow and
click Delete.

3. Click Delete.

Office 2007 deletes your chosen item.

4. Click the Close box to tuck the Office Clipboard out of sight.

If you click the Clear All button, you can delete every item currently stored on the Office Clipboard.

Make sure you really want to delete an item from the Office Clipboard because after you delete it, you can't retrieve it.

Chapter 3

Getting Help from Office 2007

. . . .

In This Chapter

▶ Opening and browsing the Help window

▶ Searching the Help window

▶ Changing the appearance of the Help window

. . . .

Microsoft designed Office 2007 to be the easiest version of Office ever. Yet, despite these improvements in Office 2007's user interface, you may still need help in using one of the many Office programs once in a while.

To help answer your questions, Office 2007 provides a Help system, which lets you browse through different help topics until you (hopefully) find the answer you need. There are two ways to use the Help system. One, you can browse through the various topics displayed until you find the answer you want. This can take time to search but can also show you related help that you might find useful.

A second way to use the Help system is to type a query such as **Page margins** or **Font size**. The Help system will then display all topics related to your query. This can be a fast way to search for help, but if you don't type the right terms that the Help system recognizes, this method may not find the exact help you need.

Browsing the Help Window

Each Office 2007 program comes with its own help files that you can access at any time. To browse through the Help system, follow these steps:

1. **Choose one of the following to display the Help window, as shown in Figure 3-1:**

   • Click the Help icon.

   • Press F1.

Forward

Back | Home

Help

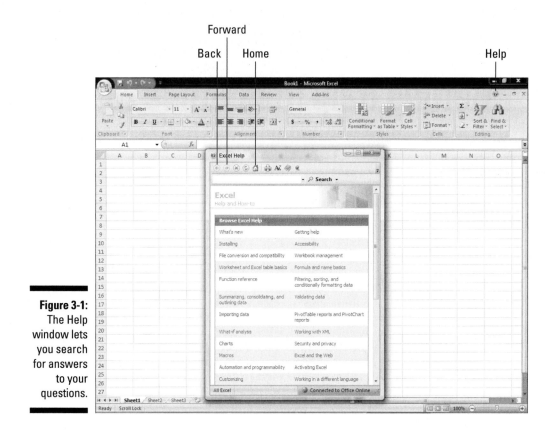

Figure 3-1:
The Help
window lets
you search
for answers
to your
questions.

2. **Click a topic.**

   The Help window either displays a list of subcategories or a list of Help topics (that appear with a question mark icon in the left margin), as shown in Figure 3-2. If a list of subcategories appears, you may have to click a subcategory until the Help window displays a list of help topics.

3. **Click a Help topic identified by a question mark icon in the left margin.**

   The Help window displays step-by-step explanations.

4. **Click the Close box when you're done to make the Help window go away.**

If you click the Back icon, you can view the previous text displayed in the Help window. If you click the Forward icon (after clicking the Back icon at least once), you can return forward to the text that you were looking at before you clicked the Back icon. If you click the Home icon, you can view the Help window's list of topics that appear every time you open the Help window.

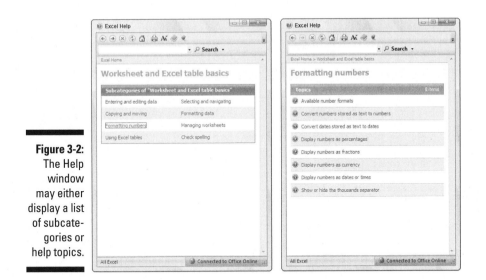

Figure 3-2:
The Help window may either display a list of subcategories or help topics.

Searching in the Help Window

Rather than browse through one or more subcategories to find help, you might want to search for help by typing in one or more keywords. Such keywords can identify a specific topic such as *Printing* or *Editing charts*.

If you misspell a topic, the Help system may not understand what you want to find, so check your spelling.

To search the Help window by typing in a keyword or two, follow these steps:

1. **Choose one of the following methods to display the Help window (refer to Figure 3-1):**
   - Click the Help icon.
   - Press F1.
2. **Click in the Search list box and type one or more keywords, such as** Formatting **or** Aligning text.
3. **Click Search.**

   The Help window displays a list of topics, as shown in Figure 3-3.
4. **Click a Help topic.**

   The Help window displays step-by-step instructions for your chosen topic.
5. **Click the Close box when you're done to make the Help window go away.**

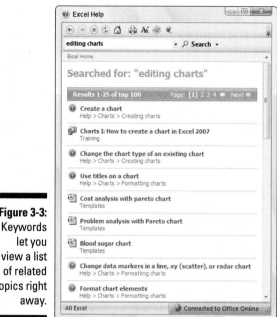

Figure 3-3:
Keywords
let you
view a list
of related
topics right
away.

Making the Help Window Easier to Read

One problem with the Help window is that it may appear too small to read comfortably. To get around this problem, you have two choices:

- ✔ Resize the Help window.
- ✔ Expand the size of the text inside the Help window.

Resizing the Help window

You can resize the Help window just like any other window by clicking one of the following icons in the upper-right corner:

- ✔ **Minimize:** Shrinks the Help window to an icon on the Windows taskbar
- ✔ **Maximize:** Expands the Help window to fill the entire screen
- ✔ **Restore Down:** Shrinks a maximized window to a smaller window that you can move and resize

You can also resize a window by moving the mouse pointer over one edge or bottom corner, holding down the left mouse button, and dragging (moving) the mouse.

Enlarging the text in the Help window

In addition to, or as an alternative to, resizing the Help window, you can enlarge the text inside the Help window to make it larger (or smaller) so you can read it easier or so you can cram more text within the limited confines of the Help window. To change the size of the text inside the Help window, follow these steps:

1. **Click the Help icon or press F1 to open the Help window.**
2. **Click the Change Font Size icon.**

   A pull-down menu appears, as shown in Figure 3-4.
3. **Choose an option, such as Smaller or Largest.**

   The Help window text changes in size.

Keep on Top icon

Figure 3-4: Clicking the Change Font Size icon lets you make text bigger or smaller.

Keeping the Help window visible at all times

Office 2007 offers a Keep on Top icon that you can choose to keep the Help window visible while letting you use the Office 2007 program underneath. That way you can read and follow the instructions in the Help window while using your program at the same time.

If you turn the Keep on Top feature off, the Help window will appear; but, the moment you click in your Office 2007 program underneath, the Help window disappears from sight.

To turn the Keep on Top feature on (or off), click the Keep on Top icon in the Help window (refer to Figure 3-4).

Printing the text in the Help window

Sometimes you may find the step-by-step instructions in the Help window so useful that you may want to reference them again. Rather than open the Help window each time, you can print the step-by-step instructions so you'll always have them at your fingertips when you need them.

To print the text displayed in the Help window, follow these steps:

1. **Click the Help icon or press F1 to open the Help window.**
2. **Make sure your printer is connected to your computer and turned on.**
3. **Click the Print icon (refer to Figure 3-4).**

   The Print dialog box appears.
4. **Choose any options in the Print dialog box (such as choosing a printer to use), and then click OK to print the current contents of the Help window.**

Viewing the Table of Contents

One problem with searching through the Help window is that you can easily lose track of which subcategory or category led you to view the current contents of the Help window. To avoid this confusion, you can expand the Help window to display two panes. The left pane displays a table of contents while the right pane displays additional information, as shown in Figure 3-5.

Show/Hide Table of Contents

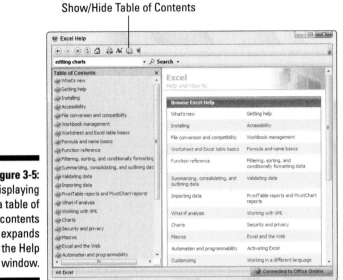

Figure 3-5:
Displaying
a table of
contents
expands
the Help
window.

To view the Table of Contents, follow these steps:

1. **Click the Help icon or press F1 to open the Help window.**

2. **Click the Show Table of Contents icon.**

   The Help window expands into two panes.

3. **Click a Help topic (which appears with a closed book icon in the left margin).**

   A list of subcategories (closed book icon) or Help topics (question mark icon) appears. You may need to click one or more additional subcategory icons until you see a list of Help topics.

4. **Click a Help topic.**

   The right pane of the Help window displays step-by-step instructions.

5. **(Optional) Click the Hide Table of Contents icon.**

   If you leave the Table of Contents pane visible, the next time you open the Help window, you'll see the table of contents in the left pane.

6. **Click the Close box to make the Help window go away.**

Part II
Working with Word

"I love the way Word justifies the text in my resume. Now if I can just get it to justify my asking salary."

In this part . . .

*W*ord processing remains the most popular use for a personal computer (right after playing games and wasting hours exploring the Internet), so this part of the book gently guides you into using the powerhouse word processor known as Microsoft Word. By using the 2007 version of Word, you can create anything from a simple letter to a resume or business report.

Along the way to discovering how to use Word's powerful features, you also encounter the more basic features, such as how to write, edit, spell-check, and grammar-check your writing, and how to format text to make it look really pretty.

Word may seem like an ordinary word processor at first glance, but this part of the book unlocks the techniques that summon Word to help you write, create, and print your ideas as fast as you care to type them. (Just as long as your computer doesn't crash on you, that is.)

Chapter 4

Typing Text in Word

· ·

In This Chapter

▶ Moving the cursor with the mouse and keyboard

▶ Viewing a document

▶ Navigating through a document

▶ Checking spelling and grammar

▶ Typing unusual symbols

· ·

*T*he whole purpose of Microsoft Word is to let you type text and make it look pretty so you can print or send it for other people to read. So the first step in using Microsoft Word is learning how to enter text in a Word file, called a *document.*

In every document, Word displays a blinking cursor that points to where your text will appear if you type anything. To move the cursor, you can use the keyboard or the mouse.

Moving the Cursor with the Mouse

When you move the mouse, Word turns the mouse pointer into an I-beam pointer. If you move the mouse over an area where you cannot type any text, the mouse pointer turns back into the traditional arrow, pointing up to the left.

To move the cursor with the mouse, just point and click the left mouse button once. The blinking cursor appears where you clicked the mouse.

If you have a blank page or a blank area at the end of your document, you can move the cursor anywhere within this blank area by following these steps:

1. **Move the mouse pointer over any blank area past the end of a document.**

   Word defines the *end* of a document as the spot where no more text appears. To find the end of a document, press Ctrl+End.

   • *In a new document:* The end of the document is in the upper-left corner where the cursor appears.

• *In a document with existing text:* The end of the document is the last area where text appears (including spaces or tabs).

2. **Move the mouse pointer over any blank area past the end of the document.**

   Notice that a Left, Center, or Right Justification icon appears to the right or bottom of the I-beam mouse pointer, as shown in Figure 4-1.

3. **Make sure the correct justification icon appears next to the mouse pointer.**

   For example, if you want to center-justify your text, make sure the Center Justification icon appears at the bottom of the I-beam pointer.

   Getting the Left, Center, or Right Justification icon to appear in Step 3 can be tricky. The Left Justification icon appears most of the time. To make the Center Justification icon appear, move the mouse pointer to the center of the page. To make the Right Justification icon appear, move the mouse pointer to the right edge of the page.

4. **Double-click the mouse pointer.**

   Word displays your cursor in the area you clicked. Any text you type now will appear justified according to the justification icon displayed in Step 3.

Figure 4-1:
The justification icon appears next to the mouse pointer when you move the mouse pointer past the end of a document.

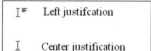

I=	Left justifcation
I	Center justification
=I	Right justification

Moving the Cursor with the Keyboard

Moving the cursor with the mouse can be fast and easy. However, touch-typists often find that moving the cursor with the keyboard is more convenient and sometimes faster too. Table 4-1 lists different keystroke combinations you can use to move the cursor.

You can move the cursor with both the keyboard and the mouse.

Table 4-1	Keystroke Shortcuts for Moving the Cursor in Word
Keystroke	*What It Does*
↑	Moves the cursor up one line
↓	Moves the cursor down one line
→	Moves the cursor right one character
←	Moves the cursor left one character
Ctrl+↑	Moves the cursor up to the beginning of the previous paragraph
Ctrl+↓	Moves the cursor down to the beginning of the next paragraph
Ctrl+→	Moves the cursor right one word
Ctrl+←	Moves the cursor left one word
Home	Moves the cursor to the beginning of the line
End	Moves the cursor to the end of the line
Ctrl+Home	Moves the cursor to the beginning of a document
Ctrl+End	Moves the cursor to the end of a document
Page Up	Moves the cursor up one screen
Page Down	Moves the cursor down one screen
Ctrl+Page Up	Moves the cursor to the top of the previous page
Ctrl+Page Down	Moves the cursor to the top of the next page

Viewing a Document

Word can display your document in one of five views, which can help you better understand the layout, margins, and page breaks in your document:

- ✔ **Print Layout:** Displays page breaks as thick, dark horizontal bars so you can clearly see where a page ends and begins. (This is the default view.)
- ✔ **Full Screen Reading:** Displays pages side by side so you see.
- ✔ **Web Layout:** Displays your document exactly as it would appear if you saved it as a Web page (looks similar to Page Layout view).
- ✔ **Outline (also called *Master Document Tools*):** Displays your document as outline headings and subheadings.
- ✔ **Draft:** Displays the document without top or bottom page margins where page breaks appear as dotted lines.

Switching between views

Microsoft Word gives you two ways to switch between different document views, as shown in Figure 4-2:

- ✔ Click the view icons in the bottom of your document window.
- ✔ Click the View tab and then click the view you want to use, such as Print Layout view.

Print Layout and Web Layout views look nearly identical, while Draft view displays your document without displaying page margins to make it easier for you to view and edit data. The two most unusual views are Full Screen Reading and Outline views.

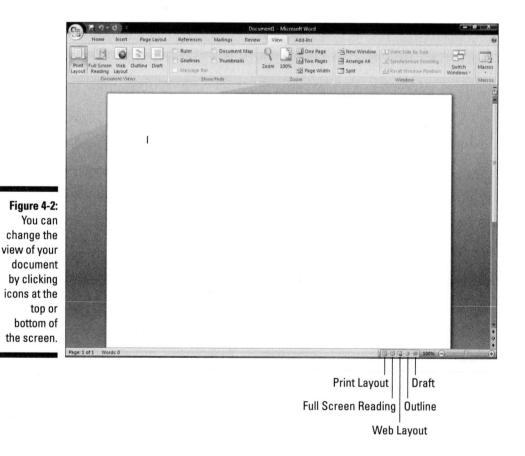

Figure 4-2: You can change the view of your document by clicking icons at the top or bottom of the screen.

Using Full Screen Reading view

Full Screen Reading view makes documents appear side by side like the pages of a book, as shown in Figure 4-3. To "turn the pages" of a document displayed in Full Screen Reading view, choose one of the following:

- ✔ Click the Previous Screen or Next Screen button.
- ✔ Click the Jump to a Page icon.

To exit Full Screen Reading view, choose one of the following:

- ✔ Press Esc.
- ✔ Click the Close button.

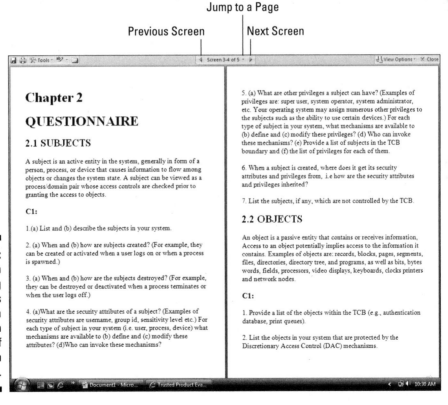

Figure 4-3: Full Screen Reading view lets you read a document in the form of an open book.

Using Outline view

Outline view divides a document into sections defined by headings and text. A *heading* represents a main idea. Text contains one or more paragraphs that are "attached" to a particular heading. A subheading lets you divide a main idea (heading) into multiple parts. A typical outline might look like Figure 4-4.

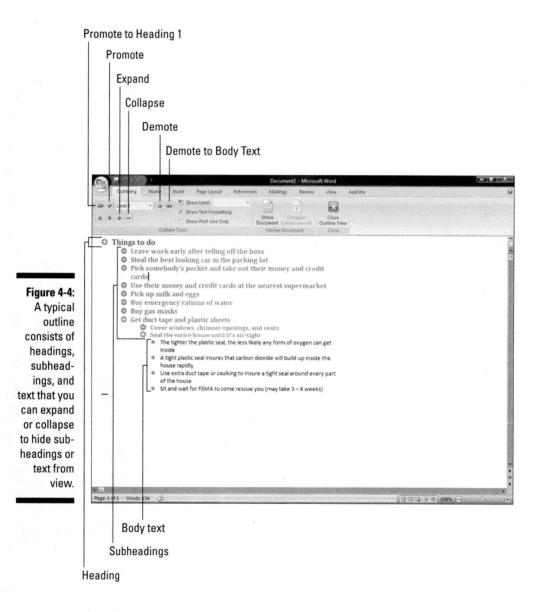

Figure 4-4:
A typical
outline
consists of
headings,
subhead-
ings, and
text that you
can expand
or collapse
to hide sub-
headings or
text from
view.

Within Outline view you can

- ✔ **Collapse headings** to hide parts (subheadings and text) temporarily from view.
- ✔ **Rearrange headings** to move subheadings and text easily within a large document.

Moving a heading automatically moves all subheadings and text. Instead of cutting and pasting multiple paragraphs, Outline view lets you rearrange a document by just moving headings around.

To switch to Outline view, click the Outline View icon at the bottom of the document window (or click the View tab and then click the Outline icon).

Defining a heading

Outline view considers each line as either a heading or text. To define a line as either a heading style (Level 1 to Level 9) or text, follow these steps:

1. **Move the cursor on the line that you want to define as a heading or text.**

2. **Click in the Outline Level list box and choose a heading level, such as Level 2.**

Word displays Level 1 headings in large type to the far left margin. Level 2 headings appear in smaller type that's slightly indented to the right, Level 3 headings appear in even smaller type that's indented further to the right, and so on, as shown in Figure 4-5.

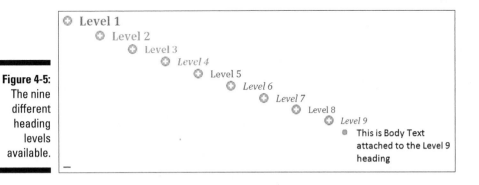

Figure 4-5:
The nine
different
heading
levels
available.

To create a heading quickly, move the cursor to the end of an existing heading and press Enter to create an identical heading. For example, if you put the cursor at the end of a Level 3 heading and press Enter, Word creates a new blank Level 3 heading.

Promoting and demoting a heading

After you define a heading (such as a Level 1 or Level 3 heading), you can always change its level, such as changing a Level 1 heading to a Level 2 heading or vice versa. When you raise a heading from one level to another (such as from Level 3 to Level 2), that's *promoting*. When you lower a heading (such as from Level 4 to Level 5), that's *demoting*.

A Level 1 heading cannot be promoted because Level 1 is the highest heading. Likewise, a Level 9 heading cannot be demoted because Level 9 is the lowest heading.

To promote or demote a heading to a different level, follow these steps:

1. **Using either the mouse or the keyboard, move the cursor to the heading you want to promote or demote.**

2. **Choose one of the following methods:**

   - Click the Outline Level list box and click a level (such as Level 2).

   - Press Tab (to promote) or Shift+Tab (to demote) the heading.

   - Click the Promote or Demote arrow.

   - Move the mouse pointer over the circle that appears to the left of the heading, hold down the left mouse button, drag the mouse right or left, and then release the left mouse button.

You can convert a heading to a Level 1 heading quickly by just clicking the Promote to Heading 1 arrow.

Promoting or demoting a heading moves any subheadings or text attached to the promoted or demoted heading.

Moving headings

You can move headings up or down within a document. To move a heading, follow these steps:

1. **Using either the mouse or the keyboard, move the cursor to the heading you want to promote or demote.**

2. **Choose one of the following methods:**

   - Click the Move Up or Move Down arrow.

   - Press Alt+Shift+↑ or Alt+Shift+↓.

   - Move the mouse pointer over the circle that appears to the left of the heading, hold down the left mouse button, drag the mouse up or down, and then release the left mouse button.

If you collapse a heading before moving it, you can move any subheadings or text underneath that heading.

Creating text

Text can consist of a single sentence, multiple sentences, or several paragraphs. Text always appears indented underneath a heading (or subheading). To create text, follow these steps:

1. **Move the cursor to the end of a heading or subheading.**

   This is the heading (or subheading) that your text will be attached to if you move the heading (or subheading).

2. **Press Enter.**

   Word creates a blank heading.

3. **Click the Demote to Body Text button.**

   Word displays a bullet indented underneath the heading you chose in Step 1.

4. **Type your text.**

Collapsing and expanding headings and subheadings

If a heading or subheading contains any subheadings or text underneath, you can collapse that heading. *Collapsing* a heading simply hides any indented subheadings or text from view temporarily. *Expanding* a heading displays any previously hidden subheadings or text.

To collapse a heading along with all subheadings or body text underneath it, double-click the plus icon that appears to the left of the heading.

If you just want to collapse the subheading or body text immediately underneath a heading, choose one of the following:

- Move the cursor anywhere in the heading you want to collapse and then click the Collapse button.
- Press Alt+Shift++ (plus sign key).

To expand a collapsed heading to reveal all subheadings and body text, double-click the plus icon that appears to the left of the heading.

If you just want to expand the subheading or body text immediately underneath a collapsed heading, choose one of the following:

- Move the cursor anywhere in the heading you want to expand and then click the Expand button.
- Press Alt+Shift+ – (minus sign key).

Navigating through a Document

If you have a large document that consists of many pages, you won't be able to see all the pages at the same time. Instead, you'll have to scroll through your document using either the mouse or the keyboard.

Navigating with the mouse

To scroll through a document with the mouse, you have two choices:

- ✔ Use the vertical scroll bar that appears on the right side of every document window.

- ✔ Use the scroll wheel of your mouse (assuming that your mouse has a scroll wheel).

Using the scroll bar

The scroll bar gives you multiple ways to navigate through a document, as shown in Figure 4-6:

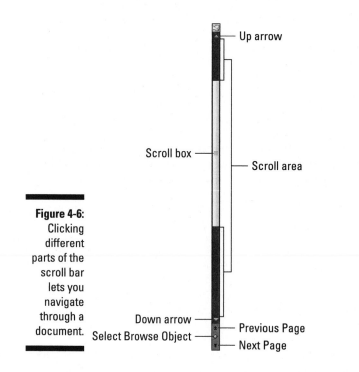

Up arrow

Scroll box

Scroll area

Figure 4-6:
Clicking
different
parts of the
scroll bar
lets you
navigate
through a
document.

Down arrow

Select Browse Object

Previous Page

Next Page

✔ **Up arrow (↑):** Moves up one line at a time.

✔ **Down arrow (↓):** Moves down one line at a time.

✔ **Scroll box:** Dragging the scroll box up displays different pages. Moving the scroll box up moves closer to the beginning; moving the scroll box down moves closer to the end.

✔ **Scroll area:** Clicking above the scroll box moves the document one screen up; clicking below the scroll box moves the document one screen down.

✔ **Previous Page:** Moves the cursor to the top of the previous page.

✔ **Next Page:** Moves the cursor to the top of the next page.

✔ **Select Browse Object:** Gives you a variety of ways to move to another part of a document such as by page, section, or heading.

Using a mouse scroll wheel

If your mouse has a scroll wheel, you can use that to scroll through a document in one of two ways:

✔ Move the mouse pointer over your document and roll the scroll wheel up or down.

✔ Move the mouse pointer over your document and click the scroll wheel; then move the mouse up or down. (The scrolling speeds up the farther up or down you move the mouse from the position where you clicked the scroll wheel.) Click the left mouse button or the scroll wheel to turn off automatic scrolling when you're done.

Using the Go To command

If you know the specific page number of your document that you want to scroll to, you can jump to that page right away by using the Go To command. To use the Go To command, follow these steps:

1. **Click the Home tab.**

2. **Choose one of the following:**

   • Click the Editing icon, click the downward-pointing arrow to the right of the Find command, and click Go To.

   • Click the Page button in the bottom-left corner.

   • Click the Select Browse Object icon and then click the Go To icon.

   • Press Ctrl+G.

   The Find and Replace dialog box appears with the Go To tab selected, as shown in Figure 4-7.

Figure 4-7:
The Go To
tab displays
a menu of
different
searching
options.

Find and Replace			
Find	Replace	Go To	

Go to what:
Page
Section
Line
Bookmark
Comment
Footnote

Enter page number:
4

Enter + and – to move relative to the current location. Example: +4 will move forward four items.

Previous   Go To   Close

3. **Click in the Enter Page Number text box and type a page number.**

If you type a plus sign (+) or a minus sign (–) in front of a number, you can scroll that many pages forward or backward from the currently displayed page. For example, if the displayed page is 5, typing **–2** displays page 3 and typing **+12** displays page 17.

4. **Click the Go To button.**

Word displays your chosen page.

5. **Click Close to make the Find and Replace dialog box disappear.**

Finding and Replacing Text

To help you find text, Word offers a handy Find feature. Not only can this Find feature search for a word or phrase, but it also offers a Replace option so you can make Word find certain words and replace them with other words automatically.

Using the Find command

The Find command can search for a single character, word, or a group of words. To make searching faster, you can either search an entire document or just a specific part of a document. To use the Find command, follow these steps:

1. **Click the Home tab.**

2. **Click the Editing icon and then click the Find command.**

The Find and Replace dialog box appears.

3. **Click in the Find What text box and type a word or phrase to find.**

4. **(Optional) Click the More button and select any additional options, as shown in Figure 4-8:**

   • *Match Case:* Finds text that exactly matches the upper- and lower-case letters you type

   • *Find Whole Words Only:* Finds text that is not part of another word. Searching for *on* will not find words like *onion*

   • *Use Wildcards:* Lets you use the single character (?) or multiple character (*) wildcards, such as searching for *d?g,* which will find *dog* or *dig;* or *b*t,* which will find *but, butt,* or *boost*

   • *Sounds Like:* Searches for words based on their phonetic pronunciation such as finding *elephant* when searching for *elefant*

   • *Find All Word Forms:* Finds all variations of a word, such as finding *run, ran,* and *running*

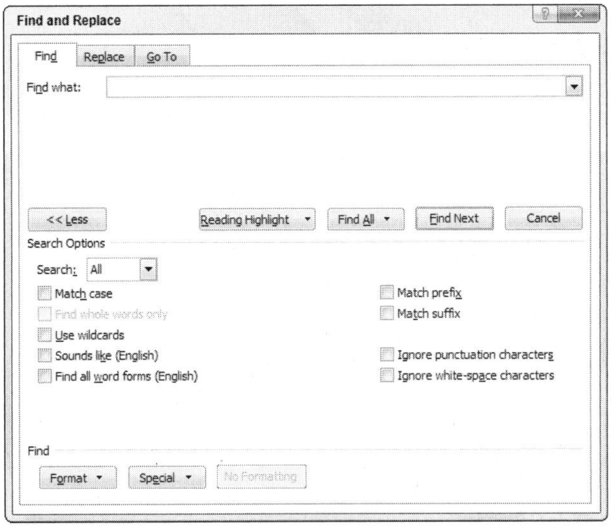

Figure 4-8:
The More button lets you choose additional options for searching for text.

5. **Click one of the following buttons:**

   • *Find All:* Searches the entire document

   • *Find Next:* Searches from the current cursor location to the end of the document

6. **Click Find Next to search for additional occurrences of the text you typed in Step 3.**

7. **Click Cancel to make the Find and Replace dialog box disappear.**

Using the Find and Replace command

Rather than just find a word or phrase, you may want to find that text and replace it with something else. To use the Find and Replace command, follow these steps:

1. **Click the Home tab.**

2. **Click the Editing icon and then click the Replace command. (You can also press Ctrl+H.)**

   The Find and Replace dialog box appears.

3. **Click in the Find What text box and type a word or phrase to find.**

4. **Click in the Replace With text box and type a word or phrase to replace the text you typed in Step 3.**

5. **(Optional) Click the More button and choose any additional options (refer to Figure 4-8).**

6. **Click one of the following buttons:**

   - *Replace All:* Searches and replaces text throughout the entire document

   - *Replace:* Replaces the currently highlighted text

   - *Find Next:* Searches from the current cursor location to the end of the document

7. **Click Find Next to search for additional occurrences of the text you typed in Step 3.**

8. **Click Cancel to make the Find and Replace dialog box disappear.**

Checking Your Spelling

As you type, Word tries to correct your spelling automatically. (Try it! Type **tjhe**, and Word will automatically change it to *the* in the blink of an eye.) If you type something that Word doesn't recognize, it underlines it with a red squiggly line.

Just because Word underlines a word doesn't necessarily mean that the word is spelled wrong. It could be a proper name, a foreign word, or just a word that Word isn't smart enough to recognize.

To correct any words that Word underlines with a red squiggly line, follow these steps:

1. **Right-click any word underlined with a red squiggly line.**

   A pop-up menu appears, as shown in Figure 4-9.

2. **Choose one of the following:**

   - *The word you want:* Click the correct spelling of the word that appears in bold in the pop-up menu.

   - *Ignore All:* This tells Word to ignore this word throughout your document.

   - *Add to Dictionary:* This tells Word to remember this word and never flag it again as a misspelled word.

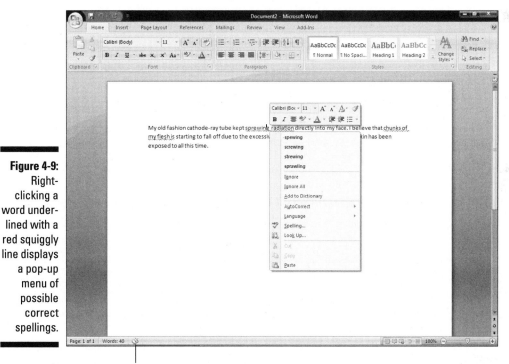

Figure 4-9: Right-clicking a word under-lined with a red squiggly line displays a pop-up menu of possible correct spellings.

Proofing icon

Checking Your Grammar

Sometimes Word may underline one or more words with a green squiggly line to highlight possible grammar errors. To correct any grammar errors, follow these steps:

1. **Right-click any text underlined with a green squiggly line.**

   A pop-up menu appears.

2. **Choose one of the following:**

   - *What you want:* Click the correct grammar that appears in bold in the pop-up menu.

   - *Ignore All:* This tells Word to ignore this type of grammatical error throughout your document.

   - *Add to Dictionary:* This tells Word to remember this grammatical construct and never flag it again as incorrect.

Proofreading Your Document

Besides checking for spelling or grammatical mistakes, Word can also proofread your document to highlight other possible problems, such as misplaced commas or correctly spelled words that may be used incorrectly. To make Word proofread your document, follow these steps:

1. **Click the Proofing icon at the bottom of the document window.**

   Word highlights a possible error and displays a pop-up menu offering options similar to the options displayed in Figure 4-9.

2. **Choose one of the following:**

   - *What you want:* Click the correct word that appears in bold in the pop-up menu.

   - *Ignore Once:* This tells Word to ignore this error.

 By default, Word automatically checks for spelling and grammatical mistakes. If this bothers you, you can turn these features off by right-clicking the status bar; when a pop-up menu appears, remove the check mark from the Spelling and Grammar Check check box.

Typing Symbols

Most keyboards display a limited number of characters you can type, but what if you want to create unusual symbols such as Π or ©? To create these symbols, Word can display a list of common symbols and let you click the one you want to insert in your document.

To insert an unusual symbol in a document, follow these steps:

1. **Move the cursor where you want to insert a character that you can't type from the keyboard.**
2. **Click the Insert tab.**
3. **Click the Symbol icon in the Symbols group.**

   A pull-down menu appears, as shown in Figure 4-10.

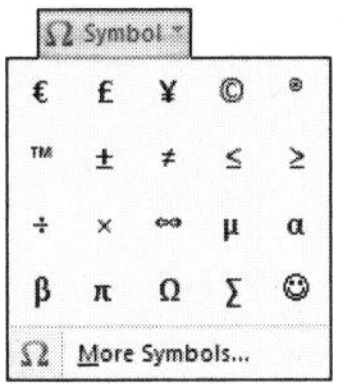

Figure 4-10: The Symbol menu lists common symbols.

4. **Click the symbol you want.**

   Word inserts your chosen symbol in your document.

5. **(Optional) If you don't see the symbol you want to add**

   a. *Click More Symbols.*

      Word displays a Symbol dialog box, as shown in Figure 4-11.

   b. *Click a symbol you want to use and then click Close.*

Word can also insert mathematical equations into a document if you click Equations instead of Symbol in Step 3.

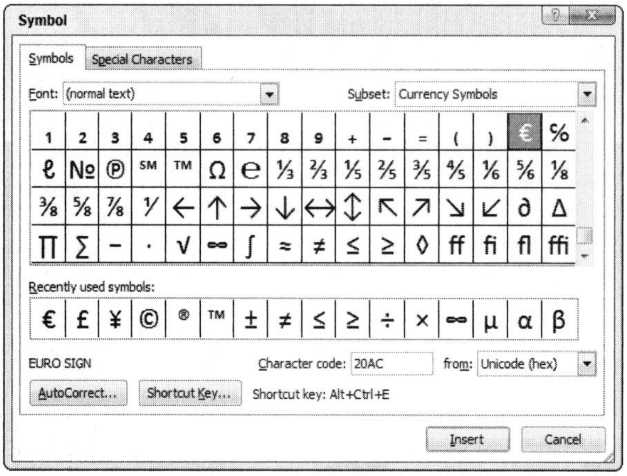

Figure 4-11:
The Symbol
dialog box
displays
every pos-
sible symbol
Word can
insert in a
document.

Chapter 5

Formatting Text

In This Chapter

▶ Changing fonts

▶ Changing the font size

▶ Using text styles

▶ Coloring text

▶ Justifying text

▶ Creating lists

▶ Clearing formatting

*A*fter you type text into a document, edit it, and check it for spelling or grammatical errors, you're ready to make it look pretty, a process known as *formatting text*. A properly formatted document can make your text easy to read, while a poorly formatted document can make even the best writing difficult or confusing to read.

The Home tab groups Word's formatting tools into three categories:

✔ **Font:** Defines the font, font size, color, highlighting, and style (bold, italic, underline, strikethrough, superscript, subscript, and case)

✔ **Paragraph:** Defines justification (left, center, or right), line spacing, shading, borders, indentation, formatting symbols, and list style (bullets, numbered, and outline)

✔ **Styles:** Displays predefined formatting that you can apply to your text

To format any text, you must follow these steps:

1. **Select the text you want to format.**

2. **Choose a formatting tool.**

When you choose most formatting commands, that command stays on until you turn it off by choosing the same command again.

As soon as you select text, Word displays the most commonly used formatting tools in a floating toolbar, as shown in Figure 5-1. You can click any icon on this floating toolbar rather than click the same icon stored at the top of the screen.

Figure 5-1:
Format text
with the
floating
toolbar.

Formatting Text

Changing the Font

The most common way to format text is to change the font. The font defines the uniform style and appearance of letters such as Baskerville, Courier, Old English, or **STENCIL**.

To change the font, follow these steps:

1. **Click the Home tab.**
2. **Select the text you want to change.**
3. **Click the Font list box.**

   A list of available fonts on your computer appears, as shown in Figure 5-2.

4. **Move the mouse pointer over each font.**

   Word temporarily changes your selected text (from Step 1) so you can see how the currently highlighted font will look.

5. **Click the font you want to use.**

   Word changes your text to appear in your chosen font.

As a general rule, try not to use more than three fonts in a document. If you use too many fonts, the overall appearance can be annoying and distracting.

Not all computers have the same lists of fonts, so if you plan on sharing documents with others, stick with common fonts that everybody's computer can display.

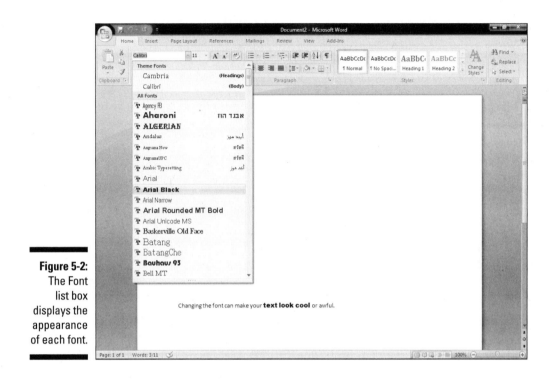

Figure 5-2:
The Font
list box
displays the
appearance
of each font.

Changing the Font Size

The *font* changes the appearance of text, but the *font size* defines how big (or small) the text may look. To change the font size, you have two choices:

✔ Select a numeric size from the Font Size list box.

✔ Choose the Grow Font/Shrink Font commands.

You can use both methods to change the font size of text. For example, you may use the Font Size list box to choose an approximate size for your text, and then use the Grow Font/Shrink Font commands to fine-tune the font size.

To change the font size, follow these steps:

1. **Click the Home tab.**

2. **Select the text you want to change.**

3. **Choose one of the following:**

   • Click the Font Size list box and then click a number, such as 12 or 24, as shown in Figure 5-3.

   • Click the Grow Font or Shrink Font icon.

Shrink Font

Grow Font

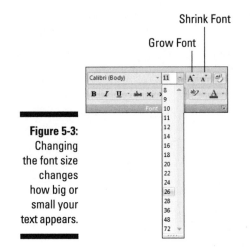

Figure 5-3:
Changing
the font size
changes
how big or
small your
text appears.

Changing the Text Style

The text style defines the appearance of text in one or more of the following ways:

- ✔ **Bold:** Press Ctrl+B.
- ✔ *Italic:* Press Ctrl+I.
- ✔ <u>Underline</u>: Press Ctrl+U.
- ✔ ~~Strikethrough~~: This formatting draws a line through text.
- ✔ Subscript: Use this to create text that falls below the text line, as in the 2 in H_2O.
- ✔ Superscript: Use this to create text that sits higher than the top of the text line, as in the 2 in $E = mc^2$.

To change the style of text, follow these steps:

1. **Click the Home tab.**
2. **Select the text you want to change.**
3. **Click a Style icon, such as Bold or Underline.**
4. **Repeat Step 3 for each additional style you want to apply to your text (<u>such as *italic* and underlining</u>).**

If you select any style change without selecting any text, Word applies your style changes to any new text you type from the cursor's current position.

Changing Colors

Color can emphasize text. There are two ways to use color:

- ✔ Change the color of the text (Font color).
- ✔ Highlight the text with a different color (Text Highlight color).

Changing the color of text

When you change the color of text, you're physically displaying a different color for each letter. Normally, Word displays text in black, but you can change the color to anything you want, such as bright red or dark green.

If you choose a light color for your text, it may be hard to read against a white background.

To change the color of text, follow these steps:

1. **Click the Home tab.**
2. **Select the text you want to color.**
3. **Click the downward-pointing arrow to the right of the Font Color icon.**

   A color palette appears, as shown in Figure 5-4.
4. **Click a color.**

   Word displays your selected text (from Step 1) in your chosen color.

After you choose a color, that color appears directly on the Font Color icon. Now you can select text and click directly on the Font Color icon (not the downward-pointing arrow) to color your text.

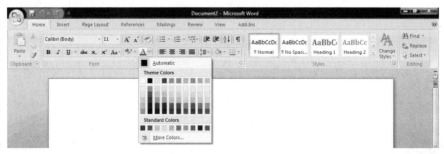

Figure 5-4: Coloring text in different ways can emphasize parts of your document.

Highlighting text

Highlighting text mimics coloring chunks of text with a highlighting marker that students often use to emphasize passages in a book. To highlight text:

1. **Click the Home tab.**

2. **Select the text you want to highlight.**

3. **Click the downward-pointing arrow to the right of the Text Highlight Color icon.**

   A color palette appears, as shown in Figure 5-5.

Figure 5-5:
The Text
Highlight
Color palette
lets you
choose a
highlighting
color.

4. **Click a color.**

   Word highlights your selected text (from Step 2) in your chosen color.

5. **Press Esc (or click the Text Highlight Color icon again) to turn off the Text Highlight Color command.**

To remove a highlight, select the text and choose No Color (or just choose the same color again).

If no text is selected and the Text Highlight Color currently displays a color you want to use (such as yellow), you can click the Text Highlight Color icon (not its downward-pointing arrow). This turns the mouse pointer into a marker icon. Now you can select and highlight text in one step.

Justifying Text Alignment

Word can align text in one of four ways, as shown in Figure 5-6:

- ✔ **Left:** Text appears flush against the left margin but ragged on the right margin.

- ✔ **Center:** Every line appears centered within the left and right margins.

> ✔ **Right:** Text appears flush against the right margin but ragged on the left margin.
>
> ✔ **Justified:** Text appears flush against both the left and right margins.

To align text, follow these steps:

1. **Click the Home tab.**

2. **Move the cursor anywhere in the text you want to align.**

3. **Click one of the alignment icons, such as Center or Justify.**

Rather than click an alignment icon, you can use one of the alignment keystroke shortcuts as follows: Align Left (Ctrl+L), Center (Ctrl+E), Align Right (Ctrl+R), or Justify (Ctrl+J).

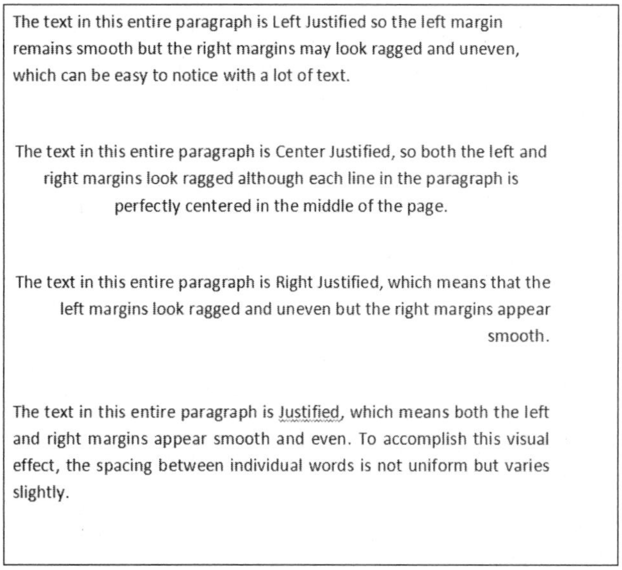

Figure 5-6: The four different alignment styles display text in different ways.

The text in this entire paragraph is Left Justified so the left margin remains smooth but the right margins may look ragged and uneven, which can be easy to notice with a lot of text.

The text in this entire paragraph is Center Justified, so both the left and right margins look ragged although each line in the paragraph is perfectly centered in the middle of the page.

The text in this entire paragraph is Right Justified, which means that the left margins look ragged and uneven but the right margins appear smooth.

The text in this entire paragraph is Justified, which means both the left and right margins appear smooth and even. To accomplish this visual effect, the spacing between individual words is not uniform but varies slightly.

Adjusting Line Spacing

Line spacing defines how close lines appear stacked on top of each other. To change the line spacing of text, follow these steps:

1. **Click the Home tab.**

2. **Select the text that you want to adjust the line spacing.**

3. **Click the Line Spacing icon.**

   A pull-down menu appears, as shown in Figure 5-7.

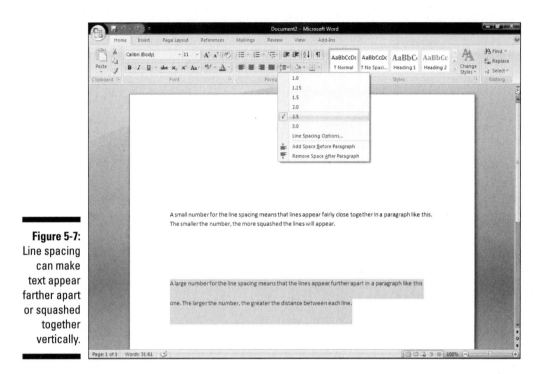

Figure 5-7:
Line spacing
can make
text appear
farther apart
or squashed
together
vertically.

4. Click the line spacing you want, such as 1 (single spacing) or 3 (triple spacing).

If you click the More option in the pull-down menu, you can precisely define your own line spacing, such as 2.75 or 3.13.

Making Lists

Word can organize and arrange text in three types of lists:

- ✔ Bullets (like this list)
- ✔ Numbering
- ✔ Multilevel list

You can create a list from scratch or convert existing text into a list. To create a list from scratch, follow these steps:

1. Click the Home tab.

2. Move the cursor where you want to create a list.

3. **Click the Bullets, Numbering, or Multilevel List icon.**

   Word creates your list (bulleted or numbered).

4. **Type your text and press Enter to create another blank item in your list.**

5. **Repeat Step 4 for each additional bullet or numbered item you want to make.**

If you have existing text, you can convert it into a list by following these steps:

1. **Click the Home tab.**

2. **Select the text you want to convert into a list.**

3. **Click the Bullets, Numbering, or Outline Numbering icon.**

   Word converts your selected text into your chosen list where each paragraph appears as a separate item in the list.

Indenting list items

After you create a list, you may want to indent one list item underneath another one. To indent an item in a list, follow these steps:

1. **Move the cursor anywhere in the text in the list item you want to indent.**

2. **Press the Home key to move the cursor to the front of the line.**

3. **Press the Tab key to indent an item to the right (or press the Shift+Tab keystroke combination to indent an item to the left).**

   When you indent a list, Word changes the number or bullet style to set the line apart from the rest of your list.

Converting list items back into text

If you have a list, you may want to convert one or more items back into ordinary text. To convert a list item into plain text, follow these steps:

1. **Click the Home tab.**

2. **Select the list items you want to convert into plain text.**

3. **Click the appropriate Bullets, Numbering, or Outline Numbering icon.**

   If you want to convert a bullet list item into text, you would click the Bullets icon.

Customizing a list

When you create a bullet or numbered list, you can choose from a variety of different styles. To choose a numbering style, follow these steps:

1. **Click the downward-pointing arrow to the right of a list icon, such as the Bullet or Numbering icon.**

   Make sure you don't click the Numbering icon itself.

   A pull-down menu appears listing all the different numbering styles available, as shown in Figure 5-8.

2. **Click the numbering style you want.**

   The next time you click the Numbering icon, Word will use the numbering style you chose.

The changes you make to the numbering or bullet style will only apply to your current document.

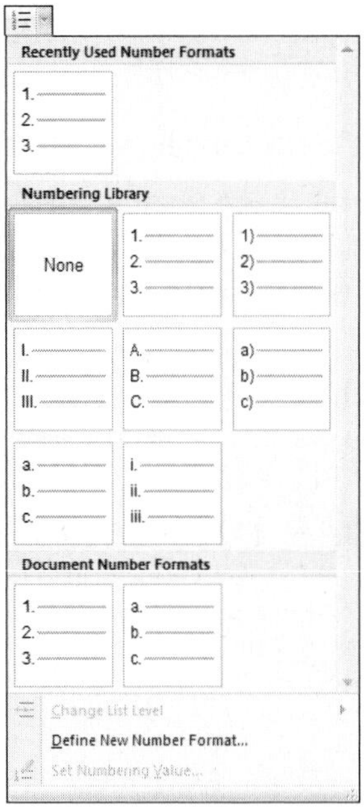

Figure 5-8:
The different numbering styles you can choose for creating numbered lists.

Renumbering numbered lists

Number lists can cause special problems when dividing or copying them because the numbering may get out of sequence, or you may want to start numbering from a number other than one.

To change the starting number of a numbered list, follow these steps:

1. **Right-click the item that you want to renumber.**

   If you want to renumber your entire list, right-click the first item at the top of the numbered list.

   A pop-up menu appears, as shown in Figure 5-9.

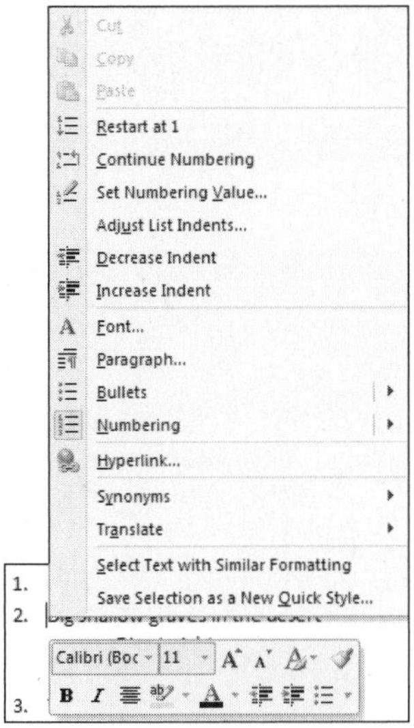

Figure 5-9: Right-clicking a numbered list item to see options for renumbering your list.

2. **Choose one of the following:**

   • *Restart at 1:* Changes the numbering of the current list item to 1, the list item directly below to 2, and so on. (This option does not appear if you right-click the first item in a number list.)

   • *Continue Numbering:* Changes the number of the current list item to one greater than the last numbered list item earlier in the document.

   • *Set Numbering Value:* Displays the Set Numbering Value dialog box, as shown in Figure 5-10, so you can change the current list item to a specific number such as 34 or 89.

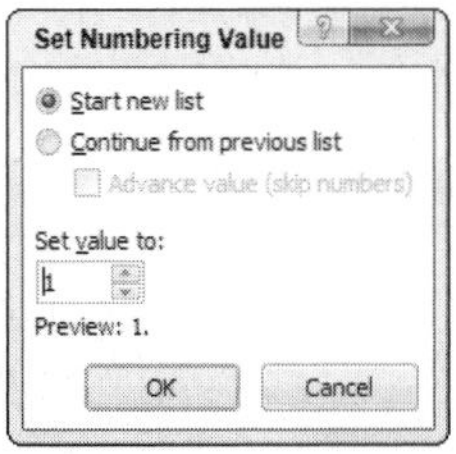

Figure 5-10: Choose a number for your list.

Using the Ruler

When you create a document, Word creates page margins automatically. However, if you want to adjust the left and right page margins, or define how far the Tab key indents text, you need to use the Ruler.

By default, Word hides the Ruler to avoid cluttering up the screen. To display the Ruler, click the View Ruler icon, as shown in Figure 5-11.

To hide the Ruler from view, just click the View Ruler icon again.

View Ruler icon

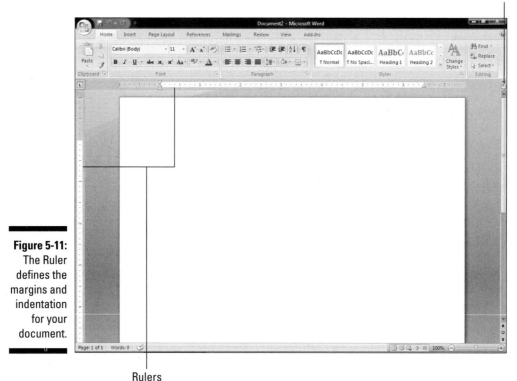

Figure 5-11: The Ruler defines the margins and indentation for your document.

Rulers

Adjusting left and right paragraph margins

The Ruler defines the left and right margins for your paragraphs. To change these paragraph margins, follow these steps:

1. **Make sure the Ruler appears visible.**

2. **Select any text.**

3. **Move the mouse pointer over the Left Indent icon on the Ruler, hold down the left mouse button, and drag (move) the mouse to the right to adjust the left paragraph margin.**

   Word displays a dotted vertical line to show you where the new left paragraph margin will be, as shown in Figure 5-12.

Figure 5-12:
Dragging the Left Indent icon lets you define a new left page margin for an entire document or just selected text.

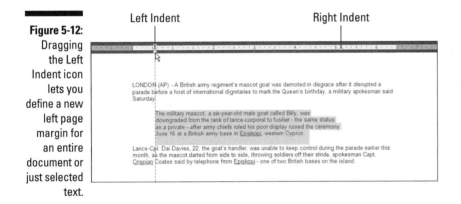

4. **Release the left mouse button when you're happy with the position of the left paragraph margin.**

5. **Move the mouse pointer over the Right Indent icon on the Ruler, hold down the left mouse button, and drag (move) the mouse to the left to adjust the right paragraph margin.**

   Word displays a dotted vertical line to show you where the new right paragraph margin will be.

6. **Release the left mouse button when you're happy with the position of the right paragraph margin.**

Defining indentation with the Ruler

The two icons on the Ruler that define indentation are the First Line Indent and the Hanging Indent icons. The First Line Indent icon defines the position of (what else?) the first line of every paragraph. The Hanging Indent icon defines the position of every line of text except for the first line, as shown in Figure 5-13.

Figure 5-13:
Drag
the icons
to set the
indentation.

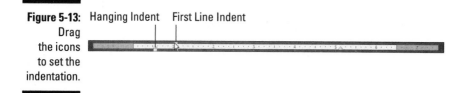

Hanging Indent   First Line Indent

To define the first line and hanging indent, follow these steps:

1. **Make sure the Ruler appears visible.**

2. **Select any text.**

3. **Move the mouse pointer over the Left Indent icon on the Ruler, hold down the left mouse button, and drag (move) the mouse to the right.**

   Word displays a dotted vertical line to show you where the new indentation margin will be.

4. **Release the left mouse button when you're happy with the position of the left indentation of your text.**

5. **Move the mouse pointer over the First Line Indent icon on the Ruler, hold down the left mouse button, and drag (move) the mouse to the right (or left).**

   Word displays a dotted vertical line to show you where the new first line indentation will be.

6. **Release the left mouse button when you're happy with the position of the first line indent position.**

Showing Formatting Marks

If you need to precisely align text, you may want to display Word's special formatting symbols. These symbols show you the exact position of spaces, tabs, and the ends of paragraphs.

To show (or hide) formatting marks, follow these steps:

1. **Click the Office Button.**

   A pull-down menu appears.

2. **Choose Word Options.**

   The Word Options dialog box appears.

3. **Click Display.**

   The Word Options dialog box displays check boxes to define which types of characters you want to make visible in your document.

4. **Mark (click) the check boxes of the formatting symbols you want to display, such as Spaces or Tab Characters, as shown in Figure 5-14.**

   Word displays your document with the formatting marks you want to display.

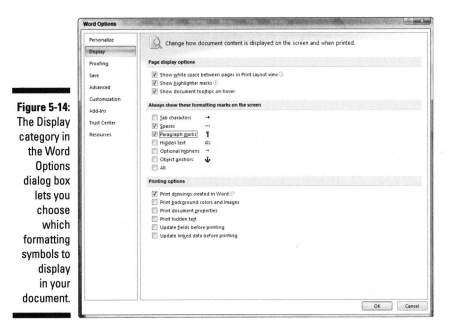

Figure 5-14: The Display category in the Word Options dialog box lets you choose which formatting symbols to display in your document.

5. **Click OK.**

For a faster way to turn on/off formatting marks, click the Home tab and then click the Show/Hide Paragraph Marks icon in the Paragraph group. This turns on all formatting marks, unlike Steps 1–5, which allow you to selectively choose which formatting marks to display, such as Spaces or Return characters.

Using Format Painter

Formatting can be simple, such as underlining text, or fairly complicated, such as underlining text while also changing its font and font size. After you format one chunk of text a certain way, you may want to format other parts of your document the exact same way.

Although you could take time to format text manually, it's much easier to use Format Painter instead. Format Painter tells Word, "See the way I formatted that chunk of text over there? Apply that same formatting to a new chunk of text."

To use Format Painter, follow these steps:

1. **Click the Home tab.**

2. **Select the text that contains the formatting you want to copy.**

3. **Click the Format Painter icon, as shown in Figure 5-15.**

4. **Select the text that you want to format. (Move the mouse pointer over the beginning of the text you want to format, hold down the left mouse button, and drag the mouse until you reach the end of the text you want to format.)**

   Word applies your formatting to your text.

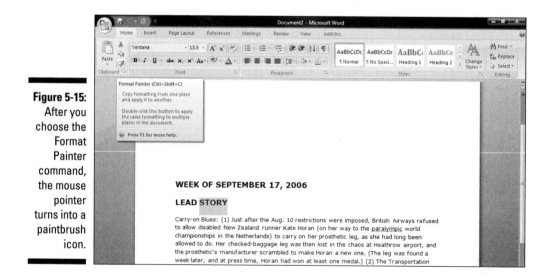

Figure 5-15:
After you choose the Format Painter command, the mouse pointer turns into a paintbrush icon.

Using Styles

As an alternative to choosing fonts, font sizes, and text styles (like bold) individually, Word offers several predefined formatting styles. To apply a style to your text, follow these steps:

1. **Click the Home tab.**

2. **Select the text that you want to format.**

3. **Click the up/down arrows of the Styles scroll bar to scroll through the different styles available. Or click the More button to display a pull-down menu of all the Quick Formatting styles, as shown in Figure 5-16.**

4. **Move the mouse pointer over a style.**

   Word displays what your text will look like if you choose this style.

5. **Click the style you want to use, such as Heading 1, Title, or Quote.**

   Word formats your text.

For another way to use a style, click on the diagonal button that appears in the bottom-right corner of the Styles group. This will open a Styles window that displays a list of available styles. (You can click on the close box of the Styles window to make it go away when you're done using it.)

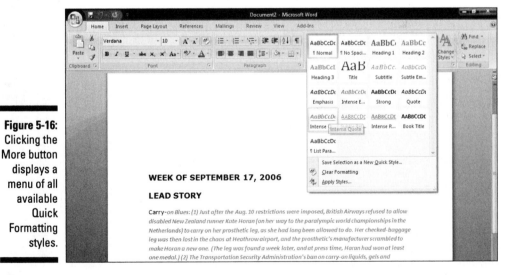

Figure 5-16: Clicking the More button displays a menu of all available Quick Formatting styles.

Using Templates

In case you need to format an entire document a certain way, you may want to use templates instead. *Templates* act like preformatted documents. Word comes with several templates, but Microsoft offers several through its Web site as well.

Creating a new document from a template

The easiest time to use a template is before you've typed any text. To create a new document from a template, follow these steps:

1. **Click the Office Button and then choose New.**

   A New Document window appears.

2. **Click one of the following in the left pane of the New Document window:**

   - *Installed Templates:* Displays templates installed on your computer

   - *Any category* under the Microsoft Office Online heading, such as Brochures or Forms

   The New Document window displays a list of available templates so you can see how they format text, as shown in Figure 5-17. If you don't choose a template, Word chooses the Normal template by default.

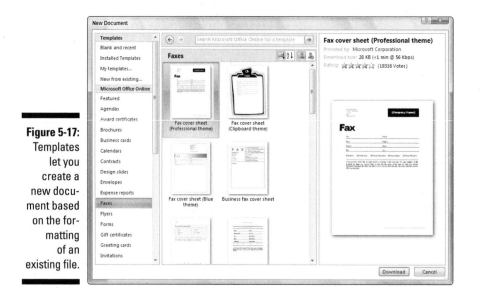

Figure 5-17: Templates let you create a new document based on the formatting of an existing file.

3. **Click a template and then click Create or Download.**

   Word creates a blank document with "dummy" text to show you how the formatting looks.

4. **Type new text and use the Style icons to apply the predefined formatting from your template to your text.**

Creating a document based on an existing document

If you already have a document that's formatted perfectly, you may want to use that document as a template for creating a new document. This essentially copies an existing document, including all its text and formatting, and creates a new document for you to edit and save under a new name.

To create a new document based on an existing one, follow these steps:

1. **Click the Office Button and then choose New.**

   A New Document window appears.

2. **Click the Featuring pane in the Installed Templates list.**

3. **Click New from Existing Document.**

   The New from Existing Document dialog box appears.

4. **Click the file that contains the formatting you want to duplicate in a new document.**

5. **Click Create New.**

   Word displays a copy of the file you chose in Step 4.

6. **Save this document under a new name and edit the current text.**

Removing Formatting from Text

After you format text, you can always remove that formatting. The simplest way to do this is to apply the same formatting you want to remove. For example, if you underline text, you can remove the underlining by highlighting all the underlined text and choosing the underline command (by pressing Ctrl+U or by clicking the Underline icon).

If you want to remove multiple formatting from text, you could remove each formatting style one by one, but it's much easier just to use the Clear Formatting command instead, which removes all formatting on text no matter how much formatting there may be.

To use the Clear Formatting command, follow these steps:

1. **Click the Home tab.**
2. **Select the text that contains the formatting you want to remove.**
3. **Click the Clear Formatting icon, as shown in Figure 5-18.**

   Word removes all formatting from your selected text.

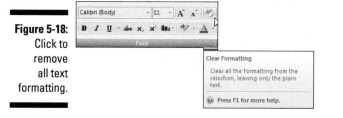

Figure 5-18: Click to remove all text formatting.

The Clear Formatting command will not remove any highlighting you may have applied over text.

Chapter 6

Designing Your Pages

· ·

In This Chapter

▶ Inserting pages

▶ Organizing text in tables

▶ Displaying text as WordArt

▶ Creating text boxes

▶ Dividing text into columns

▶ Adding pictures

▶ Printing

· ·

*T*o design the overall layout of your pages by adding columns or headers and footers that display titles or page numbers, you use the Insert and Page Layout tabs.

The Insert tab provides commands for inserting items into a document, such as new pages, tables, pictures, and headers and footers.

The Page Layout tab provides commands for defining how your pages look, such as creating columns; defining top, bottom, left, and right page margins; as well as defining how text wraps around pictures or other objects you place in the middle of a page.

Inserting New Pages

Word automatically adds new pages to your document as you write. However, Word also gives you the option of adding a new page in the middle or the beginning of your document.

To insert a new, blank page in your document, follow these steps:

1. **Click the Insert tab.**

2. **Move the cursor where you want to insert the new page.**

3. **Click the Blank Page icon in the Pages group.**

Word adds a blank page to your document.

You don't need to add a page to the end of a document. Just move the cursor to the end of your document (Ctrl+End), start typing, and Word adds new pages at the end of your document automatically.

Adding (And Deleting) a Cover Page

Rather than add more pages to type text, you may just need a cover page that is the first page that anyone can read. To create a cover page, follow these steps:

1. **Click the Insert tab.**

2. **Click the Cover Page icon in the Pages group.**

Word displays a list of cover page designs, as shown in Figure 6-1.

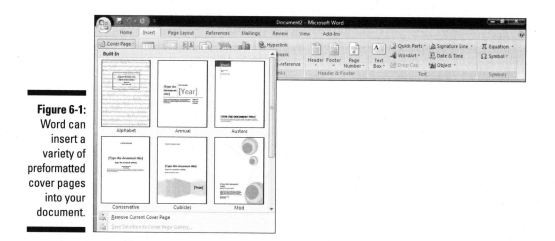

Figure 6-1:
Word can insert a variety of preformatted cover pages into your document.

3. **Click a cover page design.**

Word adds your chosen cover page as the first page of your document.

A document can have only one cover page at a time. If you choose another cover page, Word deletes your current cover page and replaces it with the new one you chose.

After you add a cover page, you may want to delete it later. To delete a cover page, follow these steps:

1. **Click the Insert tab.**
2. **Click Cover Page in the Pages group.**

   A pull-down menu appears (refer to Figure 6-1).

3. **Choose Remove Current Cover Page.**

   Word deletes your cover page.

Inserting Page Breaks

Rather than insert a new page, you may want to break text on an existing page into two pages. To insert a page break in your document, follow these steps:

1. **Click the Insert tab.**
2. **Move the cursor where you want to break your document into two pages.**
3. **Click the Page Break icon in the Pages group.**

   Word breaks your document into two pages.

To delete a page break, move the cursor to the top of the page directly following the page break you want to delete. Then press Backspace.

As an alternative to following Steps 2 and 3 in the preceding step list, you can just press Ctrl+Enter to create a page break at the cursor's current location.

Inserting Headers and Footers

Headers and footers appear at the top (headers) and bottom (footers) on one or more pages of your document. Headers and footers can display information such as titles, chapter names, dates, and page numbers.

Creating a header (or footer)

To create a header or footer, follow these steps:

1. **Click the Insert tab.**
2. **Click the Header or Footer icon in the Header & Footer group.**

   A pull-down menu appears.

3. **Click Edit header (or Edit footer).**

   Word displays your header or footer.

   Headers and footers are visible only when you display a document in Print Layout view.

4. **Type, edit, or delete any text you want to change.**

6. **(Optional) Click the Date & Time or Page Number icons of the Design contextual tools to insert the date and time or page numbers, respectively.**

7. **Click the Close Header and Footer icon.**

   Word dims your header and footer text.

Defining which pages to display a header (or footer)

Usually when you define a header or footer, Word displays that header or footer on every page of your document. However, Word gives you the option of displaying a different header and footer for your first page only, or displaying different headers and footers for odd and even pages.

Creating a unique header or footer for your first page

Often, you want a header or footer to display page numbers and document or chapter titles — just not on the first page of your document. To create a unique header or footer that appears only on your first page, follow these steps:

1. **Switch to Print Layout view (click the View tab and click Print Layout, or click the Print Layout icon near the bottom-right corner of the screen).**

2. **Click the Insert tab, click the Header icon in the Header & Footer group, and choose Edit Header.**

   The Design tab appears.

3. **Select the Different First Page check box in the Options group.**

   Word displays a header or footer with the name `First Page Header` or `First Page Footer`.

4. **Click the Close Header and Footer icon.**

   Word dims your header and footer text.

You can clear the Different First Page check box to keep Word from displaying your separate first page header and footer.

Creating unique headers and footers for odd and even pages

Sometimes you may want different headers or footers to appear on even or odd pages. In most books, even page numbers (headers) appear in the upper-left corner while odd page numbers (headers) appear in the upper-right corner. To create this effect in your own documents, you need to create different headers to appear on odd and even pages.

To create a different header or footer for even and odd numbered pages, follow these steps:

1. **Switch to Print Layout view (click the View tab and click Print Layout, or click the Print Layout icon near the bottom-right corner of the screen).**

2. **Click the Insert tab, click the Header icon in the Header & Footer group, and choose Edit Header.**

   The Design tab appears.

3. **Select the Different Odd & Even Pages check box in the Options group.**

   Word displays a header or footer with the name `Odd Page Header` or `Even Page Footer`.

4. **Click the Close Header and Footer icon.**

5. **Switch to another page and repeat Steps 2 through 4 to define the other odd or even header.**

   If an odd page number originally appeared in Step 1, switch to an even page number (or vice versa).

You can clear the Different Odd & Even Pages check box to keep Word from displaying your separate odd and even page headers and footers.

Deleting a header (or footer)

In case you want to get rid of a header or footer, you can always delete it by following these steps:

1. **Click the Insert tab.**

2. **Switch to Print Layout view (click the View tab and click Print Layout, or click the Print Layout icon near the bottom-right corner of the screen).**

3. **Click the Header or Footer icon in the Header & Footer group.**

   A pull-down menu appears.

4. **Click Remove Header (or Remove Footer).**

   Word removes your header or footer.

Organizing Text in Tables

Tables organize text into rows and columns, which can make it easy to type, edit, and format text while spacing it correctly in your document. Tables organize text in cells, where a cell is the intersection of a row and a column.

Word provides four ways to create a table:

- Click the Insert tab, click the Table icon, and then highlight the number of rows and columns for your table (up to a maximum of eight rows and ten columns).
- Use the Insert Table dialog box.
- Draw the size and position of the table with the mouse.
- Convert existing text (divided by a delimiter character such as a Tab or comma).

Creating a table by highlighting rows and columns

Creating a table by highlighting rows and columns can be fast, but it limits the size of your table to a maximum of eight rows and ten columns. To create a table by highlighting rows and columns, follow these steps:

1. **Click the Insert tab.**

2. **In your document, move the cursor where you want to insert a table.**

3. **Click the Table icon.**

   A pull-down menu appears, as shown in Figure 6-2.

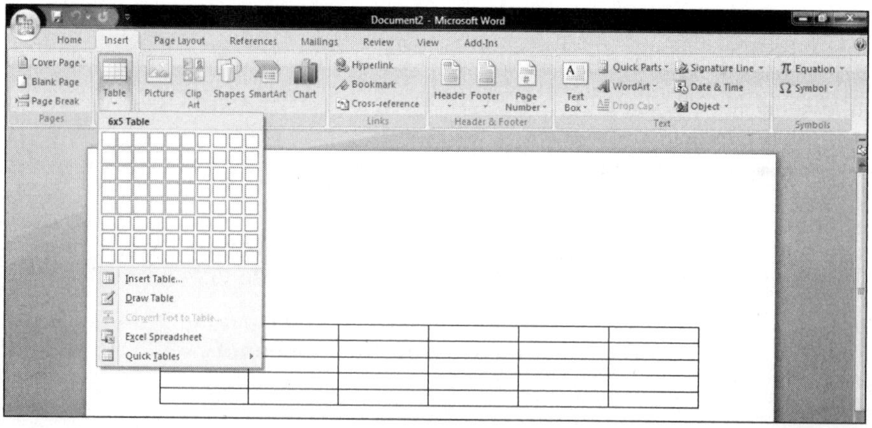

Figure 6-2:
The Table pull-down menu displays squares that represent the number of rows and columns for your table.

4. **Move the mouse pointer to highlight the number of rows and columns you want to create for your table.**

   When you highlight rows and columns, Word displays your table directly in your document so you can see exactly what your table will look like.

5. **Click the left mouse button when you're happy with the size of your table.**

Creating a table with the Insert Table dialog box

Creating a table by highlighting the number of rows and columns can be fast, but it limits the size of your table to a maximum of eight rows and ten columns. To create a table by defining a specific number of rows and columns (up to a maximum of 63 columns) and a column width, follow these steps:

1. **Click the Insert tab.**

2. **Move the cursor where you want to insert a table.**

3. **Click the Table icon.**

   A pull-down menu appears (refer to Figure 6-2).

4. **Click Insert Table.**

   The Insert Table dialog box appears, as shown in Figure 6-3.

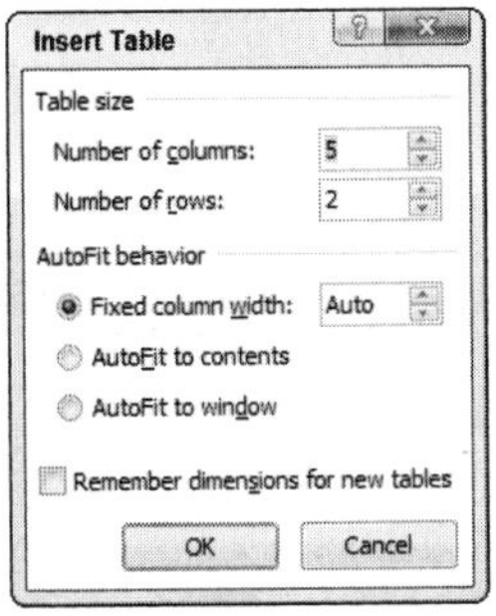

Figure 6-3: Specify an exact number of rows and columns.

5. **Click in the Number of Columns text box and type a number between 1 and 63, or click the up/down arrows to define the number of columns.**

6. **Click in the Number of Rows text box and type a number or click the up/down arrows to define the number of rows.**

7. **Select one of the following radio buttons in the AutoFit Behavior group:**

   • *Fixed Column Width:* Defines a fixed size for the column widths, such as 0.3 inches

   • *AutoFit to Contents:* Defines the width of a column based on the width of the largest item stored in that column

   • *AutoFit to Window:* Expands (or shrinks) the table to fit within the current size of the document window.

8. **Click OK.**

   Word draws the table in your document.

Creating a table with the mouse

Drawing a table can be especially useful when you want to place a table in the middle of a page and create rows and columns of different sizes, as shown in Figure 6-4.

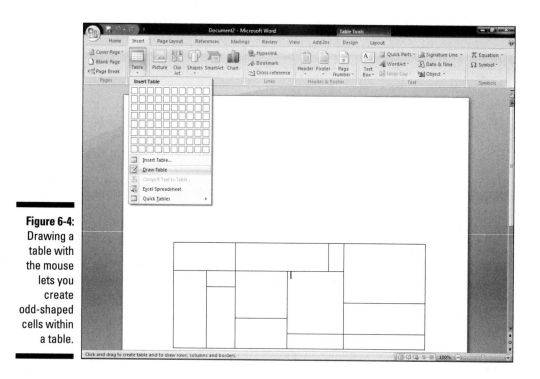

Figure 6-4:
Drawing a table with the mouse lets you create odd-shaped cells within a table.

To draw a table in your document, follow these steps:

1. **Click the Insert tab.**
2. **Click the Table icon.**

   A pull-down menu appears.
3. **Click Draw Table.**

   The mouse pointer turns into a pencil icon.
4. **Move the mouse pointer where you want to draw your table, hold down the left mouse button, and drag (move) the mouse to draw your table.**

   Word draws a rectangular dotted box to show you where your table will appear.
5. **Release the left mouse button when you're happy with the size and position of your table.**
6. **Move the mouse pointer to the top/bottom or left/right side of the table, hold down the left mouse button, and drag (move) the mouse up and down (or right and left) to draw the boundaries for your table's rows and columns.**
7. **Press Esc or double-click to turn the mouse pointer from a pencil icon back to an I-beam pointer.**

Creating a table from existing text

If you have existing text that you'd like to turn into a table, you need to first separate text into chunks so Word knows how to place the text into individual cells in a table. To define how text appears in a table, Word uses the following criteria:

✔ **Paragraphs appear in separate rows.**

   See the top example in Figure 6-5. You can change the delimiter character to commas, tabs, or any other character, such as # or *.

✔ **Tabbed text appears in separate columns, as in the bottom example of Figure 6-5.**

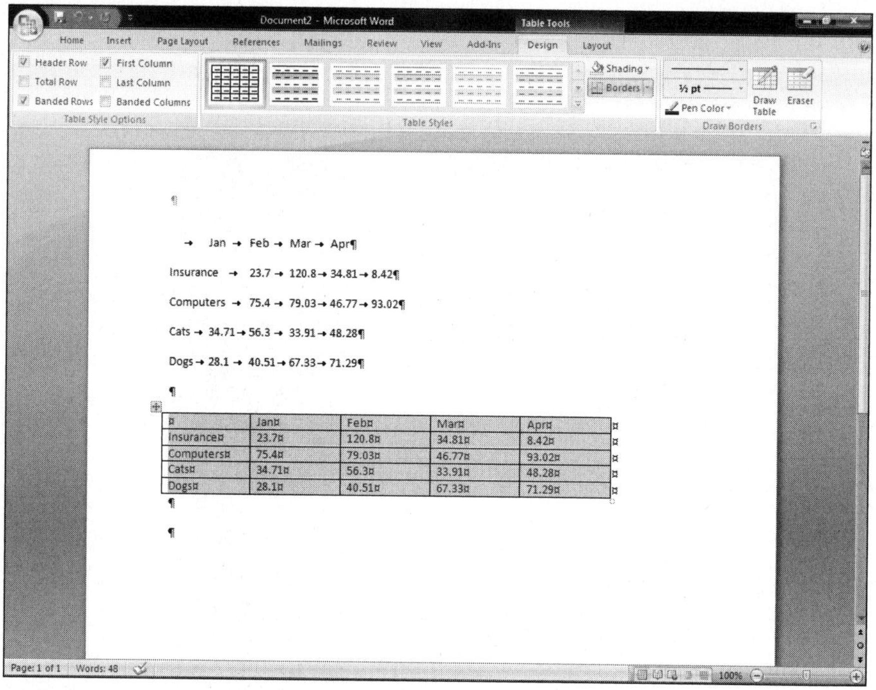

Figure 6-5:
How Word converts text into tables.

To convert existing text into a table, follow these steps:

1. **Click the Insert tab.**

2. **Select the text that you want to convert into a table.**

3. **Click the Table icon.**

   A pull-down menu appears (refer to Figure 6-2).

4. **Click the Convert Text to Table command.**

   The Convert Text to Table dialog box appears, as shown in Figure 6-6.

5. **(Optional) Select a radio button in the Separate Text At group, such as Paragraphs, Tabs, or Commas.**

   You must choose the option that corresponds to the way you divided your text. So if you divided your text by tabs, you would click the Tabs radio button.

6. **Click OK.**

   Word converts your text into a table.

Figure 6-6:
Define how
to convert
your text
into a table.

You can also convert a table into text. To convert a table into text, follow these steps:

1. **Click anywhere inside the table you want to convert into text.**

   The Layout tab appears.

2. **Click the Layout tab.**

3. **Click Convert to Text.**

   The Convert Table to Text dialog box appears, as shown in Figure 6-7.

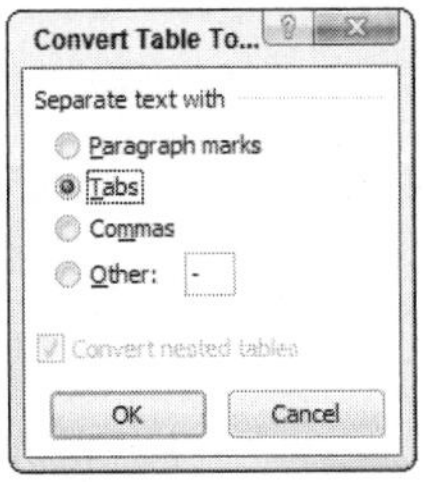

Figure 6-7:
The Convert
Table to Text
dialog box
lets you
specify how
to divide up
a table.

4. **Select a radio button to define how you want to divide your table into text, such as by Commas, Tabs, Paragraph Marks, or other symbol, as shown in Figure 6-8.**

5. **Click OK.**

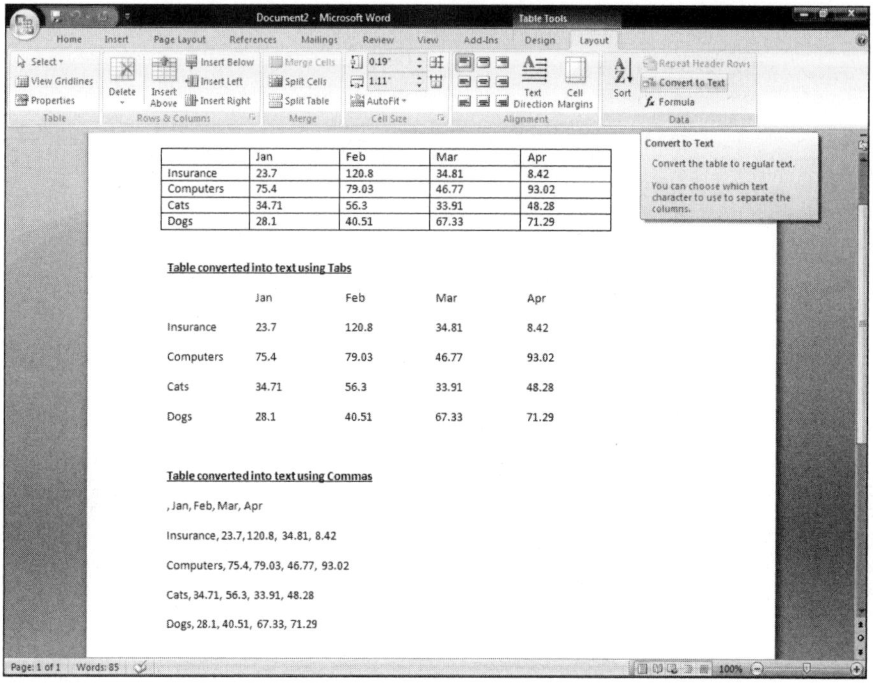

Figure 6-8:
When you
convert a
table to text,
the text
appears
different
depending
on how you
choose to
divide text.

Formatting and Coloring a Table

After you create a table, you can format individual *cells* (the intersection of a
row and column) or entire rows and columns by aligning text in cells, resizing
columns and rows, and adding borders, shading, or colors, all of which can
make the text inside easier to read.

Selecting all or part of a table

To format and color a table, you must first select the table, row, column, or
cell that you want to modify. To select all or part of a table, follow these steps:

1. **Click in the table, row, column, or cell you want to modify.**

   The Table Tools tab appears.

2. **Click the Layout tab.**

3. **Click Select in the Table group.**

   A pull-down menu appears, as shown in Figure 6-9.

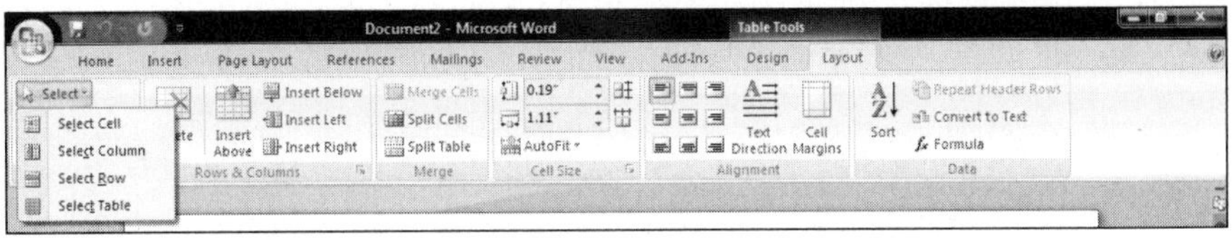

Figure 6-9:
Select a row,
column, or
entire table.

4. Choose an option, such as Select Row or Select Column.

Word highlights your chosen item in the table.

Aligning text in a table cell

You can align text in a table cell in nine different ways: Top Left (the default alignment), Top Center, Top Right, Center Left, Center, Center Right, Bottom Left, Bottom Center, and Bottom Right, as shown in Figure 6-10.

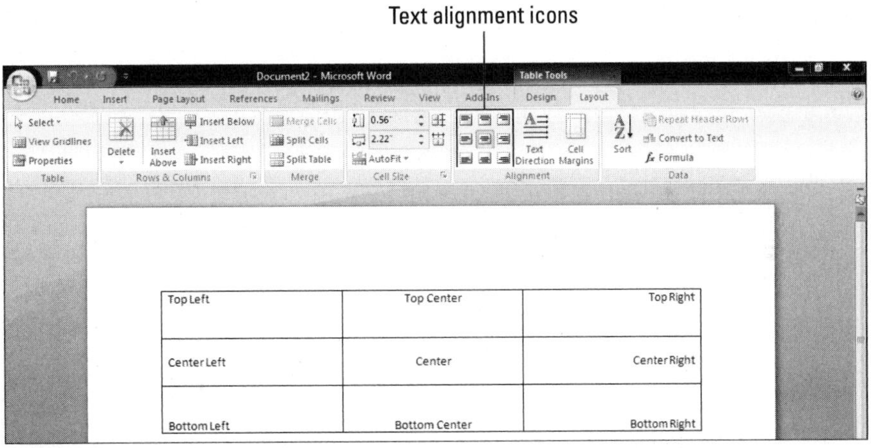

Text alignment icons

Figure 6-10:
Tables can
align text
within cells
in nine
different
ways.

To align one or more cells, follow these steps:

1. Click in the cell that contains text that you want to align.

The Table Tools tab appears.

2. Click the Layout tab.

3. Click an alignment icon in the Alignment group (refer to Figure 6-10) such as Top Right or Bottom Center.

Word aligns your text. If you changed the alignment of blank cells, any new text you type in those blank cells will appear according to the alignment you chose.

Coloring all or part of a table

Colors can make the text inside rows and columns easier to read, such as coloring every other row. To color all or part of a table, follow these steps:

1. **Select a table, row, column, or cell that you want to modify by following the steps in the earlier section, "Selecting all or part of a table."**

   Word highlights your chosen table, row, column, or cell.

2. **Click the Design tab that appears under the Table Tools tab.**

3. **Click Shading.**

   A color palette appears, as shown in Figure 6-11.

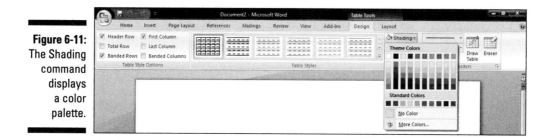

Figure 6-11: The Shading command displays a color palette.

4. **Move the mouse pointer over a color.**

   Word automatically displays your chosen color in the selected part of your table. Each time you point to a different color, Word displays a different color in the table.

5. **Click a color in the palette when you're happy with a particular color.**

Adding borders

Borders can emphasize parts of your table, such as a particular row or column. To add a border to a table, you need to define the following:

- Where you want the border to appear (on the bottom of a row, on the left of a cell, on the top of a column, and so on)
- The border color
- The border line style
- The border line thickness

To add a border, follow these steps:

1. **Move the cursor to the row, column, cell, or table where you want to add borders.**

2. **Click the Design tab that appears under the Table Tools tab.**

3. **Click Pen Color.**

   A color palette appears.

4. **Click a color for your border.**

5. **Click the Line Style list box.**

   A pull-down menu appears with different line styles, such as dotted lines or triple lines, as shown in Figure 6-12.

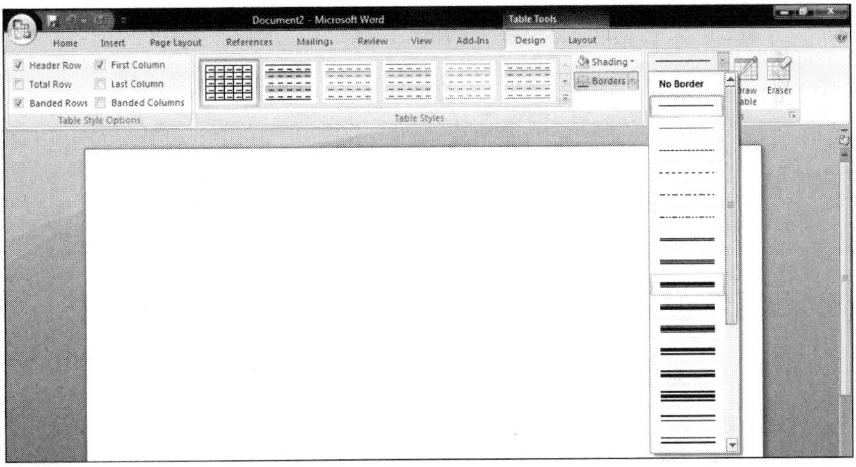

Figure 6-12:
The Line Style list box displays different types of lines.

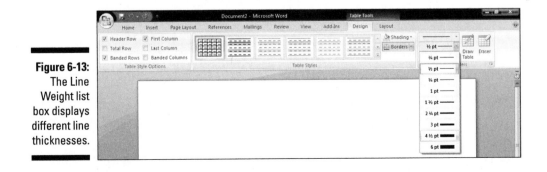

6. **Click a line style.**

7. **Click the Line Weight list box.**

   A pull-down menu appears with different line thicknesses such as ½ or 2¼ point, as shown in Figure 6-13.

Figure 6-13:
The Line Weight list box displays different line thicknesses.

8. **Click a line weight (thickness).**

9. **Click Borders.**

   A pull-down menu appears, as shown in Figure 6-14.

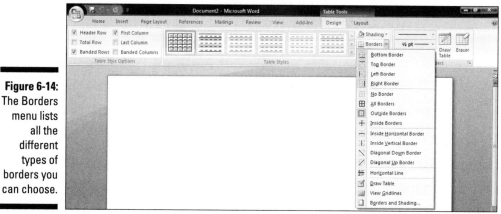

Figure 6-14: The Borders menu lists all the different types of borders you can choose.

10. **Click a border, such as All Borders or Right Border.**

    Word displays your chosen border in the color and thickness (weight) you chose.

Picking a table style

By coloring rows or columns and adding borders, you can customize the appearance of your tables. However, for a faster method, you can just use a predesigned table style instead, which can automatically format your text, color rows, and add borders to your tables.

To choose a table style, follow these steps:

1. **Move the cursor inside the table you want to modify.**

2. **Click the Design tab.**

3. **(Optional) Click or clear check boxes under the Table Style Options group, such as the Header Row or Last Column check box.**

4. **Click the More button on the Table Styles group.**

   A pull-down menu of all available styles appears, as shown in Figure 6-15. As you move the mouse pointer over a table style, Word displays a live preview of how your table will look.

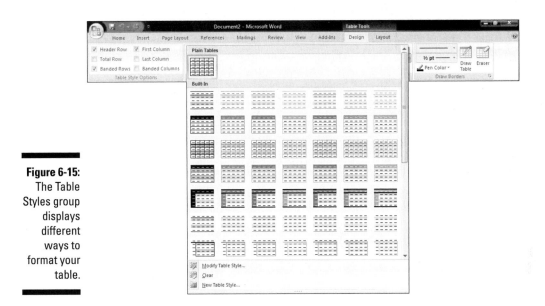

Figure 6-15:
The Table
Styles group
displays
different
ways to
format your
table.

5. **Click a table style.**

   Word formats your table according to the style you chose.

Resizing columns and rows

You may need to resize a column or row in your table to expand or shrink it so your text doesn't appear crowded or surrounded by empty space. You can resize a column or row by using the mouse or by defining row heights and column widths.

To resize a row or column with the mouse, follow these steps:

1. **Move the mouse over the row or column border that you want to resize.**

   The mouse pointer turns into a two-way pointing arrow.

2. **Hold the left mouse button down and drag (move) the mouse to resize the row or column.**

3. **Release the left mouse button when you're happy with the size of the row or column.**

Using the mouse to resize a row or column can be fast, but if you want to resize a row or column to a specific height or width, you can type in the specific dimensions by following these steps:

1. **Select the row, column, or table that you want to modify. (If you select the entire table, you can adjust the width or height of rows and columns for your entire table.)**

2. **Click the Layout tab under the Table Tools tab (refer to Figure 6-10).**

   If you want to define the width or height of multiple rows or columns equally, click the Distribute Columns or Distribute Rows icon.

3. **To precisely define a column's width, click the Width list box and type a value (or click the up/down arrows to choose a value).**

4. **To precisely define a row's height, click the Height list box and type a value (or click the up/down arrows to choose a value).**

5. **(Optional) Click AutoFit and choose one of the following:**

   • *AutoFit Contents:* Shrinks your columns or rows to largest cell

   • *AutoFit Window:* Expands the table to fit the width of the current document window

Defining cell margins

Another way to modify the appearance of a table is to change the space that appears between items in a cell, known as the *cell margin*. Cell margins simply add blank space between text and cell borders. To define cell margins in a table, follow these steps:

1. **Move the cursor inside any cell in the table you want to modify.**

2. **Click the Layout tab under the Table Tools tab.**

3. **Click the Cell Margins icon in the Alignment group.**

   The Table Options dialog box appears, as shown in Figure 6-16.

Figure 6-16: The Table Options dialog box lets you define the margins inside cells.

Table Options				
Default cell margins				
Top:	0"	Left:	0.08"	
Bottom:	0"	Right:	0.08"	
Default cell spacing				
☐ Allow spacing between cells		0"		
Options				
☑ Automatically resize to fit contents				
	OK	Cancel		

4. **Click in the Top, Bottom, Left, or Right text box and type a value (or click the up/down arrows to increase or decrease the currently displayed value).**

5. **Click OK.**

   Word displays your table with text moved away from the borders, as shown in Figure 6-17.

Figure 6-17: Cell margins can make the text inside a table easier to read.

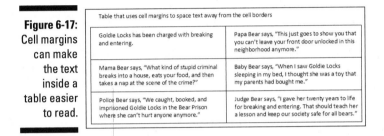

Table that uses cell margins to space text away from the cell borders

Goldie Locks has been charged with breaking and entering.	Papa Bear says, "This just goes to show you that you can't leave your front door unlocked in this neighborhood anymore."
Mama Bear says, "What kind of stupid criminal breaks into a house, eats your food, and then takes a nap at the scene of the crime?"	Baby Bear says, "When I saw Goldie Locks sleeping in my bed, I thought she was a toy that my parents had bought me."
Police Bear says, "We caught, booked, and imprisoned Goldie Locks in the Bear Prison where she can't hurt anyone anymore."	Judge Bear says, "I gave her twenty years to life for breaking and entering. That should teach her a lesson and keep our society safe for all bears."

Defining cell spacing

Defining cell margins can move text away from cell borders to make a table easier to read. For another way to separate cells in a table, you can define the cell spacing. The greater the cell spacing, the farther apart individual cells appear from one another, as shown in Figure 6-18.

Figure 6-18: Cell spacing can separate cells in a table.

Table with cell spacing so cells appear away from each other

Goldie Locks has been charged with breaking and entering|	Papa Bear says, "This just goes to show you that you can't leave your front door unlocked in this neighborhood anymore."
Mama Bear says, "What kind of stupid criminal breaks into a house, eats your food, and then takes a nap at the scene of the crime?"	Baby Bear says, "When I saw Goldie Locks sleeping in my bed, I thought she was a toy that my parents had bought me."
Police Bear says, "We caught, booked, and imprisoned Goldie Locks in the Bear Prison where she can't hurt anyone anymore."	Judge Bear says, "I gave her twenty years to life for breaking and entering. That should teach her a lesson and keep our society safe for all bears."

To define cell spacing in a table, follow these steps:

1. **Move the cursor inside any cell in the table you want to modify.**

2. **Click the Layout tab under the Table Tools tab.**

3. **Click the Cell Margins icon in the Alignment group.**

   The Table Options dialog box appears (refer to Figure 6-16).

4. **Select the Allow Spacing between Cells check box and type a value (or click the up/down arrows to increase or decrease the currently displayed value).**

5. **Click OK.**

   Word displays your table with cells spaced apart.

Splitting (and merging) cells

Splitting a cell divides the cell into multiple rows or columns. Merging cells combines two or more cells to create one big cell. Splitting or merging calls typically creates unusual tables without uniform rows and columns, as shown in Figure 6-19.

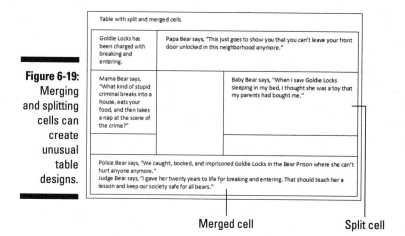

Figure 6-19: Merging and splitting cells can create unusual table designs.

Merged cell   Split cell

To split a cell, follow these steps:

1. **Move the cursor to the cell you want to divide in half.**

2. **Click the Layout tab under the Table Tools tab.**

3. **Click the Split Cells icon in the Merge group.**

   The Split Cells dialog box appears, as shown in Figure 6-20.

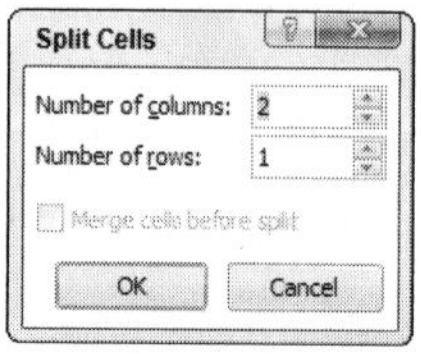

Figure 6-20: The Split Cells dialog box.

4. **Click in the Number of Columns text box and type a number (or click the up/down arrows to define a number).**

5. **Click in the Number of Rows text box and type a number (or click the up/down arrows to define a number).**

6. **Click OK.**

   Word splits your cell into the number of rows and columns you defined in Steps 4 and 5.

To merge cells, follow these steps:

1. **Select adjacent cells that you want to merge into a single cell.**

2. **Click the Layout tab under the Table Tools tab.**

3. **Click the Merge Cells icon in the Merge group.**

   Word merges your selected cells into one big cell.

Sorting a Table

Tables can not only organize data, but they can also sort your data alphabetically as well. To sort a table, you need to specify a single column of data to sort. When Word sorts the data in this column, it automatically sorts every row in the table as well, as shown in Figure 6-21.

Figure 6-21: Sorting data in a column rearranges every row in a table.

Unsorted table

Customer ID	Name	Nickname
452	Bill Smith	Moron
101	John Dole	Scumbag
9	Mary Daniels	Loser

Sorted table

Customer ID	Name	Nickname
9	Mary Daniels	Loser
101	John Dole	Scumbag
452	Bill Smith	Moron

To sort a table, follow these steps:

1. **Select the column that contains the data you want to sort.**

2. **Click the Layout tab under the Table Tools tab.**

3. **Click the Sort icon in the Data group.**

   The Sort dialog box appears, as shown in Figure 6-22.

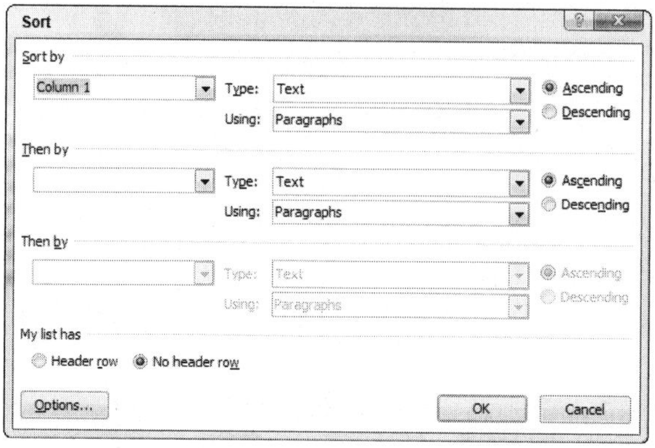

Figure 6-22:
The Sort dialog box lets you specify whether to sort by ascending or descending order.

4. **Click in the top Type list box and choose the type of data you want to sort: Text, Number, or Date.**

5. **Select either the Ascending or Descending radio button.**

6. **Click OK.**

Word sorts your entire table based on the data in the column you selected.

Deleting Tables

After you create a table, you can delete the entire table, delete one or more rows or columns, or just delete individual cells along with their data.

Deleting an entire table

Word gives you two choices in deleting a table. First, you can wipe out just the data inside the table while leaving the table itself intact. Second, you can wipe out both the data and the table at the same time.

To delete just the data in a table, follow these steps:

1. **Select every row and column in the table.**

2. **Press Delete.**

Word wipes out all your data and leaves an empty table.

To delete both your table and all the data stored in it at the same time, follow these steps:

1. **Move the cursor into the table you want to wipe out.**
2. **Click the Layout tab under the Table Tools tab.**
3. **Click the Delete icon in the Rows & Columns group.**

   A pull-down menu appears, as shown in Figure 6-23.

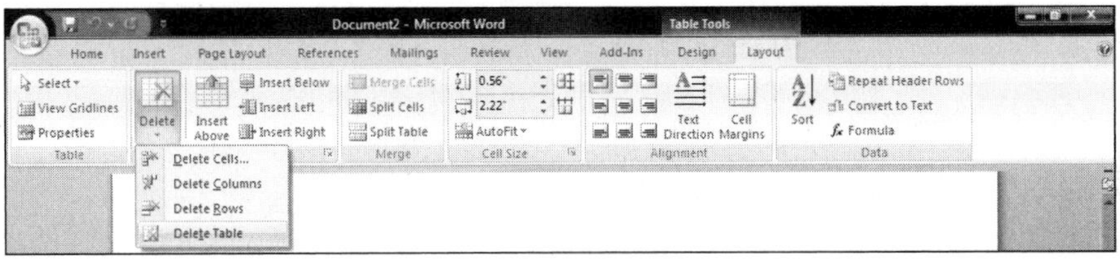

Figure 6-23:
The Delete
icon displays
commands
for deleting
parts of a
table.

Figure 6-23:
The Delete
icon displays
commands
for deleting
parts of a
table.

4. **Choose Delete Table.**

   Word wipes out your table and all the data stored in it.

Deleting rows and columns

Rather than delete an entire table, you can also delete rows and columns. When you delete a row or column, you wipe out any data stored inside that row or column.

To delete a row or column, follow these steps:

1. **Move the cursor into the row or column you want to delete.**
2. **Click the Layout tab under the Table Tools tab.**
3. **Click the Delete icon.**

   A pull-down menu appears (refer to Figure 6-23).

4. **Choose Delete Columns or Delete Rows.**

   Word deletes your chosen column or row.

Deleting cells

You can delete data in cells just by selecting the data and pressing the Delete key. If you want to delete data and the cell itself, you have two options:

- ✓ **Delete a cell and shift adjacent rows or columns.** This creates an odd-shaped table.
- ✓ **Delete the data and cell borders.** This keeps the table symmetrical but often merges cells.

To delete a cell and change the physical layout of a table, follow these steps:

1. **Select the cell or cells you want to delete.**

2. **Click the Layout tab under the Table Tools tab.**

3. **Click the Delete icon in the Rows & Columns group.**

   A pull-down menu appears (refer to Figure 6-23).

4. **Choose Delete Cells.**

   The Delete Cells dialog box appears.

5. **Select the radio button for Shift Cells Left or Shift Cells Up.**

6. **Click OK.**

   Word deletes your chosen cells and shifts cells left or up, creating an odd-shaped table in the process, as shown in Figure 6-24.

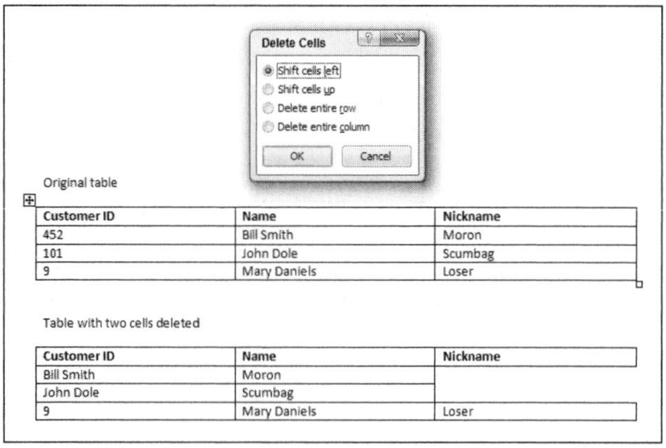

Figure 6-24: When you delete a cell, Word shifts any remaining cells left or up.

Delete Cells

- ⦿ Shift cells left
- ○ Shift cells up
- ○ Delete entire row
- ○ Delete entire column

OK | Cancel

Original table

Customer ID	Name	Nickname
452	Bill Smith	Moron
101	John Dole	Scumbag
9	Mary Daniels	Loser

Table with two cells deleted

Customer ID	Name	Nickname
Bill Smith	Moron	
John Dole	Scumbag	
9	Mary Daniels	Loser

Deleting cell borders

Word also lets you delete individual cell lines by using the mouse. By using the mouse, you can delete borders and merge adjacent cells at the same time.

To use the mouse to delete cell lines, follow these steps:

1. **Move the cursor into the table you want to modify.**
2. **Click the Design tab under the Table Tools tab.**
3. **Click the Eraser icon in the Draw Borders group.**

   The mouse pointer turns into an eraser icon.
4. **Choose one of the following:**

   • *Click a cell border to delete it.*

   or

   a. *Move the mouse pointer near a cell line to delete, hold down the left mouse button, and drag (move) the mouse to highlight one or more cell lines.*

   Word highlights any cell lines you select.

   b. *Release the left mouse button.*

   Word deletes the selected cell lines and any data stored in adjacent cells.
5. **Press Esc or double-click the mouse to turn off the Eraser and convert the mouse pointer back into an I-beam cursor.**

Making Text Look Artistic

To spice up the appearance of individual paragraphs, Word lets you add drop caps, text boxes, or WordArt. *Drop caps* make the first letter of a paragraph appear huge. *WordArt* displays text as graphical images. Text boxes let you display chunks of text in separate boxes that you can arrange anywhere in your document.

Creating drop caps

To create a drop cap, follow these steps:

1. **Click the Insert tab.**

2. **Move the cursor anywhere inside the paragraph where you want to create a drop cap.**

3. **Click Drop Cap.**

   The Drop Cap menu appears, as shown in Figure 6-25.

Figure 6-25:
The Drop
Cap menu
lists different
drop cap
styles you
can choose.

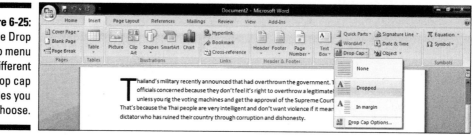

4. **Move the mouse pointer over the drop cap style you want to use.**

   Word shows you what your drop cap will look like.

5. **Click the drop cap style you want to use.**

Creating WordArt

WordArt is Microsoft's fancy term for displaying text in different graphical styles that you can stretch or resize on a page. You can crate WordArt from scratch or from existing text.

To create WordArt, follow these steps:

1. **(Optional) Select the text you want to convert into WordArt. (If you skip this step, you have to type in text later.)**

2. **Click the Insert tab.**

3. **Click WordArt.**

   The WordArt menu appears, as shown in Figure 6-26.

4. **Click a WordArt style.**

   The Edit WordArt Text dialog box appears, as shown in Figure 6-27.

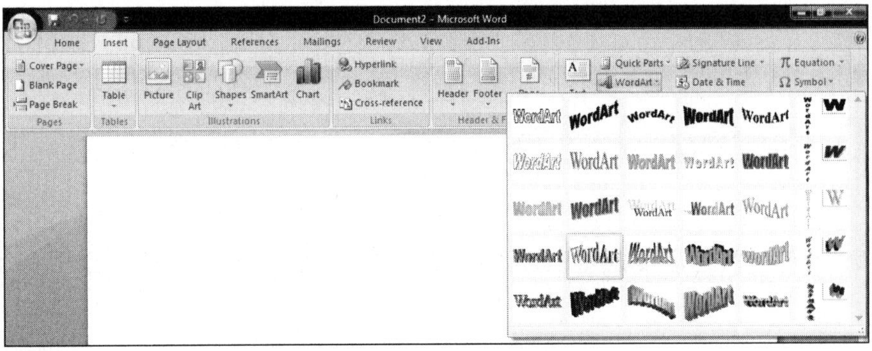

Figure 6-26:
The WordArt
menu
displays
different
graphical
styles
to display
your text.

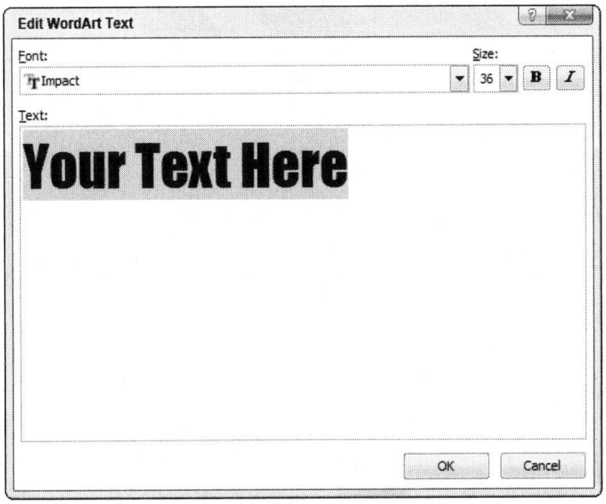

Figure 6-27:
The Edit
WordArt
Text dialog
box lets you
type or
edit text.

5. **Type or edit text and then click OK.**

   Word displays your text as WordArt in your document.

6. **(Optional) Move the mouse pointer over a WordArt handle (on the edge or the corner), hold down the left mouse button, and drag (move) the mouse to resize your WordArt.**

To edit your WordArt, right-click the WordArt. From the pop-up menu that appears, choose Edit Text. The Edit WordArt Text dialog box appears so you can edit your text.

You can delete WordArt by clicking it and then pressing Delete.

Dividing Text into Columns

When you type, Word normally displays your text to fill the area defined by the left and right margins. However, you can also divide a page into two or three columns, which can be especially handy for printing newsletters.

To divide a document into columns, follow these steps:

1. **Click the Page Layout tab.**

2. **Select the text that you want to divide into columns. (Press Ctrl+A to select your entire document.)**

3. **Click the Columns icon.**

   A pull-down menu appears that lists different column styles, as shown in Figure 6-28.

Figure 6-28:
The Columns menu lists different types of columns you can use.

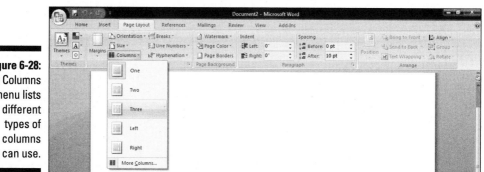

4. **Click a column style.**

   Word changes your document to display columns.

Editing columns

After you create two or three columns in your document, you may want to modify their widths, modify the spacing between columns, and choose whether to display a vertical line between columns. To edit columns, follow these steps:

1. **Move the cursor to the text divided into columns that you want to modify.**

2. **Click the Page Layout tab.**

3. **Click the Columns icon.**

   A pull-down menu appears (refer to Figure 6-28).

4. **Click More Columns.**

   The Columns dialog box appears, as shown in Figure 6-29.

5. **(Optional) Click in the Number of Columns text box and click the up/down arrows to define how many columns you want (from 1 to 9).**

6. **(Optional) Click in the Width Text box and type a value or click the up/down arrows to define a width for column 1.**

7. **(Optional) Click in the Spacing Text box and type a value or click the up/down arrows to define the spacing width to the right of column 1.**

8. **(Optional) Repeat Steps 6 and 7 for each additional column you want to modify.**

9. **(Optional) Select the Line Between check box to display a vertical line between your columns.**

10. **(Optional) Click the Apply To list box and choose Whole Document or This Point Forward (to define how columns appear from the current cursor position to the end of the document).**

11. **Click OK.**

    Word displays the changes for your columns.

Removing columns

If you decide you don't want to display text in columns any more, you can remove columns throughout your entire document or just from the current cursor position to the end of the document.

To remove columns, follow these steps:

1. **Move the cursor to the page where you want to remove columns from this page to the end of a document.**
2. **Click the Page Layout tab.**
3. **Click the Columns icon.**

   A pull-down menu appears (refer to Figure 6-28).

4. **Click One.**

   Word removes columns from the current cursor position to the end of the document.

Previewing a Document before Printing

Before you print your document, you may want to preview how it will look so you don't waste paper printing something you can't use anyway. After you see that your pages will look perfect, then you can finally print out your document for everyone to read.

Defining page size and orientation

If you need to print your documents on different sizes of paper, you may need to define the page size and paper orientation. By doing this, Word can accurately show you what your text may look like when printed on an 8.5" x 11" page compared with an 8.27" x 11.69" page.

To define the Page Size, follow these steps:

1. **Click the Page Layout tab.**
2. **Click the Size icon in the Page Setup group.**

   A pull-down menu appears, as shown in Figure 6-30.

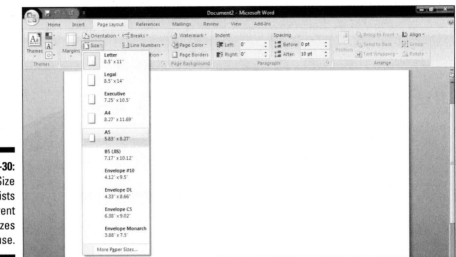

Figure 6-30:
The Size
menu lists
different
page sizes
you can use.

3. Click the page size you want.

Word displays your document based on the new page size.

Normally, Word assumes you want to print in *portrait orientation,* where the height of the paper is larger than its width. However, you may also want to print in *landscape orientation,* where the height of the paper is smaller than its width.

To define the orientation, follow these steps:

1. Click the Page Layout tab.

2. Click the Orientation icon in the Page Setup group.

A pull-down menu appears, as shown in Figure 6-31.

Figure 6-31:
Choose
a page
orientation.

3. Click either Portrait or Landscape orientation.

Word displays your document based on the new paper orientation.

Using Print Preview

Print Preview lets you browse through your document so you can see how every page will look including any headers and footers, cover pages, and pictures you may have added. To use Print Preview, follow these steps:

1. **Click the Office Button and then click the right-pointing arrow that appears to the right of the Print command.**

   The Print t menu appears, as shown in Figure 6-32.

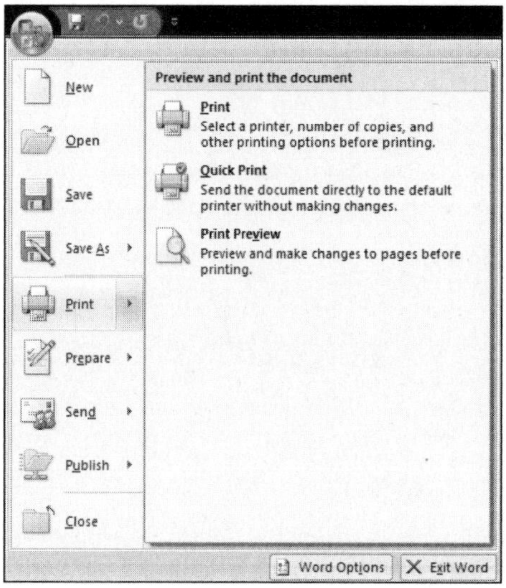

Figure 6-32:
The Print menu displays the Print Preview command.

2. **Click Print Preview.**

   The Print Preview window appears, and the mouse pointer turns into a magnifying glass icon, as shown in Figure 6-33.

3. **(Optional) Click Next Page/Previous Page or use the vertical scroll bar to browse through all the pages of your document.**

   If you select the Magnifier check box, you can click on your pages to zoom in or zoom out so you can examine the details of your document.

4. **Click Close Print Preview to return to your document, or click Print to start printing.**

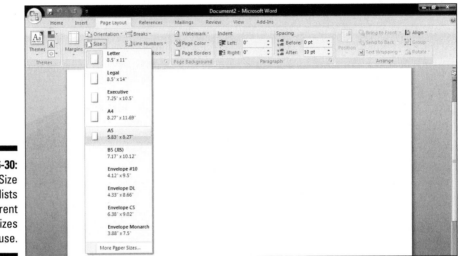

Figure 6-30:
The Size
menu lists
different
page sizes
you can use.

3. Click the page size you want.

Word displays your document based on the new page size.

Normally, Word assumes you want to print in *portrait orientation,* where the height of the paper is larger than its width. However, you may also want to print in *landscape orientation,* where the height of the paper is smaller than its width.

To define the orientation, follow these steps:

1. Click the Page Layout tab.

2. Click the Orientation icon in the Page Setup group.

A pull-down menu appears, as shown in Figure 6-31.

Figure 6-31:
Choose
a page
orientation.

3. Click either Portrait or Landscape orientation.

Word displays your document based on the new paper orientation.

Using Print Preview

Print Preview lets you browse through your document so you can see how every page will look including any headers and footers, cover pages, and pictures you may have added. To use Print Preview, follow these steps:

1. **Click the Office Button and then click the right-pointing arrow that appears to the right of the Print command.**

   The Print t menu appears, as shown in Figure 6-32.

Preview and print the document

Print
Select a printer, number of copies, and other printing options before printing.

Quick Print
Send the document directly to the default printer without making changes.

Print Preview
Preview and make changes to pages before printing.

New
Open
Save
Save As
Print
Prepare
Send
Publish
Close

Word Options   Exit Word

2. **Click Print Preview.**

   The Print Preview window appears, and the mouse pointer turns into a magnifying glass icon, as shown in Figure 6-33.

3. **(Optional) Click Next Page/Previous Page or use the vertical scroll bar to browse through all the pages of your document.**

   If you select the Magnifier check box, you can click on your pages to zoom in or zoom out so you can examine the details of your document.

4. **Click Close Print Preview to return to your document, or click Print to start printing.**

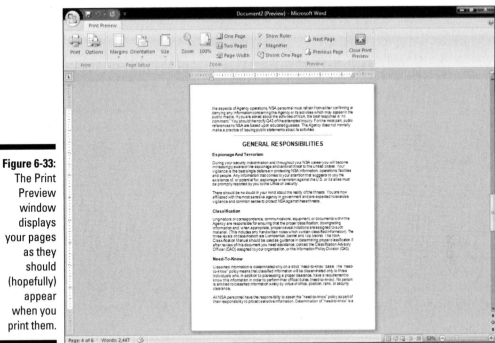

Figure 6-33:
The Print
Preview
window
displays
your pages
as they
should
(hopefully)
appear
when you
print them.

Printing

When you're happy with the way your document looks, you can finally print it. To print your document, follow these steps:

1. **Choose one of the following methods:**
   - **Click the Office Button and then click Print.**
   - **Press Ctrl+P.**
   - **From within the Print Preview window, click the Print icon.**

   The Print dialog box appears, as shown in Figure 6-34.

2. **Click in the Name list box and choose the printer you want to use.**

3. **Select one of the following radio buttons from the Page Range group:**
   - *All:* Prints your entire document
   - *Current Page:* Prints the page that currently fills the screen

- *Selection:* Prints only the currently selected text
- *Pages:* Lets you type specific pages to print (such as 4, 35, 89) or a specific page range (such as 3–9)

4. Click OK.

Word prints your document.

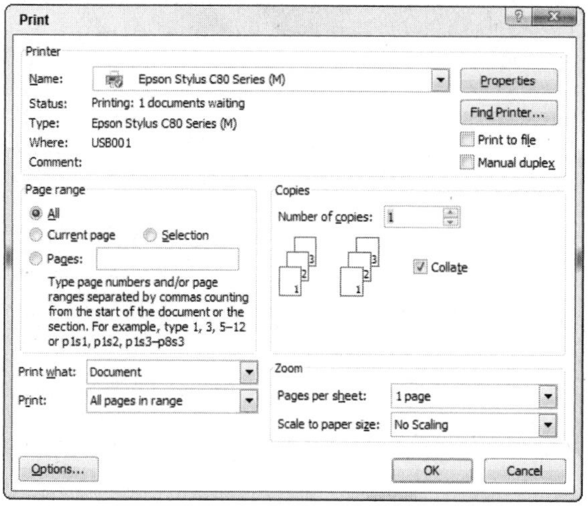

Figure 6-34:
The Print dialog box lets you control which pages to print and which printer to use.

Part III

Playing the Numbers with Excel

The 5th Wave — By Rich Tennant

©RICHTENNANT

"No, that's not the icon for Excel, it's the icon for Excuse, the database of reasons why you haven't learned the other programs in Office."

In this part . . .

*I*f adding, subtracting, multiplying, or dividing long lists of numbers sounds scary, relax. Microsoft endowed Office 2007 with the world's most popular spreadsheet program, dubbed Microsoft Excel. By using Excel, you can create budgets, track inventories, calculate future profits (or losses), and design bar, line, and pie charts so you can see what your numbers are really trying to tell you.

Think of Excel as your personal calculating machine that plows through your numbers for you — whether you need to manage something as simple as a home budget or something as wonderfully complex as an annual profit-and-loss statement for a Fortune 500 corporation.

By tracking numbers, amounts, lengths, measurements, or money with Excel, you can quickly predict future trends and likely results. Type in your annual salary along with any business expenses you have, and you can calculate how much income tax your government plans to steal from you in the future. Or play "What if?" games with your numbers and ask questions such as "Which sales region sells the most useless products?" "How much can I avoid paying in taxes if my income increases by 50 percent?" and "If my company increases sales, how much of an annual bonus can I give myself while letting my employees starve on minimum wages?"

So if you want to get started crunching numbers, this is the part of the book that shows you how to use Excel effectively.

Chapter 7

The Basics of Spreadsheets: Numbers, Labels, and Formulas

In This Chapter

▶ Typing and formatting data

▶ Moving around a spreadsheet

▶ Searching a spreadsheet

▶ Editing a spreadsheet

▶ Printing

*E*veryone needs to perform simple math. Businesses need to keep track of sales and profits, and individuals need to keep track of budgets. In the old days, people not only had to write down numbers on paper, but they also had to do all their calculations by hand (or with the aid of a calculator).

That's why people use Excel. Instead of writing numbers on paper, they can type numbers on the computer. Instead of adding or subtracting columns or rows of numbers by hand, Excel can do it for you automatically. Basically, Excel makes it easy to type and modify numbers and then calculate new results accurately and quickly.

Understanding Spreadsheets

Excel organizes numbers in rows and columns. An entire page of rows and columns is called a *spreadsheet* or a *worksheet.* (A collection of one or more worksheets is stored in a file called a *workbook.*) Each row is identified by a number such as 1 or 249; and each column is identified by letters, such as A, G, or BF. The intersection of each row and column defines a *cell,* which contains one of three items:

- ✔ Numbers
- ✔ Text (labels)
- ✔ Formulas

Numbers provide the data, and *formulas* calculate that data to produce a useful result, such as adding sales results for the week. Of course, just displaying numbers on the screen may be confusing if you don't know what those numbers mean, so labels simply identify what numbers represent. Figure 7-1 shows the parts of a typical spreadsheet.

Formulas usually appear as numbers, so at first glance, it may be difficult to tell the difference between ordinary numbers and numbers that represent a calculation by a formula.

The strength of spreadsheets comes by playing "What-if?" games with your data, such as "What if I gave myself a $20-per-hour raise and cut everyone else's salary by 25%? How much money would that save the company every month?" Because spreadsheets can rapidly calculate new results, you can experiment with different numbers to see how they create different answers.

Figure 7-1:
The parts
of a typical
spreadsheet.

	1st Quarter Results		
	Jan	Feb	Mar
Leo Fontaine	245.25	748.01	452.32
Mike Baum	782.01	421.95	747.58
Darrell Joyce	741.02	554.21	941.21
Bo Katz	145.25	954.25	142.25
Mary Shelley	847.54	145.26	198.57
Gorgeous George	174.25	946.26	810.54
Mickey Mouse	800.47	567.26	418.59
Total =	3735.79	4337.2	3711.06

Labels   Formulas   Numbers

Storing Stuff in a Spreadsheet

Every cell can contain a number, a label, or a formula. To type anything into a spreadsheet, you must first select or click in the cell (or cells) and then type a number or text.

Typing data into a single cell

To type data in a single cell, follow these steps:

1. **Choose one of the following to select a single cell:**

   • Click a cell.

   • Press the up/down/right/left arrow keys to highlight a cell.

2. **Type a number (such as** 34.29 **or** 198**), a label (such as** Tax Returns**), or a formula.**

   You can see how to create formulas in Chapter 8.

Typing data in multiple cells

After you type data in a cell, you can press one of the following four keystrokes to select a different cell:

✔ **Enter:** Selects the cell below in the same column

✔ **Tab:** Selects the cell to the right in the same row

✔ **Shift+Enter:** Selects the cell above in the same column

✔ **Shift+Tab:** Selects the cell to the left in the same row

If you type data in cell A1 and press Enter, Excel selects the next cell below, which is A2. If you type data in A2 and press Tab, Excel selects the cell to the right, which is B2.

However, what if you want to type data in a cell such as A1 and then have Excel select the next cell to the right (B1)? Or what if you want to type data in cells A1 and A2 but then jump back up to type additional data in cells B1 and B2?

To make doing this easy, Excel lets you select a range of cells, which essentially tells Excel, "See all the cells I just highlighted? I only want to type data in those cells." After you select multiple cells, you can type data and press Enter. Excel selects the next cell down in that same column. When Excel reaches the last cell in the column, it selects the top cell of the column to the right.

To select multiple cells for typing data in, follow these steps:

1. **Highlight multiple cells by choosing one of the following:**

   • Move the mouse pointer over a cell, hold down the left mouse button, and drag (move) the mouse to highlight multiple cells. Release the left mouse button when you've selected enough cells.

   • Hold down the Shift key and press the up/down/right/left arrow keys to highlight multiple cells. Release the Shift key when you've selected enough cells.

   Excel selects the cell that appears in the upper-left corner of your selected cells.

2. **Type a number, label, or formula.**

3. **Press Enter.**

   Excel selects the cell directly below the previous cell. If the previous cell appeared at the bottom of the selected column, Excel highlights the top cell in the column that appears to the right.

4. **Repeat Steps 2 and 3 until you fill your selected cells with data.**

5. **Click outside the selected cells or press an arrow key to tell Excel not to select the cells any more.**

Typing in sequences with AutoFill

If you need to type the names of successive months or days in a row or column (such as January, February, March, and so on), Excel offers a shortcut to save you from typing all the day or month names yourself. With this shortcut, you just type one month or day and then drag the mouse to highlight all the adjacent cells. Then Excel types the rest of the month or day names in those cells automatically.

To use this shortcut, follow these steps:

1. **Click a cell and type a month (like** January **or just** Jan**) or a day (like** Monday **or just** Mon**).**

   The Fill Handle, a block box, appears in the bottom-right corner of the cell.

   You can also type in a sequence of numbers in Step 1. So if you typed the numbers 2, 4, and 6 in adjacent cells, highlighted all these adjacent cells, and grabbed the Fill Handle, Excel is smart enough to detect the pattern and display the numbers 8, 10, and 12 in the next three adjacent cells.

2. **Move the mouse pointer over the Fill Handle until the mouse pointer turns into a black crosshair icon.**

3. **Hold down the left mouse button and drag (move) the mouse down a column or across the row.**

   As you drag the mouse, Excel automatically types in the remaining month or day names, as shown in Figure 7-2.

Figure 7-2:
By dragging the Fill Handle, Excel enters the names of the month or days automatically.

| January | | | | | Step 1: Type the name of a month or day in a cell. |

| January | | | | May | Step 2: Drag the Fill Handle to tell Excel how many cells you want to fill automatically with additional month or day names. |

| January | February | March | April | May | Step 3: Release the left mouse button. Excel automatically fills your selected cells. |

Formatting Numbers and Labels

When you first create a spreadsheet, numbers and labels appear as plain text. Plain labels might look boring, but plain numbers (such as 8495 or 0.39) can be difficult to read and understand if the numbers are supposed to represent currency amounts ($8,495) or percentages (39%).

To make labels visually interesting and numbers appear more descriptive of what they actually represent, you need to format your data after you type it into a spreadsheet.

You can format a cell or range of cells after you've already typed in data or before you type in any data. If you format cells before typing any data, any data you type in will appear in your chosen format.

Formatting numbers

To format the appearance of numbers, follow these steps:

1. **Select one or more cells using the mouse or keyboard.**

   To select multiple cells, drag the mouse or hold the Shift key while pressing the arrow keys.

2. **Click the Home tab.**

3. **Click the Number Format list box in the Number group.**

   A pull-down menu appears, as shown in Figure 7-3.

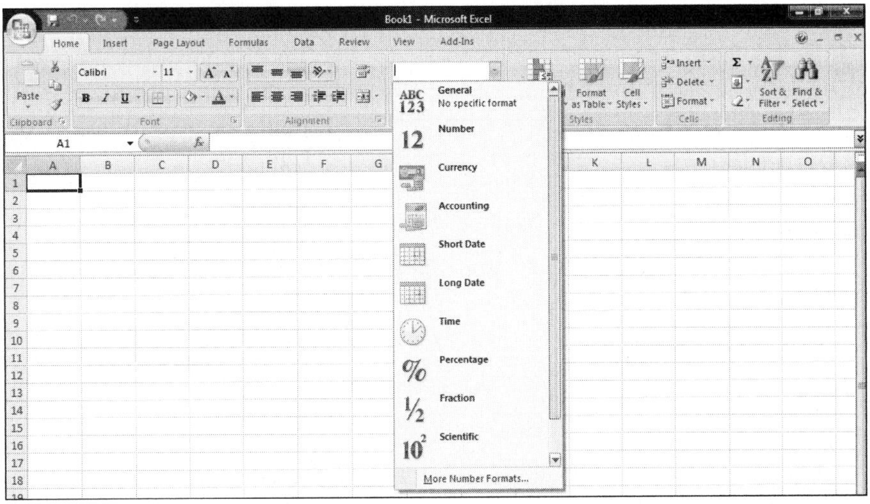

Figure 7-3: The Number Format list box lists the different ways you can format the appearance of numbers.

TIP

The Number group also displays three icons that let you format numbers as Currency, Percentage, or with Commas in one click, as shown in Figure 7-4. If you click the downward-pointing arrow to the right of the Accounting Number Format icon, you can choose different currency symbols to use such as $, £, or €.

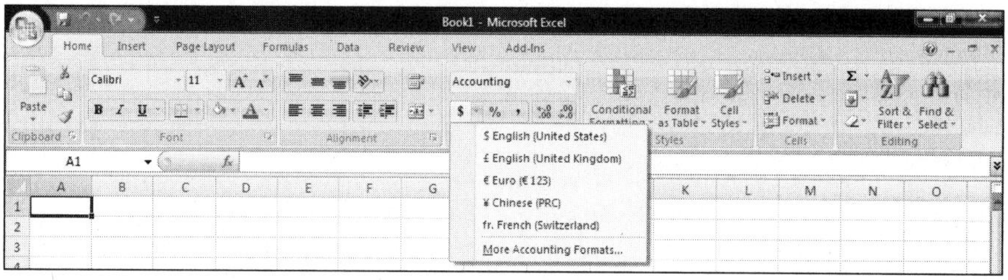

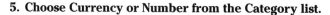

Figure 7-4:
The different
ways you
can format
money.

4. **Click a number format style, such as Percentage or Scientific.**

   Excel displays your numbers in your chosen format.

Displaying negative numbers

Because many people use spreadsheets for business, they often want negative numbers to appear highlighted so they can see them easier. Excel can display negative numbers in parentheses (–23) or in red so you can't miss them.

To define how negative numbers appear in your spreadsheet, follow these steps:

1. **Select the cell or range of cells that you want to modify.**

2. **Click the Home tab.**

3. **Click the Format icon in the Cells group.**

   A pop-up menu appears, as shown in Figure 7-5.

4. **Choose Cells.**

   The Format Cells dialog box appears, as shown in Figure 7-6.

REMEMBER

5. **Choose Currency or Number from the Category list.**

   You can choose how to format negative numbers only if you format your numbers using the Currency or Number category.

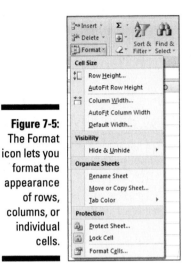

Figure 7-5:
The Format
icon lets you
format the
appearance
of rows,
columns, or
individual
cells.

6. **Click a negative number format and then click OK.**

   If any of your numbers become negative in the cell or cells you selected
   in Step 1, Excel automatically displays those negative numbers in the
   negative number format you chose.

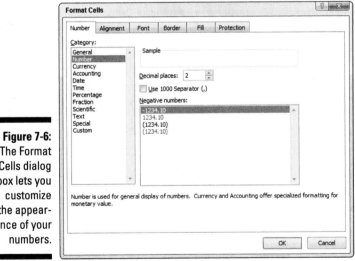

Figure 7-6:
The Format
Cells dialog
box lets you
customize
the appear-
ance of your
numbers.

Formatting decimal numbers

If you format cells to display numbers with decimal places, such as 23.09 or 23.09185, you can modify how many decimal places appear. To define the number of decimal places, follow these steps:

1. **Select the cell or cells that contain the numbers you want to format.**

2. **Click the Home tab.**

3. **Click in the Number Format list box (refer to Figure 7-3) and choose a format that displays decimal places, such as Number or Percentage.**

   Excel formats the numbers in your chosen cells.

You can click the Increase Decimal (increases the number of decimal places displayed) or Decrease Decimal icon (decreases the number of decimal places displayed), as shown in Figure 7-7.

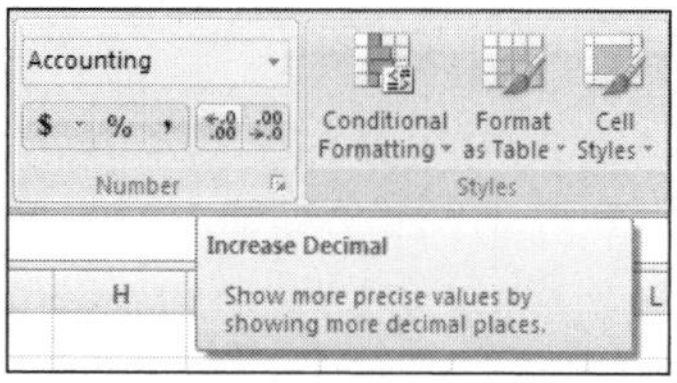

Figure 7-7:
Click to quickly change the number of decimal places displayed.

Formatting cells

To make your data look prettier, Excel can format the appearance of cells to change the font, background color, text color, or font size used to display data in a cell.

Excel provides two ways to format cells: You can use Excel's built-in formatting styles, or you can apply different types of formatting individually. Some of the individual formatting styles you can choose include

- ✔ Font and font size
- ✔ Text styles (underlining, italic, and bold)
- ✔ Text and background color
- ✔ Borders
- ✔ Alignment
- ✔ Text wrapping and orientation

Formatting cells with built-in styles

Excel provides a variety of predesigned formatting styles that you can apply to one or more cells. To format cells with a built-in style, follow these steps:

1. **Select the cell or cells that you want to format with a built-in style.**

2. **Click the Home tab.**

3. **Click the Cell Styles icon in the Styles group.**

   A pull-down menu appears listing all the different styles you can choose, as shown in Figure 7-8.

4. **Move the mouse pointer over a style.**

   Excel displays a Live Preview of how your selected cells will look with that particular style.

5. **Click the style you want.**

   Excel applies your chosen style to the selected cells.

Figure 7-8: The Cell Styles menu offers different ways to format your cells quickly.

Formatting fonts and text styles

Different fonts can emphasize parts of your spreadsheet, such as using one font to label columns and rows and another font or font size to display the actual data. Text styles (bold, underline, and italic) can also emphasize data that appears in the same font or font size.

To change the font, font size, and text style of one or more cells, follow these steps:

1. **Select the cell or cells that you want to change the font and font size.**

   2. Click the Home tab.

   3. Click the Font list box.

   A pull-down menu of different fonts appears.

   4. Click the font you want to use.

   5. Choose one of the following methods to change the font size:

   - Click the Font Size list box and then choose a font size, such as 12 or 16.

   - Click the Font Size list box and type a value such as 7 or 15.

   - Click the Increase Font Size or Decrease Font Size icon until your data appears in the size you want.

   6. Click one or more text style icons (Bold, Italic, Underline).

Formatting with color

Each cell displays data in a Font color and a Fill color. The *Font color* defines the color of the numbers and letters that appear inside a cell. (The default Font color is black.) The *Fill color* defines the color that fills the background of the cell. (The default Fill color is white.)

To change the Font and Fill colors of cells, follow these steps:

   1. Select the cell or cells that you want to color.

   2. Click the Home tab.

   3. Click the downward-pointing arrow that appears to the right of the Font Color icon.

   A color palette appears, as shown in Figure 7-9.

   4. Click the color you want to use for your text.

   The color you select appears directly on the Font Color icon. The next time you want to apply this same color to a cell, you can click the Font Color icon directly instead of the downward-pointing arrow to the right of the Font Color icon.

   5. Click the downward-pointing arrow that appears to the right of the Fill Color icon.

   A color palette appears.

   6. Click a color to use to fill the background of your cell.

   The color you select appears directly on the Fill Color icon. The next time you want to apply this same color to a cell, you can click the Fill Color icon directly instead of the downward-pointing arrow to the right of the Fill Color icon.

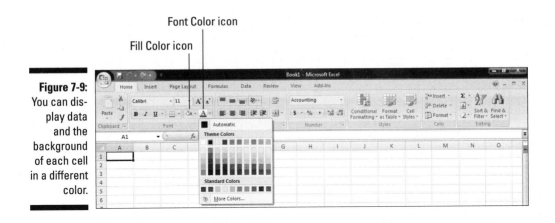

Figure 7-9:
You can dis-
play data
and the
background
of each cell
in a different
color.

Adding borders

For another way to highlight one or more cells, you can add borders. Borders
can surround the entire cell or just the top, bottom, left, or right side of a cell.
To add borders to a cell, follow these steps:

1. **Select one or more cells.**

2. **Click the Home tab.**

3. **Click the downward-pointing arrow to the right of the Border icon.**

   A pull-down menu appears, as shown in Figure 7-10.

4. **Click a border style.**

   Excel displays your chosen borders around the cells you selected in Step 1.

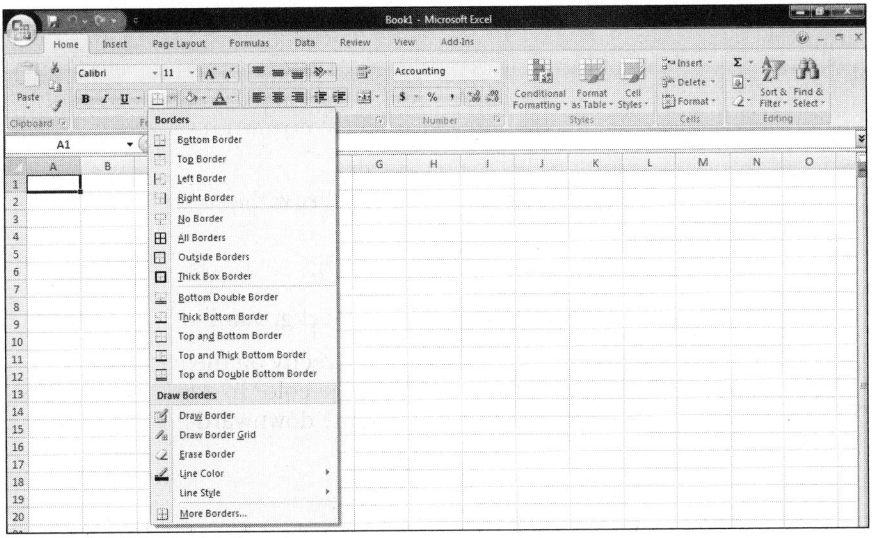

Figure 7-10:
The Border
menu lists
different
ways to
place
borders
around cells.

Navigating a Spreadsheet

If you have a large spreadsheet, chances are good that information may be hidden by the limitations of your computer screen. To help you view and select cells in different parts of your spreadsheet, Excel offers various ways to navigate a spreadsheet using the mouse and keyboard.

Using the mouse to move around in a spreadsheet

To navigate a spreadsheet with the mouse, you can click the scroll bars or use the scroll wheel on your mouse, if you have one. To use the scroll bars, you have three choices:

- **Click the up/down or right/left arrows on the horizontal or vertical scroll bars.**

  This moves the spreadsheet one row (up or down) or column (right or left) at a time.

- **Drag the scroll box of a scroll bar.**

- **Click the scroll area (any area to the left/right or above/below the scroll box on the scroll bar).**

  This moves the spreadsheet one screen left/right or up/down.

If your mouse has a scroll wheel, you can use this wheel to move through a spreadsheet by two methods:

- Roll the mouse's scroll wheel up or down to scroll your spreadsheet up or down.

- Press the scroll wheel to display a four-way pointing arrow, then move the mouse up, down, right, or left. (When you're done, click the scroll wheel again.)

Using the keyboard to move around a spreadsheet

Using the mouse can be faster to jump from one place in a spreadsheet to another, but sometimes using the mouse can be frustrating, trying to line it up just right. For that reason, you can also use the keyboard to move around a spreadsheet. Some of the common ways to move around a spreadsheet are shown in Table 7-1.

Table 7-1	Using the Keyboard to Navigate a Spreadsheet
Pressing This	*Does This*
Up arrow (↑)	Moves up one row
Down arrow (↓)	Moves down one row
Left arrow (←)	Moves left one column
Right arrow (→)	Moves right one column
Ctrl+↑	Jumps up to the top of a column that contains data
Ctrl+↓	Jumps down to the bottom of a column that contains data
Ctrl+←	Jumps to the left of a row that contains data
Ctrl+→	Jumps to the right of a row that contains data
Page Up	Moves up one screen
Page Down	Moves down one screen
Ctrl+Page Up	Displays the previous worksheet
Ctrl+Page Down	Displays the next worksheet
Home	Moves to the A column of the current row
Ctrl+Home	Moves to the A1 cell
Ctrl+End	Moves to the bottom right cell of your spreadsheet

If you know the specific cell you want to move to, you can jump to that cell by using the Go To command. To use the Go To command, follow these steps:

1. **Click the Home tab.**

2. **Click the Find & Select icon in the Editing group.**

   A pull-down menu appears.

3. **Click Go To.**

   The Go To dialog box appears, as shown in Figure 7-11.

   You can also choose the Go To command by pressing Ctrl+G.

4. **Click in the Reference text box and type the cell you want to move to, such as C13 or F4.**

5. **Click OK.**

   Excel highlights the cell you typed in Step 4.

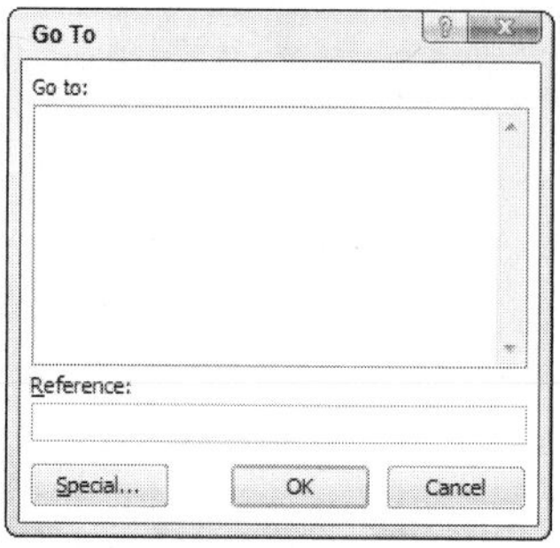

Figure 7-11:
The Go To
dialog box
lets you
jump to a
specific cell.

Naming cells

One problem with the Go To command is that most people won't know which
cell contains the data they want to find. For example, if you want to view the
cell that contains your total amount of money you owe for your income taxes,
you probably don't want to memorize that this cell is G68.

To help you identify certain cells, Excel lets you give them descriptive names.
To name a cell or range of cells, follow these steps:

1. **Select the cell or cells that you want to name.**

2. **Click in the Name box, as shown in Figure 7-12.**

3. **Type a descriptive name without any spaces and then press Enter.**

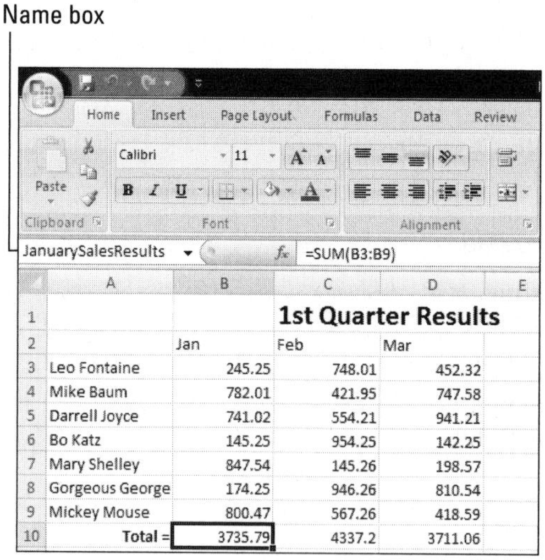

Name box

Figure 7-12:
You can type
a descriptive
name
for your
cells in the
Name box.

	A	B	C	D	E
1			**1st Quarter Results**		
2		Jan	Feb	Mar	
3	Leo Fontaine	245.25	748.01	452.32	
4	Mike Baum	782.01	421.95	747.58	
5	Darrell Joyce	741.02	554.21	941.21	
6	Bo Katz	145.25	954.25	142.25	
7	Mary Shelley	847.54	145.26	198.57	
8	Gorgeous George	174.25	946.26	810.54	
9	Mickey Mouse	800.47	567.26	418.59	
10	Total =	3735.79	4337.2	3711.06	

JanuarySalesResults f_x =SUM(B3:B9)

After you name a cell, you can jump to it quickly by following these steps:

1. **Click the downward-pointing arrow to the right of the Name box.**

   A list of named cells appears.

2. **Click the named cell you want to view.**

   Excel displays your chosen cell.

Eventually, you may want to edit or delete a name for your cells. To delete or edit a name, follow these steps:

1. **Click the Formulas tab.**

2. **Click the Name Manager icon.**

   The Name Manager dialog box appears, as shown in Figure 7-13.

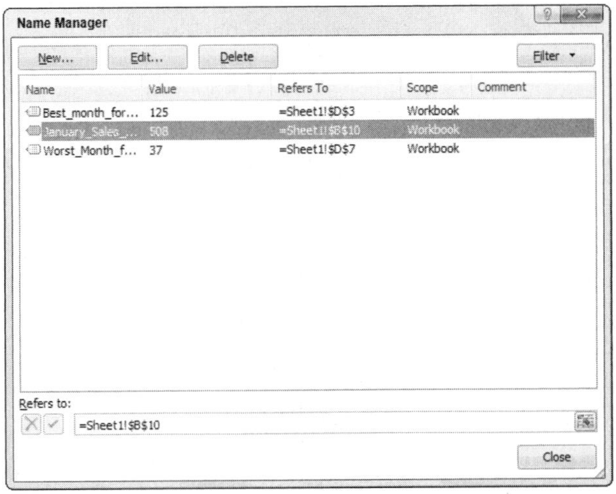

Figure 7-13: The Name Manager dialog box lets you rename or delete previously named cells.

3. **Edit or delete the named cell as follows:**

   • To edit the name, click the cell name you want to edit and then click the Edit button. An Edit Name dialog box appears, where you can change the name or the cell reference.

   • To delete the name, click the cell name you want to delete and then click the Delete button.

4. **Click Close.**

Searching a Spreadsheet

Rather than search for a specific cell, you may want to search for a particular label or number in a spreadsheet. Excel lets you search for the following:

- Specific text or numbers
- All cells that contain formulas
- All cells that contain conditional formatting

Searching for text

You can search for a specific label or number anywhere in your spreadsheet. To search for text or numbers, follow these steps:

1. **Click the Home tab.**

2. **Click the Find & Select icon in the Editing group.**

   A pull-down menu appears.

3. **Click Find.**

   The Find and Replace dialog box appears, as shown in Figure 7-14.

   If you click the Replace tab, you can define the text or number to find and new text or numbers to replace it.

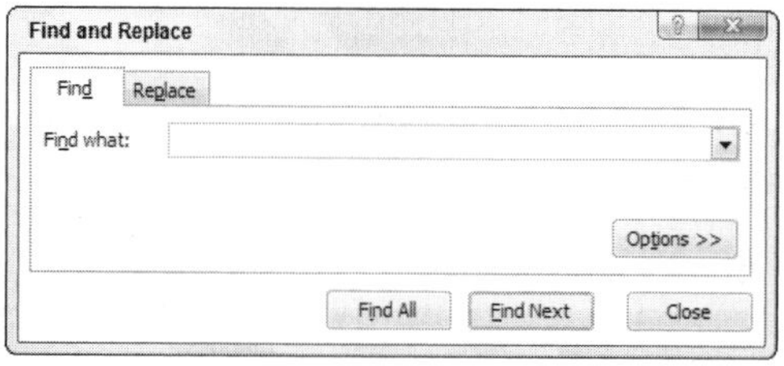

Figure 7-14: The Find and Replace dialog box lets you search your worksheet.

Find and Replace
Find   Replace
Find what:
Options >>
Find All   Find Next   Close

4. **Click in the Find What text box and type the text or number you want to find.**

   If you click the Options button, the Find and Replace dialog box expands to provide additional options for searching, such as searching in the displayed sheet or the entire workbook.

5. **Click one of the following:**

- *Find Next:* Finds and selects the first cell, starting from the currently selected cell that contains the text you typed in Step 4

- *Find All:* Finds and lists all cells that contain the text you typed in Step 4, as shown in Figure 7-15

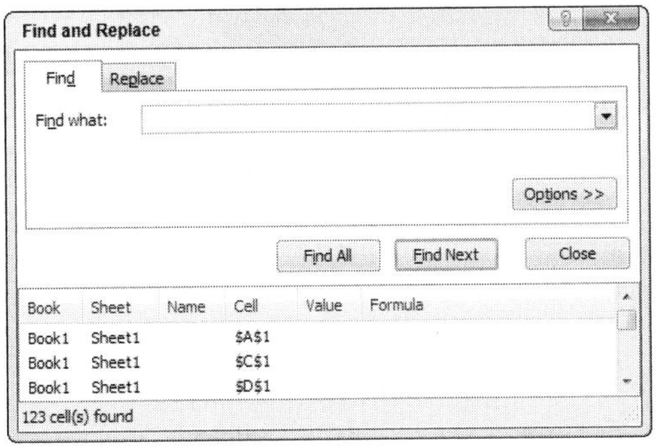

Figure 7-15:
The Find All button names all the cells that contain the text or number you want to find.

6. **Click Close to make the Find and Replace dialog box go away.**

Searching for formulas

Formulas appear just like numbers; to help you find which cells contain formulas, Excel gives you two choices:

- ✔ Display formulas in your cells (instead of numbers)
- ✔ Highlight the cells that contain formulas

To display formulas in a spreadsheet, press Ctrl+` (an accent grave character, which appears on the same key as the ~ sign and often appears to the left of the number 1 key near the top of a keyboard). Figure 7-16 shows what a spreadsheet looks like when formulas appear inside of cells.

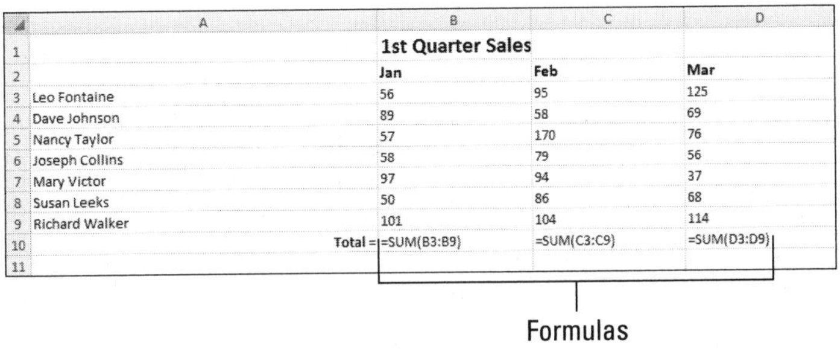

Figure 7-16:
By displaying formulas in cells, you can identify which cells display calculations.

Formulas

To highlight all cells that contain formulas, follow these steps:

1. **Click the Home tab.**

2. **Click the Find & Select icon in the Editing group.**

   A pull-down menu appears.

3. **Click Formulas.**

   Excel highlights all the cells that contain formulas.

Editing a Spreadsheet

The two ways to edit a spreadsheet are

✔ Edit the data itself, such as the labels, numbers, and formulas that make up a spreadsheet.

✔ Edit the physical layout of the spreadsheet, such as adding or deleting rows and columns, or widening or shrinking the width or heights of rows and columns.

Editing data in a cell

To edit data in a single cell, follow these steps:

1. **Double-click the cell that contains the data you want to edit.**

   Excel displays a cursor in your selected cell.

2. **Edit your data by using the Backspace or Delete key, or by typing new data.**

If you click a cell, Excel displays the contents of that cell in the Formula bar. You can click and edit data directly in the Formula bar, which can be more convenient for editing large amounts of data.

Changing the size of rows and columns with the mouse

Using the mouse can be a quick way to modify the sizes of rows and columns. To change the height of a row or the width of a column, follow these steps:

1. **Move the mouse pointer over the bottom line of a row heading, such as the 2 or 18 heading. (Or move the mouse pointer over the right line of the column heading, such as A or D.)**

   The mouse pointer turns into a two-way pointing arrow.

2. **Hold down the left mouse button and drag (move) the mouse.**

   Excel resizes your row or column.

3. **Release the left mouse button when you're happy with the size of your row or column.**

Typing the size of rows and columns

If you need to resize a row or column to a precise value, it's easier to type a specific value into the Row Height or Column Width dialog box instead. To type a value into a Row Height or Column Width dialog box, follow these steps:

1. **Click the Home tab.**

2. **Click the row or column heading that you want to resize.**

   Excel highlights your entire row or column.

3. **Click the Format icon that appears in the Cells group.**

   A pull-down menu appears.

4. **Click Height (if you selected a row) or Width (if you selected a column).**

   The Row Height or Column Width dialog box appears, as shown in Figure 7-17.

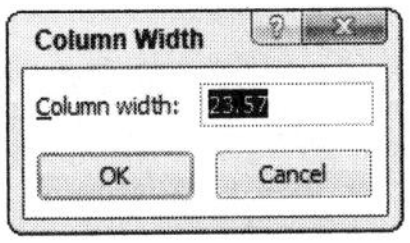

Figure 7-17:
Enter a width for the column.

Column Width

Column width: 23.57

OK   Cancel

5. **Type a value and then click OK.**

   Excel resizes your row or column.

Excel measures column width in characters. (A cell defined as 1 character width can display a single letter or number.) Excel measures row height by points where 1 point equals $\frac{1}{72}$ inch.

Adding and deleting rows and columns

After you type in labels, numbers, and formulas, you may suddenly realize that you need to add or delete extra rows or columns. To add a row or column, follow these steps:

1. **Click the Home tab.**

2. **Click the row or column heading where you want to add another row or column.**

3. **Click the Insert icon in the Cells group.**

   Inserting a row adds a new row above the selected row. Inserting a column adds a new column to the left of the selected column.

To delete a row or column, follow these steps:

1. **Click the Home tab.**

2. **Click the row or column heading that you want to delete.**

3. **Click the Delete icon in the Cells group.**

Deleting a row or column deletes any data stored in that row or column.

Adding sheets

For greater flexibility, Excel lets you create individual spreadsheets that you can save in a single workbook (file). When you load Excel, it automatically provides you with three sheets, but you can add more if you need them.

To add a new sheet, choose one of the following:

- ✔ **Click the Insert Worksheet icon.**
- ✔ **Click the Home tab, click the downward-pointing arrow next to the Insert icon in the Cells group, and then choose Insert Sheet, as shown in Figure 7-18.**

Renaming sheets

By default, Excel gives each sheet a generic name such as Sheet1. To give your sheets a more descriptive name, follow these steps:

1. **Choose one of the following:**

    - *Double-click the sheet tab that you want to rename.*

      Excel highlights the entire sheet name.

    - *Click the sheet tab you want to rename, click the Home tab, click the Format icon in the Cells group, and choose Rename Sheet.*

    - *Right-click the sheet tab you want to rename; when a pop-up menu appears, choose Rename.*

2. **Type a new name for your sheet and press Enter when you're done.**

    Your new name appears on the sheet tab.

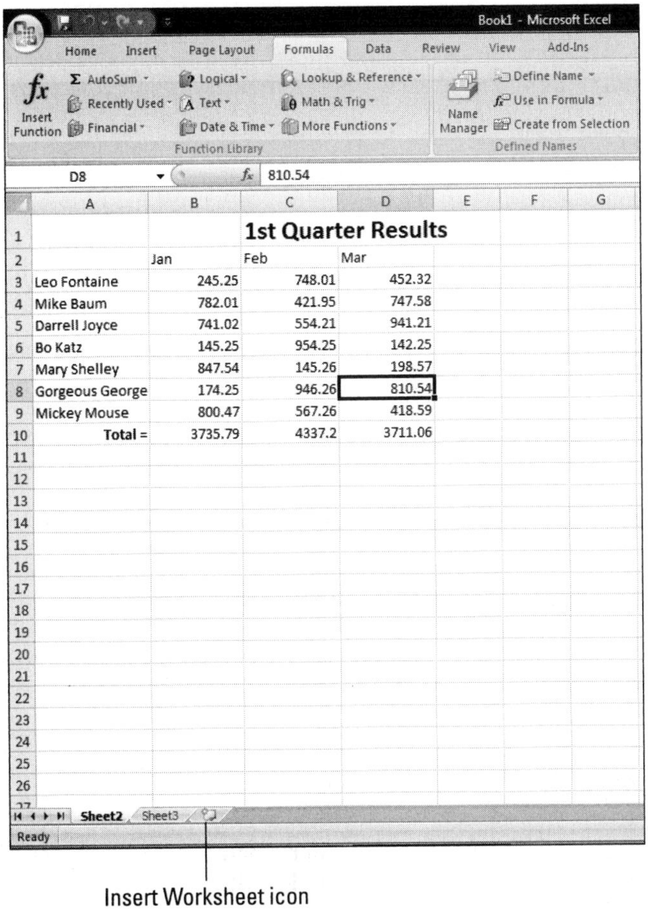

Figure 7-18:
Excel displays the names of individual sheets as tabs.

Insert Worksheet icon

Rearranging sheets

You can rearrange the order that your sheets appear in your workbook. To rearrange a sheet, follow these steps:

1. **Move the mouse pointer over the sheet tab that you want to move.**

2. **Hold down the left mouse button and drag (move) the mouse.**

   The downward-pointing black arrow points where Excel will place your sheet.

3. **Release the left mouse button to place your sheet in a new order.**

Deleting a sheet

Using multiple sheets may be handy, but you may want to delete a sheet if you don't need it.

If you delete a sheet, you also delete all the data stored on that sheet.

To delete a sheet, follow these steps:

1. **Choose one of the following:**

   - *Right-click the tab of the sheet you want to delete. When a pop-up menu appears, click Delete.*

   - *Click the Home tab, click the downward-pointing arrow that appears to the right of the Delete icon in the Cells group, and choose Delete Sheet.*

   If your sheet is empty, Excel deletes the sheet right away. If your sheet contains data, a dialog box appears to warn you that you'll lose any data stored on that sheet.

2. **Click Delete.**

   Excel deletes your sheet along with any data on it.

Clearing Data

After you create a spreadsheet, you may need to delete data, formulas, or just the formatting that defines the appearance of your data. To clear out one or more cells of data, formatting, or both data and formatting, follow these steps:

1. **Click the Home tab.**

2. **Select the cell or cells that contain the data you want to clear.**

3. **Click the downward-pointing arrow to the right of the Clear icon in the Editing group.**

   A pull-down menu appears, as shown in Figure 7-19.

Figure 7-19:
The Clear menu provides different ways to clear out a cell.

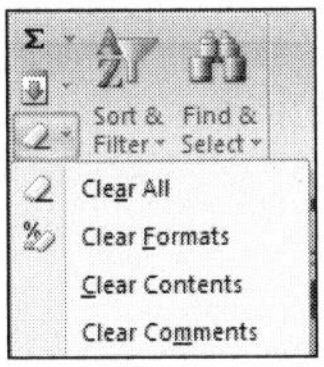

4. **Choose one of the following:**

   • *Clear All:* Deletes the data and any formatting applied to that cell or cells

   • *Clear Formats:* Leaves the data in the cell but strips away any formatting

   • *Clear Contents:* Leaves the formatting in the cell but deletes the data

   • *Clear Comments:* Leaves data and formatting but deletes any comments added to the cell

Printing Workbooks

After you create a spreadsheet, you can print it out for others to see. When printing spreadsheets, you need to take special care how your spreadsheet appears on a page because a large spreadsheet will likely get printed on two or more sheets of paper.

This can cause problems if an entire spreadsheet prints on a one page but a single row of numbers appears on a second page, which can make reading and understanding your spreadsheet data confusing. When printing spreadsheets, take time to align your data so that it prints correctly on every page.

Using Page Layout view

Excel can display your spreadsheets in two ways: Normal view and Page Layout view. Normal view is the default appearance, which simply fills your screen with rows and columns so you can see as much of your spreadsheet as possible.

Page Layout view displays your spreadsheet exactly as it will appear if you print it. Not only can you see where your page breaks occur, but you can also add any headers to the top of your spreadsheet as well.

To switch back and forth from Normal view to Page Layout view, follow these steps:

1. **Click the View tab.**

2. **Click the Normal or Page Layout View icon in the Workbook Views group, as shown in Figure 7-20.**

You can also click the Normal or Page Layout View icons in the bottom-right corner of the Excel window.

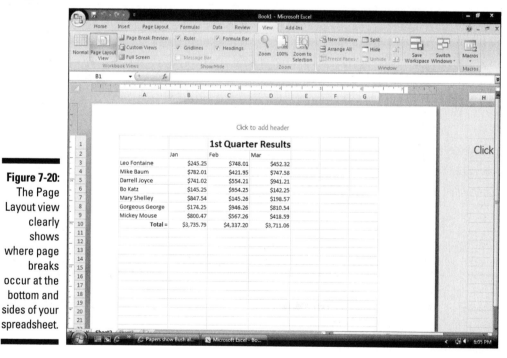

Figure 7-20:
The Page Layout view clearly shows where page breaks occur at the bottom and sides of your spreadsheet.

Adding a header (or footer)

Headers and footers are useful when printing out your spreadsheet. A header may explain the information in the spreadsheet, such as *2007 Tax Return Information,* and a footer may display page numbers. To create a header or footer, follow these steps:

1. **Click the Insert tab.**

2. **Click the Header & Footer icon in the Text group.**

   Excel displays the Design contextual tools tab and creates a text box for your header and footer, as shown in Figure 7-21.

3. **Type your header text in the header text box.**

4. **Click the Go To Footer icon in the Navigation group.**

   Excel displays your footer text box.

5. **Type your footer text in the footer text box.**

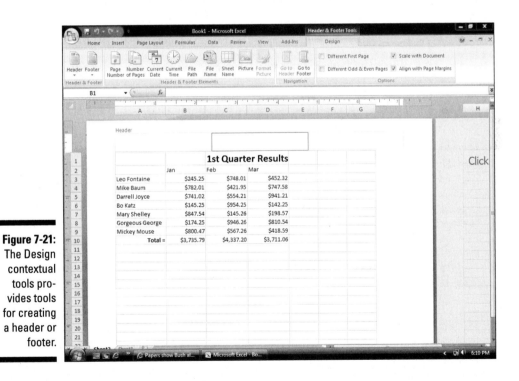

Figure 7-21:
The Design contextual tools pro-vides tools for creating a header or footer.

Printing gridlines

Gridlines help you understand how your numbers, labels, and formulas are aligned with one another. If you need to print a large spreadsheet, you may want to print gridlines to make it easier to understand.

To print gridlines and/or row and column headings, follow these steps:

1. **Click the Page Layout tab.**
2. **(Optional) Select the Print check box under the Gridlines category.**
3. **(Optional) Select the Print check box under the Heading category.**

Defining a print area

Sometimes you may not want to print your entire spreadsheet but just a certain part of it, called the *print area.* To define the print area, follow these steps:

1. **Select the cells that you want to print.**
2. **Click the Page Layout tab.**
3. **Click the Print Area icon in the Page Setup group.**

   A pull-down menu appears, as shown in Figure 7-22.

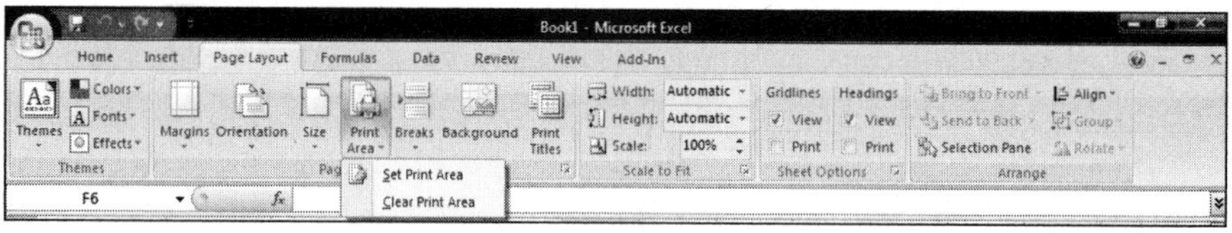

Figure 7-22:
The Print Area menu lets you define or clear the printable cells.

4. **Choose Set Print Area.**

   Excel displays a dotted line around your print area.

5. **Click the Office Button and then click the right-pointing arrow that appears to the right of Print.**

   A print menu appears.

6. **Choose Quick Print (to print) or Print Preview (to see what your spreadsheet will look like before you print it).**

After you define a print area, you can see which cells are part of your print area by clicking the downward-pointing arrow of the Name box and choosing Print_Area.

After you define a print area, you can always add to it by following these steps:

1. **Select the cells adjacent to the print area.**

2. **Click the Page Layout tab.**

3. **Click the Print Area icon in the Page Setup group.**

   A pull-down menu appears.

4. **Choose Add to Print Area.**

   Excel displays a dotted line around your newly defined print area.

After you define the print area, you can always remove it by following these steps:

1. **Click the Page Layout tab.**

2. **Click Print Area.**

   A pull-down menu appears (refer to Figure 7-22).

3. **Choose Clear Print Area.**

Inserting (and removing) page breaks

One problem with large spreadsheets is that when you print them out, parts may get cut off when printed on separate pages. To correct this problem, you can tell Excel exactly where page breaks should occur.

To insert page breaks, follow these steps:

1. **Move the cursor in the cell to define where the vertical and horizontal page breaks will appear.**

2. **Click the Page Layout tab.**

3. **Click the Breaks icon in the Page Setup group.**

   A pull-down menu appears, as shown in Figure 7-23.

4. **Choose Insert Page Break.**

   Excel inserts a horizontal page directly above the cell you selected in Step 1 and a vertical page break to the left of that cell, too.

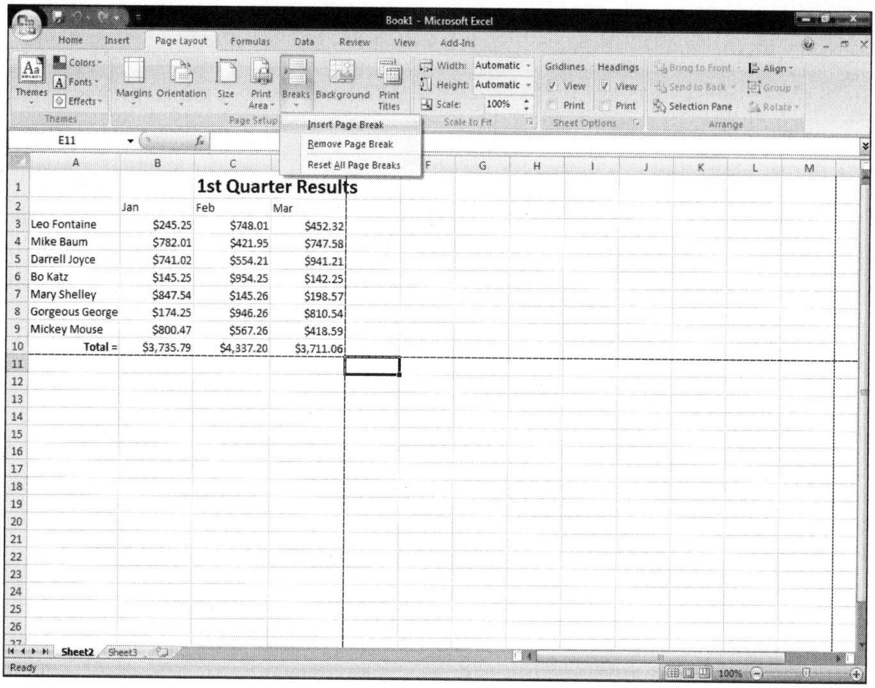

Figure 7-23:
The Breaks
menu lets
you insert a
page break.

To remove a page break, follow these steps:

1. **Choose one of the following:**

   - *To remove a horizontal page break:* Click in any cell that appears directly below that horizontal page break.

   - *To remove a vertical page break:* Click in any cell that appears directly to the right of that horizontal page break.

   - *To remove both a vertical and horizontal page break:* Click in the cell that appears to the right of the vertical page break and directly underneath the horizontal page break.

2. **Click the Page Layout tab.**

3. **Click the Breaks icon in the Page Setup group.**

   A pull-down menu appears (refer to Figure 7-23).

4. **Choose Remove Page Break.**

   Excel removes your chosen page break.

Printing row and column headings

If you have a large spreadsheet that fills two or more pages, Excel may print your spreadsheet data on separate pages. Although the first page may print your labels to identify what each row and column may represent, any additional pages that Excel prints won't bear those same identifying labels. As a result, you may wind up printing rows and columns of numbers without any labels that identify what those numbers mean.

To fix this problem, you can define labels to print on every page by following these steps:

1. **Click the Page Layout tab.**
2. **Click the Print Titles icon in the Page Setup group.**

   The Page Setup dialog box appears, as shown in Figure 7-24.

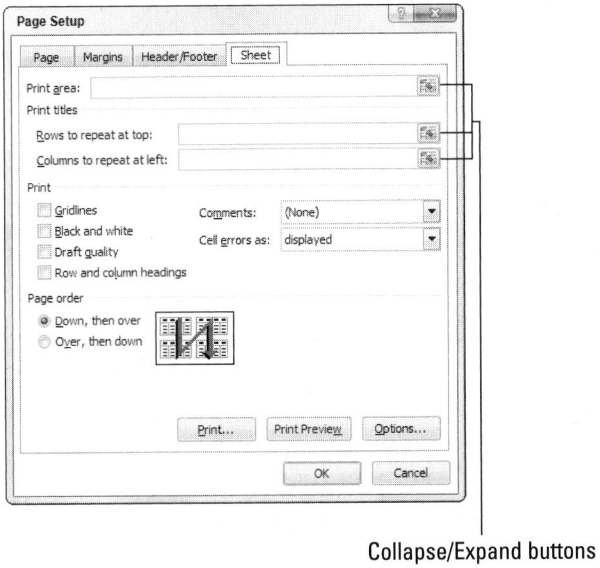

Figure 7-24:
The Page Setup dialog box lets you define the row and column headings to print on every page.

Collapse/Expand buttons

3. **Click the Collapse/Expand button that appears to the far right of the Rows to Repeat at Top text box.**

   The Page Setup dialog box shrinks.

4. **Click in the row that contains the labels you want to print at the top of every page.**

5. **Click the Collapse/Expand button again.**

   The Page Setup dialog box reappears.

6. **Click the Collapse/Expand button that appears to the far right of the Columns to Repeat at Left text box.**

   The Page Setup dialog box shrinks.

7. **Click in the column that contains the labels you want to print on the left of every page.**

8. **Click the Collapse/Expand button again.**

   The Page Setup dialog box reappears.

9. **Click OK.**

Defining printing margins

To help you squeeze or expand your spreadsheet to fill a printed page, you can define different margins for each printed page. To define margins, follow these steps:

1. **Click the Page Layout tab.**

2. **Click the Margins icon in the Page Setup group.**

   A pull-down menu appears, as shown in Figure 7-25.

3. **Choose a page margin style you want to use.**

If you choose Custom Margins in Step 3, you can define your own margins for a printed page.

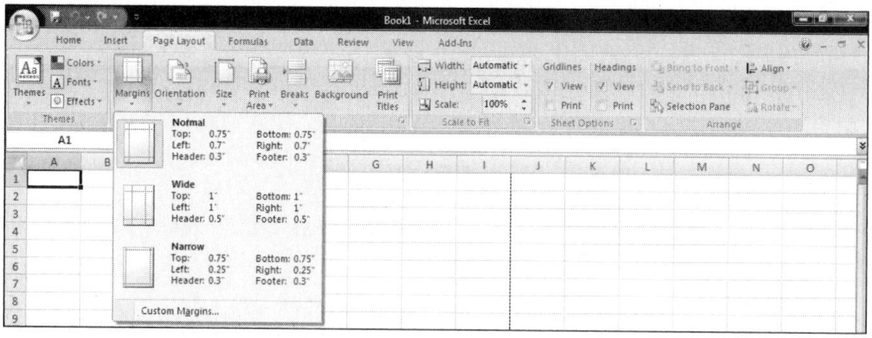

Figure 7-25:
The Margins icon lists different predefined margins you can choose.

Defining paper orientation and size

Paper *orientation* can be either *landscape* (the paper width is greater than its height) or *portrait* mode (the paper width is less than its height). Paper *size* defines the physical dimensions of the page.

To change the paper orientation and size, follow these steps:

1. **Click the Page Layout tab.**

2. **Click the Orientation icon in the Page Setup group.**

   A pull-down menu appears, as shown in Figure 7-26.

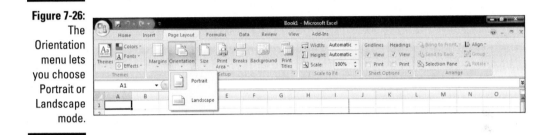

Figure 7-26:
The Orientation menu lets you choose Portrait or Landscape mode.

3. **Choose Portrait or Landscape.**

4. **Click the Size icon in the Page Setup group.**

   A pull-down menu appears, as shown in Figure 7-27.

5. **Click a paper size.**

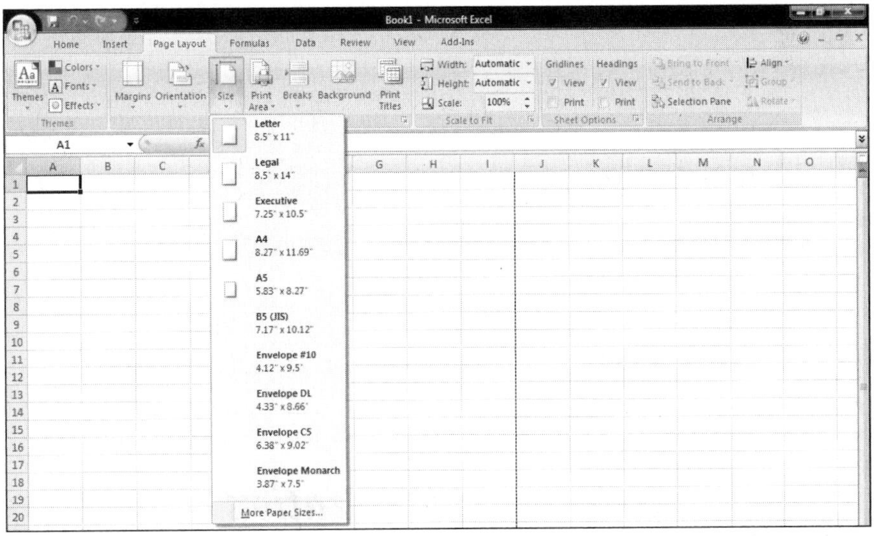

Figure 7-27:
The Size menu lists different paper sizes you can use.

Printing in Excel

When you finish defining how to print your spreadsheet, you can either print right away or view a Print Preview of your spreadsheet just to make sure everything's going to print correctly.

To print a spreadsheet right away, click the Office Button, click the right-pointing arrow that appears to the right of Print, and then choose Quick Print.

To display the Print Preview before printing, follow these steps:

1. **Click the Office Button and then choose Print.**

   The Print dialog box appears.

2. **Click the Preview button.**

   The Print Preview window appears, as shown in Figure 7-28.

   If you click the Show Margins icon, the Print Preview window displays your page margins as dotted lines, which you can drag to move and redefine new page margins before printing.

3. **Click Close Print Preview (to close the Print Preview window) or Print (to close the Print Preview window and print your spreadsheet).**

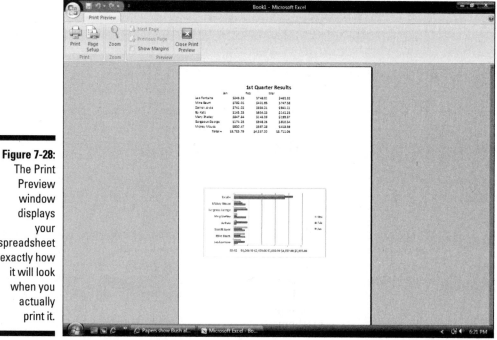

Figure 7-28:
The Print Preview window displays your spreadsheet exactly how it will look when you actually print it.

Chapter 8

Playing with Formulas

- -

In This Chapter

▶ Creating formulas

▶ Using functions

▶ Editing formulas

▶ Manipulating data with goal seeking

▶ Creating multiple scenarios

▶ Auditing formulas

▶ Validating data

- -

*E*xcel can manipulate your data by using formulas. Formulas can be as simple as adding two or more numbers together or as complicated as determining the calculation of a second-order differential equation.

Formulas use data, stored in other cells, to calculate a new result that appears in another cell. To create even more complicated spreadsheets, you can even make a formula use data from other formulas so that changes in a single cell can ripple throughout an entire spreadsheet.

Creating a Formula

Formulas consist of three crucial bits of information:

✔ An equal sign (=)

✔ One or more cell references

✔ The type of calculation to do on the data (addition, subtraction, and so on)

A *cell reference* is simply the unique row and column heading that identifies a single cell, such as A4 or D9. The four common calculations that a formula can use are addition (+), subtraction (–), multiplication (*), and division (/). Table 8-1 lists other mathematical operators you can use in a formula.

Table 8-1	Common Mathematical Operators Used to Create Formulas		
Operator	*What It Does*	*Example*	*Result*
+	Addition	=5+3.4	8.4
–	Subtraction	=54.2-2.1	52.1
*	Multiplication	=1.2*4	4.8
/	Division	=25/5	5
%	Percentage	=42%	0.42
^	Exponentiation	=4^3	64
=	Equal	=6=7	False
>	Greater than	=7>2	True
<	Less than	=9<8	False
>=	Greater than or equal to	=45>=3	True
<=	Less than or equal to	=40<=2	False
<>	Not equal to	=5<>7	True
&	Text concatenation	="Bo the "& "Cat"	Bo the Cat

A simple formula uses a single mathematical operator and two cell references such as:

=A4+C7

This formula consists of three parts:

- ✔ **The = sign:** This identifies your formula. If you type just **A4+C7** into a cell, Excel treats it as ordinary text.
- ✔ **Two cell references:** In this example, A4 and C7.
- ✔ **The addition (+) mathematical operator.**

To type a formula in a cell, follow these steps:

1. **Click in the cell where you want to store the formula.**

   You can also select a cell by pressing the arrow keys.

   Excel highlights your selected cell.

2. **Type the equal sign (=).**

   This tells Excel that you are creating a formula.

3. **Type your formula that includes one or more cell references that identify cells that contain data, such as A4 or E8.**

   For example, if you want to add the numbers stored in cells A4 and E8, you would type =**A4+E8**.

4. **Press Enter.**

Typing cell references can get cumbersome because you have to match the row and column headings of a cell correctly. As a faster alternative, you can use the mouse to click any cell that contains data; then Excel types that cell reference into your formula automatically.

To use the mouse to click cell references when creating a formula, follow these steps:

1. **Click in the cell where you want to store the formula. (You can also select the cell by pressing the arrow keys.)**

   Excel highlights your selected cell.

2. **Type the equal sign (=).**

   This tells Excel that anything you type after the equal sign is part of your formula.

3. **Type any mathematical operators and click any cells that contain data, such as A4 or E8.**

   If you want to create the formula =A4+E8, you would do the following:

   a. Type =.

      This tells Excel that you're creating a formula.

   b. Click cell A4.

      Excel types the A4 cell reference in your formula automatically.

   c. Type +.

   d. Click cell E8.

      Excel types in the E8 cell reference in your formula automatically.

4. **Press Enter.**

After you finish creating a formula, you can type data into the cell references used in your formula to calculate a new result.

Organizing formulas with parentheses

Formulas can be as simple as a single mathematical operator such as =D3*E4. However, you can also use multiple mathematical operators, such as

=A4+A5*C7/F4+D9

There are two problems with using multiple mathematical operators. First, they make a formula harder to read and understand. Second, Excel calculates mathematical operators from left to right, based on precedence, which means a formula may calculate results differently than you intended.

Precedence tells Excel which mathematical operators to calculate first, as listed in Table 8-2. For example, Excel calculates multiplication before it calculates addition. If you had a formula like

=A3+A4*B4+B5

Excel first multiplies A4*B4 and then adds this result to A3 and B5.

Table 8-2	Operator Precedence in Excel
Mathematical Operator	*Description*
: (colon) (single space) , (comma)	Reference operators
–	Negation
%	Percent
^	Exponentiation
* /	Multiplication and division
+ –	Addition and subtraction
&	Text concatenation
= < > <= >= <>	Comparison

Typing parentheses around cell references and mathematical operators not only organizes your formulas but also tells Excel specifically how you want to calculate a formula. In the example =A3+A4*B4+B5, Excel multiplies A4 and B4 first. If you want Excel to first add A3 and A4, then add B4 and B5, and finally multiply the two results together, you have to use parentheses, like this:

=(A3+A4)*(B4+B5)

Copying formulas

In many spreadsheets, you may need to create similar formulas that use different data. For example, you may have a spreadsheet that needs to add the same number of cells in adjacent columns.

You could type nearly identical formulas in multiple cells, but that's tedious and error-prone. For a faster way, you can copy a formula and paste it in another cell; then Excel automatically changes the cell references, as shown in Figure 8-1.

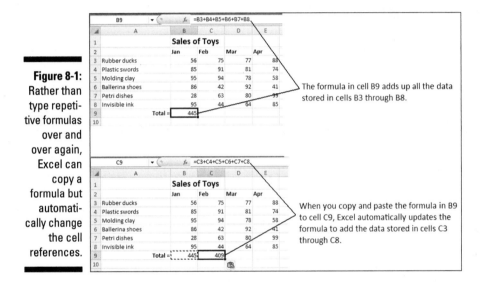

Figure 8-1: Rather than type repetitive formulas over and over again, Excel can copy a formula but automatically change the cell references.

The formula in cell B9 adds up all the data stored in cells B3 through B8.

When you copy and paste the formula in B9 to cell C9, Excel automatically updates the formula to add the data stored in cells C3 through C8.

From Figure 8-1, you can see that cell B9 contains the formula =B3+B4+B5+ B6+B7+B8, which simply adds the numbers stored in the six cells directly above the cell that contains the formula (B9). If you copy this formula to another cell, that new formula will also add the six cells directly above it. Copy and paste this formula to cell C9, and Excel changes the formula to =C3+C4+C5+C6+C7+C8.

To copy and paste a formula so that each formula changes cell references automatically, follow these steps:

1. **Select the cell that contains the formula you want to copy.**

2. **Press Ctrl+C (or click the Copy icon under the Home tab).**

   Excel displays a dotted line around your selected cell.

3. **Select the cell (or cells) where you want to paste your formula.**

   If you select multiple cells, Excel pastes a copy of your formula in each of those cells.

4. **Press Ctrl+V (or click the Paste icon under the Home tab).**

   Excel pastes your formula and automatically changes the cell references.

5. **Press Esc or double-click away from the cell with the dotted line to make the dotted line go away.**

Using Functions

Creating simple formulas is easy, but creating complex formulas is hard. To make complex formulas easier to create, Excel comes with prebuilt formulas called functions. Table 8-3 lists some of the many functions available.

Table 8-3	Common Excel Functions
Function Name	*What It Does*
AVERAGE	Calculates the average value of numbers stored in two or more cells
COUNT	Counts how many cells contain a number instead of a label (text)
MAX	Finds the largest number stored in two or more cells
MIN	Finds the smallest number stored in two or more cells
ROUND	Rounds a decimal number to a specific number of digits
SQRT	Calculates the square root of a number
SUM	Adds the values stored in two or more cells

Excel literally provides hundreds of functions that you can use by themselves or as part of your own formulas. A function typically uses one or more cell references:

✔ **Single cell references,** such as =ROUND(C4,2), which rounds the number found in cell C4 to two decimal places

✔ *Contiguous* **(adjacent) cell ranges,** such as =SUM(A4:A9), which adds all the numbers found in cells A4, A5, A6, A7, A8, and A9

✔ **Noncontiguous cell ranges,** such as =SUM(A4,B7,C11), which adds all the numbers found in cells A4, B7, and C11

To use a function, follow these steps:

1. **Click in the cell where you want to create a formula using a function.**

2. **Click the Formulas tab.**

3. **Click one of the following function icons in the Function Library group:**

   - *Financial:* Calculates business-related equations, such as the amount of interest earned over a specified time period

   - *Logical:* Provides logical operators to manipulate True and False (also known as *Boolean*) values

   - *Text:* Searches and manipulates text

   - *Date & Time:* Provides date and time information

   - *Lookup & Reference:* Provides information about cells, such as their row headings

   - *Math & Trig:* Offers mathematical equations

   - *More Functions:* Provides access to statistical and engineering functions

4. **Click a function category, such as Financial or Math & Trig.**

   A pull-down menu appears, as shown in Figure 8-2.

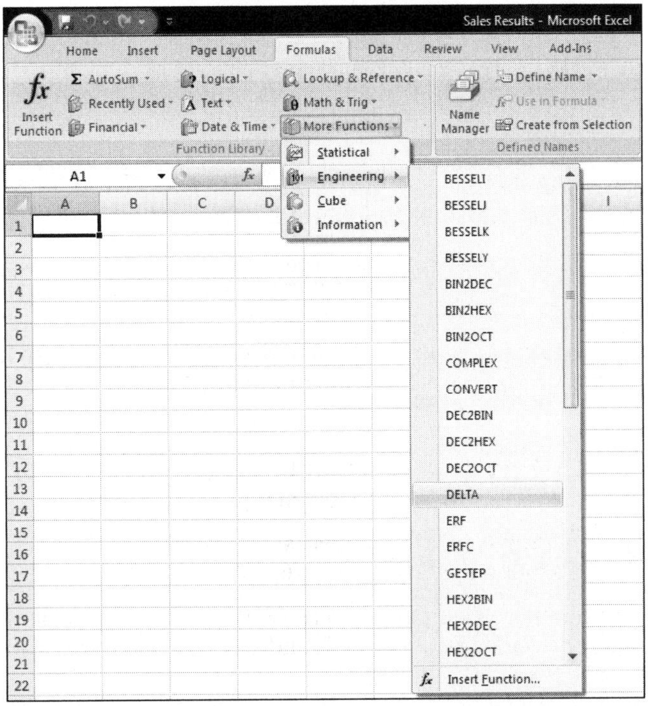

Figure 8-2:
Clicking a function library icon displays a menu of available functions you can use.

5. Click a function.

The Function Arguments dialog box appears, as shown in Figure 8-3.

6. Click the cell references you want to use.

7. Repeat Step 6 as many times as necessary.

8. Click OK.

Excel displays the calculation of your function in the cell you selected in Step 1.

Using the AutoSum command

One of the most useful and commonly used command is the AutoSum command. The *AutoSum command* uses the SUM function to add two or more cell references without making you type those cell references yourself. The most common use for the AutoSum function is to add a column or row of numbers.

To add a column or row of numbers with the AutoSum function, follow these steps:

1. Create a column or row of numbers that you want to add.

2. Click at the bottom of the column or the right of the row.

3. Click the Formulas tab.

4. Click the AutoSum icon in the Function Library group.

Excel automatically creates a SUM function in the cell you chose in Step 2 and highlights all the cells where it will retrieve data to add, as shown in Figure 8-4. (If you accidentally click the downward-pointing arrow under the AutoSum icon, a pull-down menu appears. Just choose Sum.)

5. Press Enter.

Excel automatically sums all the cell references.

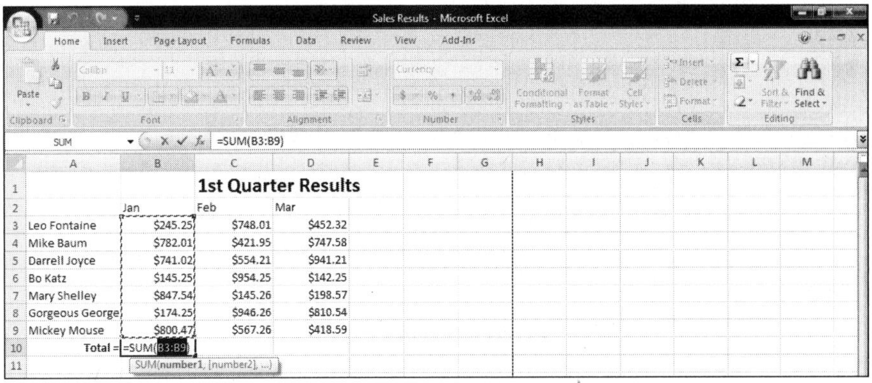

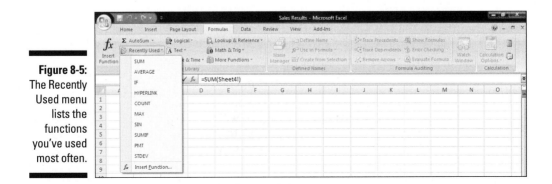

Figure 8-4:
The
AutoSum
command
automat-
ically
creates cell
references
for the SUM
function.

The AutoSum icon also appears on the Home tab in the Editing group.

Using recently used functions

Digging through all the different function library menus can be cumbersome, so Excel tries to make your life easier by creating a special Recently Used list that contains (what else?) a list of the functions you've used most often. From this menu, you can just see a list of your favorite functions and ignore the other hundred functions that you may never need in a million years.

To use the list of recently used functions, follow these steps:

1. **Click the cell where you want to store a function.**

2. **Click the Formulas tab.**

3. **Click the Recently Used icon in the Function Library group.**

   A pull-down menu appears, as shown in Figure 8-5.

4. **Choose a function.**

Figure 8-5:
The Recently
Used menu
lists the
functions
you've used
most often.

The more functions you use, the more your list will vary from what you see in Figure 8-5.

Editing a Formula

After you create a formula, you can always edit it later. You can edit a formula in two places:

- In the Formula bar
- In the cell itself

To edit a formula in the Formula bar, follow these steps:

1. **Select the cell that contains the formula you want to edit.**

   Excel displays the formula in the Formula bar.

2. **Click in the Formula bar and edit your formula using the Backspace and Delete keys.**

To edit a formula in the cell itself, follow these steps:

1. **Double-click in the cell that contains the formula you want to edit.**

   Excel displays a cursor in the cell you selected.

2. **Edit your formula using the Backspace and Delete keys.**

Because formulas display their calculations in a cell, it can be hard to tell the difference between cells that contain numbers and cells that contain formulas. To make formulas visible, press Ctrl+` (an accent grave character, which appears on the same key as the ~ symbol).

Goal Seeking

Usually after you can create a formula, you can type in new data to see how the formula calculates a new result. However, Excel also offers a feature known as *Goal Seeking*. With Goal Seeking, you specify the value you want a formula to calculate, and then Excel changes the data in the formula's cell references to tell you what values you need to achieve that goal.

For example, suppose you have a formula that calculates how much money you make every month by selling a product such as cars. Change the number of cars you sell, and Excel calculates your monthly commission. But if you use Goal Seeking, you can specify you want to earn $5,000 for your monthly commission, and Excel will work backward to tell you how many cars you need to sell. As its name implies, Goal Seeking lets you specify a goal and see what number, in a specific cell, needs to change to help you reach your goal.

To use Goal Seeking, follow these steps:

1. **Click in the cell that contains a formula.**
2. **Click the Data tab.**
3. **Click the What-If Analysis icon in the Data Tools group.**

   A pull-down menu appears, as shown in Figure 8-6.

Figure 8-6: The What-If Analysis icon displays the Goal Seek command.

4. **Click Goal Seek.**

   The Goal Seek dialog box appears, as shown in Figure 8-7.

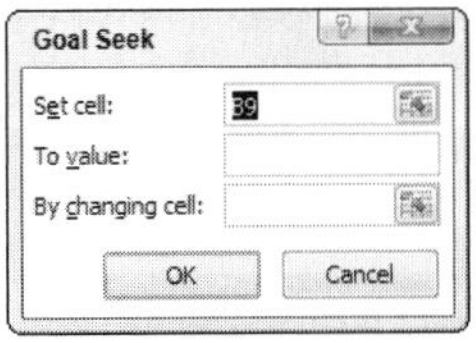

Figure 8-7: Define your goal in a cell containing a formula.

5. **Click in the To Value text box and type a number that you want to appear in the formula stored in the cell that you clicked in Step 1.**
6. **Click in the By Changing Cell text box and click one cell that contains data used by the formula you chose in Step 1.**

   Excel displays your cell reference, such as B5, in the Goal Seek dialog box.

7. **Click OK.**

   The Goal Seek Status dialog box changes the data in the cell you chose in Step 6, as shown in Figure 8-8.

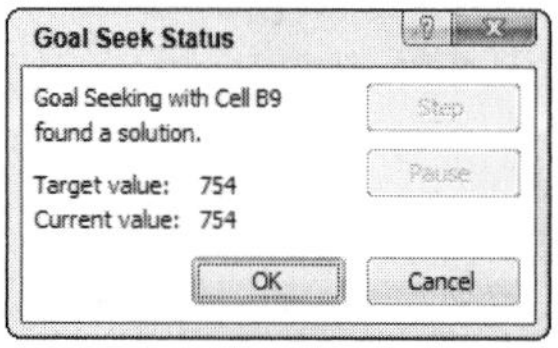

Figure 8-8:
The Goal
Seek Status
dialog box
changes the
data to
reach your
desired goal.

Goal Seek Status

Goal Seeking with Cell B9 found a solution.

Target value: 754
Current value: 754

Step
Pause
OK   Cancel

8. **Click OK (to keep the changes) or click Cancel (to display the original values your spreadsheet had before you chose the Goal Seek command).**

Creating Multiple Scenarios

Spreadsheets show you what happened in the past. However, you can also use a spreadsheet to help predict the future by typing in data that represents your best guess of what might happen.

When you use a spreadsheet as a prediction tool, you may create a best-case scenario (where customers flood you with orders) and a worst-case scenario (where hardly anybody buys anything). You could type in different data to represent multiple possibilities, but then you'd wipe out your old data. For a quick way to plug different data in the same spreadsheet, Excel offers scenarios.

A *scenario* lets you define different data for multiple cells. That way, you can choose a scenario to plug in one set of data, and then switch back to your original data without retyping everything.

Creating a scenario

Before you can create a scenario, you must first create a spreadsheet with data and formulas. Then you can create a scenario to define the data to plug into one or more cells.

To create a scenario, follow these steps:

1. **Click the Data tab.**

2. Click the What-If Analysis icon in the Data Tools group.

A pull-down menu appears.

3. Click Scenario Manager.

The Scenario Manager dialog box appears.

4. Click Add.

The Add Scenario dialog box appears, as shown in Figure 8-9.

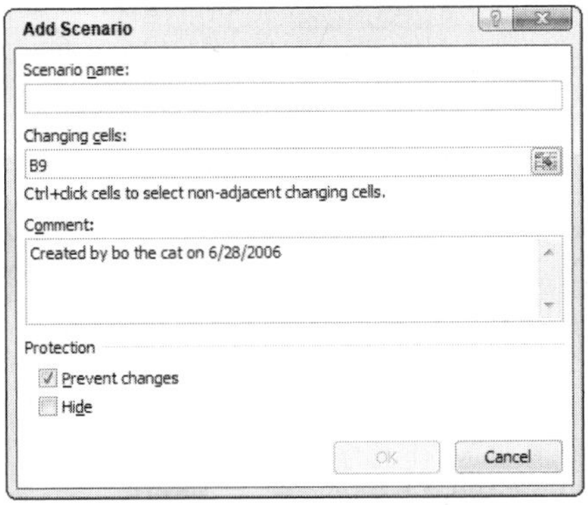

Figure 8-9:
Define a
scenario
name, the
cells you
want to
change, and
any com-
ments you
want to
include.

5. Click in the Scenario Name text box and type a descriptive name for your scenario, such as *Worst-case* or *Best-case*.

6. Click in the Changing Cells text box.

7. Click a cell in your spreadsheet that you want to display different data. If you want to choose multiple cells, hold down the Ctrl key and click multiple cells.

8. Click in the Comment text box and type any additional comments you want to add to your scenario, such as any assumptions your scenario made.

9. Click OK.

The Scenario Values dialog box appears, as shown in Figure 8-10.

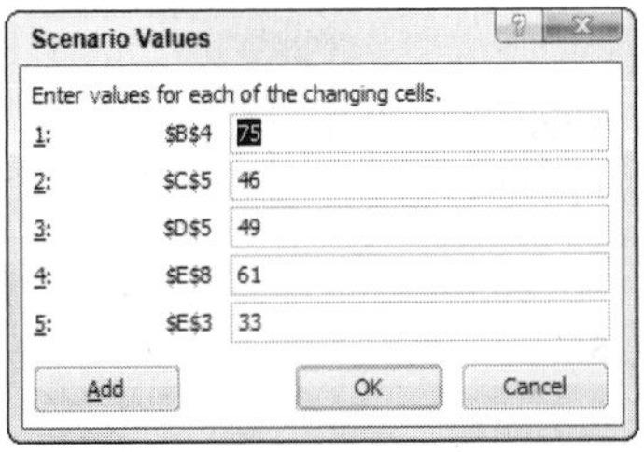

Figure 8-10:
Type in new
values for
your
selected
cells.

10. **Type a new value for each cell.**

11. **Click OK.**

    The Scenario Manager dialog box appears, as shown in Figure 8-11.

12. **Click Show.**

    Excel replaces any existing data with the data you typed in Step 10.

13. **Click Close.**

    The data from your scenario remains in the spreadsheet.

Viewing a scenario

After you create one or more scenarios, you can view them and see how they affect your data. To view a scenario, follow these steps:

1. **Click the Data tab.**

2. **Click the What-If Analysis icon in the Data Tools group.**

    A pull-down menu appears.

3. **Choose Scenario Manager.**

    The Scenario Manager dialog box appears (refer to Figure 8-11).

4. **Click the name of the scenario you want to view.**

5. **Click Show.**

    Excel shows the values in the cells defined by your chosen scenario.

6. **Click Close.**

Editing a scenario

After you create a scenario, you can always change it later by defining new data. To edit a scenario, follow these steps:

1. **Click the Data tab.**

2. **Click the What-If Analysis icon in the Data Tools group.**

   A pull-down menu appears.

3. **Choose Scenario Manager.**

   The Scenario Manager dialog box appears.

4. **Click the name of the scenario you want to edit and click Edit.**

   The Edit Scenario dialog box appears, as shown in Figure 8-12.

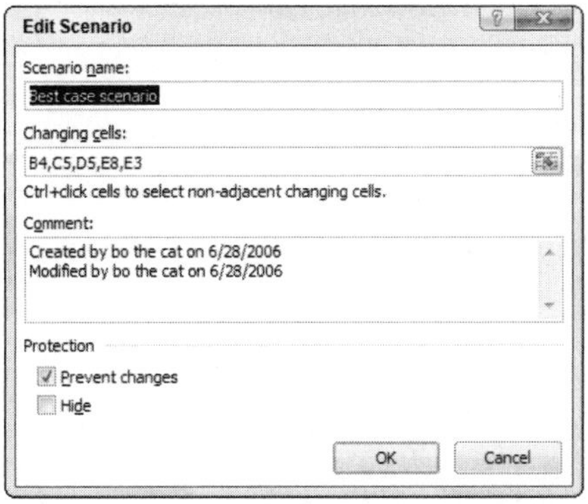

Figure 8-12: Define new cells to modify and new data to appear in those cells.

5. **(Optional) Edit the name of the scenario.**

6. **Click in the Changing Cells text box.**

   Excel displays dotted lines around all the cells that the scenario will change.

7. **Press Backspace to delete cells, or hold down the Ctrl key and click additional cells to include in your scenario.**

8. **Click OK.**

   The Scenario Values dialog box appears (refer to Figure 8-10).

9. **Type new values for your cells and click OK when you're done.**

   The Scenario Manager dialog box appears again.

10. **Click Show to view your scenario, or click Close to make the Scenario Manager dialog box disappear.**

Viewing a scenario summary

If you have multiple scenarios, it can be hard to switch back and forth between different scenarios and still understand which numbers are changing. To help you view the numbers that change in all your scenarios, you can create a scenario summary.

A *scenario summary* displays your original data along with the data stored in each scenario in a table. By viewing a scenario summary, you can see how the values of your spreadsheet can change depending on the scenario, as shown in Figure 8-13.

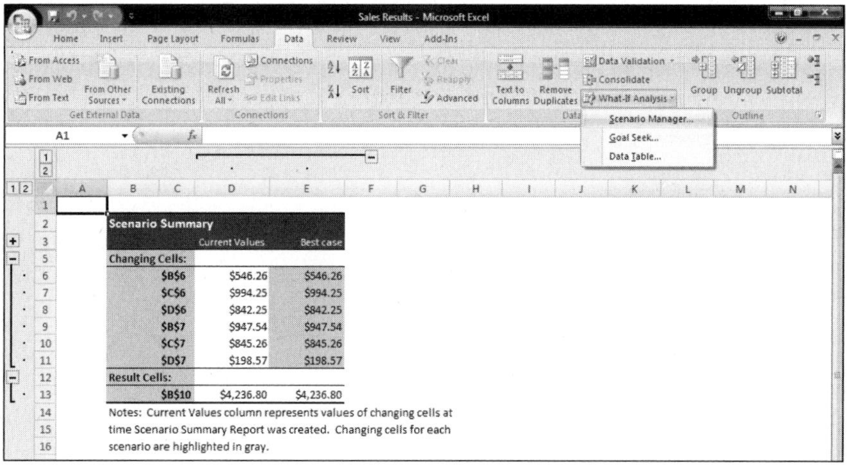

Figure 8-13:
A scenario summary compares your original data with all the data from your scenarios in an easy to read chart.

To create a scenario summary on a separate sheet in your workbook, follow these steps:

1. **Click the Data tab.**

2. **Click the What-If Analysis icon in the Data Tools group.**

   A pull-down menu appears.

3. **Choose Scenario Manager.**

   The Scenario Manager dialog box appears.

4. **Click Summary.**

   The Scenario Summary dialog box appears, as shown in Figure 8-14.

5. **Select the Scenario Summary radio button.**

6. **Click in the Result Cells text box and then click in a cell that contains a formula that your scenario affects.**

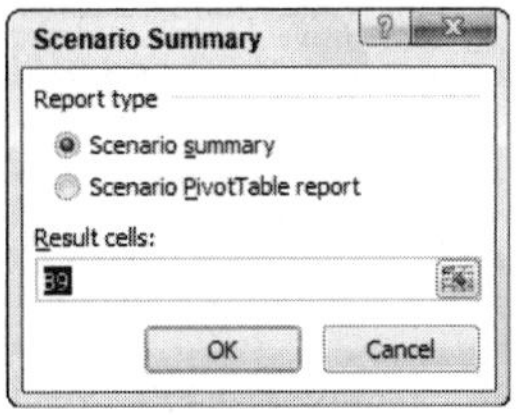

Figure 8-14:
Define the
type of
summary
to create.

7. **Click OK.**

Auditing Your Formulas

Your spreadsheet results are only as good as the data you give it and the formulas you create. Feed a spreadsheet the wrong data, and it will obviously calculate the wrong result. More troublesome is when you feed a spreadsheet the right data but your formula is incorrect, which produces a misleading and incorrect result.

Even if Excel appears to be calculating your formulas correctly, recheck your calculations just to make sure. Some common errors that can mess up your formulas include

- **Missing data:** The formula isn't using all the data necessary to calculate the proper result.
- **Incorrect data:** The formula is getting data from the wrong cell.
- **Incorrect calculation:** Your formula is incorrectly calculating a result.

If a formula is calculating data incorrectly, you probably didn't type the formula correctly. For example, you may want a formula to add two numbers, but you accidentally typed in the formula to multiply two numbers instead. To check whether a formula is calculating data incorrectly, give it data that you already know what the result should be. For example, if you typed the numbers 4 and 7 into a formula that should add two numbers, but it returns 28 instead, you know it's not calculating correctly.

If your formula is correct but it's still not calculating the right result, chances are good it's not getting the data it needs from the correct cells. To help you trace whether a formula is receiving all the data it needs, Excel offers auditing features that visually show you which cells supply data to which formulas. By using Excel's auditing features, you can

- Make sure your formulas are using data from the correct cells.
- Find out instantly whether a formula could go haywire if you change a cell reference.

Finding where a formula gets its data

If a formula is retrieving data from the wrong cells, it's never going to calculate the right result. By tracing a formula, you can see all the cells that a formula uses to retrieve data.

Any cell that supplies data to a formula is a *precedent*.

To trace a formula, follow these steps:

1. **Click a cell that contains the formula you want to check.**
2. **Click the Formulas tab.**
3. **Click the Trace Precedents icon in the Formula Auditing group.**

   Excel draws arrows that show you all the cells that feed data into the formula you chose in Step 1, as shown in Figure 8-15.

4. **Click the Remove Arrows button to make the auditing arrows go away.**

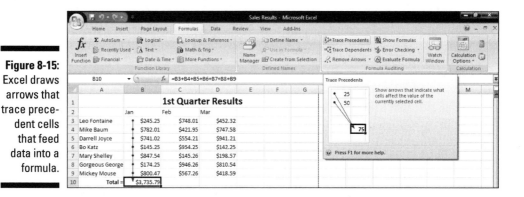

Figure 8-15: Excel draws arrows that trace precedent cells that feed data into a formula.

Finding which formula(s) a cell can change

Sometimes you may be curious how a particular cell might affect a formula stored in your worksheet. Although you could just type a new value in that cell and look for any changes, it's easier (and more accurate) to identify all formulas that are dependent on a particular cell.

Any formula that receives data is *a dependent*.

To find one or more formulas that a single cell might affect, follow these steps:

1. **Click any cell that contains data (not a formula).**

2. **Click the Formulas tab.**

3. **Click Trace Dependents.**

   Excel draws an arrow that points to a cell that contains a formula, as shown in Figure 8-16. This tells you that if you change the data in the cell you chose in Step 1, it will change the calculated result in the cell containing a formula.

4. **Click the Remove Arrows icon in the Formula Auditing group to make the arrows go away.**

Figure 8-16:
Excel can identify which formulas a particular cell can change.

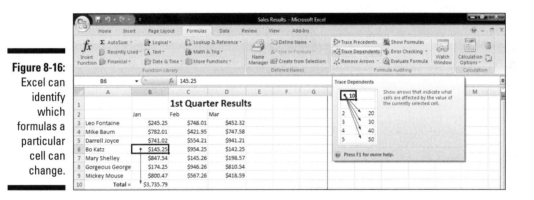

Data Validation

Because formulas are only as accurate as the data they receive, it's important that your spreadsheet contains only valid data. Examples of invalid data might be a negative number (such as –9) for a price or a decimal number (such as 4.39) for the number of items a customer bought.

To keep your spreadsheet from accepting invalid data, you can define a cell to accept only certain types of data, such as numbers that fall between 30 and 100. The moment someone tries to type invalid data into a cell, Excel immediately warns you, as shown in Figure 8-17.

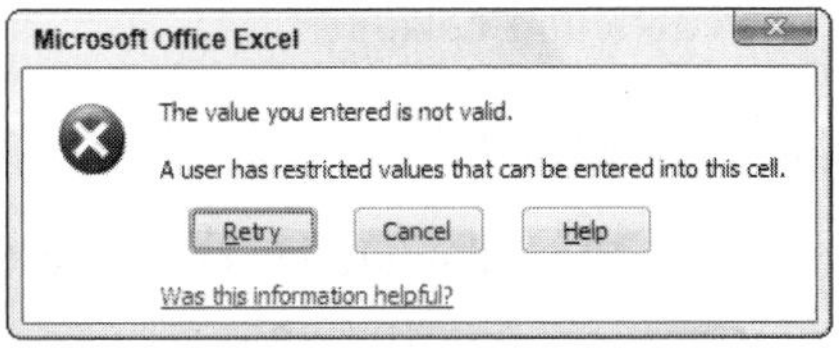

Figure 8-17:
Excel warns you if you type invalid data in a cell.

Microsoft Office Excel

The value you entered is not valid.

A user has restricted values that can be entered into this cell.

Retry   Cancel   Help

Was this information helpful?

To define valid types of data for a cell, follow these steps:

1. **Click a cell that contains data used by a formula.**
2. **Click the Data tab.**
3. **Click the Data Validation icon in the Data Tools group.**

    The Data Validation dialog box appears, as shown in Figure 8-18.

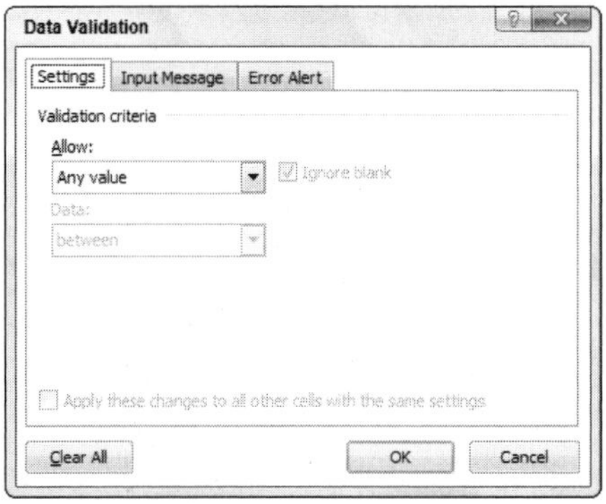

Figure 8-18:
Define the
type and
range of
acceptable
data allowed
in a cell.

Data Validation

| Settings | Input Message | Error Alert |

Validation criteria

Allow:

Any value   ☑ Ignore blank

Data:

between

☐ Apply these changes to all other cells with the same settings

Clear All   OK   Cancel

4. **Click the Allow list box and choose one of the following:**

    - *Any Value:* The default value accepts anything the user types
    - *Whole Number:* Accepts only whole numbers, such as 47 and 903
    - *Decimal:* Accepts whole and decimal numbers, such as 48.01 or 1.00
    - *List:* Allows you to define a list of valid data
    - *Date:* Accepts only dates
    - *Time:* Accepts only times
    - *Text length:* Defines a minimum and maximum length for text
    - *Custom:* Allows you to define a formula to specify valid data

    Depending on the option you choose, you may need to define Minimum and Maximum values and whether you want the data to be equal to, less than, or greater than a defined limit.

5. **Click the Input Message tab in the Data Validation dialog box, as shown in Figure 8-19.**
6. **Click in the Title text box and type a title.**

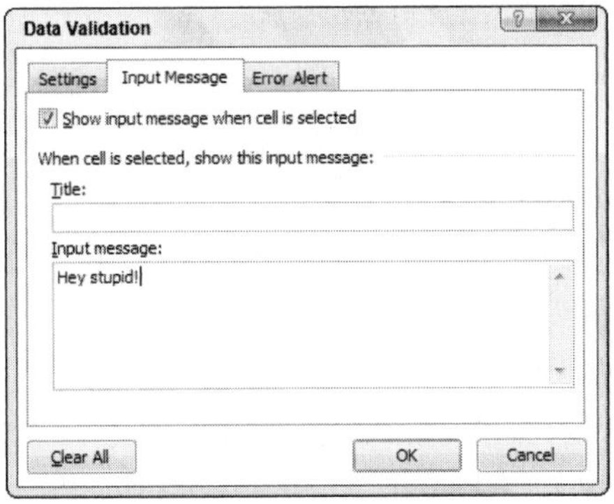

Figure 8-19:
The Input Message tab lets you display a message explaining the type of valid data a cell can hold.

7. **Click in the Input Message text box and type a message you want to display when someone selects this particular cell.**

8. **Click the Error Alert tab in the Data Validation dialog box, as shown in Figure 8-20.**

9. **Click the Style list box and choose an alert icon, such as Stop or Warning.**

10. **Click in the Title text box and type a title for your error message.**

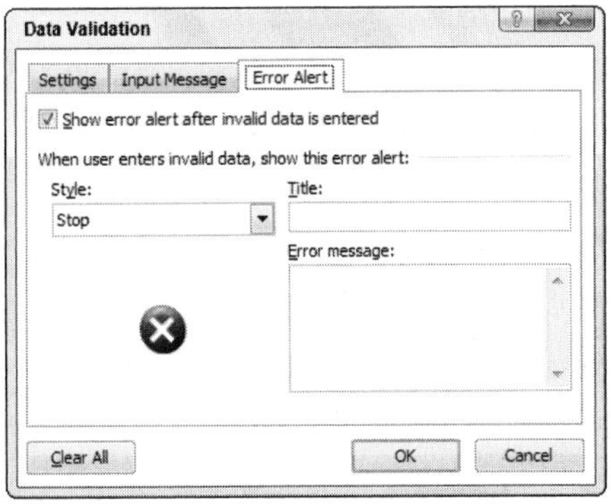

Figure 8-20:
Define an error message to show if the user types invalid data into the cell.

11. **Click in the Error Message text box and type the message to appear if the user types invalid data into the cell.**

12. **Click OK.**

After you define data validation for a cell, you can always remove it later. To remove validation for a cell, follow these steps:

1. **Click in the cell that contains data validation.**
2. **Click the Data tab.**
3. **Click the Data Validation icon in the Data Tools group.**

   The Data Validation dialog box appears (refer to Figure 8-18).

4. **Click Clear All and then click OK.**

   Excel clears all your data validation rules for your chosen cell.

Chapter 9

Charting and Analyzing Data

• •

In This Chapter

▶ Understanding the parts of a chart

▶ Creating a chart

▶ Editing a chart

▶ Modifying the parts of a chart

▶ Playing with pivot tables

• •

*I*f you stare at an Excel spreadsheet long enough, you may ask yourself, "What do these numbers really mean?"

To help you analyze and understand what rows and columns of numbers might mean, Excel offers the ability to convert your data into a variety of charts such as pie charts, bar charts, and line charts. By letting you visualize your data, Excel helps you quickly understand what your data means so you can spot trends and patterns.

Understanding the Parts of a Chart

To create charts that clarify your data (rather than confuse you even more), you need to understand the parts of a chart and their purpose, as shown in Figure 9-1:

✔ **Data Series:** The numeric data that Excel uses to create the chart

✔ **X-axis:** Defines the width of a chart

✔ **Y-axis:** Defines the height of a chart

✔ **Legend:** Provides text to explain what each visual part of a chart means

✔ **Chart Title:** Explains the purpose of the entire chart

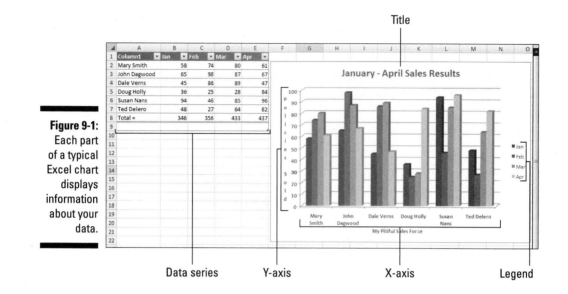

Figure 9-1:
Each part
of a typical
Excel chart
displays
information
about your
data.

Charts typically use two data series to create a chart. For example, one data series may be sales made that month, while a second data series may be the names of each salesperson.

The X-axis of such a chart would list the names of each salesperson while the Y-axis would list a range of numbers that represent dollar amounts. The chart itself could display different colors that represent different products sold, and the legend would explain what each color represents (such as red measuring life insurance policies sold, green measuring auto insurance policies sold, and yellow measuring health insurance policies sold).

By glancing at the column chart in Figure 9-1, you can quickly identify

- Total sales contributed by each salesperson every month
- Which salesperson is selling the most (and which is selling the least)
- Whether a particular salesperson is improving (or getting worse) at selling

All this data came from the spreadsheet, also shown in Figure 9-1. Looking at the numbers in this spreadsheet, trying to identify the above information is nearly impossible. However, with the aid of a chart, identifying this type of information is so simple even your boss could do it.

Although Figure 9-1 shows a column chart, Excel can create a variety of other types of charts so you can look at your data in different ways, as shown in Figure 9-2. Some of the other types of charts Excel can create include

- **Column chart:** Displays quantities as vertical columns that "grow" upward. Useful for creating charts that compare two items, such as sales per month or sales per salesperson.

- **Line chart:** Displays quantities as lines. Essentially shows the tops of a column chart.

- **Area chart:** Identical to a line chart except that it shades the area underneath each line.

- **Bar chart:** Essentially a column chart turned on its side where bars "grow" from left to right.

- **Pie chart:** Compares multiple items in relation to a whole, such as which product sales make up a percentage of a company's overall profits.

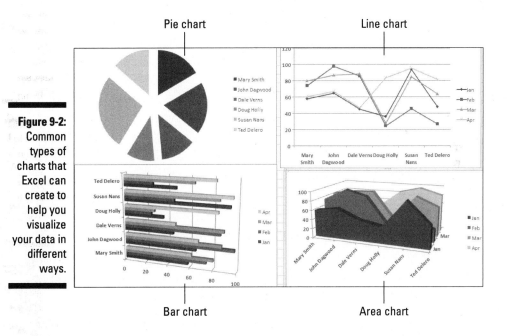

Figure 9-2: Common types of charts that Excel can create to help you visualize your data in different ways.

Excel can create both two and three-dimensional charts. A 3-D chart can look neat, but sometimes the 3-D visual can obscure the true purpose of the chart, which is to simplify data and make it easy for you to understand in the first place.

Creating a Chart

Before you create a chart, you need to type in some numbers and identifying labels because Excel will use those labels to identify the parts of your chart. (You can always edit your chart later if you don't want Excel to display certain labels or numbers.)

To create a chart, follow these steps:

1. **Select the numbers and labels that you want to use to create a chart.**
2. **Click the Insert tab.**

   A list of chart type icons appears, as shown in Figure 9-3.

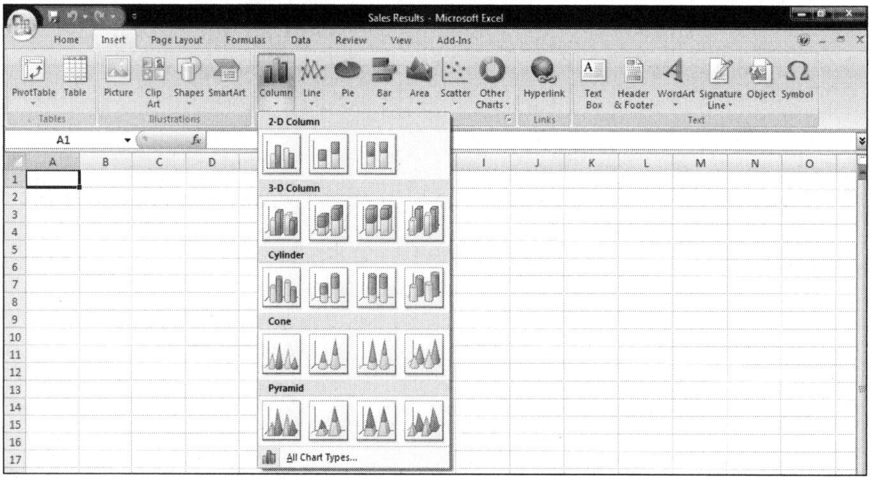

Figure 9-3: The Insert tab displays icons for creating different types of charts.

3. **Click a Chart icon, such as the Pie or Line icon.**

   The Create Chart gallery appears (see Figure 9-3).

4. **Click a chart type.**

   Excel creates your chart and displays a Chart Tools tab, as shown in Figure 9-4.

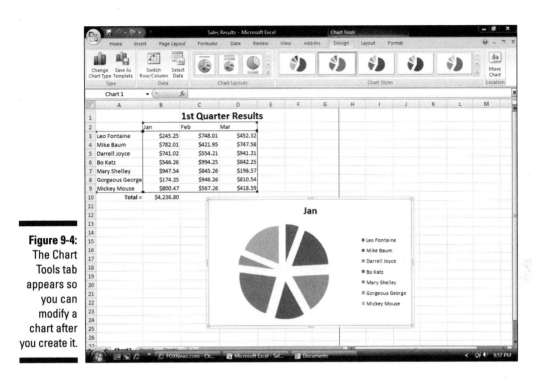

Figure 9-4:
The Chart
Tools tab
appears so
you can
modify a
chart after
you create it.

Editing a Chart

After you create a chart, you may want to edit it. Editing a chart can mean moving it to a new location, changing the data source (the numbers that Excel uses to create the chart), modifying parts of the chart itself (such as switching to a different chart type), or editing text (such as the chart title or legend).

Moving a chart on a worksheet

When you create a chart, Excel plops it right on your displayed spreadsheet, which may not be exactly where you want it to appear. Excel gives you the option of moving a chart to a different place on the current worksheet page or on a different worksheet page altogether.

To move a chart to a different location on the same worksheet, follow these steps:

1. **Move the mouse pointer over the border of the chart until the mouse pointer turns into a four-way pointing arrow.**

2. **Hold down the left mouse button and drag (move) the mouse.**

   The chart moves with the mouse.

3. **Move the chart where you want it to appear and release the left mouse button.**

Moving a chart to a new sheet

Rather than move a chart on the same sheet where it appears, you can also move the chart to another worksheet. That way your data can appear on one worksheet, and your chart can appear on another.

To move a chart to an entirely different sheet, follow these steps:

1. **Click the chart you want to move to another worksheet.**

   The Chart Tools tab appears.

2. **Click the Design contextual tools tab.**

3. **Click the Move Chart icon in the Location group.**

   The Move Chart dialog box appears, as shown in Figure 9-5.

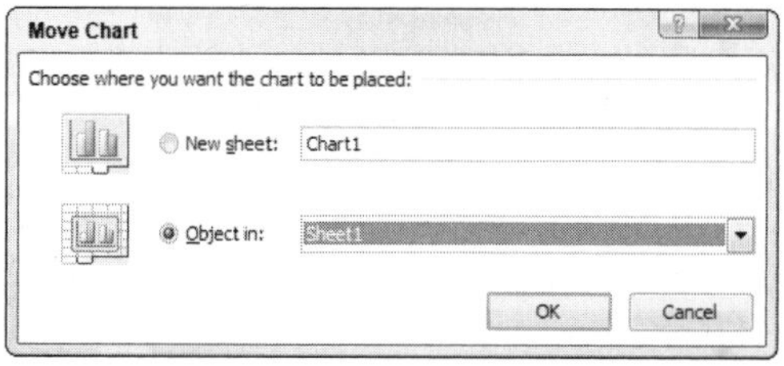

Figure 9-5:
Specify a
worksheet
where you
want to
move your
chart.

Move Chart		
Choose where you want the chart to be placed:		
	⃝ New sheet:	Chart1
	◉ Object in:	Sheet1
		OK Cancel

As an alternative to Steps 1–3, you can right-click a chart; then, when the pop-up menu appears, choose Move Chart.

4. **Select one of the following radio buttons:**

   • *New Sheet:* Creates a new worksheet and lets you name it

   • *Object In:* Lets you choose the name of an existing worksheet

5. **Click OK.**

   Excel moves your chart.

Resizing a chart

You can always resize any chart to make it bigger or smaller. To resize a chart, follow these steps:

1. **Move the mouse pointer over any corner of the chart until the mouse pointer turns into a two-way pointing arrow.**

2. **Hold down the left mouse button and drag (move) the mouse to shrink or expand your chart.**

3. **Release the left mouse button when you're happy with the new size of your chart.**

Using the Chart Tools

As soon as you create a chart or click on an existing chart, Excel displays the Chart Tools tab, which provides tools organized into four categories:

✔ **Type:** Lets you change the chart type

✔ **Data:** Lets you change the source where the chart retrieves its data or switch the data from appearing along the X-axis to the Y-axis and vice versa

✔ **Chart Layouts:** Lets you change the individual parts of a chart, such as the chart title, X- or Y-axis labels, or the placement of the chart legend (top, bottom, left, right)

✔ **Chart Styles:** Provides different ways to change the appearance of your chart

Changing the chart type

After you create a chart, you can experiment with how your data may look when displayed as a different chart, such as switching your chart from a bar chart to a pie chart. To change chart types, follow these steps:

1. **Click the chart you want to change.**

   The Chart Tools tab appears.

2. **Click the Design contextual tools tab under the Chart Tools tab.**

3. **Click the Change Chart Type icon in the Type group.**

   The Change Chart Type dialog box appears, as shown in Figure 9-6.

Figure 9-6: The Change Chart Type dialog box lets you pick a different chart.

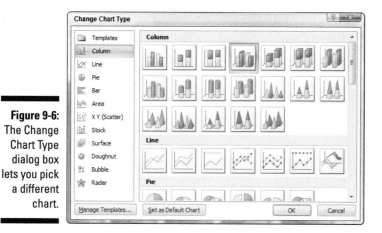

4. **Click a chart type, such as Pie or Column.**

   The dialog box displays a list of chart designs in the right panel of the dialog box.

5. **Click the chart design you want in the right panel.**

6. **Click OK.**

   Excel displays your new chart.

If you don't like how your chart looks, just press Ctrl+Z to return your chart back to its original design.

Changing the data source

Another way to change the appearance of a chart is to change its *data source* (the cells that contain the actual data that the chart uses). To change a chart's data source, follow these steps:

1. **Click the chart you want to change.**

   The Chart Tools tab appears.

2. **Click the Design contextual tools tab under the Chart Tools tab.**

3. **Click the Select Data icon in the Data group.**

   The Select Data Source dialog box appears, as shown in Figure 9-7.

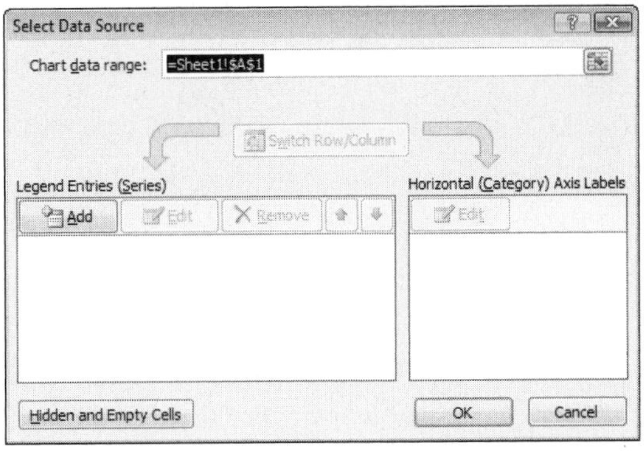

Figure 9-7: Choose new data to create a chart.

4. **(Optional) Click the Shrink Dialog Box icon to shrink the Change Data Source dialog box so you can see more of your spreadsheet.**

5. **Select all the cells that contain data to create a chart, including any cells that contain labels, numbers, and formulas.**

6. **Click OK.**

   Excel displays your chart using the data you specify in Step 5.

Switching rows and columns

When Excel creates a chart, it displays your data's labels on the X- and Y-axes. However, you can switch these around, and Excel can show you how your chart may change.

To switch the rows and columns used to create a chart, follow these steps:

1. **Click the chart you want to change.**

   The Chart Tools tab appears.

2. **Click the Design contextual tools tab under the Chart Tools tab.**

3. **Click the Switch Row/Column icon in the Data group.**

   Excel switches the X-axis data to appear on the Y-axis and vice versa.

Changing the parts of a chart

To make your charts more informative, you can add additional text, such as

- A chart title
- A legend
- Data labels
- Axis labels
- Axes
- Gridlines

With each part of a chart, Excel can either hide it completely or move it to a different location. To modify any part of a chart, follow these steps:

1. **Click the chart you want to change.**

   The Chart Tools tab appears.

2. **Click the Layout contextual tools tab under the Chart Tools tab.**

3. **Click the icon that identifies the part of the chart you want to modify, such as Chart Title or Axis Titles.**

   A menu of different options appears, as shown in Figure 9-8.

4. **Click an option, such as None.**

   Excel shows your modified chart.

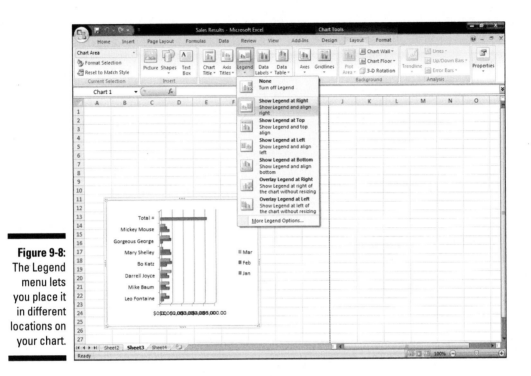

Figure 9-8:
The Legend
menu lets
you place it
in different
locations on
your chart.

Designing the layout of a chart

Although you could add and modify the individual parts of a chart yourself, such as the location of the chart title or legend, you may find it faster to choose a predefined layout for your chart. To choose a predefined chart layout, follow these steps:

1. **Click the chart you want to modify.**

   The Chart Tools tab appears.

2. **Click the Design contextual tools tab under the Chart Tools tab.**

3. **Click the More button in the Chart Layouts group, as shown in Figure 9-9.**

   A pull-down menu appears.

Click the More button to see additional layouts.

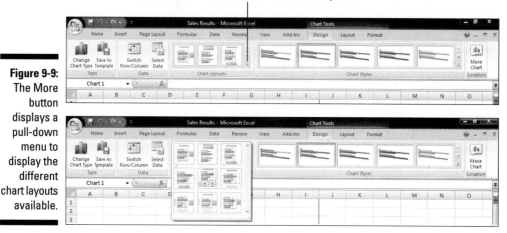

Figure 9-9:
The More
button
displays a
pull-down
menu to
display the
different
chart layouts
available.

4. **Click a chart layout.**

Excel changes your chart.

Deleting a chart

Charts may be nice to look at, but eventually you may want to delete them. To delete a chart, follow these steps:

1. **Click the chart you want to delete.**

2. **Press Delete.**

You can also right-click a chart; then, when the pop-up menu appears, choose Cut.

Organizing Lists in Pivot Tables

Ordinary spreadsheets let you compare two sets of data such as sales versus time or products sold versus the salesperson who sold them. Unfortunately, if you want to know how many products each salesperson sold in a certain month, deciphering this information from a spreadsheet may not be easy.

That's where pivot tables come in. A *pivot table* lets you yank data from your spreadsheet and organize it in different ways in a table. By rearranging (or "pivoting") your data from a row to a column (and vice versa), pivot tables can help you spot trends that may not be easily identified trapped within the confines of an ordinary spreadsheet.

Creating a pivot table

Pivot tables use the column headings of a spreadsheet to organize data in a table. Ideally, each column in the spreadsheet should identify a different type of data, such as the name of each salesperson, the sales region he or she works in, and the total amount of sales made, as shown in Figure 9-10.

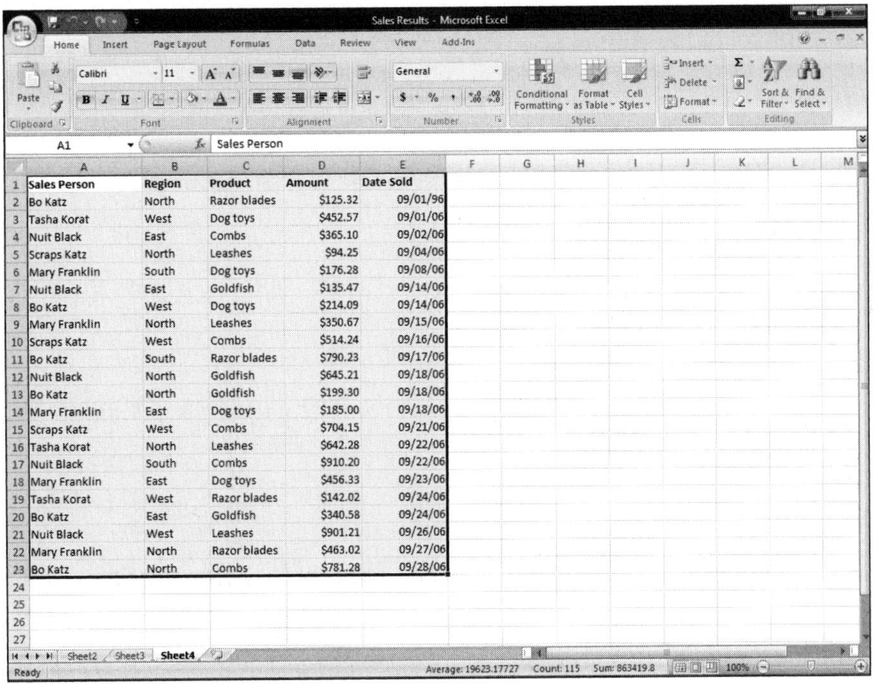

Figure 9-10: Before you create a pivot table, you must create a spreadsheet where each column identifies a different set of data.

After you design a spreadsheet with multiple columns of data, follow these steps to create a pivot table:

1. **Select the cells (including column labels) that you want to include in your pivot table.**

2. **Click the Insert tab.**

3. **Click the PivotTable icon in the Tables group.**

   The Create PivotTable dialog box appears, as shown in Figure 9-11.

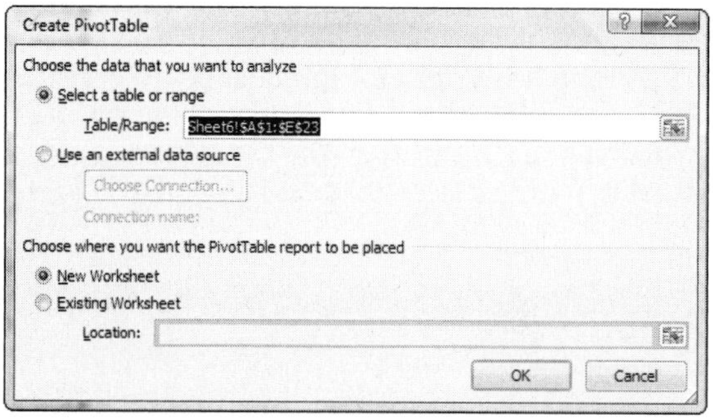

Figure 9-11:
Define the cells to use and a location to place your pivot table.

Create PivotTable
Choose the data that you want to analyze
○ Select a table or range
Table/Range: Sheet6!$A$1:$E$23
○ Use an external data source
Choose Connection...
Connection name:
Choose where you want the PivotTable report to be placed
○ New Worksheet
○ Existing Worksheet
Location:
OK   Cancel

4. **(Optional) Select the cells that contain the data you want to use in your pivot table.**

   You only need to follow Step 4 if you didn't select any cells in Step 1, or if you change your mind and want to select different cells than the ones chosen in Step 1.

5. **Select one of the following radio buttons:**

   • *New Worksheet:* Puts the pivot table on a new worksheet

   • *Existing Worksheet:* Puts the pivot table on an existing worksheet

6. **Click OK.**

   Excel displays a PivotTable Field List pane, as shown in Figure 9-12.

7. **Mark (select) one or more check boxes inside the PivotTable Field List pane.**

   Each time you select another check box, Excel modifies how data appears in your pivot table, as shown in Figure 9-13.

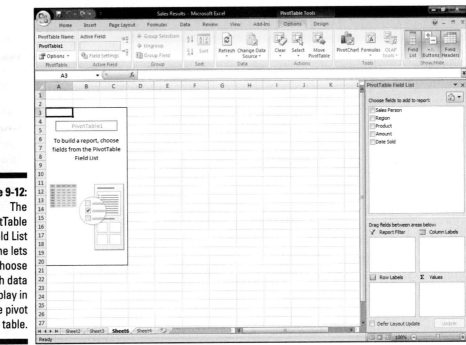

Figure 9-12:
The
PivotTable
Field List
pane lets
you choose
which data
to display in
the pivot
table.

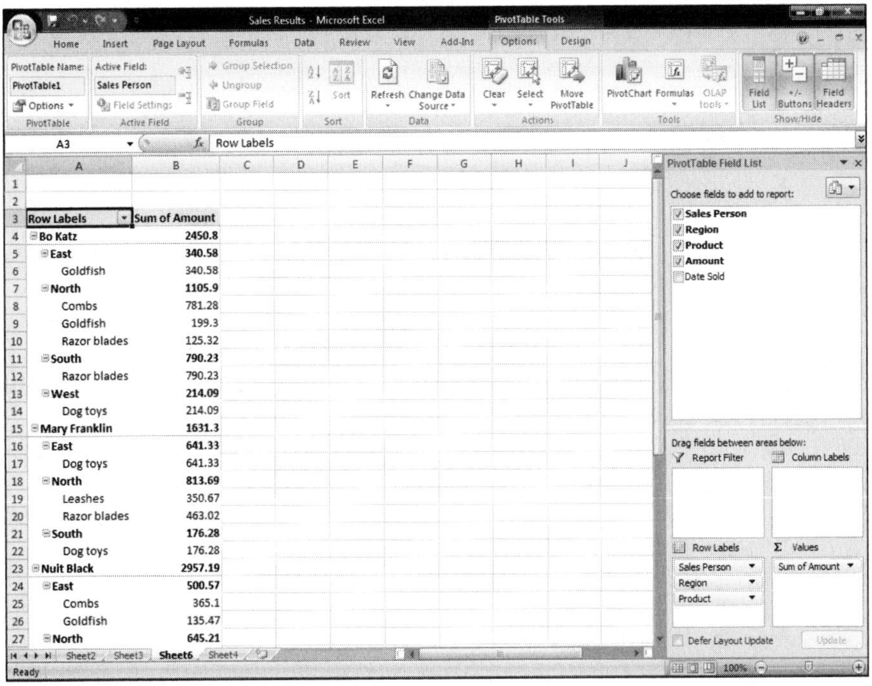

Figure 9-13:
Adding
column
headings
increases
the infor-
mation a
pivot table
displays.

Rearranging labels in a pivot table

A pivot table organizes data according to your spreadsheet's column headings (which appear in a pivot table as row labels). The pivot table shown in Figure 9-13 shows sales divided by salesperson. Each salesperson's amounts are further divided by sales region, and the names of the products sold.

However, you may be more interested in seeing the sales organized by sales region. To do this, you can modify which column heading your pivot table uses to organize your data first. To rearrange column headings in a pivot table, follow these steps:

1. **Click the pivot table you want to rearrange.**

   The PivotTable Field List pane appears.

2. **Click the downward-pointing arrow of a label that appears under the Row Labels group.**

   A pop-up menu appears, as shown in Figure 9-14.

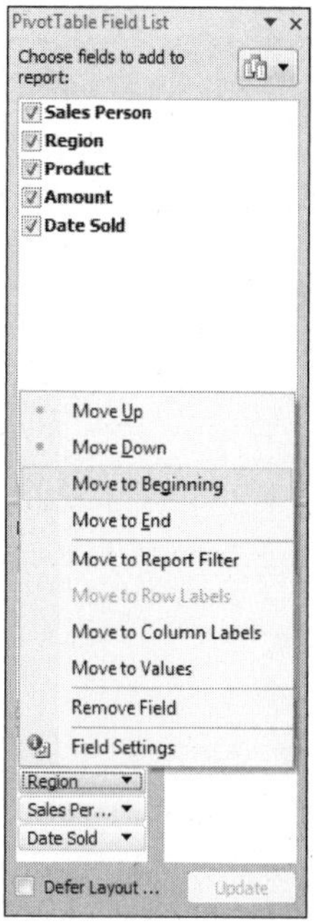

Figure 9-14:
By rearranging labels in a pivot table, you can view your data in different ways.

Select one of the following:

- *Move Up:* Moves the label one level closer to the beginning

- *Move Down:* Moves the label one level down to the end

- *Move to Beginning:* Makes the label the dominant criteria for sorting data

- *Move to End:* Makes the label the last criteria for sorting data

Figure 9-15 shows different ways a pivot table can organize the same data.

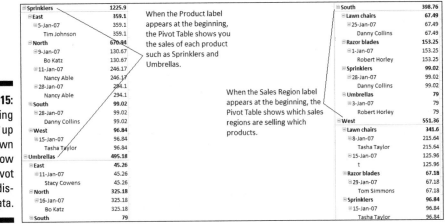

Figure 9-15: Moving labels up or down defines how the pivot table displays data.

Modifying a pivot table

Row labels let you organize data according to different criteria, such as sales per region and then by product. For greater flexibility, you can also turn a row label into a column heading. Figure 9-16 shows a pivot table where row labels are stacked on top of each other, and then the same pivot table where one row label (Products) is turned into a column heading.

To turn row labels into column headings in a pivot table (or vice versa), follow these steps:

1. **Click the pivot table you want to modify.**

    The PivotTable Field List pane appears.

2. **Click a heading.**

    A pop-up menu appears.

3. **Choose Move to Column Labels (or Row Labels).**

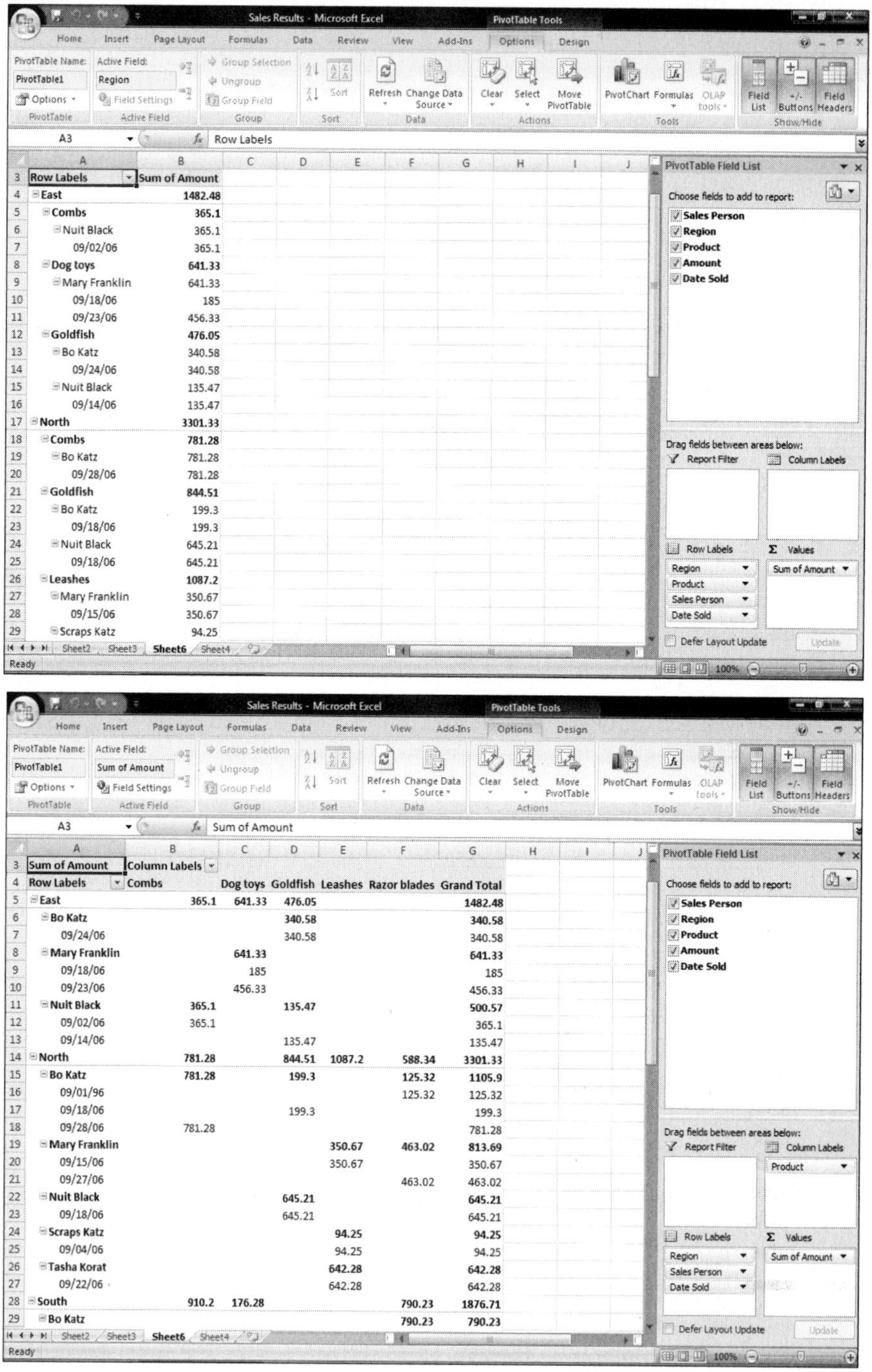

Figure 9-16: Displaying row labels as column headings can compare spreadsheet data in multiple ways.

Filtering a pivot table

The more information your pivot table contains, the harder it can be to make sense of any of the data. To help you out, Excel lets you filter your data to view only certain information, such as sales made by each salesperson or total sales within a region. To filter a pivot table, follow these steps:

1. **Click the pivot table you want to filter.**

   The PivotTable Field List pane appears.

2. **Click a heading in the Row Labels or Column Labels group in the PivotTable Field List pane.**

   A pop-up menu appears.

3. **Click Move to Report Filter.**

   Excel moves your chosen label into the Report Filter group in the PivotTable Field List pane and displays a filter list box at the top of your pivot table, as shown in Figure 9-17.

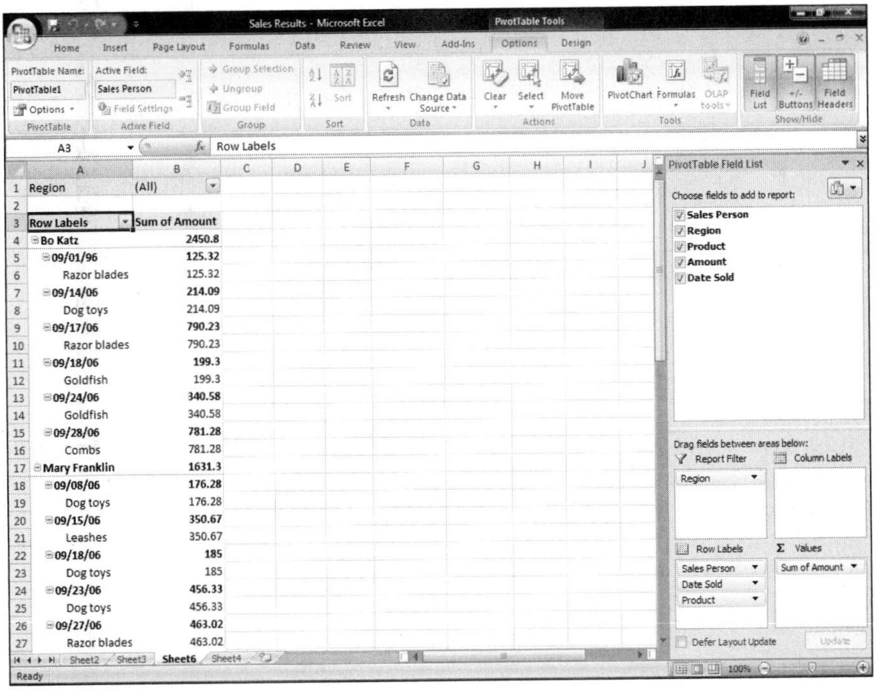

Figure 9-17: A filter lets you selectively hide information in a pivot table.

4. Click in the filter list box at the top of the pivot table.

The list box displays a list of items that you can choose to view, as shown in Figure 9-18.

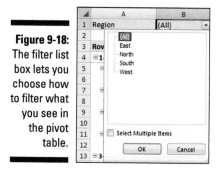

Figure 9-18:
The filter list box lets you choose how to filter what you see in the pivot table.

5. Click an item to filter your data.

If you mark the Select Multiple Items check box, you can select two or more items to filter your data.

6. Click OK.

Excel displays your filtered pivot table, as shown in Figure 9-19.

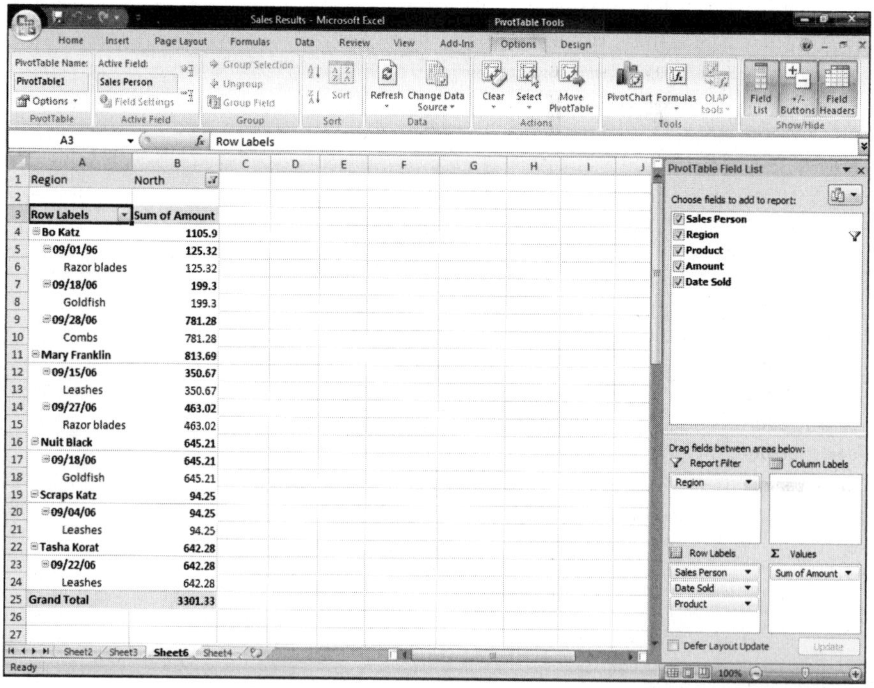

Figure 9-19:
A filtered pivot table displays only the information you want to see, such as showing you only sales results for the Southern sales region.

Summing a pivot table

A pivot table not only displays information, but it can also count the number of occurrences of information, such as the number of sales per sales region. To display a count of data, you need to move a heading in the Values group inside the PivotTable Field List pane by following these steps:

1. **Click the pivot table you want to modify.**

   The PivotTable Field List pane appears.

2. **Click a heading that you want to count in the PivotTable Field List pane.**

   A pop-up menu appears.

3. **Click Move to Values.**

   Excel moves your chosen heading to the Values group inside the PivotTable Field List pane and displays a count of items under your chosen heading, as shown in Figure 9-20.

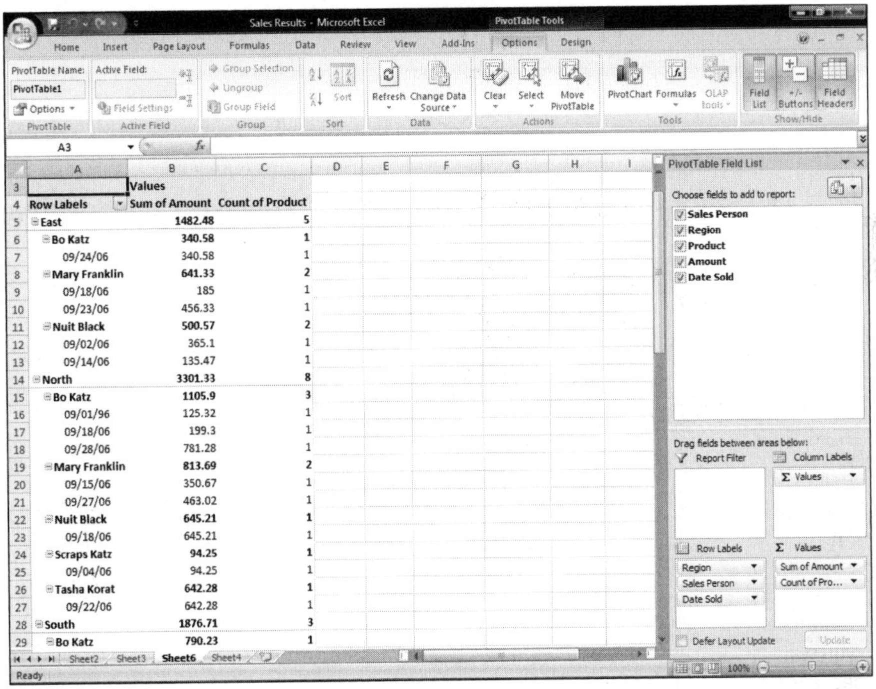

Figure 9-20: A pivot table can count occurrences of certain data, such as the number of different products sold by each salesperson.

Part IV
Making Presentations with PowerPoint

The 5th Wave   By Rich Tennant

"You know kids — you can't buy them just _any_ slideshow presentation software."

In this part . . .

The fear of public speaking is the number one fear of most people — with the fear of death running a distant second. Although Microsoft Office 2007 can't help you overcome your fear of death, it can help you overcome your fear of public speaking and giving presentations with the help of Microsoft PowerPoint. PowerPoint can help you organize and design a presentation that can keep others so amused that they won't even bother looking in your direction.

When you use PowerPoint to create a presentation, you won't need to rely on mere words, pointless hand gestures, or crudely drawn diagrams scribbled on a white board. With PowerPoint, you can give flawless presentations consisting of text, graphics, and even sound effects that people will remember.

The next time you need to dazzle an audience (with facts, rumors, or blatant lies dressed up to look like facts), flip through this part of the book and see how PowerPoint can help you create dazzling slide show presentations and handouts that can clarify, emphasize, or entertainingly distort topics for your audience until you have a chance to sneak out of the room.

Chapter 10

Creating a PowerPoint Presentation

In This Chapter

▶ Designing a presentation

▶ Creating a PowerPoint presentation

▶ Using different views to create a presentation

▶ Adding text

*P*owerPoint works as a visual aid for giving presentations. (If you never give presentations, you probably don't need PowerPoint.) Rather than fumble around creating, organizing, and displaying transparencies with an overhead projector, you can use PowerPoint on your computer to create, organize, and display slides that display information organized as text and graphics.

Besides displaying slides on the screen, PowerPoint also lets you add notes that only you can see to each slide and turn your entire slide show presentation into printed handouts so the audience can review your presentation and take notes next to a printed copy of each slide. The next time you need to convince or inform an audience, use PowerPoint to create and deliver your presentation. (Just make sure you never use PowerPoint to propose marriage.)

Defining the Purpose of Your Presentation

PowerPoint can make creating and delivering a presentation easy, but before you start creating fancy visuals with eye-popping graphics and colors, step away from your computer, put down your copy of PowerPoint, and place your hands in the open where anyone can see them.

Rushing into PowerPoint to create a presentation is likely to create a dazzling array of colors, fonts, and graphics that may look interesting but won't convey your message effectively. The best way to create an effective presentation is to take some time to think about the following:

- ✔ **What is your point?** Define the single most important idea of your presentation.

- ✔ **Who is the target audience?** A presentation given to engineers and scientists will look different than the same presentation given to CEOs and venture capital executives.

- ✔ **What do you want the audience to do?** A speaker may present new ideas to a conference while a politician may present ideas designed to sway the audience to take certain actions, such as voting a specific way.

After you understand the purpose of your presentation, your audience, and what you hope your presentation will do, you're ready to go through the physical steps of creating a presentation in PowerPoint.

Creating a PowerPoint Presentation

A PowerPoint *presentation* consists of one or more slides where each slide can display text and graphics. Creating a presentation means adding slides and typing text or pasting graphics on each slide.

When you first start PowerPoint, the program loads a blank presentation that you can modify right away.

If you've been working on another presentation in PowerPoint and you need to start a new, blank presentation from scratch, follow these steps:

1. **Click the Office Button and then choose New.**

   A New Presentation dialog box appears.

2. **Click Blank Presentation and then click Create.**

   PowerPoint displays a blank slide with a title and subtitle box, as shown in Figure 10-1.

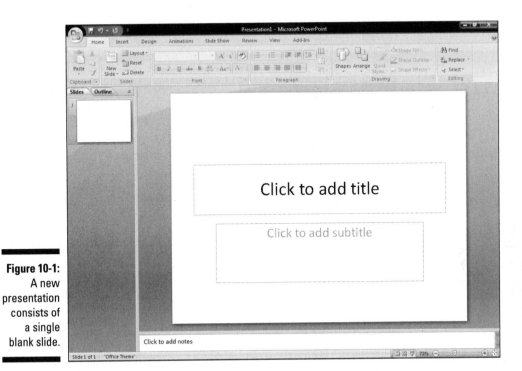

Figure 10-1:
A new
presentation
consists of
a single
blank slide.

After you create a new presentation, you need to fill it with *content* (text and graphics). PowerPoint gives you two ways to view, edit, and design your presentation:

- ✔ Slide view
- ✔ Outline view

Both views let you add, delete, rearrange, and edit slides. The main difference is that *Slide view* lets you add graphics and modify the visual appearance of a slide. *Outline view* displays your entire presentation as an outline where each slide appears as an outline heading, and additional text on each slide appears as a subheading. Outline view makes it easy to rearrange and organize the slides in your presentation without the distraction of the visual appearance of each slide.

You can create an entire presentation in Slide view without ever using Outline view at all (or use Outline view without ever using Slide view at all). Outline view is most useful for creating and organizing a presentation. Slide view is most useful for viewing the appearance of multiple slides at once.

Designing a presentation with Slide view

Slide view shows your entire slide show as thumbnails in the left pane and the currently selected slide in full size view in the right pane, as shown in Figure 10-2.

Creating a new slide

To create a new slide within Slide view, follow these steps:

1. **Click an existing slide in the thumbnail pane.**

2. **Click the Home tab.**

3. **Click New Slide in the Slides group.**

   PowerPoint inserts your new slide after the slide you selected in Step 1.

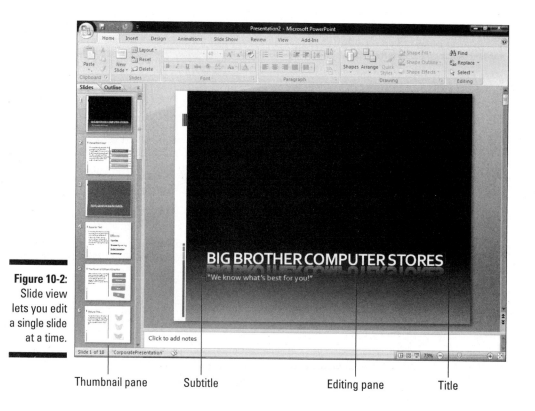

Figure 10-2:
Slide view
lets you edit
a single slide
at a time.

Thumbnail pane   Subtitle   Editing pane   Title

Rearranging slides

You can rearrange the order of your slides by following these steps:

1. **In the thumbnail pane, click the slide that you want to move to a new position in your presentation.**

2. **Hold down the left mouse button and drag (move) the mouse up or down within the thumbnail pane.**

   PowerPoint displays a horizontal line between slides to show you where your slide will appear. If you drag the mouse to the top or bottom of the thumbnail pane, PowerPoint automatically scrolls up or down the list.

3. **Release the left mouse button when you're happy with the slide's new position.**

Hiding and deleting a slide

If you have a slide that you no longer want in your presentation, you can either hide or delete it. Hiding a slide keeps the slide but doesn't display that slide when you give your presentation. You may want to hide a slide in case you need it later or so you can reference the information on this slide with the rest of your presentation.

To hide a slide, follow these steps:

1. **Click the slide in the thumbnail pane that you want to hide.**

2. **Click the Slide Show tab.**

3. **Click Hide Slide in the Set Up group.**

   PowerPoint dims your chosen slide and highlights the Hide Slide icon.

To unhide a slide, repeat the above steps.

If you're sure you want to get rid of a slide, you can just delete it. To delete a slide, follow these steps:

1. **Click the slide in the thumbnail pane that you want to delete.**

2. **Click the Home tab.**

3. **Click Delete in the Slides group.**

   PowerPoint deletes your chosen slide.

If you press Ctrl+Z or click the Undo icon right away, you can recover a deleted slide.

Designing a presentation with Outline view

Outline view shows the title and subtitle text of each slide in the left pane and the currently selected slide in full size view in the right pane, as shown in Figure 10-3.

The biggest advantage of Outline view is that it lets you rearrange and organize your slides by focusing on their content (title and subtitles). To switch from Slide view to Outline view, click the Outline tab. To switch from Outline view to Slide view, click the Slides tab.

Title

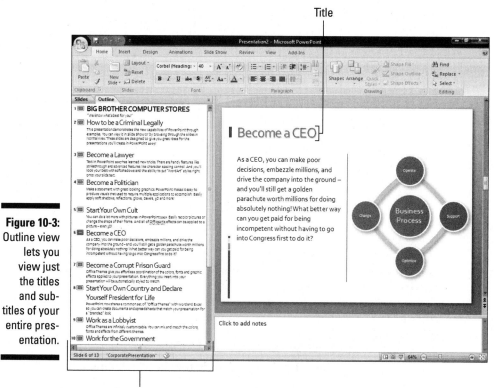

Figure 10-3: Outline view lets you view just the titles and subtitles of your entire presentation.

Ouline pane

Creating a new slide

In Outline view, each outline heading represents a slide title and each sub-heading represents a slide's subtitles. To create a new slide in Outline view, follow these steps:

1. **Click the Outline tab to switch to Outline view.**

2. **Click a slide title in the Outline pane.**

3. **Choose one of the following:**

   - *Press Home to move the cursor to the front of the outline heading.* This creates a new slide before the currently displayed slide.

   - *Press End to move the cursor to the end of the outline heading.* This creates a new slide after the currently displayed slide.

4. **Press Enter.**

   PowerPoint adds a new, blank slide to your presentation.

Creating subtitles on a slide

Outline view lets you create slides and add subtitles to each slide as well. To add a subtitle to a slide, follow these steps:

1. **Click the Outline view tab to display the Outline pane.**

2. **Click a slide title and then press End to move the cursor to the end of the slide title.**

3. **Press Enter.**

   PowerPoint creates a blank slide title underneath.

4. **Press Tab.**

   PowerPoint indents your slide title and turns it into subtitle text under the previous outline heading.

Collapsing and expanding subtitles

A large presentation consisting of multiple slides with subtitles can be hard to read. To simplify the appearance of your outline, PowerPoint lets you collapse or expand outline headings. To collapse or expand an outline heading, follow these steps:

1. **Click the Outline tab to display the Outline pane.**

2. **Double-click the slide icon of a slide title in the Outline pane.**

PowerPoint collapses any subtitles that appear under your chosen outline heading and displays a gray line under your outline heading to let you know that its subtitle text is *collapsed* (hidden), as shown in Figure 10-4.

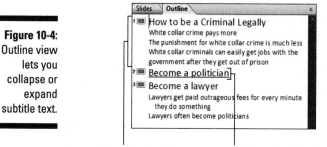

Figure 10-4:
Outline view lets you collapse or expand subtitle text.

Expanded outline heading   Collapsed outline heading

To expand a collapsed slide title, just double-click its slide icon.

Rearranging slides

Outline view makes it easy to rearrange slides just by moving slide titles up or down. To move a slide title, follow these steps:

1. **Move the mouse pointer over the slide icon that appears to the left of the slide title that you want to move.**

   The mouse turns into a two-way pointing arrow.

2. **Hold down the left mouse button and drag (move) the mouse up or down.**

   PowerPoint displays a horizontal gray line to show where the new position of the slide will appear in your presentation.

3. **Release the left mouse button.**

   PowerPoint moves your outline heading to its new position in your presentation.

Deleting a slide

To delete a slide in Outline view, follow these steps:

1. **Click the slide icon that appears to the left of the slide title you want to delete.**

2. **Press Delete.**

Working with Text

Most slides contain exactly one title and one subtitle text box. The title text box typically defines the information that the slide presents, while the subtitle text box displays supporting information.

When you create a new slide, both the title and subtitle text boxes will be empty, although they'll both display the message Click here to add title or Click here to add subtitle. (This text won't appear on your slides if you don't type anything there.)

If you delete all the text inside of a title or subtitle text box, PowerPoint automatically displays the Click here to add title or Click here to add subtitle text in the empty text boxes.

To add text inside a title or subtitle text box, follow these steps:

1. **Click in the title or subtitle text box, directly on the slide.**

   PowerPoint displays a cursor in your chosen text box.

2. **Type your text.**

You can also create title and subtitle text in Outline view as explained in the earlier section, "Designing a presentation with Outline view."

Typing text in a text box

A typical PowerPoint slide lets you type text in the Title text box or the Subtitle text box. When you type text in the Title or Subtitle text box, the contents appear as slide titles and subheadings within Outline view.

However, PowerPoint also offers you a third option for displaying text on a slide: You can create your own text box and place it anywhere on the slide.

When you create your own text box and fill it with text, this text will not appear within Outline view.

To create and place a text box on a slide, follow these steps:

1. **Click the Insert tab.**
2. **Click the Text Box icon in the Text group.**

   The mouse pointer turns into a downward-pointing arrow.

3. **Move the mouse pointer over the area on the slide where you want to create a text box.**

4. **Hold down the left mouse button and drag (move) the mouse to draw a text box on a slide.**

5. **Release the left mouse button.**

   PowerPoint displays a text box, as shown in Figure 10-5.

6. **Type your text inside the text box.**

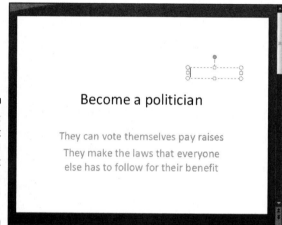

Figure 10-5: PowerPoint lets you draw text boxes directly on a slide.

Become a politician

They can vote themselves pay raises
They make the laws that everyone
else has to follow for their benefit

Any text you type into a text box that you create will not appear in Outline view.

Formatting text

After you create text in a text box, you can format it by choosing different fonts, font sizes, and colors. To change the appearance of text, follow these steps:

1. **Click the Home tab.**

2. **Click in a text box and select the text you want to format.**

3. **Click one of the following font tools, as shown in Figure 10-6:**

   • Font list box

   • Font Size list box

   • Increase Font Size

- Decrease Font Size
- Change Case
- Bold
- Italic
- Underline
- Shadow
- Strikethrough
- Character Spacing
- Font Color

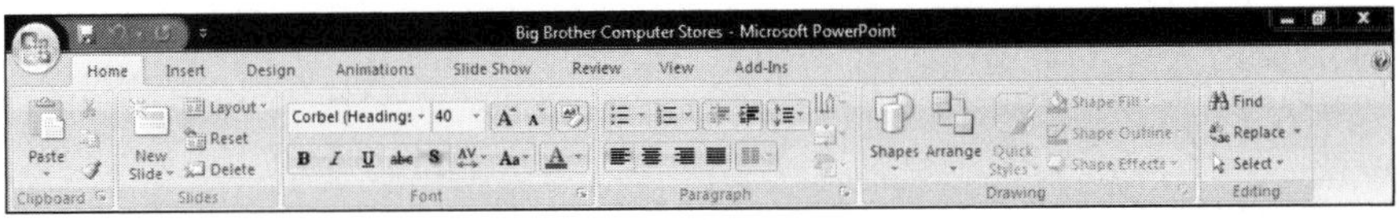

Figure 10-6:
The Home tab contains various font tools for formatting text.

Aligning text

PowerPoint can align text both horizontally and vertically inside a text box. To align text, follow these steps:

1. **Click the Home tab.**

2. **Click in a text box and select the text you want to align.**

3. **Click one of the following text alignment tools in the Paragraph group:**
   - Align Left
   - Center
   - Align Right
   - Justify
   - Align Text (Top, Middle, Bottom, Top Centered, Middle Centered, Bottom Centered)

4. **Click the Align Text icon in the Paragraph group.**

   A pop-up menu appears, as shown in Figure 10-7.

5. **Click a vertical alignment option, such as Top or Middle.**

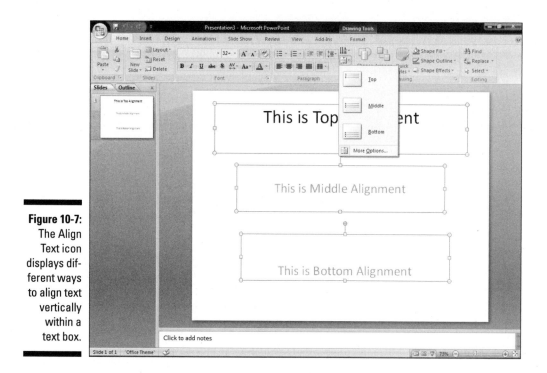

Figure 10-7:
The Align
Text icon
displays dif-
ferent ways
to align text
vertically
within a
text box.

Adjusting line spacing

Line spacing defines the space that appears between each line in a text box. To define the line space in a text box, follow these steps:

1. **Click the text box that contains text.**
2. **Click the Home tab.**
3. **Click the Line Spacing icon in the Paragraph group.**

   A pull-down menu appears, as shown in Figure 10-8.
4. **Select a line spacing value, such as 1.5 or 2.**

   PowerPoint adjusts line spacing in your chosen text box.

Figure 10-8:
The Line
Spacing icon
displays
different line
spacing
options.

Making numbered and bullet lists

PowerPoint can display text as bulleted or numbered lists. The two ways to create such a list are before you type any text or after you've already typed some text.

To create a bulleted or numbered list as you type new text, follow these steps:

1. **Click in a text box.**
2. **Click the Home tab.**
3. **Click the Bullets or Numbering icon in the Paragraph group.**

   A pull-down menu appears, as shown in Figure 10-9.
4. **Click a bullet or numbering option.**

   PowerPoint displays a bullet or number.
5. **Type any text and press Enter.**

   As soon as you press Enter, PowerPoint displays a new bullet or number.

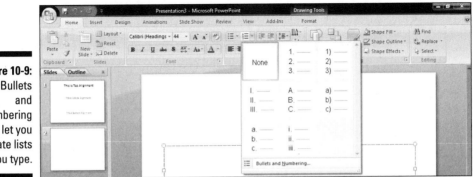

Figure 10-9:
The Bullets
and
Numbering
icons let you
create lists
as you type.

If you have existing text, you can convert it to a bullet or numbered list. To convert existing text into a list, follow these steps:

1. **Click in the text box that contains the text you want to convert into a bullet or numbered list.**

2. **Select the text you want to convert into a list.**

3. **Click the Home tab.**

4. **Click the Bullets or Numbering icon in the Paragraph group.**

   PowerPoint converts your text into a list.

PowerPoint displays each paragraph as a separate item in a bullet or numbered list. A *paragraph* is any amount of text that ends with a paragraph mark (¶), which is an invisible character that you create when you press the Enter key.

Making columns

You can divide a text box into multiple columns, which can be especially useful if you need to display large lists on a slide. To divide a text box into columns, follow these steps:

1. **Click the text box that you want to divide into columns.**

2. **Click the Home tab.**

3. **Click the Columns icon in the Paragraph group.**

   A menu appears, as shown in Figure 10-10.

4. **Click a column option, such as Two or Three.**

   PowerPoint divides your text box into columns.

Figure 10-10: You can divide any text box into multiple columns.

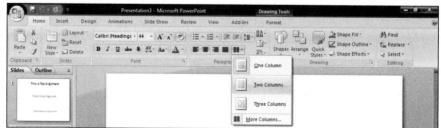

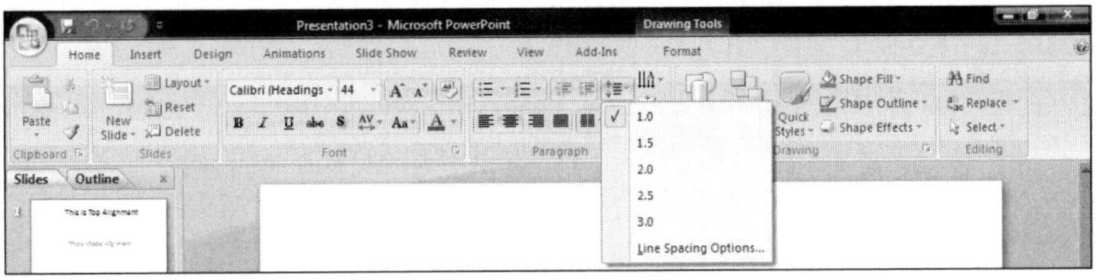

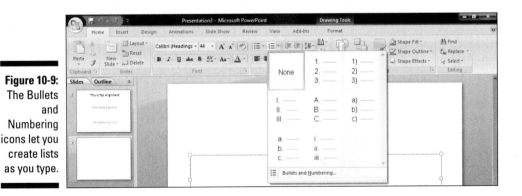

Figure 10-8:
The Line
Spacing icon
displays
different line
spacing
options.

Making numbered and bullet lists

PowerPoint can display text as bulleted or numbered lists. The two ways to create such a list are before you type any text or after you've already typed some text.

To create a bulleted or numbered list as you type new text, follow these steps:

1. **Click in a text box.**

2. **Click the Home tab.**

3. **Click the Bullets or Numbering icon in the Paragraph group.**

   A pull-down menu appears, as shown in Figure 10-9.

4. **Click a bullet or numbering option.**

   PowerPoint displays a bullet or number.

5. **Type any text and press Enter.**

   As soon as you press Enter, PowerPoint displays a new bullet or number.

Figure 10-9:
The Bullets
and
Numbering
icons let you
create lists
as you type.

If you have existing text, you can convert it to a bullet or numbered list. To convert existing text into a list, follow these steps:

1. **Click in the text box that contains the text you want to convert into a bullet or numbered list.**

2. **Select the text you want to convert into a list.**

3. **Click the Home tab.**

4. **Click the Bullets or Numbering icon in the Paragraph group.**

   PowerPoint converts your text into a list.

PowerPoint displays each paragraph as a separate item in a bullet or numbered list. A *paragraph* is any amount of text that ends with a paragraph mark (¶), which is an invisible character that you create when you press the Enter key.

Making columns

You can divide a text box into multiple columns, which can be especially useful if you need to display large lists on a slide. To divide a text box into columns, follow these steps:

1. **Click the text box that you want to divide into columns.**

2. **Click the Home tab.**

3. **Click the Columns icon in the Paragraph group.**

   A menu appears, as shown in Figure 10-10.

4. **Click a column option, such as Two or Three.**

   PowerPoint divides your text box into columns.

Figure 10-10: You can divide any text box into multiple columns.

Moving and resizing a text box

PowerPoint lets you move text boxes anywhere on the slide. To move a text box, follow these steps:

1. **Move the mouse pointer over the edge of the text box that you want to move.**

   The mouse turns into a four-way pointing arrow.

2. **Hold down the left mouse button and drag (move) the mouse to move the text box.**

3. **Release the left mouse button when you're happy with the new location of the text box.**

To resize a text box, follow these steps:

1. **Click the text box you want to resize.**

   PowerPoint displays handles around your chosen text box, as shown in Figure 10-11.

Figure 10-11:
Handles let
you resize a
text box.

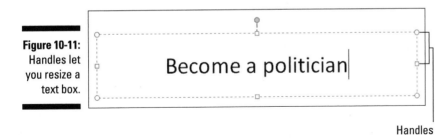

Become a politician

Handles

2. **Move the mouse pointer over a handle.**

   The mouse pointer turns into a two-way pointing arrow.

3. **Hold down the left mouse button and drag (move) the mouse.**

   PowerPoint resizes your text box in the direction you move the mouse.

4. **Release the left mouse button when you're happy with the size of the text box.**

Rotating a text box

After you type text in a title or subtitle text box, you can rotate the text box on your slide. To rotate a text box, follow these steps:

1. **Click the text box you want to rotate.**

   PowerPoint displays a rotate handle at the top of your text box, as shown in Figure 10-12.

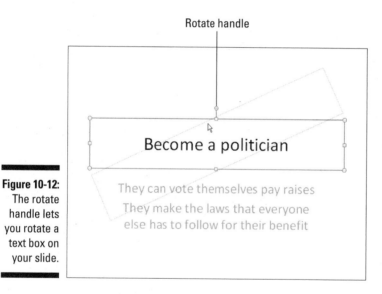

Figure 10-12:
The rotate
handle lets
you rotate a
text box on
your slide.

2. **Move the mouse pointer over the rotate handle.**

   The mouse pointer turns into a circular arrow.

3. **Hold down the left mouse button and drag (move) the mouse to rotate your text box.**

   If you hold down the Shift key while dragging the mouse, you can rotate the text box in 15 degree increments.

4. **Release the left mouse button when you're happy with the rotated position of your text box.**

You can still edit and format text in a text box that appears rotated.

Chapter 11

Adding Color and Pictures to a Presentation

· ·

In This Chapter

▶ Using themes

▶ Changing a background

▶ Adding graphics

▶ Showing movies on a slide

▶ Adding sound to a presentation

· ·

*T*o make your presentations look more visually appealing, PowerPoint lets you add color and graphics to your slides. Color and graphics can't turn a worthless presentation into an informative one, but they can enhance an informative presentation and make it easier for people to watch.

Applying a Theme

By default, PowerPoint displays each slide with a white background. Although you could change the colors and appearance of each slide individually, it's much easier to change every slide in your presentation using a theme. A *theme* provides predesigned colors and designs that are applied to each slide to give your presentation a uniform and professional look.

To define a theme for a presentation, follow these steps:

1. **Click the Design tab.**

2. **Click the More button under the Themes group.**

   A menu appears, as shown in Figure 11-1.

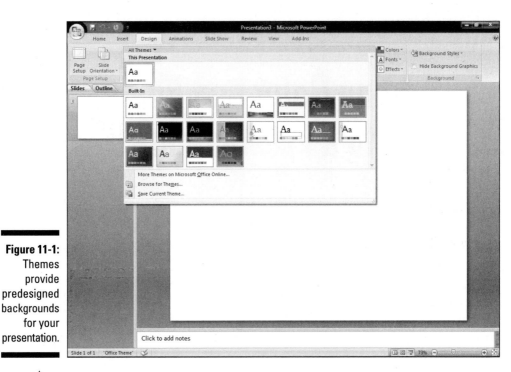

Figure 11-1:
Themes
provide
predesigned
backgrounds
for your
presentation.

If you move the mouse pointer over a theme, PowerPoint shows how your presentation will look.

3. Click a theme.

PowerPoint displays your chosen theme on your slides.

4. Click the Theme Colors icon in the Themes group.

A menu appears, listing different color variations you can choose for your presentation, as shown in Figure 11-2.

5. Click a color pattern.

PowerPoint displays your new theme colors.

6. Click the Fonts icon in the Themes group.

A menu appears listing all the default fonts for your presentation, as shown in Figure 11-3.

7. Click a font.

8. Click the Effects icon in the Themes group.

A menu appears listing all the different effects you can give your presentation, such as Metro or Currency.

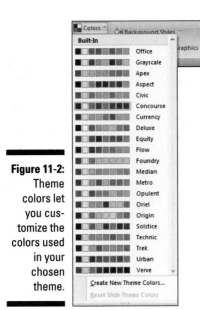

Figure 11-2:
Theme
colors let
you cus-
tomize the
colors used
in your
chosen
theme.

9. Click an effect.

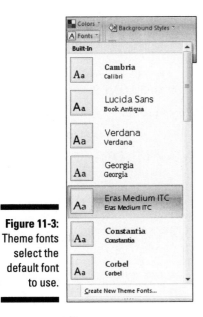

Figure 11-3:
Theme fonts
select the
default font
to use.

Changing the Background

Another way to change the appearance of your presentation is to modify the background of your slides. PowerPoint provides predefined background themes that you can choose. To choose a background theme, follow these steps:

1. **Click the Design tab.**

2. **Click Background Styles under the Background group.**

   A menu displays different backgrounds you can choose, as shown in Figure 11-4.

Figure 11-4:
The Background Styles menu lists different background designs for your slide.

3. **Click a background style.**

   PowerPoint applies your chosen background style to every slide in your presentation.

Choosing a solid color background

Rather than choose a theme, you might want to choose a solid color. If you choose a solid color background, you must make sure that any text or graphics that appear on your slides can still be seen. For example, if you choose a dark red background, any text or graphics on your slides should appear in light colors to make them visible against the dark red background.

To make sure solid background colors don't obscure your text and graphics, you can also adjust its transparency to make the color appear darker or lighter.

To change the background to a solid color, follow these steps:

1. **Click the Design tab.**

2. **Click the Background Styles icon in the Background group.**

   A pull-down menu appears (refer to Figure 11-4).

3. **Click Format Background near the bottom of the menu.**

   The Format Background dialog box appears, as shown in Figure 11-5.

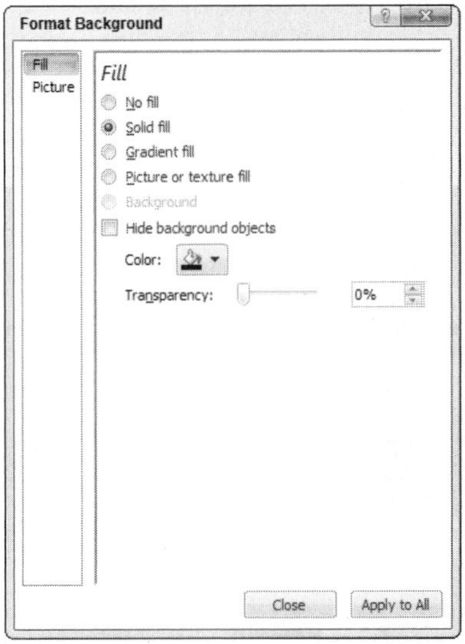

Figure 11-5:
The Format
Background
dialog box
displays a
color palette
for choosing
a solid color
background.

4. **Select the Solid Fill radio button.**

5. **Click the Color icon.**

   A pull-down menu appears, listing a palette of colors, as shown in Figure 11-6.

6. **Click a color.**

   PowerPoint fills your slide background with your chosen color.

7. **(Optional) Drag the Transparency slider left (0%) or right (100%).**

   The higher the transparency value, the lighter the background color appears.

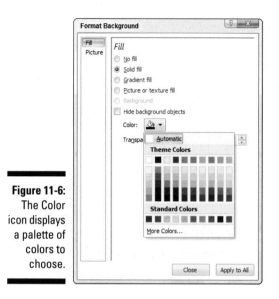

Figure 11-6:
The Color
icon displays
a palette of
colors to
choose.

8. **(Optional) Click Apply to All to change the background of every slide in your presentation.**

   If you don't click the Apply to All button, PowerPoint changes only the background of the currently selected slide.

9. **Click Close.**

Choosing a gradient background

A gradient displays one color that gradually fades into another color, such as green to orange. To define a gradient, you can define one or more stops, transparency, and the gradient direction. *Stops* define where the colors in the gradient start and end. *Transparency* defines how opaque a color appears. The *gradient direction* defines how the gradient appears, such as vertically or diagonally.

To define a gradient background, follow these steps:

1. **Click the Design tab.**

2. **Click the Background Styles icon in the Background group.**

   A pull-down menu appears (refer to Figure 11-4).

3. **Click Format Background near the bottom of the menu.**

   The Format Background dialog box appears (refer to Figure 11-5).

4. **Select the Gradient Fill radio button.**

   The Format Background dialog box displays additional options for defining a gradient, as shown in Figure 11-7.

   If you click the Preset Colors icon, you can choose from a variety of predefined gradients.

5. **Click in the Stop list box under Gradient Stops and choose Stop 1.**

6. **Click the Color icon.**

   A color palette appears.

7. **Click on a color.**

   PowerPoint displays your chosen color as a gradient on the current slide.

8. **Drag the Stop Position slider left or right.**

   The far left and far right positions of the stop position slider define where the gradient begins and ends on the slide.

9. **Drag the Transparency slider left or right.**

   The far left position (0%) displays your chosen color in full strength, and the far right position (100%) displays your chosen color to the point where it disappears from view completely (100% transparency).

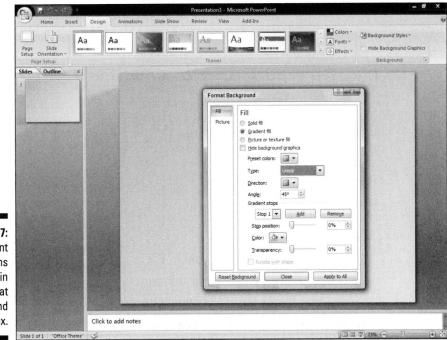

Figure 11-7:
The gradient options displayed in the Format Background dialog box.

10. **Click in the Type list box above the Gradient Direction group and choose an option, such as Radial or Linear.**

12. **Repeat Steps 5–8 to define the position of Stop 2.**

13. **(Optional) Click Apply to All if you want to apply your gradient to apply to every slide in your presentation.**

    If you don't click the Apply to All button, PowerPoint displays only the background of the currently selected slide.

14. **Click Close.**

Choosing a picture background

A picture, such as clip art or a photograph captured with a digital camera, can appear in your background. After you use a picture for the background, you can also adjust its transparency so that you can read any title or subtitle text that appears on each slide.

To add a picture background to slides, follow these steps:

1. **Click the Design tab.**

2. **Click the Background Styles icon in the Background group.**

    A pull-down menu appears (refer to Figure 11-4).

3. **Click Format Background near the bottom of the menu.**

    The Format Background dialog box appears (refer to Figure 11-5).

4. **Select the Picture or Texture Fill radio button.**

    The Format Background dialog box displays options for adding a picture to your background, as shown in Figure 11-8.

5. **Click one of the following buttons:**

    • *File:* Retrieves a graphic image stored on your computer, such as a digital photo. When the Insert Picture dialog box appears, click the picture you want to use and then click Open.

    • *Clipboard:* Pastes a previously cut or copied graphic image from another program, such as Photoshop.

    • *ClipArt:* Displays a library of clip art images you can choose. When the Select Picture dialog box appears, click the clip art image you want to use and then click OK.

6. **Drag the Transparency slider to the left or right until you're happy with the way the picture appears.**

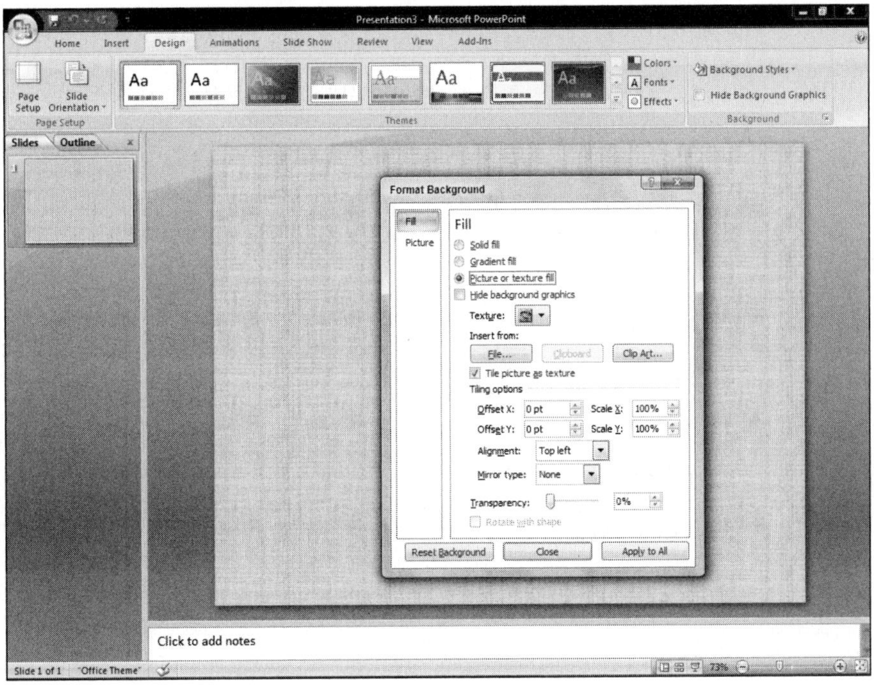

Figure 11-8:
The Picture
options let
you define
how your
picture
appears as
a slide
background.

7. **(Optional) Click Apply to All if you want to apply your picture to every slide in your presentation.**

   If you don't click the Apply to All button, PowerPoint displays only the background of the currently selected slide.

8. **Click Close.**

Adding Graphics to a Slide

Another way to spice up the appearance of your presentation is to include graphics on one or more slides. Such graphics can be informative, such as a chart that displays sales results; or they can be decorative, such as a cartoon smiley face that emphasizes the presentation's good news.

Three common types of graphics you can add to a PowerPoint slide include

- ✓ **Picture files:** Includes clip art images as well as images you may have stored on your hard disk, such as photographs from your digital camera

- ✓ **Charts:** Displays bar, column, line, pie, and other types of charts

- ✓ **WordArt:** Displays text as colorful text

Placing picture files on a slide

To liven up a presentation, you can add pictures you may have already stored on your computer. To add a picture to a slide, follow these steps:

1. **Click a slide (in either Slide or Outline view) to which you want to add a picture.**

2. **Click the Insert tab.**

3. **Click the Picture icon in the Illustrations group.**

   The Insert Picture dialog box appears, as shown in Figure 11-9. You may need to change folders or drives to find the picture file you want.

Figure 11-9: The Insert Picture dialog box lets you choose to add a picture file off your computer.

4. **Click the picture file you want and then click Open.**

   PowerPoint displays your chosen picture on the currently displayed slide. You may need to resize or move your picture.

Placing clip art on a slide

Clip art consists of drawings that come with PowerPoint. To add a clip art image to a slide, follow these steps:

1. **Click a slide (in either Slide or Outline view) to which you want to add a picture.**

2. **Click the Insert tab.**

3. **Click the Clip Art icon in the Illustrations group.**

   The Clip Art window appears on the right side of the screen, as shown in Figure 11-10.

4. **Click in the Search For text box and type a word that describes the type of image you want to find.**

5. **Click Go.**

   The Clip Art dialog box displays all the clip art images it could find that matched the descriptive word you typed in Step 4.

6. **Click the clip art image you want to use.**

   PowerPoint displays your chosen image on the current slide. (You may need to move or resize the image.)

7. **(Optional) Click the Close box of the Clip Art pane to make it go away.**

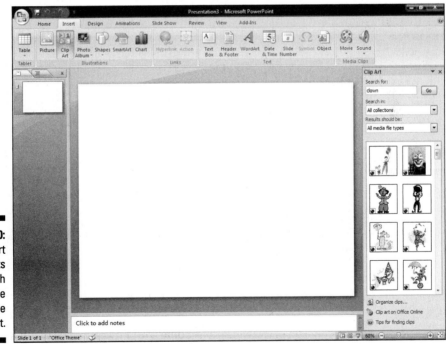

Figure 11-10:
The Clip Art pane lets you search for the type of picture you want.

Creating WordArt

WordArt provides another way to display text. Unlike ordinary text that you can format, WordArt lets you create graphically oriented text to use as head-lines for added emphasis. To create WordArt, follow these steps:

1. **Click the slide (in either Slide or Outline view) to which you want to add WordArt.**

2. **Click the Insert tab.**

3. **Click the WordArt icon in the Text group.**

   A WordArt menu appears, as shown in Figure 11-11.

4. **Click a WordArt style to use.**

   PowerPoint displays a WordArt text box on the current slide.

5. **Click in the WordArt text box and type text.**

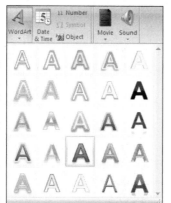

Figure 11-11:
The WordArt menu lists all the different styles you can choose to display text.

Resizing, moving, and deleting graphic images

When you add graphics to a slide, you may need to resize or move them to another location. To resize a graphic image, follow these steps:

1. **Click the graphic (picture, clip art, or WordArt) that you want to resize.**

   PowerPoint displays handles around your chosen object.

2. **Move the mouse pointer over a handle.**

   The mouse pointer turns into a two-way pointing arrow.

3. **Hold down the left mouse button and drag (move) the mouse.**

   PowerPoint resizes your chosen graphic image.

4. **Release the left mouse button when you're happy with the new size of your graphic image.**

To move a graphic image, follow these steps:

1. **Move the mouse pointer over the edge of the graphic image you want to move.**

   The mouse turns into a four-way pointing arrow.

2. **Hold down the left mouse button and drag (move) the mouse.**

   PowerPoint moves your graphic image.

3. **Release the left mouse button when you're happy with the new position of your graphic image.**

After you add a graphic image to a slide, you may later decide to delete it. To delete a graphic image, follow these steps:

1. **Click the graphic image you want to delete.**

   PowerPoint displays handles around your chosen graphic image.

2. **Press Delete.**

   PowerPoint deletes your chosen graphic image.

Rotating graphics

You may want to rotate graphic images for added visual effects. To rotate images or to flip them vertically or horizontally, follow these steps:

1. **Click the graphic image you want to rotate.**

   PowerPoint displays handles around your image along with a green rotate handle.

2. **Move the mouse pointer over the rotate handle.**

   The mouse pointer turns into a circular arrow.

3. **Hold down the left mouse button and move (drag) the mouse.**

   PowerPoint rotates your graphic image.

   If you hold down the Shift key while dragging the mouse, you can rotate an image at 15 degree increments.

4. **Release the left mouse button when you're happy with the rotation of the image.**

Layering objects

PowerPoint treats graphics and text boxes (see Chapter 10) as objects that you can move around on a slide. If you move one object over another, it may block part of another object, as shown in Figure 11-12.

When one object covers another one, PowerPoint considers the first object to be on top and the other object (the one being obscured) to be on the bottom. By moving objects from top to bottom (or vice versa), you can create unique visual effects (or just cover up parts of other objects by mistake).

To move a graphic image to the top or bottom when layered over another object, follow these steps:

1. **Click the graphic image you want to move.**

   The Format contextual tab appears.

2. **Click the Bring to Front or Send to Back icon in the Arrange group.**

   PowerPoint rearranges the layering of your graphic images.

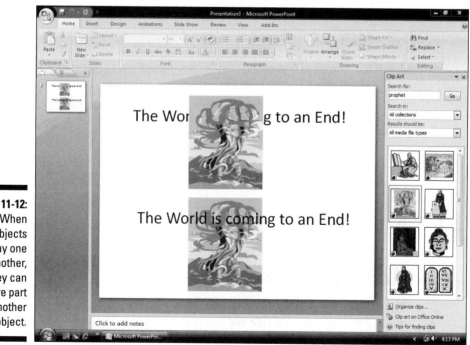

Figure 11-12:
When objects overlay one another, they can obscure part of another object.

Adding Movies to a Slide

Besides adding static graphic images, you can also add movies to a slide so that they play as part of your presentation. You can add two types of movies: simple graphic animations (animated GIF files) included with PowerPoint or movie files that you can download off the Internet or capture with a digital video camera.

Adding an animated cartoon to a slide

PowerPoint includes a library of simple animated cartoons that you can place on a slide for added visual emphasis. To include one of these animated cartoons on a slide, follow these steps:

1. **Click the slide (in either Slide or Outline view) to which you want to add an animated cartoon.**

2. **Click the Insert tab.**

3. **Click the downward-pointing arrow underneath the Movie icon in the Media Clips group.**

   A pull-down menu appears, enabling you to choose whether to select a movie from a file stored on your hard disk, or to select a movie from PowerPoint's clip organizer.

4. **Choose Movie from Clip Organizer.**

   A Clip Art window appears on the right side of the screen, as shown in Figure 11-13.

5. **Click a cartoon.**

   PowerPoint displays your cartoon on the slide. (You may need to move or resize it.)

You won't see the animated cartoon in action until you view your presentation by pressing F5.

Adding a movie to a slide

PowerPoint slides can also display a movie. When you store a movie on a slide, you can resize its size and move it anywhere on your slide. As soon as your slide appears, you have the option of having the movie play automatically or wait until you click the mouse first.

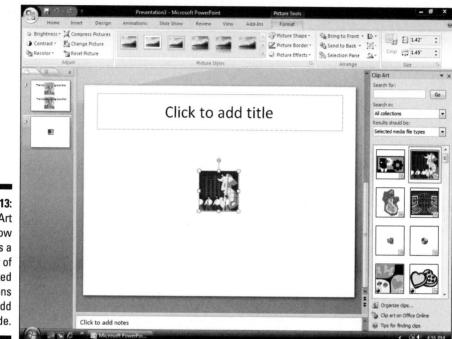

Figure 11-13:
The Clip Art window displays a variety of animated cartoons you can add to a slide.

PowerPoint can use movies stored in common Windows video formats such as AVI, MPEG, ASF (streaming video), and WMV files. If your movie is stored in a different file format, such as QuickTime, you have to convert the file first before you can add it to a PowerPoint presentation.

To add a movie to a slide, follow these steps:

1. **Click the slide (in either Slide or Outline view) to which you want to add a movie.**

2. **Click the Insert tab.**

3. **Click the Movie icon in the Media Clips group.**

   The Insert Movie dialog box appears.

   If you click the downward-pointing arrow underneath the Movie icon, a pull-down menu appears. Choose Movie from File.

4. **Click the movie file you want to add and then click OK.**

   PowerPoint displays a box on your slide where your movie will appear along with a dialog box, asking whether you want the movie to play automatically or when you click the mouse, as shown in Figure 11-14.

5. **Click Automatically or When Clicked.**

6. **Move the mouse pointer over the movie.**

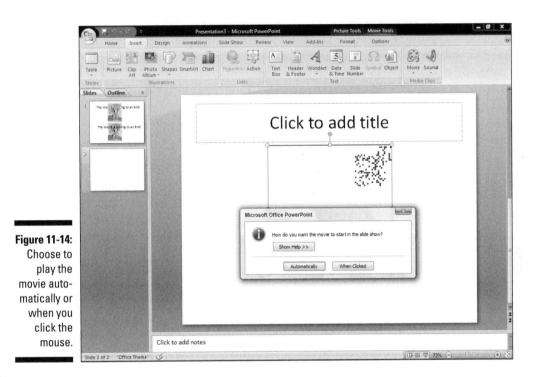

Figure 11-14:
Choose to play the movie automatically or when you click the mouse.

The mouse pointer turns into a four-way pointing arrow.

7. **Hold down the left mouse button and drag (move) the mouse to place the movie where you want it to appear on the slide.**

8. **Move the mouse pointer over one corner of the movie until the mouse pointer turns into a two-way pointing arrow.**

9. **Hold down the left mouse button and drag (move) the mouse to resize the movie.**

You won't see your movie play until you view your presentation by pressing F5.

Adding Sound to a Slide

Sound can be as simple as a sound effect (like a gun firing to wake up people in the middle of your presentation) or a recorded speech from the CEO, explaining why everyone's going to be forced to take a 25 percent pay cut while the CEO gets a golden parachute of $500,000 a year for the rest of his life.

The three types of sound files you can include in a presentation include audio files stored on your computer, sound files included with PowerPoint, and audio tracks from an audio CD in your computer.

PowerPoint can use audio files stored in common formats such as AIFF, MIDI, MP3, and WAV files. If your audio file is stored in a different file format, such as Real Audio, you'll have to convert the file first before you can add it to a PowerPoint presentation.

Adding an audio file to a presentation

If you already have music, sound effects, or a speech stored as a file, such as an MP3 file, you can add it to your presentation. To add an audio file to a slide, follow these steps:

1. **Click the slide (in either Slide or Outline view) to which you want to add an audio file.**

2. **Click the Insert tab.**

3. **Click the downward-pointing arrow underneath the Sound icon in the Media Clips group.**

   A pull-down menu appears, as shown in Figure 11-15.

Figure 11-15:
Choose the
type of audio
file to add.

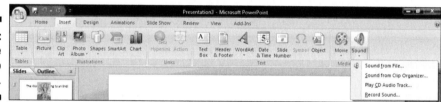

4. **Choose Sound from File.**

   The Insert Sound dialog box appears.

5. **Click the audio file you want to add and then click OK.**

   PowerPoint adds your audio file to the currently displayed slide (represented as a horn icon) and displays a dialog box, asking whether you want the sound to play automatically or when you click the mouse.

6. **Click Automatically or When Clicked.**

   PowerPoint displays your audio file as a sound icon on your slide. You may want to move the sound icon on your slide so it doesn't obscure part of your slide.

You won't hear your sound file play until you view your slide show by pressing F5.

Adding an audio clip to a presentation

PowerPoint includes a library of sound files (such as cheering or applause) that you can add to a presentation. To add a PowerPoint audio file to a slide, follow these steps:

1. **Click the slide (in either Slide or Outline view) to which you want to add an audio file.**

2. **Click the Insert tab.**

3. **Click the downward-pointing arrow underneath the Sound icon in the Media Clips group.**

   A pull-down menu appears (refer to Figure 11-15).

4. **Choose Sound from Clip Organizer.**

   The Clip Art dialog box appears.

   You can preview each sound by clicking the downward-pointing arrow on each sound icon in the Clip Organizer. When a pull-down menu appears, click Preview/Properties.

5. **Click the audio file you want to add.**

   PowerPoint adds your audio file to the currently displayed slide (represented as a horn icon) and displays a dialog box, asking whether you want the sound to play automatically or when you click the mouse.

6. **Click Automatically or When Clicked.**

   PowerPoint displays your audio file as a sound icon on your slide. You may want to move the sound icon on your slide so it doesn't obscure part of your slide.

You won't hear your sound file play until you view your slide show by pressing F5.

Adding a CD audio track to a presentation

You might have an audio CD that contains a sound that you want to play during your presentation. To play an audio CD track during a presentation, follow these steps:

1. **Click the slide (in either Slide or Outline view) to which you want to add an audio file.**

2. **Insert an audio CD in your computer's drive.**

3. **Click the Insert tab.**

4. **Click the downward-pointing arrow underneath the Sound icon in the Media Clips group.**

   A pull-down menu appears (refer to Figure 11-15).

5. **Choose Play CD Audio Track.**

   The Insert CD Audio dialog box appears, as shown in Figure 11-16.

Figure 11-16: The Insert CD Audio dialog box lets you choose which CD track to play.

6. **Click in the Start at Track and End at Track text boxes to choose one or more tracks to play.**

7. **Click in the Seconds text boxes to define the time to start playing the audio track and the time to end it.**

8. **Click OK.**

   PowerPoint adds your audio track to the currently displayed slide (represented as a horn icon) and displays a dialog box, asking whether you want the sound to play automatically or when you click the mouse.

9. **Click Automatically or When Clicked.**

   PowerPoint displays your audio file as a sound icon on your slide. You may want to move the sound icon on your slide so it doesn't obscure part of your slide.

You won't hear your sound file play until you view your slide show by pressing F5. If you copy your presentation to play on another computer, you must bring along the audio CD, too.

Be careful of copyright infringement when using audio CDs. Depending on your location and audience, using copyrighted material may not be acceptable.

Chapter 12

Showing Off a Presentation

In This Chapter

▶ Spell-checking a presentation

▶ Adding visual transitions

▶ Adding hyperlinks on a slide

▶ Viewing a presentation

▶ Printing handouts

▶ Packing a presentation on a CD

The whole point of creating a PowerPoint presentation is to show it off to an audience. So PowerPoint provides some handy Hollywood-style special effects to make your presentation look more interesting to your eyes and ears.

PowerPoint also provides features for creating handouts for your audience. Because people often want to take notes during an interesting presentation (or just doodle during a really boring presentation), PowerPoint can create handouts that you can print and distribute.

Spell-Checking Your Presentation

You could have the best presentation in the world, but it will look like the worst presentation in the world if you have misspellings and typos on your slides for everyone to snicker at. To prevent this problem from occurring, PowerPoint can spell-check your entire presentation.

PowerPoint automatically underlines all misspelled words with a red squiggly line. If you right-click any word underlined with a red squiggly line, a pop-up menu appears with a list of correctly spelled alternatives that you can choose.

To spell-check your entire presentation, follow these steps:

1. Click the Review tab.

2. Click the Spelling icon.

PowerPoint displays the Spelling dialog box when it finds a misspelled word, as shown in Figure 12-1.

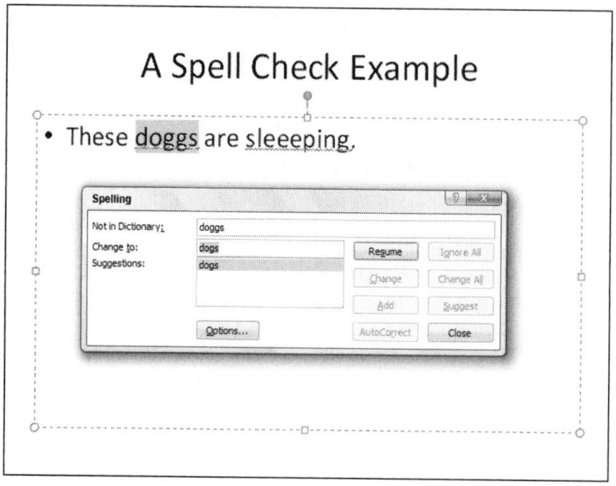

Figure 12-1:
The Spelling
dialog box
can identify
potential
misspellings
and offer
corrections.

3. Choose one of the following for each word that PowerPoint highlights as misspelled:

- *Change:* Click the correct spelling of the word and then click Change. (Click Change All to change all identical misspellings throughout your presentation.)

- *Ignore All:* Click Ignore All to ignore all instances of that word throughout your presentation.

- *Add:* Click Add to add the word to the PowerPoint dictionary so it won't flag the word as misspelled again.

4. Click Close to stop spell-checking.

PowerPoint won't recognize technical terms, proper names, or correctly spelled words used incorrectly, such as using the word *there* instead of *their,* so it's a good idea to proofread your presentation yourself.

Adding Visual Transitions

Transitions define how slides or part of a slide (text or graphics) appear during your presentation. By default, slides appear one at a time with all the text and graphics displayed at once, which can get monotonous.

To spice up your presentation, PowerPoint offers two types of transitions:

- Slide transitions
- Text and picture transitions

Use transitions sparingly. Transitions may be visually interesting, but you don't want your transitions to be distracting.

Adding slide transitions

Slide transitions can make a slide appear to melt or break into multiple pieces that slip away, revealing the next slide underneath.

When creating a transition, you need to define the following:

- The actual visual appearance of the transition
- The speed of the transition (Slow, Medium, or Fast)
- Any sound effects you want to play during the transition (these can get really annoying, so use them sparingly)
- When to display the transition (after a certain time period or when you click the mouse)

To create a slide transition, follow these steps:

1. **Click a slide (in the Slide or Outline view pane).**

   Any transition you choose will end by displaying the slide you choose in this step.

2. **Click the Animations tab.**

   PowerPoint displays the different animation (transition) tools, as shown in Figure 12-2.

Figure 12-2:
The Animations tab displays all the tools you need to create a slide transition.

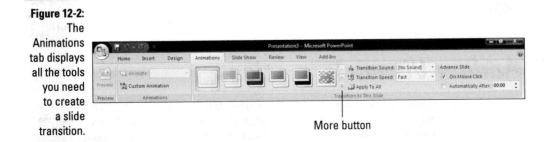

More button

3. **Click the More button of the Transition To This Slide group.**

   A pull-down menu appears listing all the different transitions available, as shown in Figure 12-3.

   If you move the mouse over a transition, PowerPoint shows you what that transition will look like on your chosen slide.

4. **Click the transition you want.**

5. **(Optional) Click in the Transition Sound list box and choose a sound, such as Cash Register or Drum Roll.**

6. **(Optional) Click in the Transition Speed list box and choose a speed (Slow, Medium, or Fast).**

7. **(Optional) Select the Automatically After or the On Mouse Click check box.**

   If you select the Automatically After check box, you have to specify a time in the Automatically After text box for the slide to wait before running the transition.

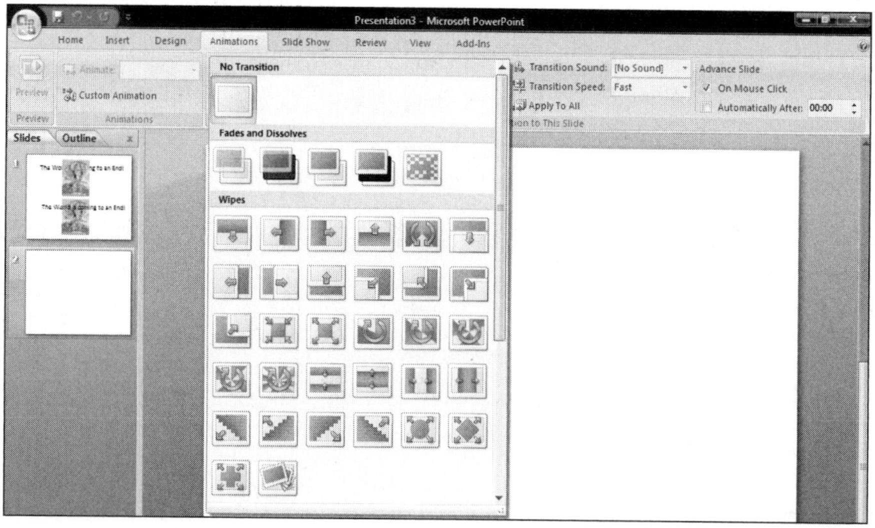

Figure 12-3:
The Transition menu displays each transition as an icon, which gives you an idea how the transition will appear.

You can select both the On Mouse Click and Automatically After check boxes, so the slide transition waits until you click the mouse or until a certain amount of time passes.

8. **(Optional) Click Apply to All to apply your transitions to every slide in your presentation.**

Applying the same transition throughout your presentation can give your slide show a consistent look, but it's best for only simple, visual transitions and not for transitions that involve noisy sound effects that get tedious after a while.

Text transitions

Besides animating how your slides appear and disappear, you can also add transitions to your text boxes or graphics so they fly or drop into place across a slide.

Use text transitions sparingly because the transitions can get distracting when people just want to read your presentation without having to watch letters zoom around the screen.

To create a simple text transition, follow these steps:

1. **Click a text box or picture on a slide.**

   PowerPoint displays handles around your chosen item.

2. **Click the Animations tab.**

3. **Click the Animate list box in the Animations group.**

   A list of different animation schemes appears, as shown in Figure 12-4.

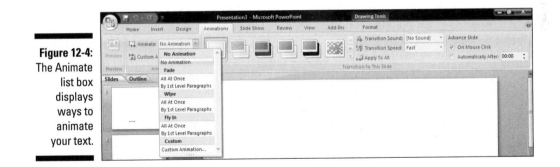

Figure 12-4: The Animate list box displays ways to animate your text.

4. **Click an animation, such as Fly In or Wipe.**

   PowerPoint animates your text so you can see how it looks.

Adding Hyperlinks

For greater flexibility in presenting information, PowerPoint lets you add hyperlinks to your slides. Hyperlinks let you open a Web page (provided you have an Internet connection), a file (such as a Word document), another slide in your current presentation, or a program. By adding hyperlinks to your slides, you can display additional information or display slides out of order.

Creating Web page hyperlinks

A Web page hyperlink lets you convert text into a hyperlink that can load your default browser and display any Web site. When you exit the browser (or just switch back to PowerPoint), you can see your slide again and continue with your presentation.

By accessing a Web site, you can avoid copying data and pasting it on a slide. For example, if you're giving a presentation about advertising, you can create Web page hyperlinks to show how your competitors use the Internet to advertise and sell their products.

To create a Web page hyperlink, follow these steps:

1. **Highlight the text in a title or subtitle text box that you want to turn into a Web page hyperlink.**

2. **Click the Insert tab.**

3. **Click the Hyperlink icon in the Links group.**

   The Insert Hyperlink dialog box appears, as shown in Figure 12-5.

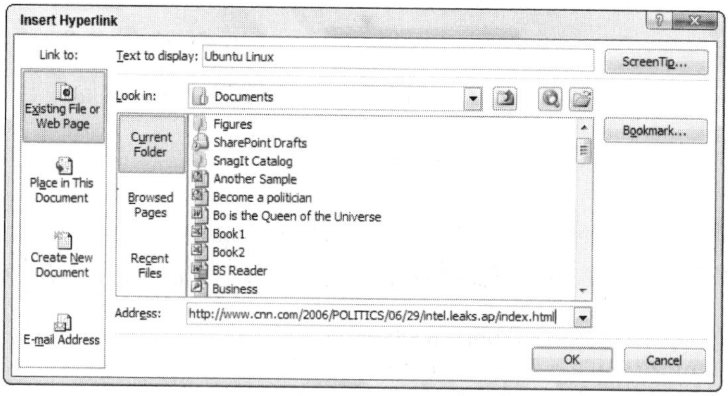

Figure 12-5:
The Insert Hyperlink dialog box lets you type in a Web site address.

4. **Click in the Address text box and type a Web site address, such as** www.microsoft.com.

5. **Click OK.**

   PowerPoint underlines the text you selected in Step 1. When you view your presentation, PowerPoint turns the mouse pointer into a hand icon when you move the mouse over the hyperlink.

Creating hyperlinks to external files

You may have data stored in another file that you want to include in your PowerPoint presentation. Rather than copy the data and paste it in your presentation, it may be easier just to display the file itself. That way you can update the file, and PowerPoint will always link to the updated file.

When you create a hyperlink to a file, PowerPoint opens that file by loading the program that created it. For example, if you want to view a Microsoft Word file, make sure you have a copy of Microsoft Word installed on your computer.

To create a hyperlink that opens an external file, follow these steps:

1. **Highlight the text in a title or subtitle text box that you want to turn into an external file hyperlink.**

2. **Click the Insert tab.**

3. **Click the Hyperlink icon in the Links group.**

   The Insert Hyperlink dialog box appears (refer to Figure 12-5).

4. **Click in the Look In list box and choose a drive and folder that holds the file you want to use.**

   You may need to click through several folders to find the file you want.

5. **Click the file you want to use and then click OK.**

If you're viewing your presentation on Windows Vista, a dialog box appears, warning you that opening a file may be unsafe. This is to protect you from opening up a file that may contain a virus or Trojan Horse.

Creating hyperlinks to different slides

You can also create hyperlinks that let you jump to a different slide in your presentation. That way you could jump from slide 2 to slide 35 and then back to slide 2 again. By doing this, you can create a slide that refers to previous information or gives viewers a peek at upcoming information.

To create a hyperlink that links to other slides in your presentation, follow these steps:

1. **Highlight the text in a text box that you want to turn into a slide hyperlink.**

2. **Click the Insert tab.**

3. **Click the Action icon in the Links group.**

   The Action Settings dialog box appears, as shown in Figure 12-6.

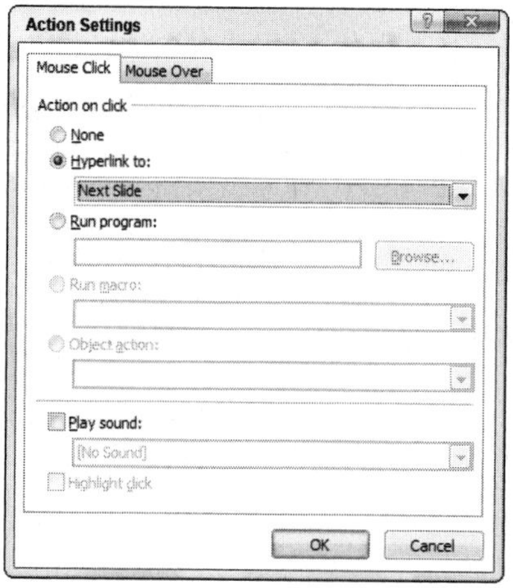

Figure 12-6:
The Action Settings dialog box lets you choose a slide to attach to your hyperlink.

4. **Select the Hyperlink To radio button.**

5. **Click the Hyperlink To list box and choose an option, such as Next Slide.**

   If you choose Slide, the Hyperlink to Slide dialog box appears, as shown in Figure 12-7.

   The Hyperlink To list box displays commands for linking to the first or last slide of your presentation. The Slide command is useful for linking to a slide in the middle of your presentation.

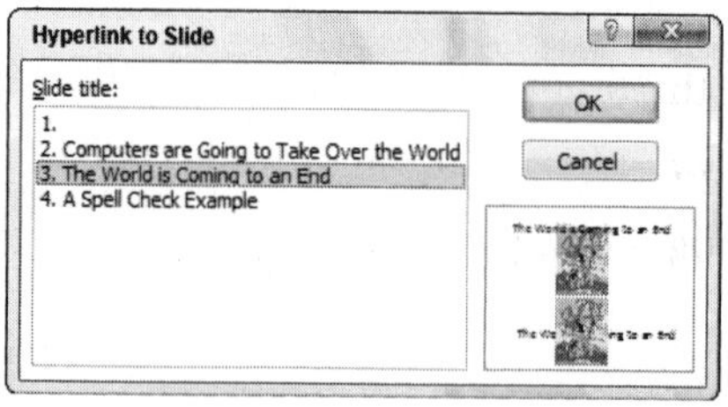

Figure 12-7:
Link to a specific slide, such as slide 3.

6. **Click a slide number, such as slide 3, and click OK.**

   The Action Settings dialog box appears again.

7. **Click OK.**

When you link to another slide, it's usually a good idea to create a second hyperlink that lets you jump back to the previous slide. Otherwise, you can jump from slide 3 to slide 60 and not be able to return back to slide 3 again to see the rest of your presentation.

Running a program through a hyperlink

A PowerPoint hyperlink can also run any program from within a presentation. For example, you could create a presentation that explains how to market a new computer program, and then create a hyperlink to that same program so you can demonstrate how that program actually works. When you exit that program, you'll return back to your PowerPoint presentation again.

Make sure your computer has enough memory to run both PowerPoint and any program you want to run.

To create a hyperlink that runs a program, follow these steps:

1. **Highlight the text in a text box that you want to turn into a program hyperlink.**

2. **Click the Insert tab.**

3. **Click the Action icon in the Links group.**

   The Action Settings dialog box appears (refer to Figure 12-6).

4. **Select the Run Program radio button.**

5. **Click Browse.**

   The Select a Program to Run dialog box appears.

6. **Click in the Look In list box to choose the drive that contains the program you want to run.**

7. **Click in the folder and then click Open to find the program you want to run.**

   You may have to repeat this step multiple times.

8. **Click the program you want to run and then click OK.**

   The Action Settings dialog box appears again.

9. **Click OK.**

Viewing a Presentation

After you finish arranging your slides, adding transitions, and adding hyperlinks, you're ready to test how your entire presentation looks. To view your entire presentation, follow these steps:

1. **Click the Slide Show tab.**

2. **Click the From Beginning icon in the Start Slide Show group, as shown in Figure 12-8.**

   PowerPoint displays the first slide of your presentation.

   You can also choose the From Beginning command by pressing F5.

3. **Choose one of the following:**

   • Click the mouse or press the spacebar to view the next slide.

   • Press Esc to exit your presentation.

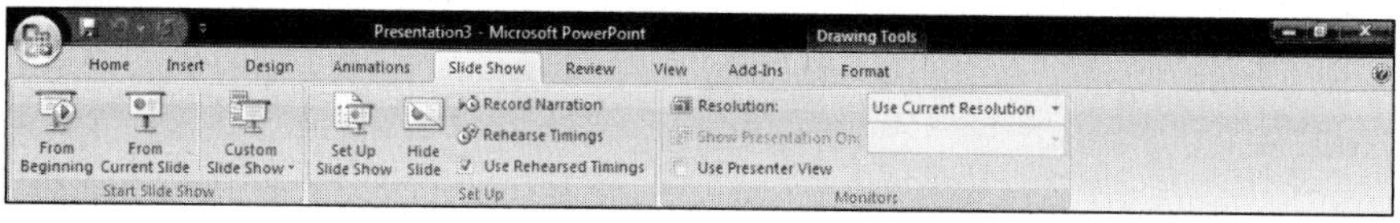

Figure 12-8:
The Slide Show tab lists tools for helping you view your presentation.

If you have a large presentation consisting of 300 slides, you may not want to view the first 290 slides just to test how your last 10 slides look. To avoid this problem, PowerPoint lets you choose to view your presentation starting with any slide.

To view your presentation starting with a slide other than the first one, follow these steps:

1. **Click the Slide Show tab.**

2. **Click the From Current Slide icon in the Start Slide Show group (refer to Figure 12-8).**

   PowerPoint displays the currently displayed slide.

3. **Choose one of the following:**

   • Click the mouse or press the spacebar to view the next slide.

   • Press Esc to exit your presentation.

Creating a custom slide show

You may have a presentation organized for one audience (engineers and scientists) but need to give the same presentation to a different audience (sales executives). Although you could copy your original presentation and then modify it, now you'll be stuck with two copies of the same information. And, if you modify the information in one presentation, you have to modify the same information in the second (or third or fourth) presentation.

To avoid this problem, PowerPoint lets you create custom slide shows based on an existing presentation. Such a custom slide show can selectively show slides in a different order. To create a custom slide show, you need to define the order you want to display the slides.

To arrange the order of a custom slide show, follow these steps:

1. **Click the Slide Show tab.**

2. **Click the Custom Slide Show icon in the Start Slide Show group.**

   A pull-down menu appears.

3. **Choose Custom Shows.**

   The Custom Shows dialog box appears, as shown in Figure 12-9.

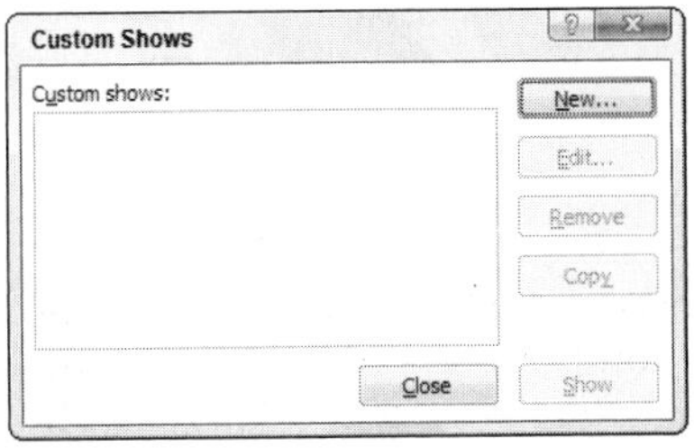

Figure 12-9: The Custom Shows dialog box lets you define a name for your custom slide show.

4. **Click New.**

   The Define Custom Show dialog box appears, as shown in Figure 12-10.

5. **Click in the Slide Show Name text box and type a name for your custom slide show.**

6. **Click a slide in the Slides in Presentation list box and then click the Add button.**

   This tells PowerPoint which existing slides you want to reuse in your custom slide show.

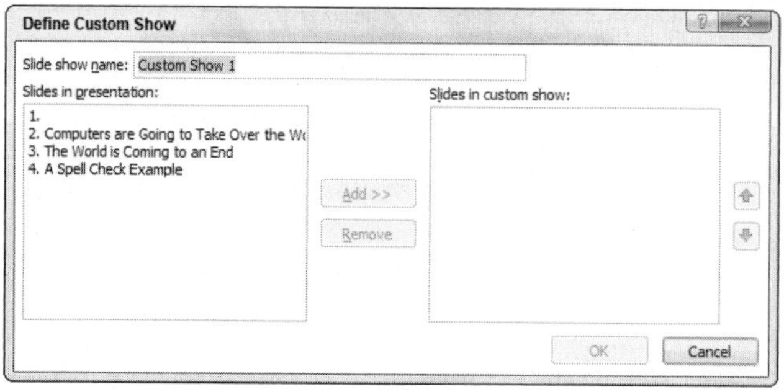

Figure 12-10:
Customize
your slide
show by
reordering
slides.

7. **Repeat Step 6 for each slide you want to include in your custom slide show.**

8. **Click a slide in the Slides in Custom Show list box and click the Up or Down arrow button to rearrange their order.**

9. **Repeat Step 8 for each slide you want to rearrange in your custom slide show.**

10. **Click OK.**

   The Custom Shows dialog box appears again.

11. **Click the name of your custom slide show and then click Show.**

   PowerPoint shows your new, customized presentation.

To present a custom slide show, follow these steps:

1. **Click the Slide Show tab.**

2. **Click the Custom Slide Show icon in the Start Slide Show group.**

   A pull-down menu appears that lists the names of all the custom slide shows you've created.

3. **Click the name of the custom slide show you want to view.**

4. **Choose one of the following:**

   - Click the mouse or press the spacebar to view the next slide.
   - Press Esc to exit your presentation.

Hiding a slide

PowerPoint can hide a slide, which lets you keep your slide but not display it during a presentation. Hiding a slide can be especially handy when you need to create a custom slide show and need a slide to appear only in the custom slide show but not the original presentation (or vice versa).

To hide a slide, follow these steps:

1. **Click the slide that you want to hide (in Slide or Outline view).**
2. **Click the Slide Show tab.**
3. **Click the Hide Slide icon in the Set Up group.**

   PowerPoint dims your selected slide.

To unhide a slide, just repeat the above three steps.

Organizing with Slide Sorter view

After you have a chance to view your presentation, you may want to rearrange or hide slides. To help you organize your presentation, switch to Slide Sorter view, which numbers each slide to show you the order that they appear, as shown in Figure 12-11.

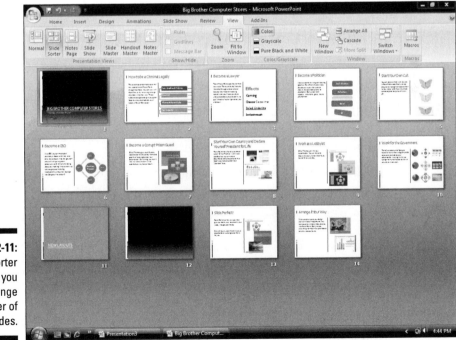

Figure 12-11:
Slide Sorter view lets you rearrange the order of your slides.

To use Slide Sorter view, follow these steps:

1. **Click the View tab.**
2. **Click the Slide Sorter view icon in the Presentation Views group.**
3. **(Optional) To delete a slide, click a slide and press Delete.**
4. **(Optional) To hide a slide, click a slide, click the Slide Show command tab, and click Hide Slide.**
5. **(Optional) To move a slide**

   a. Move the mouse pointer over a slide.

   b. Hold down the left mouse button and move (drag) the mouse.

   PowerPoint displays a vertical line where it will place your slide.

   c. Release the left mouse button.
6. **Click the Normal icon in the Presentation Views group to switch out of Slide Sorter view.**

Timing yourself

To help you practice giving a presentation, PowerPoint can time how long you've spent on each slide. Such timing can give you a rough idea of how long you want to keep each slide visible for an audience to see.

No matter how hard you may practice, the timing of your presentation by yourself will almost never be exactly the timings of your actual presentation because people may ask questions, equipment may fail, distractions may occur when the waiter drops a plate, and so on.

To time a presentation, follow these steps:

1. **Click the Slide Show tab.**
2. **Click the Rehearse Timings icon in the Set Up group.**

   PowerPoint displays the first slide of your presentation along with the Timing toolbar that shows you how long your current slide has been visible, as shown in Figure 12-12.
3. **Click the mouse or press the spacebar to view each slide in your presentation.**

Each time a new slide appears, the Timing toolbar records how long each slide remains visible.

4. **Click Esc when you reach the end of your presentation.**

   A dialog box appears, asking whether you want to keep the timings for each slide.

5. **Click Yes or No.**

   If you click Yes in Step 5, PowerPoint displays Slide Sorter view and lists the timings for each slide, as shown in Figure 12-13.

6. **Click the Normal icon in the Start Slide Show group to switch out of Slide Sorter view.**

Timing toolbar

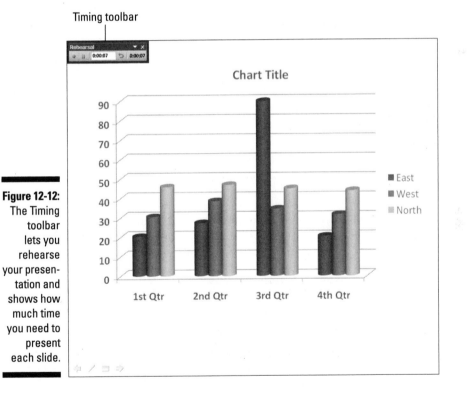

Figure 12-12: The Timing toolbar lets you rehearse your presentation and shows how much time you need to present each slide.

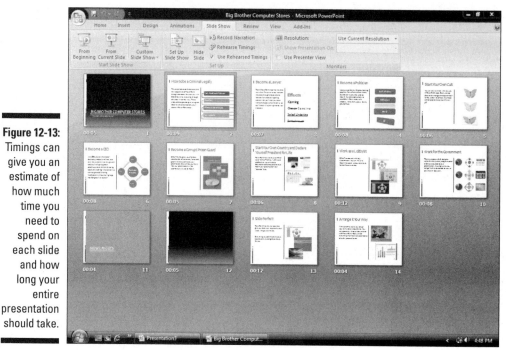

Figure 12-13:
Timings can
give you an
estimate of
how much
time you
need to
spend on
each slide
and how
long your
entire
presentation
should take.

Creating Handouts

When people view a particularly interesting presentation, they often want copies of that presentation so they can review the information later or have a place to jot down notes during the presentation itself. For that reason, PowerPoint lets you create handouts from your presentation.

Handouts typically contain a thumbnail of each slide along with blank space for jotting down notes about the information presented by that slide. To create a handout, follow these steps:

1. **Click the Office Button and choose Print⇨Print Preview.**

   The Print Preview window appears.

2. **Click the Print What list box in the Page Setup group and choose a handout style, such as Handouts (3 Slides Per Page).**

   The Print Preview window shows you what your handouts will look like, as shown in Figure 12-14.

3. **Click the Print icon when you're ready to print your handouts.**

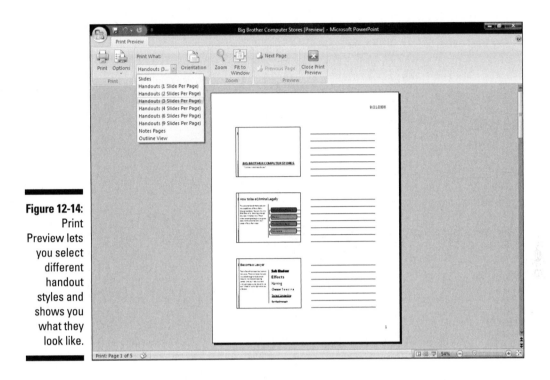

Figure 12-14:
Print
Preview lets
you select
different
handout
styles and
shows you
what they
look like.

Packing Presentations to Go

Many people use their laptops to display their PowerPoint presentations, but occasionally, you may need to use a different computer to run your presentation. Because that other computer may not have a copy of PowerPoint, you can store your entire PowerPoint presentation on a CD that you can run on another computer.

You can view your presentations only on a computer that uses Windows 2000, Windows XP, or Windows Vista.

When you package a presentation on a CD, PowerPoint includes a stripped-down version of PowerPoint designed just to run and display presentations. You won't be able to change your presentation.

To package up your presentation, follow these steps:

1. **Click the Office Button and choose Send⇨Publish for CD.**

   The Package for CD dialog box appears, as shown in Figure 12-15.

Figure 12-15:
Specify a
name for
your pre-
sentation.

Rather than save a presentation to a CD, you can click the Copy to Folder button and specify a different drive and folder, such as a USB removable drive.

2. **Click in the Name the CD text box and type a descriptive name for your presentation.**

3. **Insert a blank CD in your rewritable CD drive.**

4. **Click Copy to CD.**

   If your presentation includes hyperlinks to other programs, PowerPoint displays a dialog box to alert you. This dialog box is meant to keep you from accidentally creating a presentation that could spread viruses or Trojan Horses.

5. **Click Close.**

Part V

Getting Organized with Outlook

The 5th Wave By Rich Tennant

It's an e-mail from my mother. She wants me to know how happy she is for us.

In this part . . .

After a few days on the job, most people's desks disappear under a pile of memos, reports, and papers. If you want to actually use the top of your desk as a writing surface rather than a filing cabinet or garbage bin, you may need the help of Microsoft Outlook (a combination e-mail program and personal information organizer) to save the day.

In addition to helping you create, send, receive, and sort through your e-mail, Outlook also organizes your appointments, tasks, and important contacts. With the help of Outlook, you can track meetings and appointments you'd rather avoid, store the names of people you might forget, and organize e-mail in a single location so that you don't have to search frantically all over your hard drive for an important message that could determine the future of your career or your business.

Outlook can handle all your personal information so you can focus on doing the work that really needs to get done. Who knows? If Outlook makes you productive enough at work, you just may find that you have enough time to relax and take that extended lunch break you've needed for so long.

Chapter 13

Organizing E-Mail with Outlook

● ●

In This Chapter

▶ Configuring e-mail account settings

▶ Creating e-mail

▶ Adding file attachments

▶ Formatting e-mail text

▶ Reading e-mail

▶ Deleting e-mail

● ●

Microsoft Outlook is the personal organizer portion of Office 2007, able to handle information such as your appointments, names and addresses of important people, and list of to-do tasks. However, one of the most popular uses for Outlook is reading, writing, and organizing your e-mail.

Configuring E-Mail Settings

The first time you run Outlook, you'll need to configure your e-mail account information. To retrieve e-mail from your account within Outlook, you need to know the following:

✔ Your name

✔ The username of your e-mail account, which might be JSmith (for Joe Smith)

✔ Your e-mail address (such as JSmith@microsoft.com)

✔ Your e-mail account password

✔ Your e-mail account type (either POP3 or IMAP)

✔ Your incoming mail server name (such as pop.microsoft.com)

✔ Your outgoing mail server name (such as smtp.microsoft.com)

Outlook can often recognize many popular e-mail accounts such as HotMail, but if Outlook can't set up your e-mail account automatically, you will need to ask your Internet service provider (ISP) for all of these details.

Configuring an e-mail account the first time you run Outlook, follow these steps:

1. **Load Outlook.**

   A dialog box appears, letting you know Outlook is preparing to configure your e-mail account settings.

2. **Click Next.**

   The Account Configuration dialog box appears, as shown in Figure 13-1.

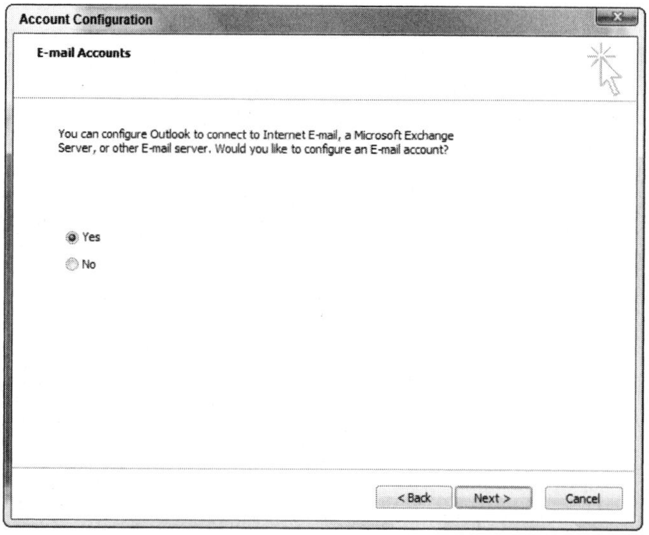

Figure 13-1:
The Account
Configu-
ration dialog
box lets you
choose
whether to
configure
Outlook to
retrieve
messages
from your
e-mail
account.

Account Configuration
E-mail Accounts
You can configure Outlook to connect to Internet E-mail, a Microsoft Exchange Server, or other E-mail server. Would you like to configure an E-mail account?
⊙ Yes
○ No
< Back   Next >   Cancel

3. **Select the Yes radio button and then click Next. (If you click the No radio button, you can always configure Outlook to access your e-mail account later.)**

   The Add New E-mail Account dialog box appears, as shown in Figure 13-2. In most cases, you'll use the default setting that has the Microsoft Exchange Server, POP3, IMAP, or HTTP radio button selected.

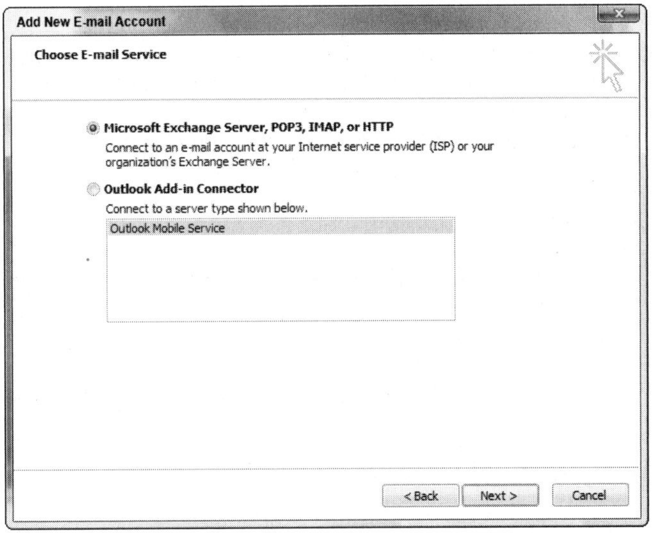

Figure 13-2:
The Add
New E-mail
Account
dialog box
lets you
choose the
type of
e-mail
service
you use.

4. **Click Next.**

   The Add New E-mail Account dialog box next asks for your name, your
   e-mail address, and your e-mail account password, as shown in Figure 13-3.

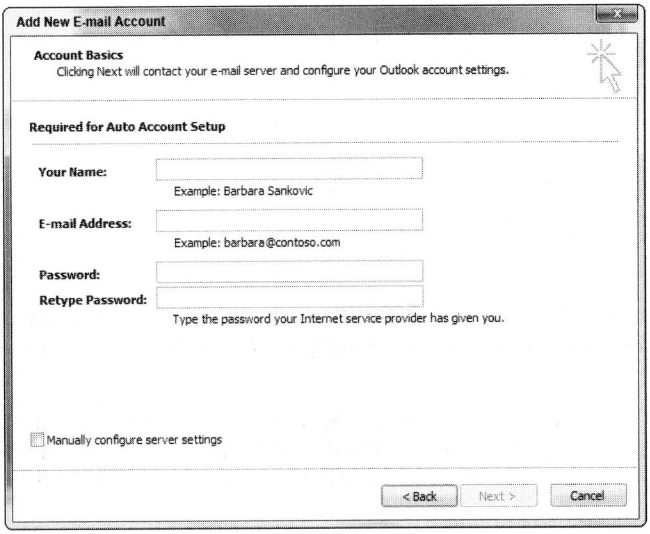

Figure 13-3:
The Add
New E-mail
Account
dialog box
displays text
boxes for
you to type
your e-mail
address and
password.

5. **Type your name, e-mail address, and password in the appropriate text boxes and then click Next.**

   Another dialog box appears, letting you know Outlook is trying to automatically detect the rest of your e-mail account settings. (If Outlook succeeds in configuring your e-mail account settings, you're done. Otherwise, continue with the rest of the steps.)

6. **Select the Manually Configure Server Settings check box and then click Next.**

   Another Add New E-mail Account dialog box appears, asking you to define the type of e-mail account you want to set up — either Internet E-mail or Microsoft Exchange Server — as shown in Figure 13-4.

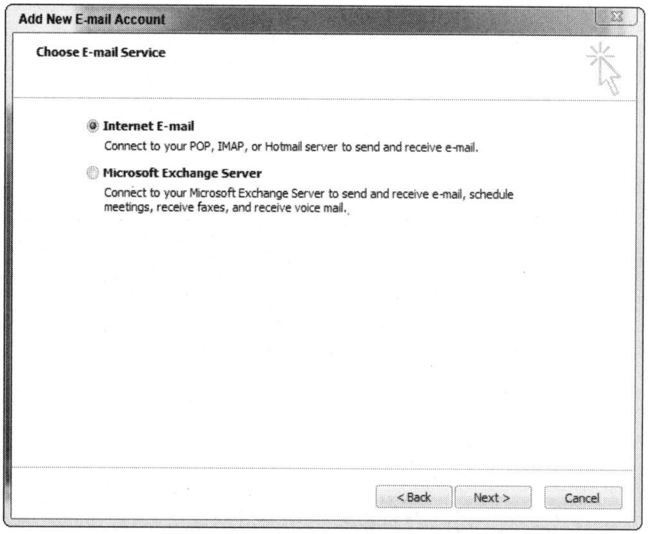

Figure 13-4:
Select the type of e-mail account you use.

Add New E-mail Account

Choose E-mail Service

◉ **Internet E-mail**
   Connect to your POP, IMAP, or Hotmail server to send and receive e-mail.

○ **Microsoft Exchange Server**
   Connect to your Microsoft Exchange Server to send and receive e-mail, schedule meetings, receive faxes, and receive voice mail.

[< Back] [Next >] [Cancel]

Most home computers connect to the Internet through the Internet E-mail option, but many corporate computers connect to the Internet through the Microsoft Exchange Server option.

7. **Click Next.**

   The Add New E-mail Account dialog box appears that displays text boxes for entering your server settings, as shown in Figure 13-5.

8. **Type in your incoming and outgoing mail server settings.**

   The incoming and outgoing mail server settings typically put the letters pop and smtp in front of your ISP's name, such as pop.isp.com and smtp.isp.com.

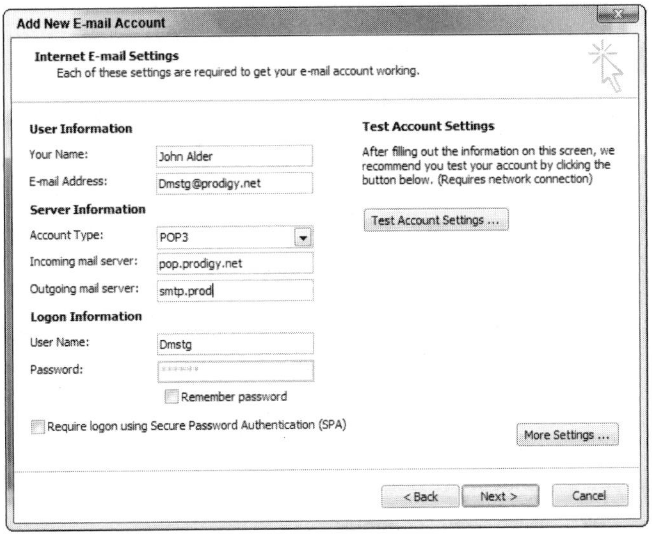

Figure 13-5:
Enter your server settings to define how to retrieve and send e-mail.

9. **Click the Test Account Settings button.**

   Outlook attempts to connect to the Internet and send a message to your e-mail account to verify that everything is working.

10. **Click Next.**

    Another dialog box appears to inform you that you're done setting up your e-mail account.

11. **Click Finish.**

Adding an e-mail account

After you configure your initial e-mail account in Outlook, you can always add (or delete) an e-mail account later. To add a new e-mail account, follow these steps:

1. **Choose Tools⇨Account Settings.**

   The Account Settings dialog box appears, as shown in Figure 13-6.

2. **Click New.**

   The Add New E-mail Account dialog box appears (refer to Figure 13-2).

3. **Follow Steps 4–10 in the preceding section, "Configuring E-Mail Settings."**

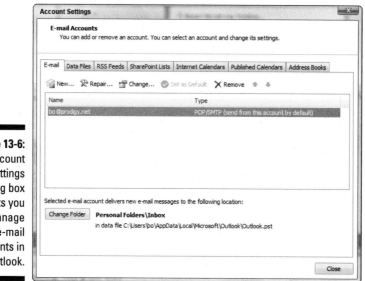

Account Settings

E-mail Accounts
You can add or remove an account. You can select an account and change its settings.

| E-mail | Data Files | RSS Feeds | SharePoint Lists | Internet Calendars | Published Calendars | Address Books |

New...   Repair...   Change...   Set as Default   ✗ Remove   ⬆ ⬇

Name	Type
bo @prodigy.net	POP/SMTP (send from this account by default)

Selected e-mail account delivers new e-mail messages to the following location:

Change Folder   **Personal Folders\Inbox**
in data file C:\Users\bo\AppData\Local\Microsoft\Outlook\Outlook.pst

Close

Figure 13-6:
The Account
Settings
dialog box
lets you
manage
your e-mail
accounts in
Outlook.

Deleting an e-mail account

You can always delete an e-mail account at any time. To delete an e-mail account, follow these steps:

1. **Choose Tools⟹Account Settings.**

   The Account Settings dialog box appears (refer to Figure 13-6).

2. **Click the e-mail account you want to delete.**

3. **Click Remove.**

   A dialog box appears, asking you to verify whether you want to delete your e-mail account.

4. **Click Yes (or No).**

   If you click Yes, Outlook removes your e-mail account.

If you delete an e-mail account, Outlook still saves any e-mail messages it has already retrieved from your account.

Editing an e-mail account

If you've already configured an e-mail account, you may need to make changes to it later, such as changing your password periodically. To edit an existing account

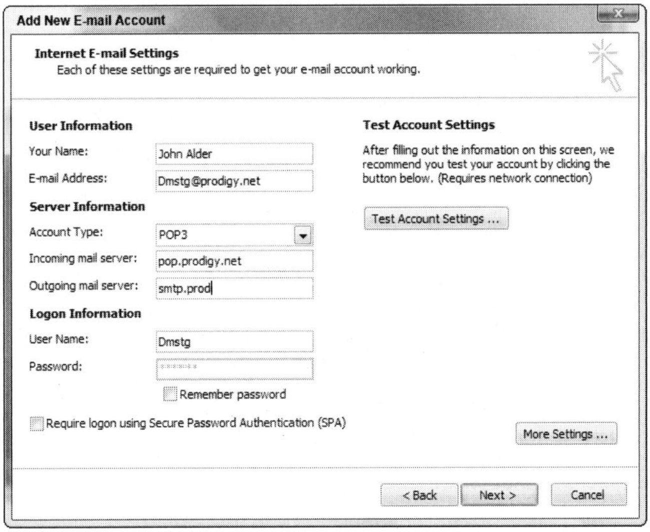

Figure 13-5:
Enter your
server
settings to
define how
to retrieve
and send
e-mail.

9. **Click the Test Account Settings button.**

   Outlook attempts to connect to the Internet and send a message to your e-mail account to verify that everything is working.

10. **Click Next.**

    Another dialog box appears to inform you that you're done setting up your e-mail account.

11. **Click Finish.**

Adding an e-mail account

After you configure your initial e-mail account in Outlook, you can always add (or delete) an e-mail account later. To add a new e-mail account, follow these steps:

1. **Choose Tools⇨Account Settings.**

   The Account Settings dialog box appears, as shown in Figure 13-6.

2. **Click New.**

   The Add New E-mail Account dialog box appears (refer to Figure 13-2).

3. **Follow Steps 4–10 in the preceding section, "Configuring E-Mail Settings."**

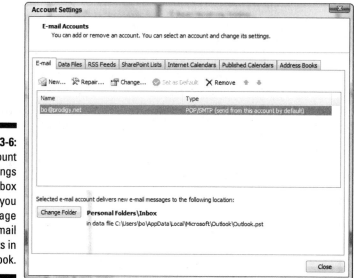

Figure 13-6:
The Account
Settings
dialog box
lets you
manage
your e-mail
accounts in
Outlook.

Deleting an e-mail account

You can always delete an e-mail account at any time. To delete an e-mail account, follow these steps:

1. **Choose Tools⇨Account Settings.**

   The Account Settings dialog box appears (refer to Figure 13-6).

2. **Click the e-mail account you want to delete.**

3. **Click Remove.**

   A dialog box appears, asking you to verify whether you want to delete your e-mail account.

4. **Click Yes (or No).**

   If you click Yes, Outlook removes your e-mail account.

If you delete an e-mail account, Outlook still saves any e-mail messages it has already retrieved from your account.

Editing an e-mail account

If you've already configured an e-mail account, you may need to make changes to it later, such as changing your password periodically. To edit an existing account

1. **Choose Tools➪Account Settings.**

   The Account Settings dialog box appears (refer to Figure 13-6).

2. **Click the e-mail account you want to edit and then click Change.**

   The Change E-mail Account dialog box appears (which displays options similar to those shown in Figure 13-5).

   As an alternative to clicking the Change icon, you can also click the Repair icon to have Outlook try to automatically configure your e-mail account settings.

3. **Make any changes, such as changing the password or incoming or outgoing mail server settings, and then click Next.**

   A dialog box appears to inform you that you've changed your settings.

4. **Click Finish.**

Creating E-Mail

After you set up an e-mail account, you can start sending e-mail. The three ways to create and send e-mail are

- ✔ **Create a message and type the recipient's e-mail address manually.**

- ✔ **Reply to a previously received message.** Outlook then adds the recipient's e-mail address automatically.

- ✔ **Create a message and use a previously stored e-mail address.** Outlook adds the e-mail address automatically.

Creating a new e-mail message

The most straightforward way to send a message is to type the recipient's e-mail address and then type your message. To create a new e-mail message and type the e-mail address, follow these steps:

1. **Choose Go➪Mail. (You can also press Ctrl+1 or click the Mail button in the lower-left corner of the Outlook window.)**

   Outlook displays the Mail pane.

2. **Choose one of the following:**

   - Click the New button (don't click the downward-pointing arrow next to the New button).

   - Choose Actions➪New Mail Message.

   - Press Ctrl+N.

The message window appears, as shown in Figure 13-7. Notice that the message window displays a Ribbon with Message, Insert, Options, and Format Text tabs.

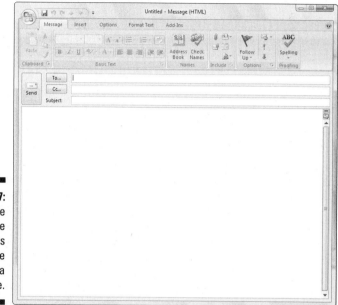

Figure 13-7: The message window lets you type and format a message.

3. **Click in the To text box and type the e-mail address of the person you want to receive your message.**

Make sure you type the e-mail address correctly. One incorrect character, and your message won't go to your intended recipient.

4. **(Optional) Click in the Cc text box and type another e-mail address to send the message to more than one person.**

5. **Click in the Subject text box and type a brief description of your message.**

Many people use spam filters that examine the Subject line of a message, so it's a good idea to not type your subject text in ALL CAPITAL LETTERS or use multiple exclamation points!!! Otherwise, your recipient's spam filter may inadvertently flag your message as spam and delete it before anyone can even read it.

6. **Click in the message text box and type your message.**

If you click the Save icon on the Quick Access toolbar, you can store the message in your Drafts folder so you can edit and send it at a later time.

7. Click the Send icon to send your message.

Replying to an e-mail message

Oftentimes. you may receive a message from someone else and want to send a reply to that person. When you send a reply, Outlook automatically copies the original message as part of your e-mail so that way the recipient can read the original message that you're responding to.

Even better, when you reply to a message, you won't have to retype the recipient's e-mail address and risk misspelling it. To reply to an e-mail message, follow these steps:

1. **Choose Go⇨Mail. (You can also press Ctrl+1 or click the Mail button in the lower-left corner of the Outlook window.)**

   Outlook displays the Mail pane.

2. **Click the Inbox folder.**

   Outlook displays the Inbox pane that lists all the messages you've received.

3. **Click a message that you wish to reply to.**

   Outlook displays the contents of that message in a pane on the right side of the Outlook window.

4. **Choose one of the following:**

   - Click the Reply icon.
   - Choose Actions⇨Reply.
   - Press Ctrl+R.

   Outlook displays a message window with the recipient's e-mail address and subject line already typed in along with a copy of the original message.

5. **Click in the message text box and type your message.**

   If you click the Save icon on the Quick Access toolbar, you can store the message in your Drafts folder so you can edit and send it at a later time.

6. **Click the Send icon.**

Using a stored e-mail address to create a new e-mail message

If you've stored names and e-mail addresses (see Chapter 14), you can retrieve an e-mail address so you don't have to type it in yourself. To retrieve a stored e-mail address, follow these steps:

1. **Choose Go⇨Mail. (You can also press Ctrl+1 or click the Mail button in the lower-left corner of the Outlook window.)**

   Outlook displays the Mail pane.

2. **Choose Actions⇨New Mail Message (or press Ctrl+N).**

   The message window appears (refer to Figure 13-7).

3. **Click the To button.**

   The Contacts dialog box appears, as shown in Figure 13-8.

4. **Click a name to select it.**

5. **Click the To button to copy your chosen e-mail address to the To text box.**

6. **(Optional) Click additional e-mail addresses and then click the Cc or Bcc button.**

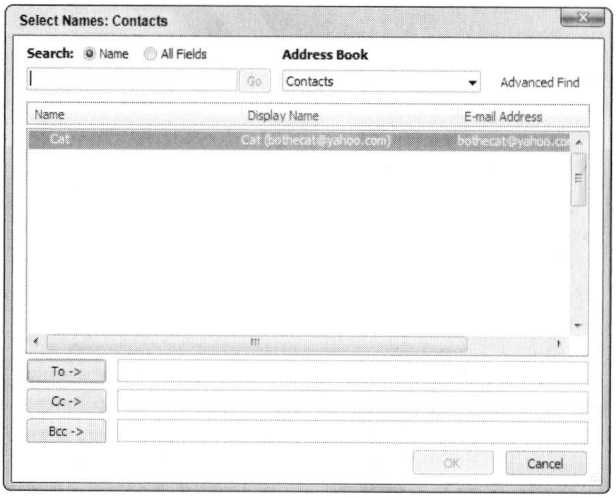

Figure 13-8:
Outlook can send your message to an e-mail address you've already stored.

Cc stands for Carbon Copy while Bcc stands for Blind Carbon Copy. Anyone on the Cc list will receive your message along with all the e-mail addresses that also received your message. Anyone on the Bcc list will just receive your message but will not be able to see any other e-mail addresses you may have sent your message to.

7. **Click OK.**

Outlook automatically enters your chosen e-mail address in the To text box.

8. **Click in the Subject text box and type a brief description of your message.**

9. **Click in the message text box and type your message.**

If you click the Save icon on the Quick Access toolbar, you can store the message in your Drafts folder so you can edit and send it at a later time.

10. **Click the Send icon to send your message.**

Forwarding an e-mail message

Sometimes you may receive a message, but rather than reply to it, you want to send it (*forward* it) to someone else. Forwarding a message essentially copies a message and sends it to someone else whom the original sender may not even know. (This can be handy for sending incriminating e-mail messages to prosecutors trying to collect evidence to put your boss in prison.)

To forward a message, follow these steps:

1. **Choose Go⇨Mail. (You can also press Ctrl+1 or click the Mail button in the lower-left corner of the Outlook window.)**

Outlook displays the Mail pane.

2. **Click a message that you want to forward to someone else.**

3. **Choose one of the following:**

   • Click the Forward icon.

   • Choose Actions⇨Forward.

   • Press Ctrl+F.

A message window appears that contains your chosen message.

If you try to forward a message that contains HTML code known as a *Web bug*, Outlook may display a dialog box warning you that the content of the forwarded message may send information back to the original sender to verify that your e-mail address is valid.

4. **Click in the To text box and type an e-mail address. (Or click the To button to choose a stored e-mail address.)**

5. **Click in the message window and type any additional text you want to send along with the forwarded message.**

6. **Click the Send icon.**

Attaching Files to Messages

Rather than just send plain text, you can also *attach* a file to your message. This file can be anything from a picture, a song (stored as an audio file), a program, or even another e-mail message.

Be careful when attaching files to messages because many ISPs put a limit on the maximum size of an e-mail message, such as 10MB. Also try to keep any file attachments small because if the recipient has a slow Internet connection, downloading a large file attachment can take a really long time.

Attaching a file to a message

If you want to send someone a picture, video, audio file, compressed file, or even an entire program, you need to attach that file to a message by following these steps:

1. **Follow the steps in the earlier section, "Creating E-Mail," to create a new e-mail message, type a subject, and type an e-mail address.**

2. **Click the Insert tab.**

3. **Click the Attach File icon.**

   The Insert File dialog box appears.

4. **Click the file you want to attach to your message and then click Insert.**

   Outlook displays an Attach button and text box in the message window, as shown in Figure 13-9.

   If you hold down the Ctrl or Shift key while clicking a file, you can select multiple files at once.

5. **(Optional) Click the Attach button to display the Insert File dialog box so you can select more files.**

6. **(Optional) Right-click any file in the Attachment text box; when a pop-up menu appears, choose Remove if you change your mind about attaching a file to a message.**

7. **Click the Send icon.**

Rather than select multiple files to attach to a message, you can compress or *zip* multiple files into a single compressed file by using a separate program like WinZip or by using the built-in Zip compression feature in Windows.

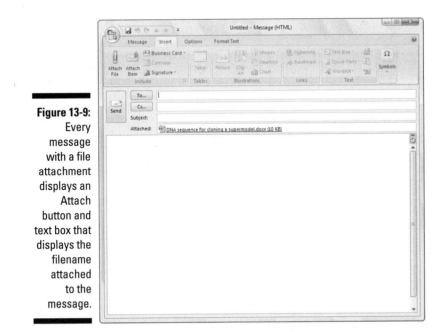

Figure 13-9:
Every message with a file attachment displays an Attach button and text box that displays the filename attached to the message.

Attaching Outlook information to another message

Rather than attach a file, you might want to send information stored in Outlook, such as contact information or a task. To attach Outlook information to a message, follow these steps:

1. **Follow the steps in the earlier section, "Creating E-Mail," to create a new e-mail message, type a subject, and type an e-mail address.**

2. **Click the Insert tab.**

3. **Click the Attach Item icon.**

   The Insert Item dialog box appears, as shown in Figure 13-10.

4. **Click a folder, such as Inbox or Contacts.**

   The dialog box displays a list of the items stored in your currently selected folder.

5. **Click an item, such as an e-mail message stored in the Inbox folder.**

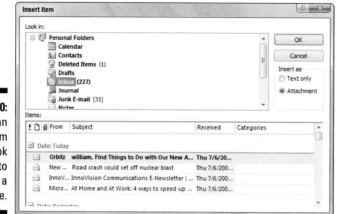

Figure 13-10:
Choose an
item from
your Outlook
folders to
attach to a
message.

6. **Click OK.**

   Outlook attaches your chosen item to the message window.

7. **Type an e-mail address, subject, and any text in the message window.**

8. **Click the Send icon.**

Formatting E-Mail

Plain e-mail will just look like black text against a white background. If you want to spice up the appearance of your e-mail messages, you can use stationery or text formatting tools. You can also use signature files to display unique information in every message you send, such as your name and phone number.

Formatting text

You can format text in an e-mail message just the same way you can format text in a Word document, such as changing fonts, choosing different colors, underlining text, or creating numbered lists.

Outlook displays basic formatting tools, such as the Font list box, on both the Message tab and the Format Text tab, as shown in Figure 13-11.

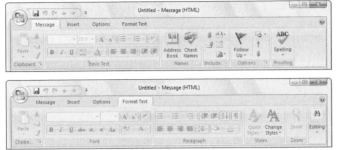

Figure 13-11:
The
Message
and Format
Text tabs
provide tools
for mod-
ifying text.

Not all computers and e-mail programs are capable of viewing formatted text.

To format text, follow these steps:

1. **Select the text you want to format.**

2. **Click the Message or Format Text tab.**

   The Format Text tab displays additional formatting tools such as creating numbered and bullet lists, and aligning text to the right, center, or left.

Adding signatures to your messages

Signatures contain text that appears at the bottom of every e-mail message you send. Signatures can be useful for displaying your name, company, Web site address, or short message that you want everyone to read when they receive a message from you.

Be careful about including personal information in a signature, such as your home phone number. If someone forwards your e-mail that has your signature at the bottom, some stranger could read your signature text and use your information against you to hack into your computer or steal your identity. As a general rule, only put information in your signature file that you don't mind sharing with a world full of strangers.

To create a signature, follow these steps:

1. **Choose Go⊅Mail. (You can also press Ctrl+1 or click the Mail button in the lower-left corner of the Outlook window.)**

   Outlook displays the Mail pane.

2. **Choose Tools⊅Options.**

   The Options dialog box appears.

3. Click the Mail Format tab, as shown in Figure 13-12.

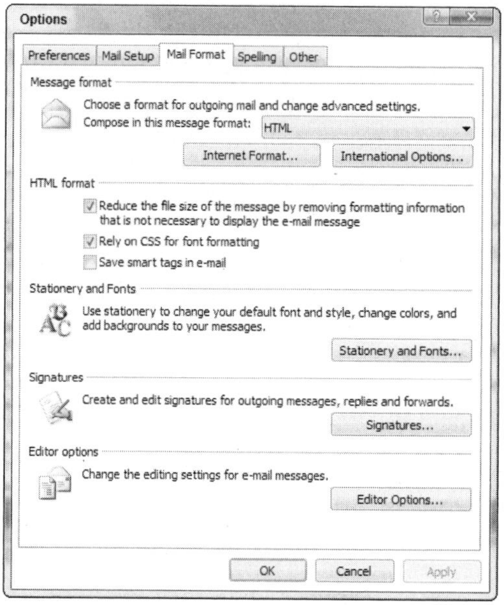

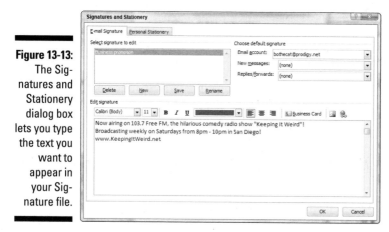

Figure 13-12:
The Options dialog box offers different ways to customize Outlook.

4. Click the Signatures button.

The Signatures and Stationery dialog box appears, as shown in Figure 13-13.

Figure 13-13:
The Signatures and Stationery dialog box lets you type the text you want to appear in your Signature file.

5. **Click the New button.**

   The New Signature dialog box appears.

6. **Type a descriptive name for your signature file and then click OK.**

7. **Click in the text box and type the text that you want to include in your signature file, such as your name, company, Web site, and so on.**

   You can also format your text at this point. Just be aware that some computers and e-mail programs may not be able to display all the formatting correctly.

8. **Click the Save button.**

9. **(Optional) Click in the Replies/Forwards list box and choose the name of your signature file that you defined in Step 6.**

10. **Click OK twice.**

    Now every time you create a new e-mail message, Outlook automatically inserts the text you saved in your signature file.

Creating and using multiple signatures

You can actually create multiple signature files although Outlook will attach only one signature file to your e-mail messages automatically. Creating multiple signature files lets you create one signature file for personal use and one for business use. (Just make sure you don't get the two of them confused and send out personal information in your signature file to your business contacts.)

To create additional signatures, follow Steps 1–10 in the preceding section, "Adding signatures to your messages." After you create multiple signature files, you can define which one to use by following these steps:

1. **Follow Steps 1–5 in the "Creating a new e-mail message" section to create a new message.**

2. **Click the Insert tab.**

3. **Click the Signature icon in the Include group.**

   A pull-down menu appears that displays a list of your existing signature files, as shown in Figure 13-14.

4. **Click the name of the signature file you want to use.**

   Outlook displays that signature file's text in your e-mail message.

5. **Type your message in the text box.**

6. **Click the Send icon to send your message.**

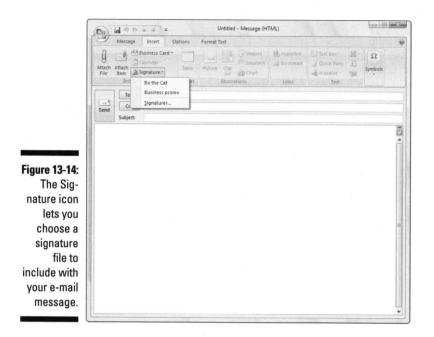

Figure 13-14:
The Signature icon lets you choose a signature file to include with your e-mail message.

Editing and deleting a signature file

You can always edit a signature file at any time to add or delete text. To edit a signature file, follow these steps:

1. **Choose Tools⇨Options.**

   The Options dialog box appears.

2. **Click the Mail Format tab.**

3. **Click the Signatures button.**

   The Signatures and Stationery dialog box appears (refer to Figure 13-13).

4. **Click a signature filename.**

   Outlook displays the contents of that signature file in the text box below.

5. **(Optional) Click the Delete button.**

   When a dialog box appears to warn you that you are about to delete the signature file, click Yes (or No).

6. **Click in the text box and edit your text.**

7. **Click the Save button to save your changes.**

8. **Click OK.**

Reading and Organizing E-Mail

When Outlook retrieves e-mail, it organizes messages according to time. Messages received today appear under the Today heading, messages received last week appear under the Last Week heading, and messages received last month appear under the Last Month heading.

Outlook gives you two ways to read an e-mail message:

- In the Preview pane
- In a separate window

The Preview pane can be handy for browsing the content of different messages to see if you really want to read them or not. Because the Preview pane shows only part of the message, some text may appear cut off.

Viewing a message in a separate window is more useful when you want to read the entire message. Figure 13-15 shows what the same message looks like in the Preview pane (top) and in a separate window (bottom).

To view an e-mail message, follow these steps:

1. **Choose Go⇨Mail. (You can also press Ctrl+1 or click the Mail button in the lower-left corner of the Outlook window.)**

    Outlook displays the Mail pane.

2. **Click a message in the Inbox pane.**

    Outlook shows your chosen message in the Preview pane.

3. **(Optional) Double-click the message in the Inbox pane.**

    Outlook displays your message in a separate window.

4. **Click the Close box to make the message window disappear.**

Categorizing messages

One problem with receiving messages is that you may have personal and business messages mixed together, and trying to find an older message later can involve tedious searching through your past messages, one by one.

To solve this problem, Outlook lets you categorize messages according to color. You may use red to highlight important messages, yellow to highlight personal messages, green to highlight business messages that involve money, and so on.

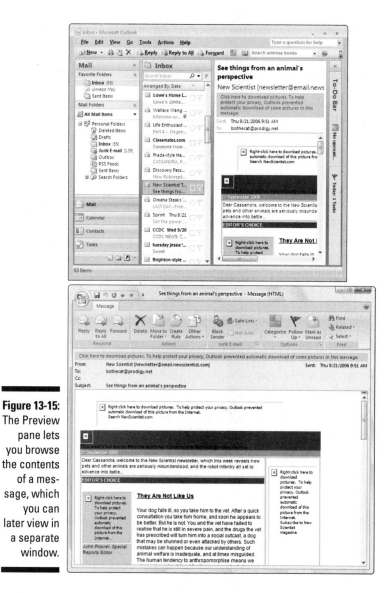

Figure 13-15:
The Preview pane lets you browse the contents of a message, which you can later view in a separate window.

Color categorizing a message

To categorize a message, follow these steps:

1. **Choose Go⇨Mail. (You can also press Ctrl+1 or click the Mail button in the lower-left corner of the Outlook window.)**

   Outlook displays the Mail pane.

2. **Click a message in the Inbox pane.**

3. **Choose Actions⇨Categorize.**

A list of different color categories appears, as shown in Figure 13-16.

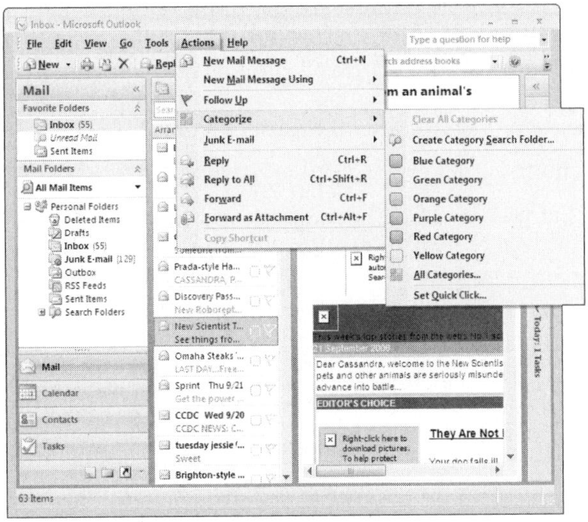

Figure 13-16:
The Categorize submenu lists all the different colors you can choose to categorize a message.

You can also see the list of different color categories if you click the Categorize icon or if you right-click a Category icon inside a message, as shown in Figure 13-17.

4. Click a category.

Outlook displays your chosen color in the Category icon of the message. (If this is the first time you've chosen a color, Outlook displays a dialog box, giving you the chance to give the color a more descriptive name.)

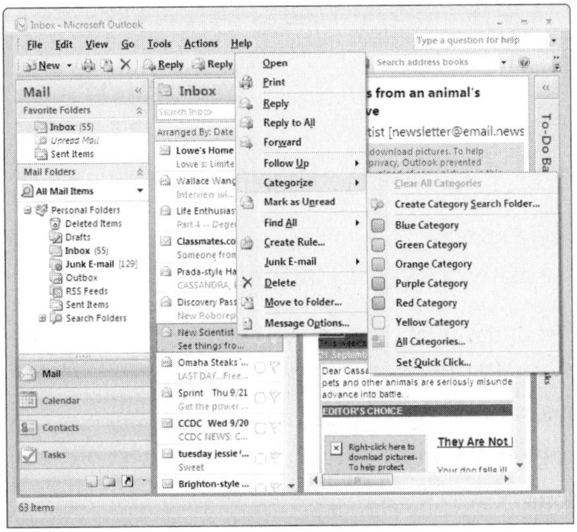

Figure 13-17:
The Categorize submenu lists all the different colors you can choose to categorize a message.

After you color-categorize your messages, you can organize them in groups by choosing View➪Arrange By➪Categories.

Clearing color categories from a message

To clear color categories from a message, follow these steps:

1. **Click a message that contains a color category.**

2. **Choose Actions➪Categorize➪All Categories.**

   The Color Categories dialog box appears, as shown in Figure 13-18.

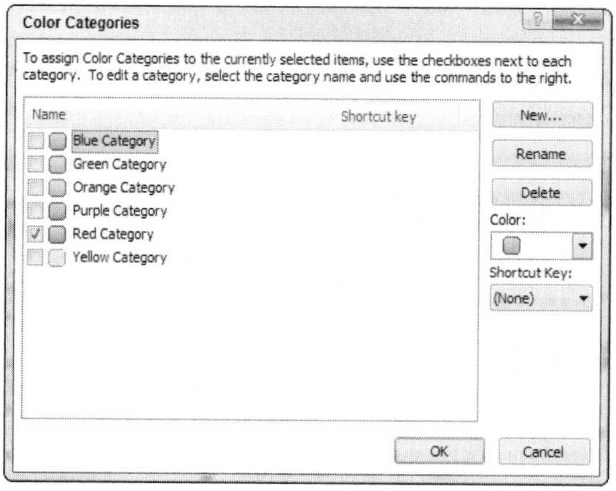

Figure 13-18: The Color Categories dialog box lets you add colors to or remove colors from a message.

3. **Select the check boxes to add or remove a color category from the message you selected in Step 1.**

4. **Click OK.**

If you want to clear color categories from all messages, choose Actions➪ Categorize➪Clear All Categories.

Retrieving a file attachment from a message

Rather than just send text, people might send you pictures, word processor documents, or databases as file attachments. When you receive a message with a file attachment, Outlook displays a paper clip icon next to the message, as shown in Figure 13-19.

Never open a file attachment unless you absolutely trust its contents. Many hackers send viruses, worms, and Trojan Horses as file attachments, so if you're not careful, you could accidentally infect your computer and lose your data.

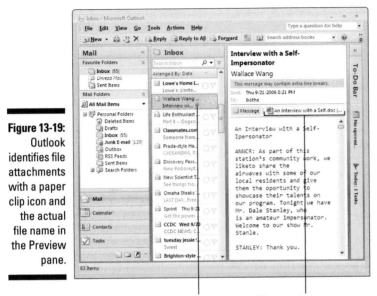

Figure 13-19:
Outlook
identifies file
attachments
with a paper
clip icon and
the actual
file name in
the Preview
pane.

Paper clip icon   File attachment name

To open a file attachment, follow these steps:

1. **Click a message that displays a paper clip icon.**

   Outlook displays the message's contents in the Preview pane along
   with displaying a file icon and the actual file attachment name (refer
   to Figure 13-21).

2. **Double-click the file icon displayed in the message's Preview pane.**

   A dialog box appears, warning you only to open files from a trusted
   source, as shown in Figure 13-20.

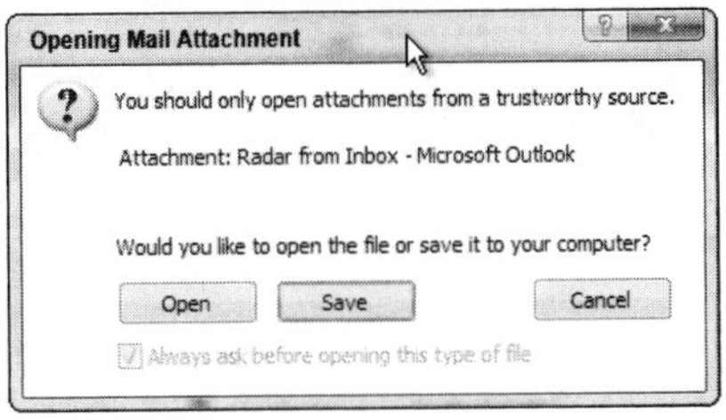

Figure 13-20:
Only open
file attach-
ments if
you're sure
they aren't
harmful.

Opening Mail Attachment

You should only open attachments from a trustworthy source.

Attachment: Radar from Inbox - Microsoft Outlook

Would you like to open the file or save it to your computer?

Open   Save   Cancel

☑ Always ask before opening this type of file

3. **Click Open.**

The Open With dialog box appears, as shown in Figure 13-21.

If you click Save, you can save the file in a folder and examine it with an antivirus or antispyware program before opening it.

Figure 13-21:
The Open
With dialog
box lets you
choose the
program to
open a file
attachment.

4. **Click a program to use and then click OK.**

Another dialog box appears, asking whether you really want to open the file.

5. **Click Yes (or Cancel if you change your mind and don't want to open the file after all).**

Your chosen program loads and displays the contents of the file attachment.

You can often open file attachments using more than one program. If you receive a text file as a file attachment, you can open it using Notepad, WordPad, or Microsoft Word.

Deleting E-Mail Messages

To keep your Inbox folder from getting too cluttered, you can always delete messages that you're sure you'll never need to read again. To delete a message, follow these steps:

1. **Choose Go⇨Mail. (You can also press Ctrl+1 or click the Mail button in the lower-left corner of the Outlook window.)**

   Outlook displays the Mail pane.

2. **Click a message in the Mail pane that you want to delete.**

3. **Press Delete or choose Edit⇨Delete.**

If you accidentally delete the wrong e-mail message, you can undelete it by pressing Ctrl+Z or choosing Edit⇨Undo right away.

When you delete messages, Outlook stores them in the Deleted Items folder so you can always retrieve them later. To retrieve a previously deleted message, follow these steps:

1. **Choose Go⇨Mail. (You can also press Ctrl+1 or click the Mail button in the lower-left corner of the Outlook window.)**

   Outlook displays the Mail pane.

2. **Click the Deleted Items icon in the Mail Folders pane.**

3. **Click a message that you want to retrieve.**

4. **Choose Edit⇨Move to Folder.**

   The Move Items dialog box appears, as shown in Figure 13-22.

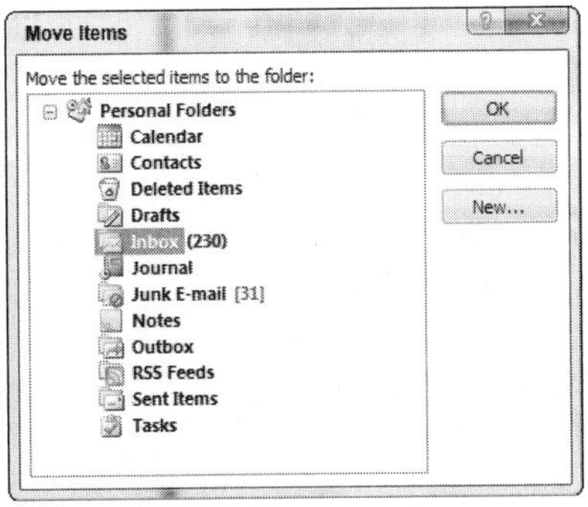

Figure 13-22:
Move an item to another folder.

Move Items

Move the selected items to the folder:

- Personal Folders
  - Calendar
  - Contacts
  - Deleted Items
  - Drafts
  - Inbox (230)
  - Journal
  - Junk E-mail [31]
  - Notes
  - Outbox
  - RSS Feeds
  - Sent Items
  - Tasks

OK   Cancel   New...

5. **Click a folder (such as Inbox) to store your message and then click OK.**

   Outlook removes your message from the Deleted Items folder and stores it in the folder you chose.

If you delete a message from the Deleted Items folder, that message will be gone for good. To clean out your Deleted Items folder (to save space or to destroy incriminating e-mail messages), follow these steps:

1. **Choose Go⇨Mail. (You can also press Ctrl+1 or click the Mail button in the lower-left corner of the Outlook window.)**

   Outlook displays the Mail pane.

2. **Choose one of the following:**

   - *Click a message.*

   - *Choose Edit⇨Select All to select all the messages stored in the Deleted Items folder.*

   - *Hold down the Ctrl key and click each message you want to delete.*

   - *Hold down the Shift key, click the first message you want to delete, and then click the last message you want to delete.*

     Outlook selects all the messages in between the first and last messages you selected.

3. **Press Delete or choose Edit⇨Delete.**

   A dialog box appears, asking whether you're sure you want to delete your selected messages.

   If you delete any messages from the Deleted Items folder, you will not be able to retrieve them ever again for the rest of eternity.

4. **Click Yes (or No).**

Chapter 14

Storing Contacts and Organizing Tasks

In This Chapter

▶ Storing contact information

▶ Searching your contacts

▶ Viewing and printing contacts

▶ Organizing contacts

▶ Sharing contact information

▶ Defining a task

*B*efore computers, most people stored the names and addresses of important people in a Rolodex file. Rolodex files are great for storing names, but it can take time to find those names again.

Obviously, such a clumsy process has no place in today's world. Rather than store names and addresses in a paper file, you can store names and addresses in Outlook. Outlook's biggest advantage is that it can store, sort, and find names and addresses in ways much faster than an ordinary Rolodex file.

If you use a Windows Mobile device, you can synchronize and share your Outlook data between your computer and your PDA (personal digital assistant) so you can keep your list of names and addresses with you at all times (or until you lose your PDA and/or computer).

Storing Contact Information

You can store as much or as little information about each contact as you wish, such as someone's name, e-mail address, street address, work number, home number, cell phone number, fax number, birthday, job title, and Web page address, and add a photograph as well.

To store names and other contact information, follow these steps:

1. **Choose Go⇨Contacts. (You can also click the Contacts button that appears on the left side of the Outlook window or press Ctrl+3.)**

   Outlook displays a list of your current contacts.

2. **Click New.**

   The Contact window appears, as shown in Figure 14-1.

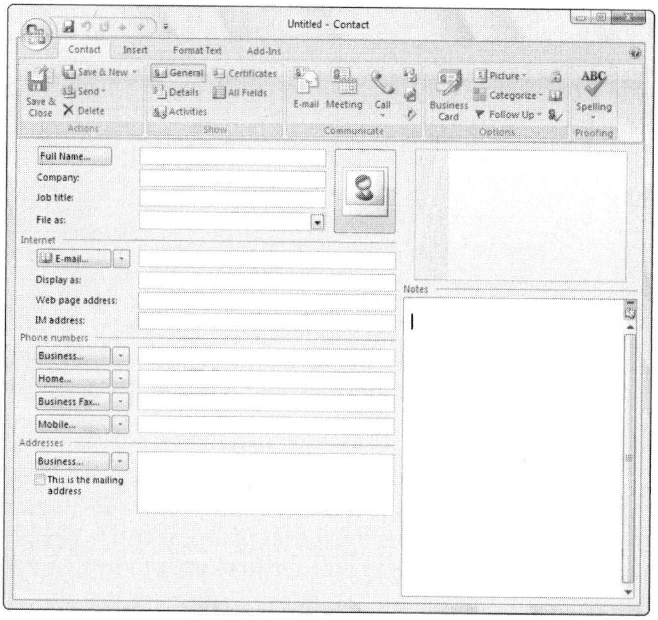

Figure 14-1: The Contact window lets you store names and other information about a person.

3. **Click in the Full Name text box and type a person's name.**

4. **(Optional) Type any additional information that you want to store about a person, such as additional telephone numbers or e-mail addresses.**

5. **Click Save & Close (to save your current contact information) or click Save & New (to save your current contact information and open a new Contact window to store another name).**

   Both the Save & Close and the Save & New icons appear in the Actions group.

Searching Contact Information

After you store names, you may have another problem. How do you find a name without browsing through your entire contact list one by one? Fortunately, you can search your list of contacts by name, by either typing the complete name or part of the name.

To search your list of contacts in Outlook, follow these steps:

1. **Choose Go⇨Contacts.**
2. **Click in the Search Contacts list box, as shown in Figure 14-2.**

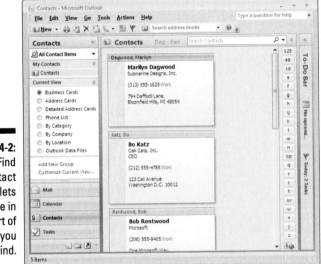

Figure 14-2:
The Find a Contact window lets you type in all or part of a name you want to find.

3. **Type all or part of a name.**

   Type only as many letters in a person's name as you know because if you misspell a name, Outlook won't find it. The more letters you type, the faster Outlook can search and the more likely it will find the name you want.

4. **Press Enter when you've typed as much of the correct spelling of a name as you can.**

   Outlook displays only those names that match the text you typed in Step 3.

5. **Click the name you want and then click OK.**

   Outlook displays your chosen name in the Contact window.

Viewing and Printing Contact Information

Outlook can display your contact list in several different views, such as showing only names and phone numbers or showing names and street addresses along with phone numbers and e-mail addresses.

After you find a view that you like, you can edit individual names or print your entire contact list. To display and print your contact list, follow these steps:

1. **Choose Go⇨Contacts.**

2. **Choose View⇨Current View (or click the Current View pane on the left side) to view the list of different viewing options displayed as radio buttons, such as Business Cards or Address Cards. (If this list is already visible, skip this step.)**

3. **Select the radio button to choose how to display your contacts, such as Business Cards.**

   Outlook displays your contacts in your chosen style, as shown in Figure 14-3.

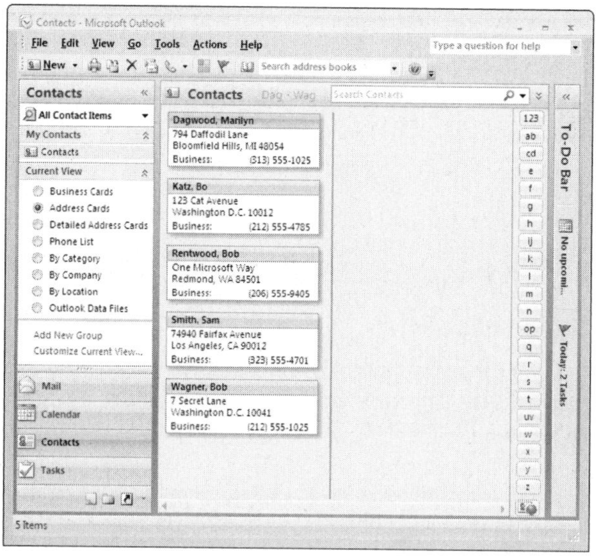

Figure 14-3: Changing how you view contacts can show you as much or as little information as you choose.

4. **Double-click a contact to open it in the Contact window so you can edit it. Then click the Save & Close icon when you're done.**

5. **Choose File⇨Print Preview.**

   Outlook shows you what your contact list will look like when printed, as shown in Figure 14-4.

6. **Click Print.**

If you just want to print information from a single contact, right-click that contact and choose Print.

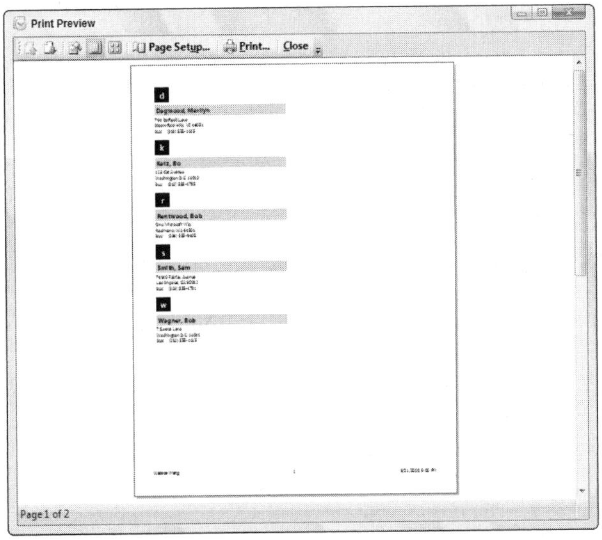

Figure 14-4:
The Print Preview window lets you see how your contact list will look before you print.

Categorizing Contact Information

If you collect enough names, your contact list may soon get unwieldy with both personal and business contact information jumbled together. To help you sort out your contact list, you can assign each contact to one or more categories.

For example, one category may be Personal Friends while another may be Customers. (You can assign a contact to multiple categories, too, such as putting someone's entry under both the Personal Friends and Customers categories.)

Creating categories

Before you organize your contacts into categories, you need to define your different categories. Outlook creates default categories that are color-coded and named Blue Category or Red Category, but you'll need to customize these categories for your own use.

To create your own categories, follow these steps:

1. **Choose Go⇨Contacts.**

2. **Click a contact.**

3. **Choose Actions⇨Categorize.**

   A menu appears, as shown in Figure 14-5.

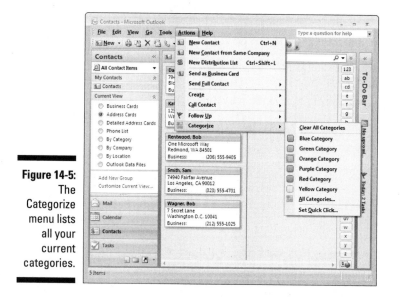

Figure 14-5: The Categorize menu lists all your current categories.

4. **Choose All Categories.**

   The Color Categories dialog box appears, as shown in Figure 14-6.

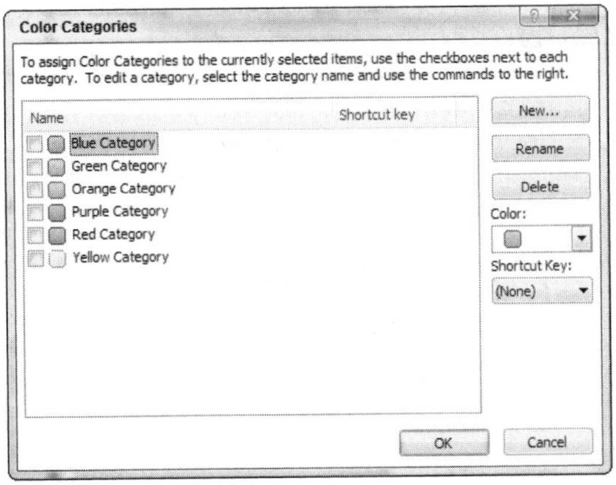

Figure 14-6:
The Color
Categories
dialog box
lets you
rename
your
category
names.

5. **Click a category (such as Blue Category) and then click the Rename button.**

   Outlook highlights the category name.

6. **Type a new name for your category, such as** Friends **or** Customers, **and then press Enter.**

7. **Repeat Steps 5 and 6 for each category you want to rename.**

8. **Click OK.**

Storing names in categories

After you give distinct names to your categories, you can assign names to one or more categories to help you search through your data.

To organize names into categories, follow these steps:

1. **Choose Go⇨Contacts.**

2. **Choose Actions⇨Categorize.**

   A menu appears listing all your available categories.

3. **Select the check box of a category.**

   Repeat this step for each additional category you want to assign the contact.

Viewing names by categories

After you assign names to different categories, you can view them organized in different categories by following these steps:

1. **Choose Go⇨Contacts.**

2. **Choose View⇨Current View to display a list of different categories, such as Phone List or By Category.**

3. **Click By Category.**

   Outlook displays your contacts organized into categories, as shown in Figure 14-7.

Figure 14-7: Categories divide your contact list into smaller, more manageable lists of related names.

Sharing Contact Information

You may have the name and address of someone like the president and want to share this information with someone else. You could just print this data and force that other person to retype all this information back into their computer all over again.

Obviously, this is a clumsy solution, so Outlook offers another way to share your contact information with others:

- ✔ As a vCard
- ✔ As an Outlook file

The *vCard* format is a standard for storing names and addresses, which many personal information-organizing programs can import. If you need to share your Outlook data with someone who isn't using Outlook, you need to store and share your data as a vCard.

If you're sharing information with someone who also uses Outlook, you can store your data as an Outlook file. Whichever format you choose (vCard or Outlook format), you can then e-mail the contact information to someone else.

To share contact information, follow these steps:

1. **Choose Go⇨Contacts.**

2. **Click the contact you want to share.**

3. **Choose Actions⇨Send Full Contact.**

   A pop-up menu appears.

4. **Choose either In vCard Format or In Outlook Format.**

   An e-mail window appears.

5. **Click in the To text box and type an e-mail address.**

6. **Click Send.**

   Outlook sends your contact information to your chosen recipient.

Defining Tasks

To help you stay focused on the important tasks you need to accomplish for each day, Outlook lets you create a to-do list. By using this list, you can see what you need to do (and get a sense of accomplishment when you can cross it off your list).

Creating a task

A *task* typically defines some action with a definite, measurable ending such as *Finish writing monthly report* or *Embezzle another $20,000 for the weekend.* To create a task, follow these steps:

1. **Choose Go⇨Tasks (or click the Tasks button that appears to the left of the Outlook window, or press Ctrl+4).**

2. **Chose Actions⇨New Task (or press Ctrl+N).**

   An empty task window appears, as shown in Figure 14-8.

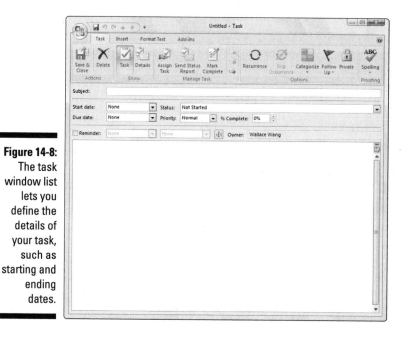

Figure 14-8: The task window list lets you define the details of your task, such as starting and ending dates.

3. **Click in the Subject text box and type a brief description of your task.**

4. **Click in the Due Date list box. (Skip Steps 4–9 if you don't want to choose a due date and a starting date.)**

   A downward-pointing arrow appears.

5. **Click the downward-pointing arrow.**

   A calendar appears.

6. **Click a due date.**

   Outlook displays your chosen date next to your task.

7. **Click in the Start Date list box.**

   A downward-pointing arrow appears.

8. **Click the downward-pointing arrow.**

   A calendar appears.

9. **Click a start date.**

   Outlook displays your chosen start date.

10. **Click in the text box below and type any additional details you want to write about your task.**

11. **Click the Save & Close icon in the Actions group.**

    Outlook closes the task window.

Editing a task

After you create a task, you can edit it later to set a reminder or track how much of the task you've completed. To edit a task, follow these steps:

1. **Choose Go⇨Contacts.**

2. **Choose View⇨Current View⇨Simple List.**

   Outlook displays a list of your tasks.

3. **Double-click a task (or click on a task and press Ctrl+O).**

   A task window appears (refer to Figure 14-8).

4. **Choose one or more of the following:**

   - *Click the Status list box and choose a status for your task, such as In Progress, Completed, or Waiting on Someone Else.* A task's status shows you how each task is progressing (or not progressing); this feature helps you manage time more effectively.

   - *Click the Priority list box and choose Low, Normal, or High.* When categorizing tasks by priority, you can identify the ones that really need to get done and the ones that you can safely ignore and hope they go away.

   - *Click the % Complete list box* to specify how much of the task you've already completed.

   - *Select the Reminder check box and specify a date and time* for Outlook to remind you of this particular task. If you click the Alarm button (it looks like a megaphone), you can specify a unique sound that Outlook plays to remind you of your task.

   - *Type your task in more detail in the big text box at the bottom of the task window.*

5. **Click the Save & Close icon in the Actions group.**

Organizing and viewing your tasks

Listing your tasks may be useful, but if you have a particularly long list of tasks (which means you either have a lot of work or you're falling way behind), you can rearrange your task list to display tasks based on their due date (such as overdue tasks, tasks that should be done within the next seven days, tasks that are already completed, and so on).

To view your task list in different ways, follow these steps:

1. **Choose Go⇨Tasks.**

2. **Choose View⇨Current View.**

   Outlook displays a list of different options such as Detailed List or Overdue Tasks, as shown in Figure 14-9.

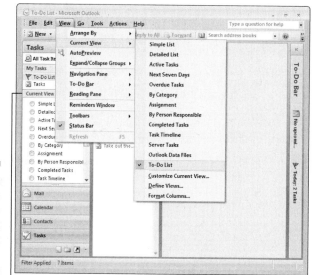

Figure 14-9: Outlook can organize your task list in different categories.

Current View tab

You can also click the Current View tab and select a radio button to choose a different way to view your tasks.

3. **Select the way you want to view your list, such as Active Tasks or Assignment.**

   Outlook changes the appearance of your task list. (The default task list style is Simple List.)

Finishing a task

Despite that natural tendency to procrastinate, many people actually do complete the tasks they set for themselves. To tell Outlook that you've joined this elite group, select the check box of the task you completed, as shown in Figure 14-10. Outlook displays a check mark in the check box, dims the task, and draws a line through the task.

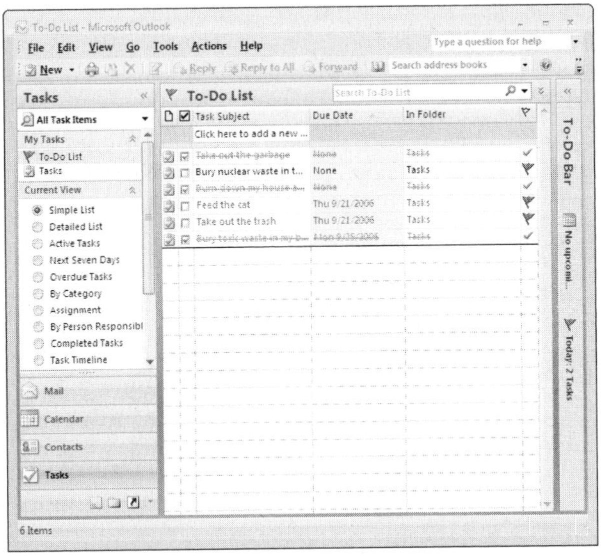

Figure 14-10: To give you a sense of accomplishment, you can check off all your completed tasks.

Deleting a task

After you complete a task (or just decide to ignore it permanently), you may want to delete it from Outlook so it doesn't clutter up your screen. Here's how:

1. **Choose Go⇨Tasks.**

2. **Choose View⇨Current View.**

   Outlook displays a list of different options, such as Detailed List or Overdue Tasks (see Figure 14-10).

3. **Click a task.**

4. **Choose Edit⇨Delete, press Ctrl+D, or click the Delete icon on the toolbar.**

   Outlook deletes your chosen task.

If you delete a task by mistake, press Ctrl+Z right away, and Outlook kindly retrieves it for you.

Chapter 15

Scheduling Your Time

. . . .

In This Chapter

▶ Setting an appointment

▶ Editing an appointment

▶ Creating a recurring appointment

▶ Printing your schedule

. . . .

*H*ow you spend your time directly determines the quality of your life. To help you spend your time wisely (or at least spend it on the tasks you want to accomplish first, whether it's wise to do so or not), you can use Outlook as your electronic Day-Timer. The key to scheduling your time is to first put down all the tasks that are most important to you, and then fill in the gaps with the less-important tasks (like the stuff you're supposed to be doing at work). In this way, you can always be sure that you set aside time for your crucial tasks first.

Setting Appointments

If you're not careful, you can overload yourself with so many appointments that you never have time to do any work, which may not be so bad if you don't like your job anyway. So to help you sort out your appointments and keep them handy, Outlook keeps track of your busy and free time.

Making a new appointment

Outlook lets you schedule appointments for tomorrow or (if you prefer the long view) decades in advance. To make an appointment in Outlook, follow these steps:

1. **Choose Go⇨Calendar (or press Ctrl+2, or click the Calendar button).**

   Calendar view appears.

2. **Click the Month tab to display the monthly calendar, as shown in Figure 15-1.**

Figure 15-1:
The monthly
Calendar
view in
Outlook.

3. **Click the day that you want to schedule an appointment.**

   Outlook displays the Day calendar view, as shown in Figure 15-2.

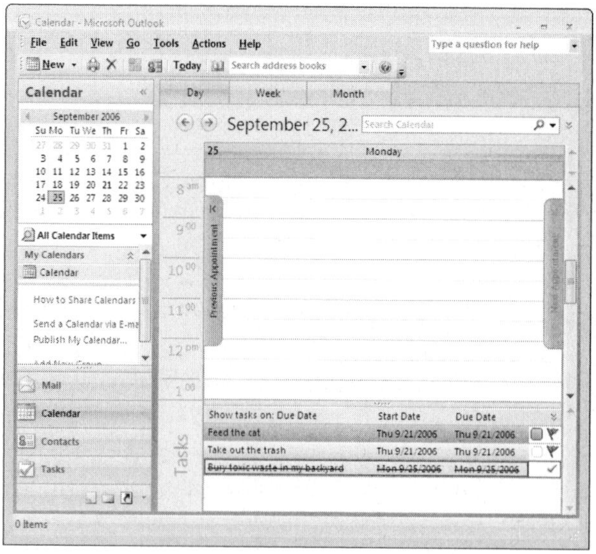

Figure 15-2:
Day view
lets you see
the day
divided into
half-hour
segments.

4. **Double-click a time, such as 10:00.**

The Appointment window appears, as shown in Figure 15-3.

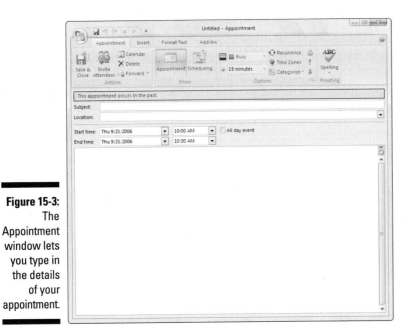

Figure 15-3:
The
Appointment
window lets
you type in
the details
of your
appointment.

5. **Click in the Subject text box and type a brief description of your appointment, such as** Another boring meeting with Mike **or** Meet with reluctant client**.**

6. **(Optional) Click in the Location text box and type the location of your appointment, such as** Break Room 10 **or** Back alley near the dumpster**.**

If you often set appointments for specific locations, Outlook will remember these locations. In the future, just click the downward-pointing arrow in the Location text box and then click a previously used location in the list that appears.

7. **Click in the second Start Time list box and choose a time. (You can also type a time directly in the Start time list box, such as** 9:53**.)**

8. **Click in the second End Time list box and choose a time. (You can also type a time directly in the End time list box, such as** 2:23**.)**

9. **Click in the big text box and type any additional information you want to store about your appointment, such as items you need to bring or information you want to remind yourself about the person you're meeting.**

10. **Click the Save & Close icon in the Actions group.**

    Outlook displays your appointment in Day, Week, or Month view of the calendar, as shown in Figure 15-4.

Editing an appointment

After you create an appointment, you may want to edit it to change the appointment location, the subject, the starting and ending times, and whether Outlook should beep a reminder before you risk missing the appointment altogether.

To edit an appointment in Outlook, follow these steps:

1. **Choose Go⇨Calendar.**

   Outlook displays calendar view.

2. **Click the Day or Week tab.**

3. **Double-click the appointment you want to modify. (You may need to scroll through the window to find the appointment you want to modify.)**

   The Appointment window appears.

4. **Follow Steps 5–10 in the preceding section, "Making a new appointment," to finish editing your appointment.**

Deleting an appointment

After an appointment has passed or been canceled, you can delete it to make room for other appointments. To delete an appointment, follow these steps:

1. **Choose Go⇨Calendar.**

   Outlook displays calendar view.

2. **Click the Day, Week, or Month tab.**

3. **Click the appointment that you want to delete.**

4. **Choose Edit⇨Delete (or press Ctrl+D).**

   Outlook deletes your appointment.

If you delete an appointment by mistake, press Ctrl+Z to recover it.

Defining a recurring appointment

A *recurring* appointment occurs regularly such as every day, week, month, or year (such as going to lunch with the boss on the first Monday of the month). Instead of typing in recurring appointments again and again, you can enter them once and then define how often they occur. Outlook automatically schedules those appointments unless you specifically tell it otherwise.

To create a recurring appointment, follow these steps:

1. **Follow Steps 1–9 in the earlier section, "Making a new appointment."**

2. **Click the Recurrence button.**

   The Appointment Recurrence dialog box appears, as shown in Figure 15-5.

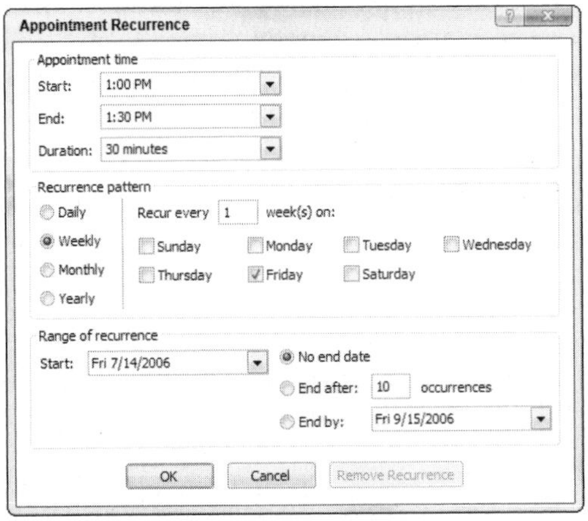

Figure 15-5:
The Appointment Recurrence dialog box lets you define how often your appointment occurs.

Appointment Recurrence		

Appointment time

Start: 1:00 PM

End: 1:30 PM

Duration: 30 minutes

Recurrence pattern

○ Daily   Recur every 1 week(s) on:

● Weekly   ☐ Sunday ☐ Monday ☐ Tuesday ☐ Wednesday

○ Monthly   ☐ Thursday ☑ Friday ☐ Saturday

○ Yearly

Range of recurrence

Start: Fri 7/14/2006   ● No end date

     ○ End after: 10 occurrences

     ○ End by: Fri 9/15/2006

OK   Cancel   Remove Recurrence

3. **Click in the Start list box in the Appointment Time group and choose a start time.**

4. **Choose one of the following:**

    • Click in the End list box and choose an ending time.

    • Click in the Duration list box and choose the length of time, such as 2 hours.

5. **Select a radio button in the Recurrence Pattern group, such as the Daily or Weekly radio button.**

6. **Click in the Start list box in the Range of Recurrence group and choose a date when your recurring appointment begins.**

7. **Choose one of the following radio buttons:**

    • *No End Date:* The recurring appointment will appear on your calendar forever.

    • *End After:* This lets you type how many times the appointment occurs, such as 10.

    • *End By:* This lets you choose a specific date to stop the appointment from occurring.

8. **Click OK.**

9. **Click the Save & Close icon in the Actions group.**

Editing a recurring appointment

If you want to edit a recurring appointment, you have two choices. First, you can edit just a single instance of a recurring appointment. When you edit a single occurrence of a recurring appointment, any future occurrences of that same appointment remain unchanged.

If you edit the series of recurring appointments, all future occurrences of that appointment will reflect your changes. To edit a recurring appointment, follow these steps:

1. **Choose Go⇨Calendar.**

    Outlook displays calendar view.

2. **Click the Day, Week, or Month tab.**

3. **Double-click the recurring appointment that you want to edit.**

   The Open Recurring Item dialog box appears, as shown in Figure 15-6.

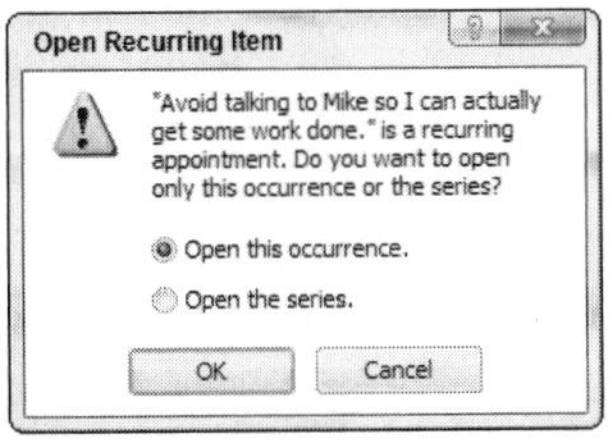

Figure 15-6:
Edit just this
occurrence
or the entire
series.

4. **Select one of the following radio buttons and then click OK to view the Appointment window:**

   • Open This Occurrence

   • Open the Series

5. **Make any changes to your appointment and then click the Save & Close icon in the Actions group when you're done.**

TIP

If you click the Recurrence button, Outlook displays the Appointment Recurrence dialog box (refer to Figure 15-5). If you click the Remove Recurrence button, you can stop your appointment from recurring on a regular basis.

Printing Your Schedule

Unless you carry a laptop computer around all day, you may occasionally need to print your appointment schedule on paper so you can look at it without using electricity or copy it for all your fans and relatives. To print your appointments, follow these steps:

1. **Choose Go⇨Calendar.**

   Outlook displays your calendar.

2. **Click the Day, Week, or Month tab.**

3. **Choose File⇨Print Preview.**

   The Print Preview window appears, as shown in Figure 15-7.

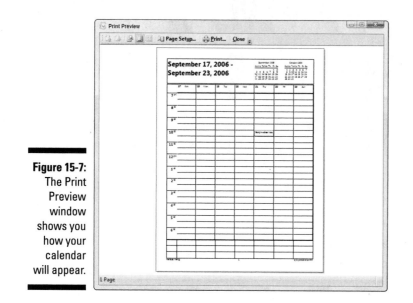

Figure 15-7:
The Print
Preview
window
shows you
how your
calendar
will appear.

4. **Click the Print button.**

The Print dialog box appears, as shown in Figure 15-8.

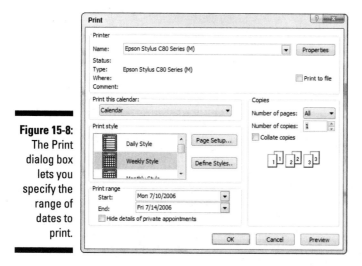

Figure 15-8:
The Print
dialog box
lets you
specify the
range of
dates to
print.

5. **Click in the Start and End list boxes under the Print Range group and define the start and end dates to print your appointments.**

6. **Click OK to start printing.**

Part VI
Storing Stuff in Access

The 5th Wave   By Rich Tennant

"Yes, I know how to query information from the program, but what if I just want to leak it instead?"

In this part . . .

Personal computers provide an excellent tool for storing large chunks of information in databases so you don't have to store this same information in filing cabinets. Databases can not only store huge amounts of data, they can also sort and search through that data, which makes them particularly valuable to businesses that need to track their customers, inventories, or assets. So it's no surprise that the more advanced (and expensive) versions of Microsoft Office 2007 include a special database program called (what's in a name?) Access.

For those of you who enjoy deciphering computer terminology, Access is a relational database. For those of you who prefer English, the previous sentence means that Access lets you store lots of stuff in a variety of ways so you can find it again — fast — when you need it.

This part of the book gets you started storing stuff in Access. The goal is to get you feeling comfortable enough to create databases with Access so you can store great huge stockpiles of useful information in your computer.

Chapter 16

Using a Database

In This Chapter

▶ Understanding how databases work

▶ Designing a database

▶ Editing a database

▶ Typing information into a database

▶ Closing a database

A database is nothing more than a program to store useful bits of information such as names, addresses, and phone numbers, or inventory part numbers, shipping dates, customer codes, and any other type of information that you think is worth storing.

To help you store information in a database, Office 2007 comes with the database program, *Access.* Access provides two huge advantages over storing information on paper. First, Access can store literally billions of chunks of information (try doing that with a Rolodex file or a filing cabinet). Second, Access makes it easy to search and sort through your information in the blink of an eye.

The three main advantages of a computer database over a paper database are

- ✔ **Massive storage:** The largest computer database can fit on a hard disk, but a paper database might take a roomful of file cabinets.

- ✔ **Fast retrieval:** Searching for a single name in a computer database is fast and easy. Doing the same thing in a paper database is difficult, error prone, and nearly impossible with a large database.

- ✔ **Reporting:** A *report* can help you make sense out of your data, such as showing a list of customers who earn a certain amount of money and live in a specific area. Trying to find this information in a paper database is time consuming and error prone.

Understanding the Basics of a Database

A database is nothing more than a file that contains useful information that you need to save and retrieve in the future. A database can consist of a single name and address, or several million names and addresses.

A typical Access database file consists of several parts:

- ✔ **Fields:** A *field* contains a single chunk of information such as name, street address, or phone number.

- ✔ **Records:** A *record* consists of one or more fields. A business card is a paper version of a database record that stores fields (name, address, phone number, and so on) about a single person (record).

- ✔ **Tables:** A *table* displays records in rows and columns, much like a spreadsheet. Tables group related records, such as records of all your customers or records of all your invoices.

- ✔ **Forms:** A *form* displays all the fields of a single record onscreen, mimicking a paper form, so that you can add, edit, or view a single record at a time.

- ✔ **Queries:** A *query* lets you retrieve certain information based on your criteria such as only retrieving names and addresses of people who earn more than $50,000 a year and have children.

- ✔ **Reports:** A *report* arranges your data in a certain way, such as showing all customers who placed over 1,000 orders last year or all customers who live within a certain ZIP code.

Access is known as a *relational* database. Basically, this means you can store data in separate tables and link or "relate" them together to avoid duplicating data in multiple tables. One table might contain customer names and addresses while a separate, related table might contain those same customers' purchase orders.

Here are the two basic steps to using a database. First, you need to design your database, which means deciding what type of information your database will hold, such as names, addresses, e-mail addresses, telephone numbers, and so on.

After you design a database, the second step is filling it with actual data, such as typing the name **Bob Jones** in the Name field or the e-mail address **BJones@somecompany.com** in the E-mail field.

The whole purpose of a database is to store information you need to retrieve in the future, such as names and phone numbers of customers. For example, there's no point in storing the fax number for people if you'll never need to send them a fax.

When you first create a database, you'll probably start out with a single table that contains customer information. Inside the Customer Information table will be multiple records where each record represents a single customer. Each record will consist of multiple fields such as First Name, Company Name, Phone Number, and E-mail Address.

To help you edit and view your database table information, you might eventually want to create a form that displays your fields on the screen mimicking a paper form that's easy to read.

If you find yourself searching for the same type of information on a regular basis, such as looking for the names of your best customers (those who order more than $1,000 worth of products from you a week), you can store this search criteria as a query. Then you can just click on the query name and make Access show you exactly what you want to find.

Finally, you may want to print out your data in a way that makes sense to you, such as printing a quarterly sales report. By saving your printing criteria in a report, you can make Access print out selected data on a page that's easy for you to read and understand.

Features like forms, queries, and reports are optional but handy. Features like tables, records, and fields are necessary to store your information in your database.

Designing a Database

To design a database, you need to first create a database table and then define the names of all the fields you want to store in that particular table. Database tables let you divide a file into separate parts. For example, one database table may hold the names and addresses of all your customers, a second database table may hold the names and addresses of all your employees, and a third database table may hold the names and addresses of your suppliers. Access stores all this related information in a single Access file that's saved on your hard disk, as illustrated in Figure 16-1.

To design your database, you can create a database from scratch or use an existing template, which you can modify. *Designing* a database means defining both the number of fields to use for storing information and the maximum amount of data each field can hold.

If you have a field that stores last names, what is the maximum number of characters you want the field to hold? If you make the field hold too few characters, people with long last names (maybe they're hyphenated) won't be able to enter their entire name. Conversely, if you make the field hold too many characters, you waste storage space.

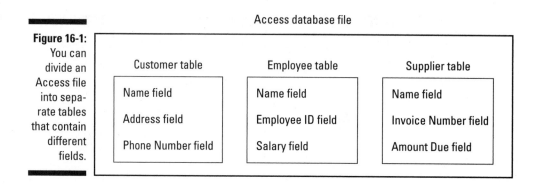

Access database file

Figure 16-1:
You can
divide an
Access file
into sepa-
rate tables
that contain
different
fields.

Customer table

Name field

Address field

Phone Number field

Employee table

Name field

Employee ID field

Salary field

Supplier table

Name field

Invoice Number field

Amount Due field

Similarly, if you have a field that stores numbers, what are the maximum and minimum limits on the numbers you want to save in that field? If you're storing someone's age, you probably don't want the field to contain negative numbers or numbers beyond 200. If your field needs to hold salaries, the field may need to hold large numbers but no negative numbers.

In general, store information in separate fields. So rather than create a single field to hold someone's full name, create two separate fields: One field holds a first name, and the second field holds the last name. By storing last names in a separate field, you can easily yank last names out of your database to create form letters that state, "The Smith family has just won $20,000 dollars in the Publisher's Sales Pitch Sweepstakes!"

Creating a database from scratch

Access can create a blank database or a database using one of many templates available from the Microsoft Web site. No matter how you create a database, you will likely need to modify it to customize it for the type of data you want to store.

To create a blank database, follow these steps:

1. **Click the Office Button and choose New.**

   The Getting Started with Microsoft Access screen appears.

2. **Click the Blank Database icon.**

   The File Name text box appears in the right corner of the screen, as shown in Figure 16-2.

3. **Type a descriptive filename for your database.**

   You may want to click the Browse icon to specify a different folder or drive to store your database.

Figure 16-2:
When you create a blank database, you can give it a descriptive filename.

4. **Click Create.**

Access displays a blank table and an Add New Field text box, as shown in Figure 16-3. Displaying your database in rows and columns is *Datasheet view.*

When you create a database, Access automatically creates a special ID field to help you sort and organize your data. (You don't have to use this ID field if you don't want to.)

Figure 16-3:
To design a database, you need to define all the fields used to store information in a table.

Creating a database from a template

Just like it's easier to copy someone else's work, it's easier to use an existing database template and modify it for your own needs.

REMEMBER

You need an Internet connection to retrieve any database templates from the Microsoft Web site.

To create a database file from a template, follow these steps:

1. **Click the Office Button and choose New.**

   The Getting Started with Microsoft Access screen appears.

2. **Click a category under the From Microsoft Office Online category, such as Business or Education.**

   A list of available templates appears, as shown in Figure 16-4.

3. **Click a template.**

   Access displays a default name in the File Name text box in the bottom-right corner of the screen.

4. **Type a descriptive name for your database in the File Name text box and then click Create.**

   Access displays your database in rows and columns *(Datasheet view)*.

Figure 16-4:
Each category of templates offers a variety of database designs you can choose from.

Editing and Modifying a Database

After you create a database from scratch or from a template, you need to modify it by giving each field a descriptive name, defining the size of each field, or adding and deleting a field.

Naming a field

If you create a database from scratch, Access displays generic field names such as *Field1*. If you create a database from a template, you'll see the descriptive field names, but you may still want to rename the fields to something else.

To rename a field, follow these steps:

1. **Click the Office Button and then choose Open.**

   The Open dialog box appears.

2. **Click the Access database file you want to modify and then click Open.**

   Access displays your chosen database.

3. **In the All Tables pane on the left of the screen, double-click the table that contains the fields you want to rename.**

   Access displays the Datasheet view of your database.

4. **Click the Datasheet tab.**

5. **Click the field (column head) that you want to rename.**

6. **Click the Rename icon in the Fields & Columns group.**

   Access highlights the field name.

7. **Type a new name for your field and then click outside the field name when you're done.**

Adding and deleting a field

Sometimes you may need to add a field to make room to store new information. Other times, you may want to delete a field that you don't really want after all. To add a field to a database table, follow these steps:

1. **Click an existing field in your database table.**

2. **Click the Datasheet tab.**

3. **Click the Insert button in the Fields & Columns group.**

   Access inserts a new field (column) in your database table.

To delete a field from a database table, follow these steps:

1. Click the field you want to delete.

Access highlights the entire column in your database table.

2. Click the Datasheet tab.

3. Click the Delete button in the Fields & Columns group.

A dialog box appears, asking whether you want to permanently delete all the data in the field, as shown in Figure 16-5.

If you delete a field, you also delete any data that may be stored in that field. Depending on how much data you have stored, you could wipe out a lot of information by deleting a single field, so be careful.

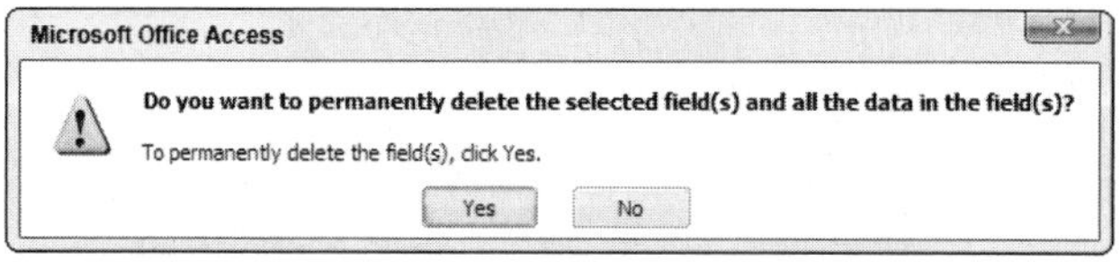

Figure 16-5:
Deleting a field also deletes any data in that field.

Microsoft Office Access

Do you want to permanently delete the selected field(s) and all the data in the field(s)?

To permanently delete the field(s), click Yes.

Yes   No

4. Click Yes (or No).

If you click Yes, Access deletes your chosen field.

Defining the type and size of a field

The *type* of a field defines the type of data the field can hold (numbers, text, dates, and so on), and the *size* of a field defines the amount of data the field can hold (no numbers larger than 250 digits, any text string fewer than 120 characters, and so on).

The purpose of defining the type and size of a field is to make sure you store only valid data in a particular field. If a field is meant to store names, you don't want someone typing in a number. If a field is meant to store a person's age, you don't want the field to accept negative numbers.

To define the type and amount of a data a field can store, follow these steps:

1. Click the Home or Datasheet tab.

2. **In the All Tables pane on the left of the screen, double-click the table that contains the fields you want to define.**

   Access displays the Datasheet view of your table.

3. **Click the downward-pointing arrow underneath the View icon, which appears in the Views group.**

   A pull-down menu appears.

4. **Click Design View.**

   Access displays the Design view of your database table, as shown in Figure 16-6.

5. **(Optional) Click in the Field Name column and edit an existing field name.**

   If you click in a blank row, you can add a field to a database table.

6. **Click in the Data Type column.**

   A downward-pointing arrow appears.

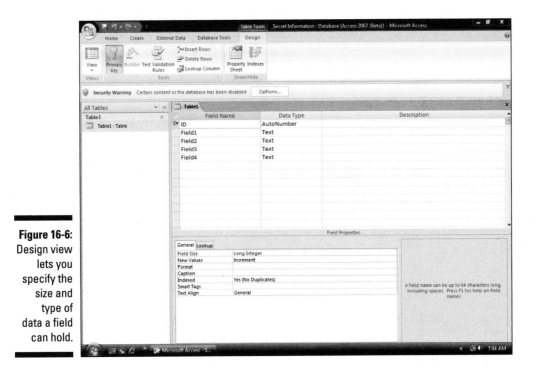

Figure 16-6: Design view lets you specify the size and type of data a field can hold.

7. **Click the downward-pointing arrow.**

A pull-down menu appears, listing all the different types of data you can define to store in a field, as shown in Figure 16-7.

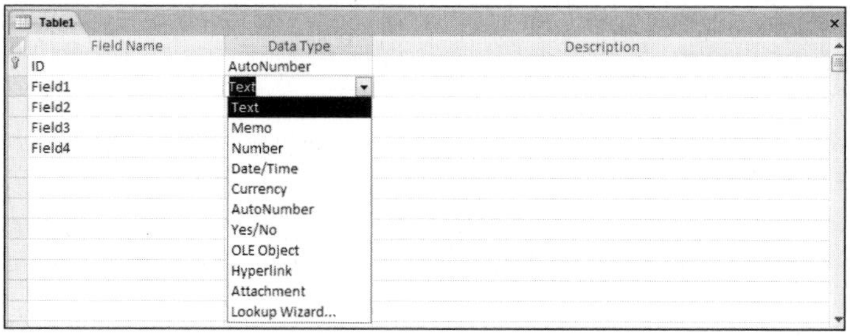

Figure 16-7:
You can choose a specific data type to make sure a field stores the correct information.

8. **Choose a data type, such as Number, Text, or Date/Time.**

Access displays a General tab that contains different options for modifying your chosen data type, as shown in Figure 16-8.

Figure 16-8:
The General tab displays options for modifying your data type.

9. **Click one of the data type options, such as Format or Input Mask, listed under the General tab.**

Sometimes you have to type a value directly into a data type option. Other times a pull-down menu appears, from which you can choose an option.

10. **Repeat Step 9 for each data type option you want to modify.**

You do not need to modify every data type option.

Typing Data into a Database

After you create a database table and define fields within that table to hold chunks of information, you're ready to type in actual names, phone numbers, and e-mail addresses into each field. Access gives you two ways to enter data:

✔ Through Datasheet view

✔ Through Form view

Datasheet view displays information in rows and columns, where each row represents a single record and each column defines a specific field name. Datasheet view can be especially handy for examining multiple records at once.

Form view displays all the fields of a single record onscreen. Form view is most useful when you just need to view or edit a single record, such as typing in the phone number of your cousin or boss.

Using Datasheet view

Datasheet view is the default view for entering data. To view and enter data in Datasheet view, follow these steps:

1. **Click the Office Button and then choose Open.**

   The Open dialog box appears.

2. **Click the Access database file you want to add or edit data in, and then click Open.**

   Access displays your chosen database.

3. **In the All Tables pane on the left of the screen, double-click a table.**

   Access displays the Datasheet view of your table.

4. **Click in a field defined by the column and row.**

   Each column defines a field, such as a name or address. Each row represents a single record.

   If you click in a field that already contains data, you can edit or delete that data.

5. **Press Tab to select the next field (or Shift+Tab to select the previous field).**

6. **Type or edit the data in the field.**

Using Form view

The biggest problem with Datasheet view is that it can be confusing to find a field for a specific record. Because most people are familiar with paper forms or index cards that arrange related data (fields) on a page, Access offers you Form view.

Form view simply displays the fields of a single record onscreen. To use Form view, you must first create a form and arrange your fields on that form. After you create a form, you can add, edit, and view data through that form.

Creating a form

The simplest way to create a form is to let Access design one for you, which you can modify. To create a form quickly, follow these steps:

1. **Click the Office Button and then choose Open.**

   The Open dialog box appears.

2. **Click the Access database file you want to add or edit data. Then click Open.**

   Access displays your chosen database.

3. **In the All Tables pane on the left of the screen, double-click a table.**

   Access displays the Datasheet view of your database.

4. **Click the Create tab.**

5. **Click the Form icon in the Forms group.**

   Access creates a form as shown in Figure 16-9. Notice that the form name automatically uses the name of the database table you chose in Step 3.

6. **Click the Office Button and then choose Save (or click the Save icon on the Quick Access toolbar).**

   The Save As dialog box appears, asking you to type a name for your form, as shown in Figure 16-10.

7. **Type a descriptive name for your form in the Form Name text box and then click OK.**

   Access displays your form's name underneath the All Tables pane. The next time you open this database and want to view the form, you can double-click the form's name in the left pane.

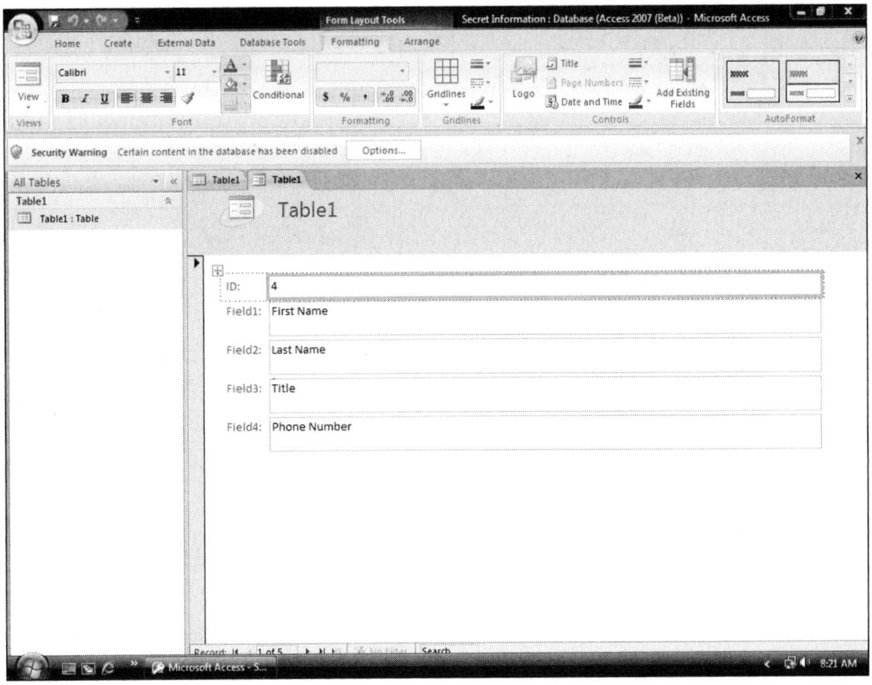

Figure 16-9: Form view displays multiple fields of a single record.

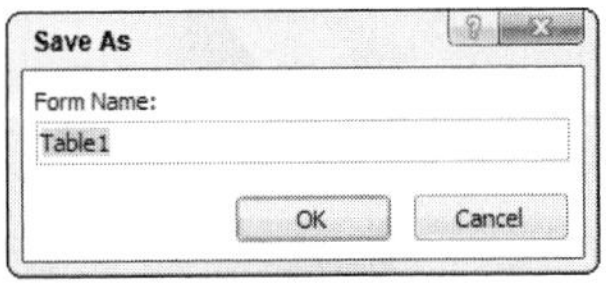

Figure 16-10: Name your form in the Save As dialog box.

Viewing and editing data in a form

After you create a form, you can use it to edit and add data at any time. To view a form, follow these steps:

1. **Click the Office Button and then choose Open.**

   The Open dialog box appears.

2. **Click the Access database file you want to add or edit data. Then click Open.**

   Access displays your chosen database.

3. **In the All Tables pane on the left of the screen, double-click the name of the form you want to use.**

   Access displays the Form view of your database.

4. **Click one of the following icons to display a record:**

   • *First Record:* Displays the first record stored in your file

   • *Previous Record:* Displays the previous record in the file

   • *Next Record:* Displays the next record in the file

   • *Last Record:* Displays the last record that contains data

   • *New (Blank) Record:* Displays a blank form so you can type in data that will create a new record in your file

5. **Click in a field and type the information you want to store, such as a name or phone number.**

You don't need to use the Save command to save your changes because Access automatically saves any data you add or edit in your file as soon as you type or edit the data and move the cursor to a new field or record.

Editing a form

A form can be a convenient way to view all the fields of a single record. However, you can always rearrange the position of certain fields onscreen (to make them easier to find), or you can delete one or more fields altogether. This can be handy to create a form that shows only a filtered view of your data, such as a form that shows you only employee names, phone numbers, and e-mail addresses rather than also showing you their salary and employee ID number at the same time.

Deleting a field

If you delete a field from a form, you simply prevent the form from displaying any data stored in that field. For example, if you don't want to see each person's hire date, you can delete the Hire Date field from your form.

Deleting a field on a form doesn't erase any data; it just keeps you from seeing that data on a particular form.

To delete a field from a form, follow these steps:

1. **Click the Office Button and then choose Open.**

   The Open dialog box appears.

2. **Click the Access database file you want to add or edit data. Then click Open.**

   Access displays your chosen database.

3. **In the All Tables pane on the left of the screen, double-click the name of the form you want to use.**

   Access displays the Form view of your database.

4. **Click the Home tab.**

5. **Click the downward-pointing arrow underneath the View icon in the Views group.**

   A pull-down menu appears.

6. **Choose Design View.**

   Access shows your chosen form in Design view, which displays a background grid to help you align fields on your form.

7. **Click a field you want to delete.**

   Access highlights your chosen field.

8. **Click the Delete icon in the Records group.**

   Access deletes your chosen field.

   If you press Ctrl+Z right away, you can undelete any field that you just deleted.

9. **Click the downward-pointing arrow underneath the View icon in the Views group.**

   A pull-down menu appears.

10. **Choose Form View.**

    Access shows your form with the deleted field missing.

Adding a field

Before you can add a field to a form, you must make sure that the field already exists in your database table. For example, if you want to add a field on a form that displays phone numbers, you must first create that field in your database table and then stuff it with actual data.

To add a new field to a database table, follow these steps:

1. **Click the Office Button and then choose Open.**

   The Open dialog box appears.

2. Click the Access database file you want to add or edit data. Then click Open.

Access displays your chosen database.

3. In the All Tables pane on the left of the screen, double-click the name of the database table that displays data through a form.

Access displays the Datasheet view, showing rows and columns.

4. Click the Add New Field column that appears to the right of your database table.

Access highlights the entire column.

5. Click the Datasheet tab.

6. Click the Rename icon in the Fields and Columns group.

The cursor appears in the column heading you chose in Step 4.

7. Type a descriptive field name, such as E-Mail **or** Birthday, **and then press Enter.**

8. Click in the column of the field you just created and named and then type new data.

After you either create a new field or verify that a field already exists in a database table, you're ready to add that field to a form.

To add a field to a form, follow these steps:

1. Click the Office Button and then choose Open.

The Open dialog box appears.

2. Click the Access database file you want to add or edit data. Then click Open.

Access displays your chosen database.

3. In the All Tables pane on the left of the screen, double-click the name of the form you want to use.

Access displays the Form view of your database.

4. Click the Home tab.

5. Click the downward-pointing arrow underneath the View icon in the Views group.

A pull-down menu appears.

6. Choose Design View.

Access displays your form in Design view.

7. Click the Design tab.

8. **Click the Add Existing Fields icon in the Tools group.**

   The Field List window appears, as shown in Figure 16-11.

9. **Double-click a field.**

   Access displays the field label and a field on your form.

10. **(Optional) Move the mouse pointer over the upper-right corner of the field label and drag the mouse (hold down the left mouse button and move the mouse) to move the field label on your form.**

11. **(Optional) Repeat Step 10, except move the field instead of the field label.**

12. **Click the downward-pointing arrow underneath the View icon in the Views group.**

    Access displays the Form view. Notice that the form displays both your newly added field and any data stored in that field.

13. **Click the Office Button and choose Save to save the changes to your form.**

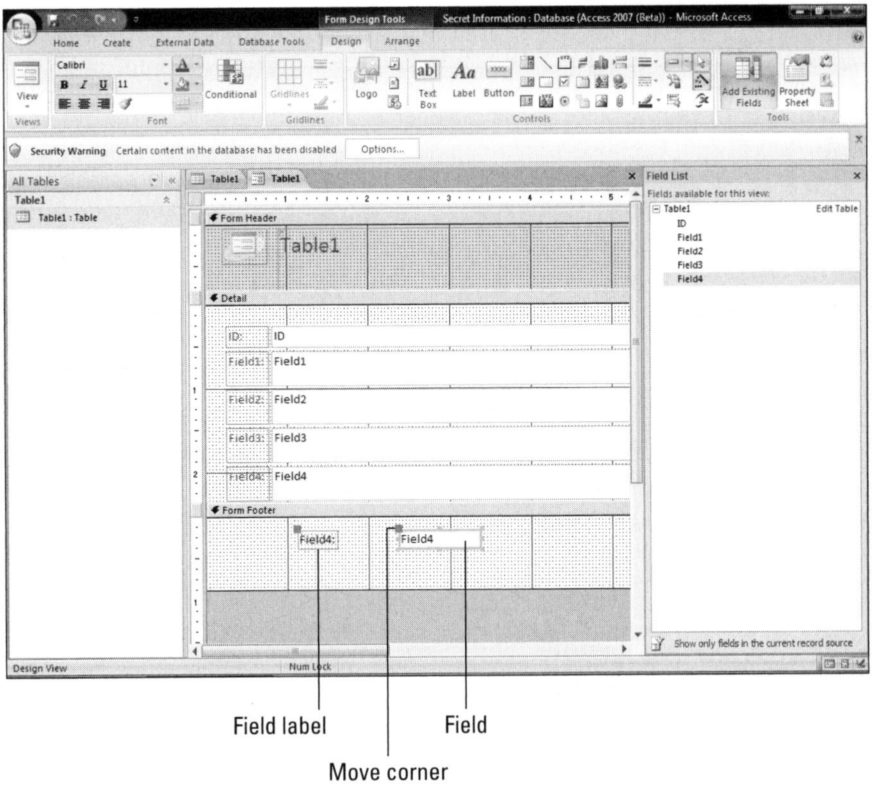

Figure 16-11: The Field List window shows you all the fields stored in your database table that you can place on the form.

Field label   Field

Move corner

Closing and Saving a Database

When you're done using a database file, you can either close it or exit Access altogether. Access gives you two options for closing a database:

- ✔ Close a single database table.
- ✔ Close the entire Access database file.

Closing a database table

Closing a single database table simply removes the data from view and leaves Access running your loaded database file. After you close a database table, you can open another one. (You don't have to close a database table to open another one, but if you know you won't need to view a particular database table, you might as well close it to get it out of the way.)

To close a database table, follow these steps:

1. Right-click the database table tab that you want to close.

A pop-up menu appears, as shown in Figure 16-12.

Figure 16-12: Choose Close to close that table from view.

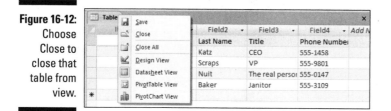

2. Choose Close.

Access closes your chosen database table.

If you choose Close All, you can close all open database tables so you won't have to right-click each tab and close the tables one at a time.

Closing a database file

Closing a database file keeps Access running so you can open another database file. To close a database file but keep Access running, follow these steps:

1. **Click the Office Button and then choose Close Database.**

   To exit Access, choose Exit Access instead.

   If you haven't saved any changes to the design of your database, a dialog box appears, asking whether you want to save your changes.

2. **Click Yes (or No).**

   Access remains running so you can load another database file.

When you save an Access database, you're saving only the changes you made to the database table or form. Access automatically saves any data you type or edit in your database file. (When you type or edit data, Access saves it as soon as you move the cursor to a new field or record.)

Chapter 17

Searching, Sorting, and Querying a Database

In This Chapter

▶ Searching and filtering a database

▶ Sorting databases

▶ Creating and using queries

*I*f you need to find a specific name in your database, searching through the database alphabetically may be tedious but possible. However, if you need to find the names of everyone who ordered more than $50,000 worth of supplies in the past three months, trying to find this information yourself would prove tedious and time-consuming. Yet, Access can search for this information at the blink of an eye.

If you search for specific types of data on a regular basis, you probably don't want to keep telling Access what to search for over and over again. To simplify this, you can create a *query*. A query lets you define specific ways to search your data and save those parameters so you can search your data in the future.

Besides searching through your data, Access can also sort your data. *Sorting* can be as simple as organizing names alphabetically, or it can be more complicated, such as sorting names according to ZIP code, annual salary, or alphabetically by last name. Sorting simply rearranges your data so you can study it from a new point of view.

By searching, sorting, and querying your data, you can extract useful information about your data.

Searching a Database

A paper database is useful for storing information, but not so useful for finding it again. If you have a thousand business cards stored in a Rolodex file, how much time do you want to waste trying to find the phone number of a single person?

Searching a database is crucial to make your data useful, so Access provides two different ways to search a database:

- ✔ Search for a specific record.
- ✔ Use a filter to show one or more records that meet a specific criterion.

Searching for a specific record

The simplest type of search looks for a specific record. To search for a record, you need to know the data stored in at least one of its fields, such as a phone number and e-mail address.

The more information you already know, the more likely Access will find the one record you want. If you search for all records that contain the first name *Bill,* Access could find dozens of records. If you just search for all records that contain the first name *Bill,* the last name *Johnson,* and a state address of *Alaska,* Access will likely find just the record you want.

To search for a specific record in a database table, follow these steps:

1. **In the All Tables pane on the left of the screen, double-click the name of the database table you want to search.**

   Access displays the Datasheet view of your database.

2. **Click the Home tab.**

3. **Click the Find icon in the Find group.**

   The Find and Replace dialog box appears, as shown in Figure 17-1.

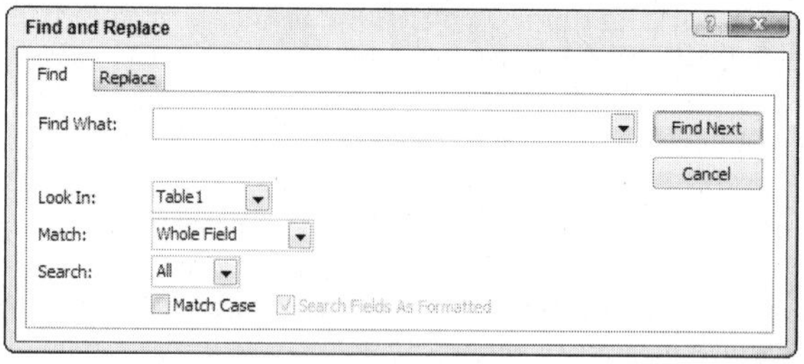

Figure 17-1:
Search for
a specific
record in a
database
table.

4. **Click in the Find What text box and type in the data you know is stored in the record you want to find.**

   For example, if you want to find the phone number of a person but you know only that person's last name, you type that person's last name in the Find What text box.

5. **Click the Look In list box and choose the name of the entire database table.**

6. **(Optional) Click in the Match list box and choose one of the following:**

   - *Any Part of Field:* The Find What text can appear in any part of a field.
   - *Whole Field:* The Find What text is the only text stored in a field.
   - *Start of Field:* The Find What text can be only at the beginning of a field.

7. **(Optional) Click in the Search list box and choose one of the following:**

   - *Up:* Searches from the record where the cursor appears, up to the beginning of the database table
   - *Down:* Searches from the record where the cursor appears, down to the end of the database table
   - *All:* Searches the entire database table

8. **Click Find Next.**

   Access highlights the field where it finds the text you typed in Step 4.

9. **Repeat Step 8 to search for more records that might contain the text you typed in Step 4.**

10. **Click Cancel or the Close button.**

Filtering a database

Searching a database is easy but somewhat limited because you can retrieve only a record that matches any text that you want to find. If you want to find multiple records, you can use a filter.

A *filter* lets you tell Access to display only those records that meet a certain criteria, such all records that contain people who earn more than $200,000 a year, are currently married, live in Las Vegas, Nevada, and own two or more cars.

To filter a database table, you must tell Access which field to use as a filter, and then you must define the criteria for that filter. For example, if you want to filter your database table to see only those records listing the names of people who are at least 65, you filter the Age field and set the criteria to *Greater than or equal to 65.*

Filtering simply hides all records in a database table that don't match your criteria. Filtering doesn't delete or erase any records.

Using an exact match for a filter

The simplest filtering criterion searches for an exact match. When you filter a field by an exact match, you're telling Access, "I want to see only those records that contain this specific chunk of data in this particular field." By using an exact match filter, you could display only those records that contain CA in the State field.

To filter a database table, follow these steps:

1. **In the All Tables pane on the left of the screen, double-click the name of the database table you want to filter.**

   Access displays the Datasheet view of your database.

2. **Click the Home tab.**

3. **Click in the field (column) that you want to use as a filter.**

4. **Click the Filter icon in the Sort & Filter group.**

   A pop-up menu appears, as shown in Figure 17-2.

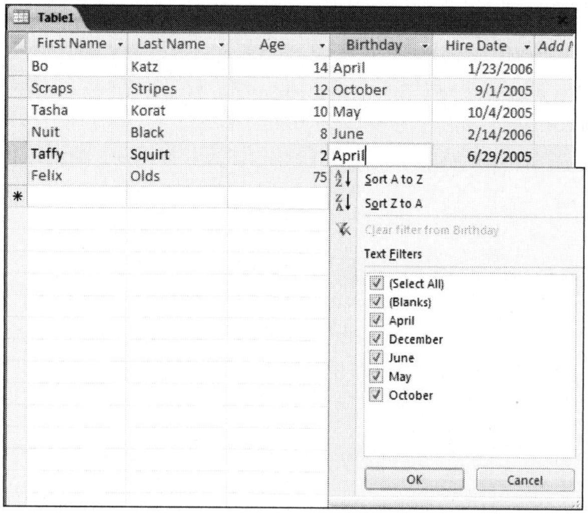

Figure 17-2:
The Filter pop-up menu lets you specify the criteria for a specific field.

First Name	Last Name	Age	Birthday	Hire Date	Add I
Bo	Katz	14	April	1/23/2006	
Scraps	Stripes	12	October	9/1/2005	
Tasha	Korat	10	May	10/4/2005	
Nuit	Black	8	June	2/14/2006	
Taffy	Squirt	2	April	6/29/2005	
Felix	Olds	75			

Sort A to Z
Sort Z to A
Clear filter from Birthday
Text Filters

☑ (Select All)
☑ (Blanks)
☑ April
☑ December
☑ June
☑ May
☑ October

OK   Cancel

5. **(Optional) Clear one or more of the check boxes that appear to the left of the list of data that appears in the field you chose in Step 3.**

6. **Click OK.**

   Access displays the filtered view of your database table.

7. **Repeat Steps 3–6 for each additional field you want to filter.**

Filtering by form

One problem with defining filters in Datasheet view is that you have all your database table records cluttering the screen. To avoid this problem, Access lets you define filters by using a *form,* which basically displays an empty record so you can click the fields that you want to use to filter your database table.

To define a filter by form, follow these steps:

1. **In the All Tables pane on the left of the screen, double-click the name of the database table that you want to filter.**

   Access displays the Datasheet view of your database.

2. **Click the Home tab.**

3. **Click the Advanced icon in the Sort & Filter group.**

   A pull-down menu appears.

4. **Choose Filter By Form, as shown in Figure 17-3.**

   Access displays a blank record.

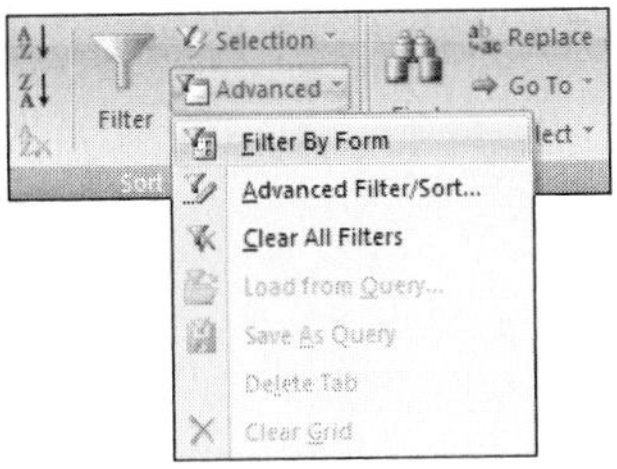

Figure 17-3:
The Advanced pop-up menu lets you specify the criteria for a specific field.

5. **Click in any field.**

   A downward-pointing arrow appears.

6. **Click the downward-pointing arrow.**

   A pull-down menu appears, listing all the data currently stored in that field, as shown in Figure 17-4.

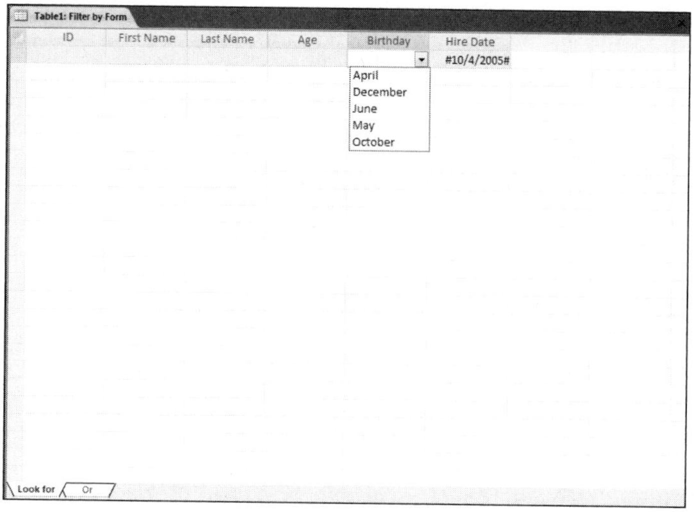

Figure 17-4:
Filtering by form lets you choose the type of data you want to view from a pull-down menu.

7. **Click the data you want.**

   You can only click on one entry in the list.

8. **Click the Toggle Filter icon in the Sort & Filter group.**

   Access displays a filtered view of your database table.

Using a filter criteria

Searching for an exact match in a field can be handy, but sometimes you may want to see records that meet certain criteria, such as finding the names of everyone whose salary is greater than $50,000 a year. Instead of filtering by an exact match, you have to define the filter criteria.

The type of data stored in each field determines the type of criteria you can create. Three common types of data stored in fields include Text, Numbers, and Dates, which you can filter in different ways, as shown in Table 17-1.

Table 17-1	Common Criteria for Filtering Different Types of Data	
Field Data Type	*Filtering Criteria*	*Description*
Text	Equals	Field must match filter text exactly.
	Does Not Equal	Field must not match filter text.
	Begins With	Field must start with the filter text.
	Does Not Begin With	Field must not begin with the filter text.
	Contains	Field must contain the filter text.
	Does Not Contain	Field must not contain any part of the filter text.
	Ends With	Field ends with the filter text.
	Does Not End With	Field does not end with the filter text.
Numbers	Equals	Field must equal filter number.
	Does Not Equal	Field must not equal filter number.
	Less Than or Equal To	Field must contain a number less than or equal to the filter number.
	Greater Than or Equal To	Field must contain a number greater than or equal to the filter number.
	Between	Field must contain a number that falls between two filter numbers.
Dates	Equals	Field must equal the filter date.
	Does Not Equal	Field must not equal the filter date.
	On or Before	Field date must be equal or earlier than the filter date.
	On or After	Field date must be equal or later than the filter date.

To create the filter criteria, follow these steps:

1. **In the All Tables pane on the left of the screen, double-click the name of the database table you want to filter.**

   Access displays the Datasheet view of your database.

2. **Click the Home tab.**

3. **Click in the field (column) that you want to use as a filter.**

4. **Click the Filter icon in the Sort & Filter group.**

   A pop-up menu appears (refer to Figure 17-2).

5. **Select the Filters option, such as Text Filters or Number Filters.**

   A submenu of filter options appears, as shown in Figure 17-5.

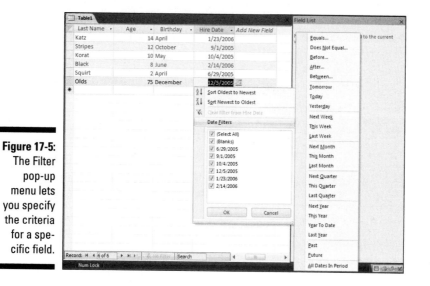

Figure 17-5:
The Filter
pop-up
menu lets
you specify
the criteria
for a spe-
cific field.

6. **Click a filter option, such as Between or Less Than.**

   The Custom Filter dialog box appears, as shown in Figure 17-6. The Custom Filter dialog box contains the name of your filter option such as Between Numbers.

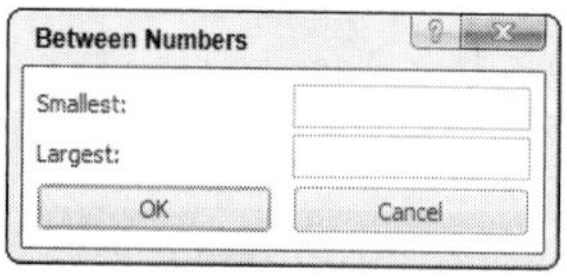

Figure 17-6:
Type in a
value for
your filter
criteria.

7. **Type in one or more values in each text box displayed in the Custom Filter dialog box and then click OK.**

    Access filters your database table according to your criteria.

8. **Repeat Steps 5–7 for each additional filter you want to add.**

Clearing a filter

When you apply a filter to a database table, you see only those records that-match that filter. Access displays a Filtered message at the bottom of the screen to let you know when you're looking at a filtered database table.

To remove a filter so you can see all the records, choose one of the following:

- ✔ Click the Toggle Filter icon in the Sort & Filter group.
- ✔ Click the Filtered or Unfiltered button on the status bar near the bottom of the screen.

Access temporarily turns off any filters so you can see all the information stored in your database table.

When you choose the Save command (Ctrl+S) to save a database table, Access also saves your last filter. The next time you open that database table, you'll be able to use the last filter you created. If you want to save multiple filters, you'll have to save them as a query (see the section "Querying a Database" later in this chapter).

Sorting a Database

Sorting simply rearranges how Access displays your information. Sorting can be especially handy for rearranging your records alphabetically by last name, by state, or by country. You can also sort data numerically so that customers who buy the most from you appear at the top of your database table while customers who don't buy as much appear near the bottom.

To sort a database table, follow these steps:

1. **In the All Tables pane on the left of the screen, double-click the name of the database table you want to sort.**

    Access displays the Datasheet view of your database.

2. **Click the Home tab.**

3. **Click in a field (column) that you want to use for sorting.**

4. **Click the Ascending or Descending icon in the Sort & Filter group.**

   Access sorts your records and displays an Ascending or Descending icon in the field name so you know you're looking at a sorted list, as shown in Figure 17-7.

5. **Click the Clear All Sorts icon in the Sort & Filter group when you don't want to view your sorted database table any more.**

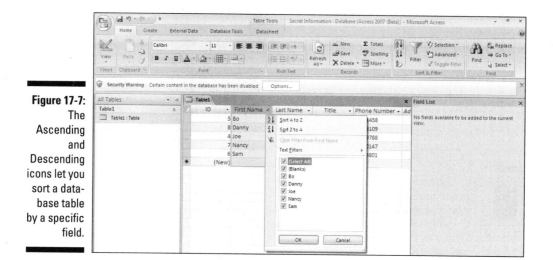

Figure 17-7:
The Ascending and Descending icons let you sort a database table by a specific field.

Querying a Database

One problem with sorting or filtering a database table is that you must constantly define what you want to sort or filter. In case you sort or filter your data a certain way on a regular basis, you can use a query instead.

A *query* is nothing more than a saved version of your sort or filter criteria. By saving the particular sort or filter criteria as a query, you can select that query by name later.

Creating a simple query

If your database table contains dozens of different fields, you may find it confusing to make sense of all your information. As an aid, a *simple query* strips away fields so you see only the fields containing data you want to see, such as a person's name and phone number but not her hire date or employee number.

To create a query, follow these steps:

1. **Click the Create tab.**

2. **Click the Query Wizard icon in the Other group.**

   The New Query dialog box appears, as shown in Figure 17-8.

Figure 17-8: The New Query dialog box lets you choose a query wizard.

3. **Click Simple Query Wizard and then click OK.**

   The Simple Query Wizard dialog box appears, as shown in Figure 17-9.

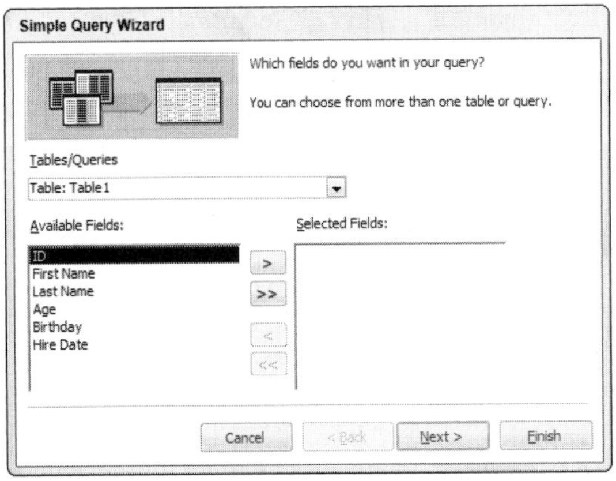

Figure 17-9: The Simple Query Wizard dialog box lets you pick the fields to use for your query.

4. **Click a field name listed in the Available Fields box and then click the > button.**

   Access displays your chosen field in the Selected Fields box.

5. **Repeat Step 4 for each field you want to use in your query.**

6. **Click Next.**

Another dialog box appears, as shown in Figure 17-10. This dialog box asks whether you want to display a Detail (shows every record) or Summary (shows numerical information such as the total number of records found, the average value, and the minimum/maximum value) view of your data.

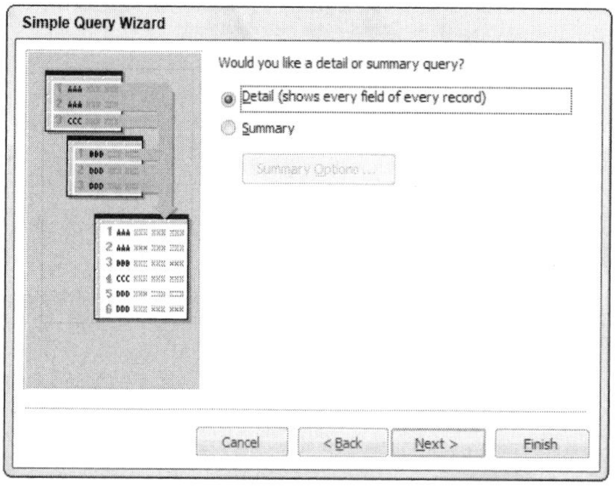

Figure 17-10:
Choose
between
viewing
Detail or
Summary
view.

7. **Select the Detail or Summary radio button and then click Next.**

Another dialog box appears, asking you to type a descriptive name for your query, as shown in Figure 17-11.

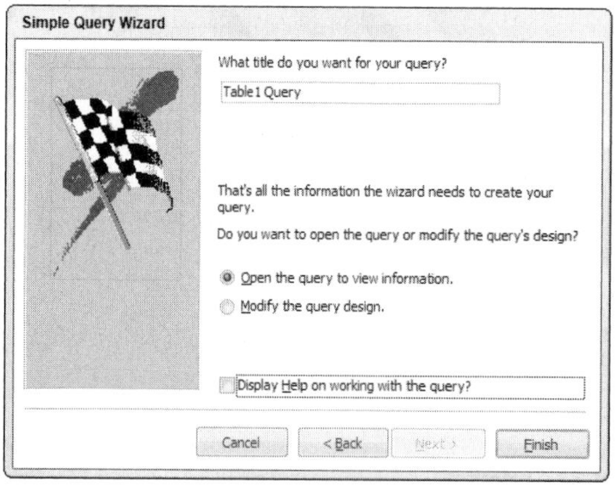

Figure 17-11:
Type a
descriptive
name for
your query.

8. **Click in the text box, type a descriptive name for your query, and then click Finish.**

   Access displays the results of your query as a separate tab.

9. **Click the Office Button and then choose Save to save your query.**

Creating a crosstab query

A *crosstab query* lets you combine two or more fields to calculate and display a calculation based on a third field. For example, if your database contains the names of salespeople and the products they sold, you can use those two fields to create a crosstab that tells you how much each salesperson sold of each product, as shown in Figure 17-12.

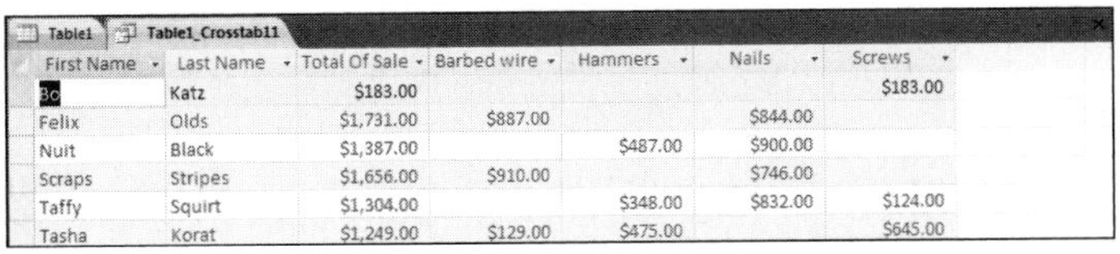

Figure 17-12:
A crosstab query extracts information by cross-referencing two or more fields.

First Name	Last Name	Total Of Sale	Barbed wire	Hammers	Nails	Screws
Bo	Katz	$183.00				$183.00
Felix	Olds	$1,731.00	$887.00		$844.00	
Nuit	Black	$1,387.00		$487.00	$900.00	
Scraps	Stripes	$1,656.00	$910.00		$746.00	
Taffy	Squirt	$1,304.00		$348.00	$832.00	$124.00
Tasha	Korat	$1,249.00	$129.00	$475.00		$645.00

To create a crosstab query, you need to identify three types of fields:

✔ One to three fields to identify each record (such as the First Name and Last Name fields)

✔ A single field to display specific data from each record (such as the Product field, which displays the actual product names like Nails, Barbed Wire, and Screws)

✔ A crosstab field that displays a calculated result (such as Sales)

To create a crosstab query, follow these steps:

1. **Click the Create tab.**

2. **Click the Query Wizard icon in the Other group.**

   The New Query dialog box appears (refer to Figure 17-8).

3. Click Crosstab Query Wizard and then click OK.

The Crosstab Query Wizard dialog box appears, as shown in Figure 17-13.

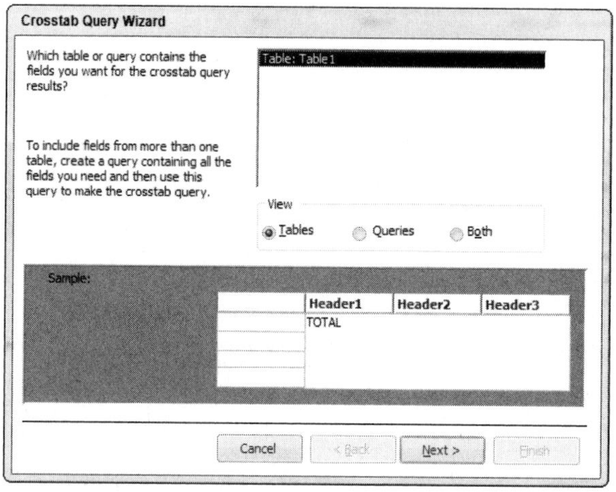

Figure 17-13: The Crosstab Query Wizard dialog box asks you to choose which database table to use.

4. Click a database table and then click Next.

Another Crosstab Query Wizard dialog box appears that asks for between one and three fields to identify each row (record), as shown in Figure 17-14.

5. Click a field in the Available Fields box and then click the > button to move your chosen field to the Selected Fields box.

6. Repeat Step 5 for each additional field you want to include.

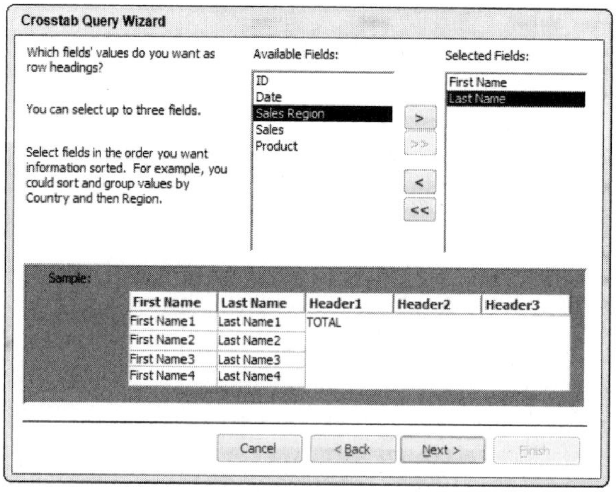

Figure 17-14: The first step to creating a crosstab query is to choose up to three fields to identify each record.

7. Click Next.

Another dialog box appears, asking for a single field to use to cross-tabulate data with the fields you chose in Steps 5 and 6, as shown in Figure 17-15.

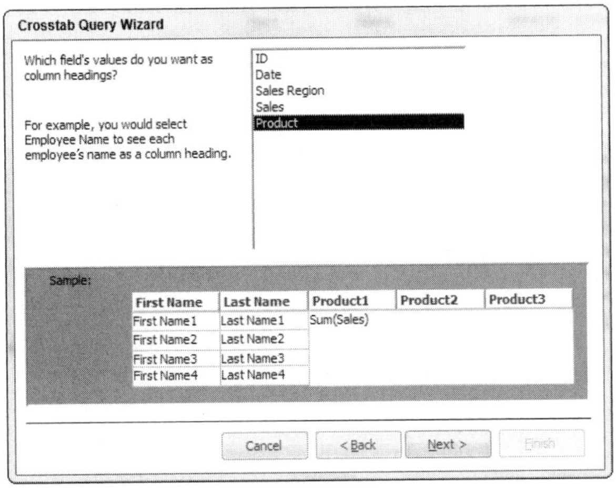

Figure 17-15:
To cross-tabulate your data, you need to choose another field.

8. Click a field name and then click Next.

Ideally, this field should consist of text information that lists different data, such as sales regions (East, West, North, or South) or products (Hammers, Screws, Nails, and so on). If you choose a field that contains numerical data, your crosstab query displays only those numbers in the column headings, which will appear meaningless. Another dialog box appears, as shown in Figure 17-16.

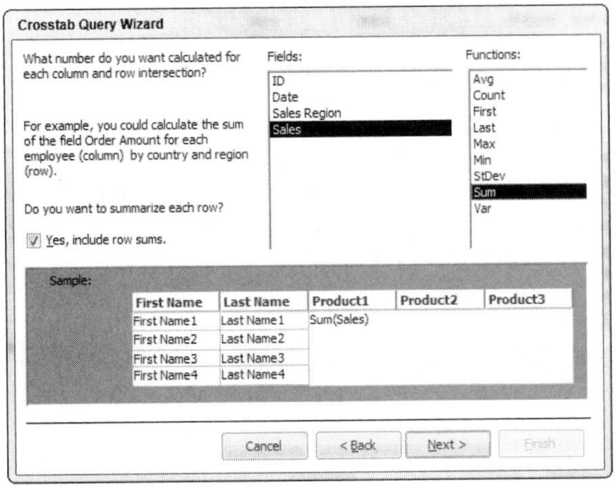

Figure 17-16:
The final field to choose must contain numerical data for the crosstab query to calculate.

9. **Click a field that contains numerical data and then click a mathematical function that you want Access to calculate, such as Sum, Avg, or Count.**

10. **Click Next.**

    Another dialog box appears, asking for a name for your query, as shown in Figure 17-17.

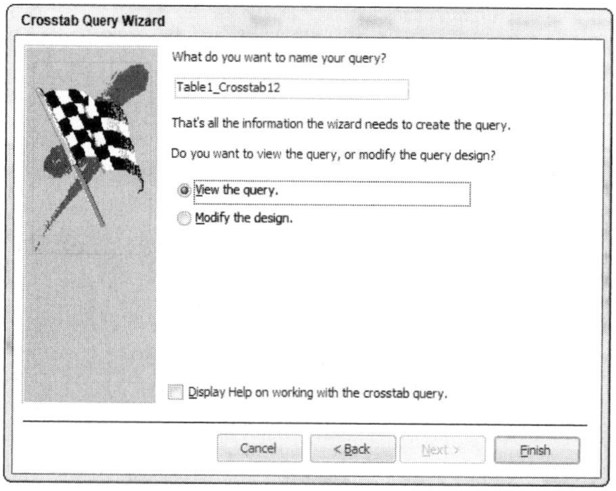

Figure 17-17:
After you create a query, give it a descriptive name.

11. **Type a descriptive name for your query in the text box at the top of the dialog box and then click Finish.**

    Access displays your crosstab query (refer to Figure 17-12).

12. **Click the Office Button and choose Save to save your query.**

Creating a query that finds duplicate field data

Suppose you sell a hundred different products. How can you tell which products customers are buying the most? To find the answer to this type of question, you could search your database manually to find a Products Sold field and then count how many times each product appears.

As a simpler solution, you can create a query that finds and counts how many times duplicate data appears. To create a query to find duplicate field data, follow these steps:

1. **Click the Create tab.**

2. **Click the Query Wizard icon in the Other group.**

   The New Query dialog box appears (refer to Figure 17-8).

3. **Click Find Duplicates Query Wizard and then click OK.**

   The Find Duplicates Query Wizard dialog box appears, asking you to choose the database table to search.

4. **Click a database table and then click Next.**

   Another dialog box appears, asking you to choose the fields to examine for duplicate data, as shown in Figure 17-18.

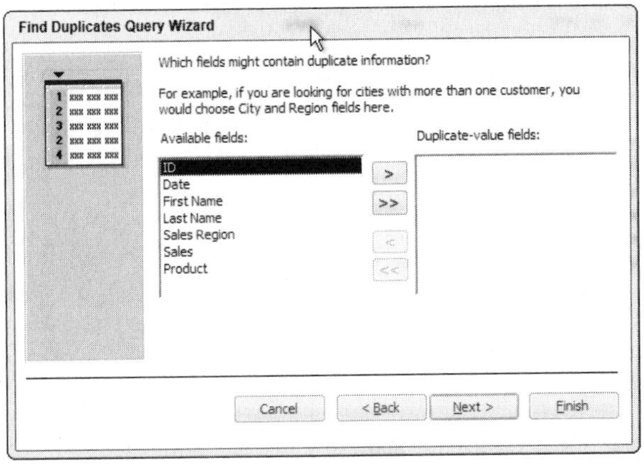

Figure 17-18: Define one or more fields to search for duplicate data.

5. **Click a field name and then click the > button. Repeat this step for each additional field you want to search.**

6. **Click Next.**

   Another dialog box appears, asking whether you want to display any additional fields. If you choose to look for duplicate data in a Product field (Step 5) to see which products are most popular, you can display additional fields such as each salesperson's name so you can also see who is responsible for selling the most products.

7. **Click a field and click the > button. Repeat this step for each additional field you want to display.**

8. **Click Next.**

   A dialog box appears, asking whether you want to give your query a descriptive name.

9. **Type a descriptive name in the top text box and then click Finish.**

   Access displays your query as a separate tab.

10. **Click the Office Button and then choose Save to save your query.**

Creating an unmatched query

Access can store huge amounts of data, but the more data you store, the harder it can be to view your data. To help you organize your data, you can divide data into separate tables. One table may contain a list of customers, and a second table may contain a list of salespeople.

When you store data in separate tables, each table may share one or more common fields. For example, a table containing customers may contain a SalesPerson field that shows which salesperson deals exclusively with which customer. A second table listing salespeople could contain the Customer field (along with additional information such as each salesperson's phone number, address, sales region, and so on).

An unmatched query examines two (or more) database tables to look for missing information. For example, you could also use an unmatched query to find customers who haven't ordered anything in the past six months, sales regions that haven't ordered certain products, or salespeople who have not been assigned to a sales region. Basically, an unmatched query can help you find missing pieces or holes in your entire database file.

To create an unmatched query, follow these steps:

1. **Click the Create tab.**

2. **Click the Query Wizard icon in the Other group.**

   The New Query dialog box appears (refer to Figure 17-8).

3. **Click Find Unmatched Query Wizard and then click OK.**

   The Find Unmatched Query Wizard dialog box appears, asking you to choose a database table that contains the unmatched records you want to find.

4. **Click a database table and then click Next.**

   Another dialog box appears, asking you to choose a database table that contains at least one field that also appears in the table you chose in Step 3.

5. **Click a second database table and then click Next.**

   Another dialog box appears, asking you to identify the field that both database tables have in common, as shown in Figure 17-19.

6. **Click the common field that both database tables share.**

7. **Click on the gray <=> button that appears between the two fields and then click Next.**

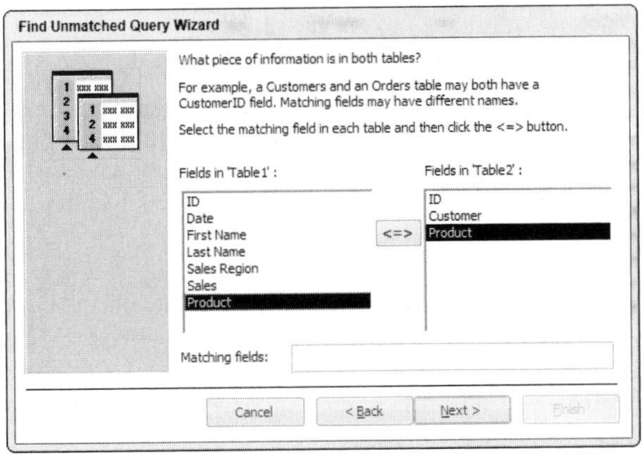

Figure 17-19:
To find
unmatched
records, you
must first
identify the
fields both
database
tables share.

A dialog box appears, asking you to identify the fields you want to display
from the database table you chose in Step 4, as shown in Figure 17-20.

8. **Click a field and then click the > button. Repeat this step for each
   additional field you want to display.**

9. **Click Next.**

   A dialog box appears, asking you to give your query a descriptive name.

10. **Type a descriptive name in the text box and then click Finish.**

    Access displays your query results, which show you only the data in
    fields you selected in Step 8.

11. **Click the Office Button and choose Save to save your query.**

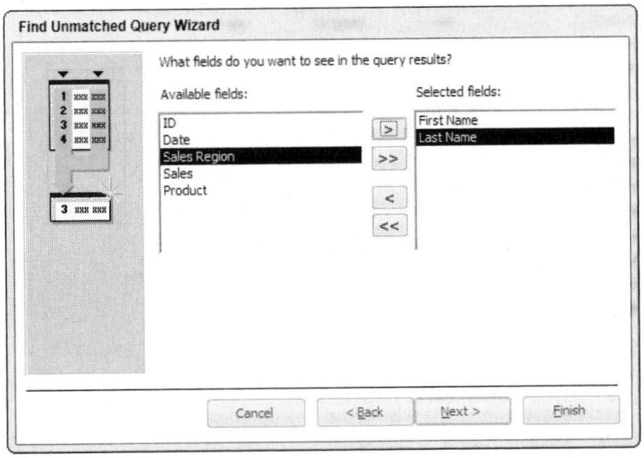

Figure 17-20:
You can
choose
which fields
you want to
display in
your query.

Viewing and deleting queries

Each time you create and save a query, Access stores it for future use. After you create and save a query, you can add or delete data from your tables and then apply your queries on the newly modified data.

To view a query, follow these steps:

1. **Click the downward-pointing arrow in the left pane.**

   A pull-down menu appears, as shown in Figure 17-21.

2. **Click Queries.**

   Access shows your list of queries.

3. **Double-click the query name you want to view.**

   Access displays your chosen query.

4. **Right-click the query tab; when a pop-up menu appears, choose Close.**

In case you need to rename your query to give it a better descriptive name, follow these steps:

1. **Click the downward-pointing arrow in the left pane.**

   A pull-down menu appears (refer to Figure 17-21).

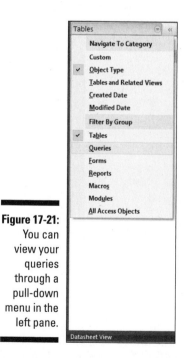

Figure 17-21:
You can
view your
queries
through a
pull-down
menu in the
left pane.

2. **Choose Queries.**

   Access shows your list of queries.

3. **Right-click a query name; when a pop-up menu appears, choose Rename.**

   Access highlights the query name.

4. **Type a new name and then press Enter.**

Eventually, you may no longer need a query. To delete it, follow these steps:

1. **Click the downward-pointing arrow in the left pane.**

   A pull-down menu appears (refer to Figure 17-21).

2. **Choose Queries.**

   Access shows your list of queries.

3. **Right-click a query name; when a pop-up menu appears, choose Delete.**

   A dialog box appears, asking whether you really want to delete your query.

4. **Click Yes (or No).**

Chapter 18

Creating a Database Report

. . . .

In This Chapter

▶ Creating a report with the Report Wizard

▶ Displaying and printing reports

▶ Modifying the appearance of a report

▶ Erasing a report

. . . .

Data is useless if you can't understand what it means, so that's why Access lets you create reports. A *report* simply provides a printed version of your data arranged in some useful way.

A report could dig through your data and print a list of your top ten salespeople. Another report may print out the top ten products you sold last year. Reports simply provide a way to make sense of your data and print it so you can examine your data on paper.

Using the Report Wizard

The easiest way to create a report is to use the Report Wizard, which guides you step by step through arranging and selecting which data to print on a report along with sorting your data at the same time. To use the Report Wizard, follow these steps:

1. **Click the Create tab.**

2. **Click the Report Wizard icon in the Reports group.**

   The Report Wizard dialog box appears, as shown in Figure 18-1.

3. **Click in the Tables/Queries list box and choose the table or query that contains the data you want to print in a report.**

4. **Click a field in the Available Fields box and then click the > button. Repeat this step for each additional field you want to display in your report.**

Figure 18-1:
The Report
Wizard lets
you choose
where to
retrieve
your data
for your
report.

5. **Click Next.**

   Another dialog box appears, asking whether you want to group your
   data by a specific filed, such as by Last Name or Employee Number, as
   shown in Figure 18-2.

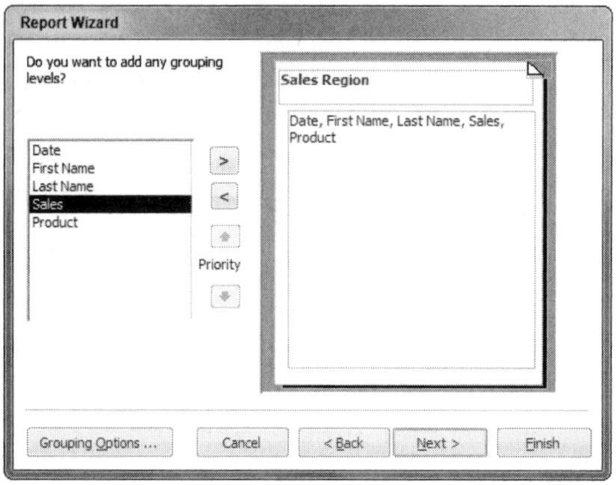

Figure 18-2:
A report can
group data
under cate-
gories so
you can see
all your data
arranged by
a specific
field.

6. **Click a field name displayed in the box and then click the > button.
   Repeat this step for each additional field you want to use to group
   your data on the report.**

7. **Click Next.**

   Another dialog box appears, asking you to choose up to four fields to
   use for sorting your data in your report, as shown in Figure 18-3.

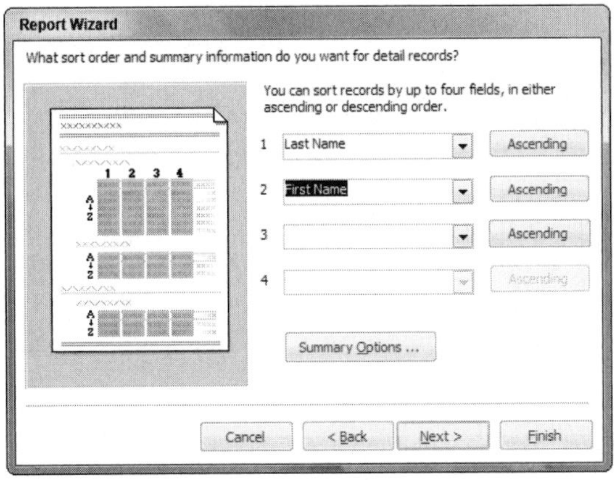

Figure 18-3:
You can sort the data in your report using up to four fields.

8. **Click in a list box and choose a field to sort your data.**

   Data will be sorted by the order chosen here for each additional field you sort on.

9. **(Optional) Click the Ascending button to change the sorting criteria from Ascending to Descending and vice versa.**

10. **Click Next.**

   Another dialog box appears, asking you how to lay out your report, as shown in Figure 18-4.

11. **Select a radio button under the Layout group, such as Stepped or Outline.**

12. **(Optional) Select on a radio button in the Orientation group, such as Portrait or Landscape.**

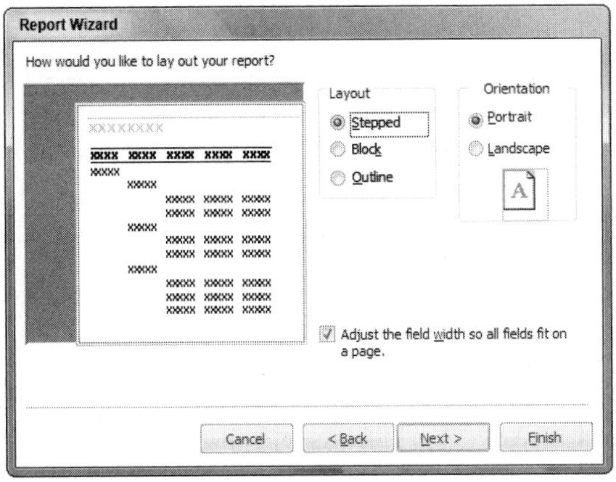

Figure 18-4:
The Report Wizard offers different options for making your report look readable.

13. Click Next.

Another dialog box appears, asking you to choose a style for your report, as shown in Figure 18-5. The preview to the left will give you an indication of what the printed report will look like.

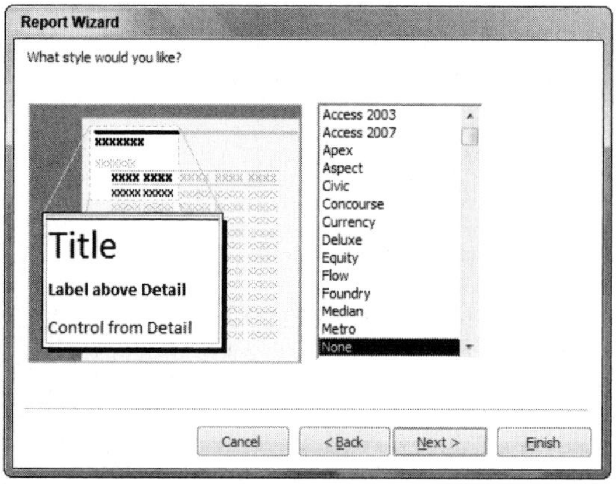

Figure 18-5:
You can choose a specific reporting style to define how your report looks.

14. Click Next.

Another dialog box appears, asking you for a descriptive name for your report, as shown in Figure 18-6.

Figure 18-6:
You can type a descriptive title for your report.

15. Type a descriptive name for your report and then click Finish.

Access displays your report, as shown in Figure 18-7.

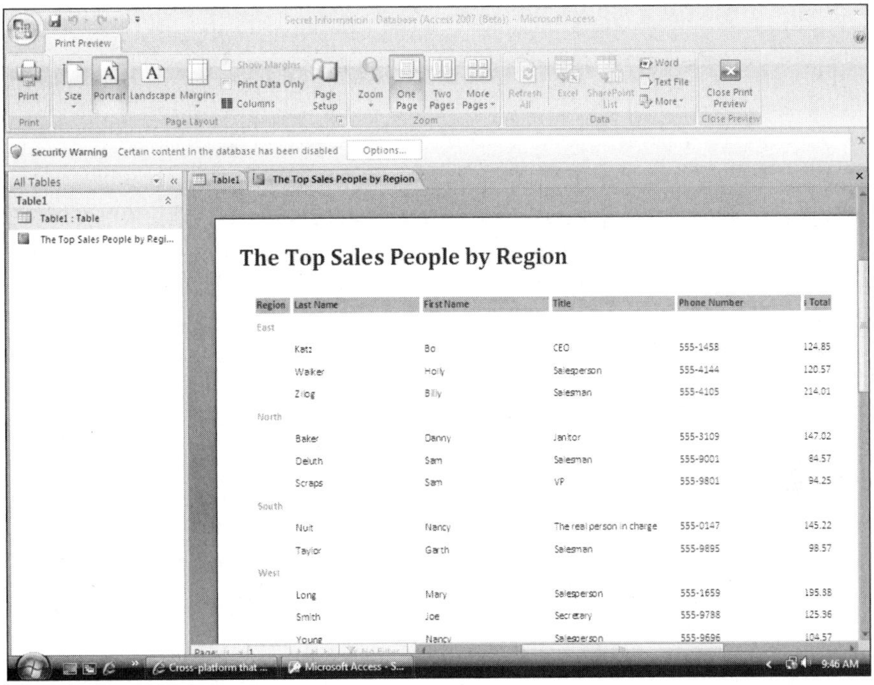

Figure 18-7:
Access
displays
your report
onscreen.

16. **Right-click the Report tab.**

    A pop-up menu appears.

17. **Click Close.**

    A dialog box appears, asking whether you want to save the design of your report.

18. **Click Yes.**

    Access saves your report for future use and removes it from view.

Viewing and Printing a Report

The first time you create a report, Access displays it on the screen right away. After you close a report, you can add, edit, or delete your data and then view your data through your report.

To view a report, follow these steps:

1. **Click the downward-pointing arrow that appears in the left pane.**

   A pull-down menu appears, as shown in Figure 18-8.

2. **Click Tables and Related Views.**

   Access displays a list of all your previously saved reports in the left pane.

3. **Double-click a report name.**

   Access displays your chosen report, displaying any new or edited data that you may have added since the last time you viewed the report.

After you display a report onscreen, you can use the Print Preview command to see exactly how your report will appear when printed. Within Print Preview, you can also modify the appearance of your report, such as adjusting page margins or paper orientation.

To preview and print a report, follow these steps:

1. **Make sure your desired report appears on the screen. (Follow Steps 1–3 of the preceding step list.)**

2. **Click the Office Button.**

   A pull-down menu appears.

3. **Click the right arrow that appears to the right of the Print command.**

   A submenu appears, displaying the Print Preview command.

4. **Click Print Preview.**

   Access displays the Print Preview tab, as shown in Figure 18-9.

5. **(Optional) Select one or more of the following:**

   • *Size:* Defines the paper size such as 8.5 x 11 or 8.5 x 14

   • *Portrait/Landscape:* Makes the report print up and down or sideways on a page

   • *Margins:* Lets you define page margins around your report

6. **Click the Print icon in the Print group to send the report to your printer.**

7. **Click the Close Print Preview icon in the Close Preview group.**

Figure 18-9:
The Print
Preview tab
provides
commands
for modifying
your printed
report.

Manipulating the Data in a Report

After you create a report, you can manipulate the data displayed in that report, such as sorting data in ascending or descending order, or applying a filter that only displays data that meets a certain criteria.

By using a report, you can get a different view of your data. By manipulating the data in a report, you can create alternate views of the same report. Some common ways to extract information from a report include

✔ Counting

✔ Sorting

✔ Filtering

To manipulate data in a report, you must first display your report in Layout view, which you can do by following these steps:

1. **Make sure your desired report appears on the screen. (Follow Steps 1–3 of the first step list in the earlier section, "Viewing and Printing a Report.")**

2. **Click the downward-pointing arrow underneath the View icon in the Views group.**

   A pull-down menu appears.

3. **Choose Layout View.**

   Access displays your report in Layout view, which highlights an entire column (field) at a time, as shown in Figure 18-10.

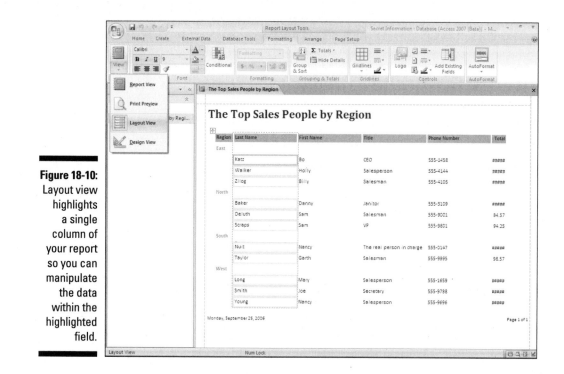

Figure 18-10:
Layout view highlights a single column of your report so you can manipulate the data within the highlighted field.

Counting records or values

To make reports more useful, you can have Access count and display information such as which products are selling the best or the total dollar amount of each sale so you could tell exactly how much money your company made during March. By counting records or adding up values stored in fields, Access can help you better interpret the data displayed in a report.

You can count values only of fields that contain numbers; you cannot count values of a field that contains text such as names.

To count the number of records or values in a report, follow these steps:

1. **Switch to the Layout view of your report by following Steps 1–3 in the preceding section, "Manipulating the Data in a Report."**

2. **Right-click in the column (field) that you want to count.**

   Access highlights your chosen column and displays a pop-up menu, as shown in Figure 18-11.

3. **Click Total.**

   The menu command displays the Total command along with the field name you right-clicked, such as Total Last Name or Total Sales.

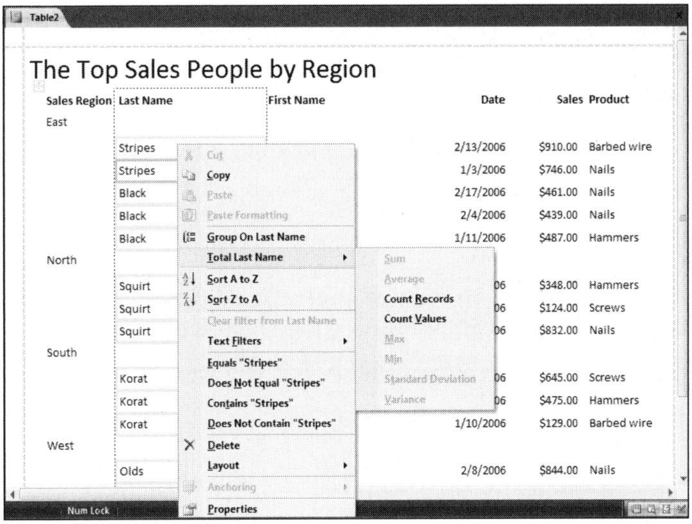

Figure 18-11:
Right-
clicking a
column
displays a
pop-up
menu for
manipulating
your data.

The figure shows a window titled "Table2" with a report "The Top Sales People by Region" and a right-click pop-up menu.

Sales Region	Last Name	First Name	Date	Sales	Product
East					
	Stripes		2/13/2006	$910.00	Barbed wire
	Stripes		1/3/2006	$746.00	Nails
	Black		2/17/2006	$461.00	Nails
	Black		2/4/2006	$439.00	Nails
	Black		1/11/2006	$487.00	Hammers
North					
	Squirt		06	$348.00	Hammers
	Squirt		06	$124.00	Screws
	Squirt		06	$832.00	Nails
South					
	Korat		06	$645.00	Screws
	Korat		06	$475.00	Hammers
	Korat		1/10/2006	$129.00	Barbed wire
West					
	Olds		2/8/2006	$844.00	Nails

Pop-up menu items:
- Cut
- Copy
- Paste
- Paste Formatting
- Group On Last Name
- Total Last Name ▶
- Sort A to Z
- Sort Z to A
- Clear filter from Last Name
- Text Filters ▶
- Equals "Stripes"
- Does Not Equal "Stripes"
- Contains "Stripes"
- Does Not Contain "Stripes"
- Delete
- Layout ▶
- Anchoring ▶
- Properties

Submenu (Total Last Name):
- Sum
- Average
- Count Records
- Count Values
- Max
- Min
- Standard Deviation
- Variance

Access displays a submenu that displays Count Records or Count Values.

4. Click either Count Records or Count Values.

Access displays the total count in your report.

If you choose the Count Records or Count Values command again, you can hide the total count in your report.

Sorting a field

Access can sort each field in ascending or descending order. *Sorting a field* simply rearranges the data in your report for your convenience. To sort a column (field) in a report, follow these steps:

1. Switch to the Layout view of your report by following Steps 1–3 in the earlier section, "Manipulating the Data in a Report."

2. Right-click in the column (field) that you want to sort.

Access highlights your chosen column and displays a pop-up menu (refer to Figure 18-11).

3 Choose one of the following:

- *Sort A to Z:* Sorts in ascending order
- *Sort Z to A:* Sorts in descending order

Access sorts your chosen data in your report.

Filtering a field

Filtering can tell Access to only display data that meets certain criteria, such as a fixed amount. For example, if you have a report that lists all the sales of products, you could filter your report to show only those products that sold over a fixed amount, such as $1,000.

To filter data in a field, follow these steps:

1. **Switch to the Layout view of your report by following Steps 1–3 in the previous section "Manipulating the Data in a Report."**

2. **Right-click in the column (field) that you want to filter.**

   Access highlights your chosen column and displays a pop-up menu (refer to Figure 18-11).

3. **Click Filters.**

   Depending on the type of data your column contains, the Filter command may appear as Text Filters or Number Filters.

   A submenu appears, as shown in Figure 18-12.

4. **Click a filter criteria, such as Equals or Less Than.**

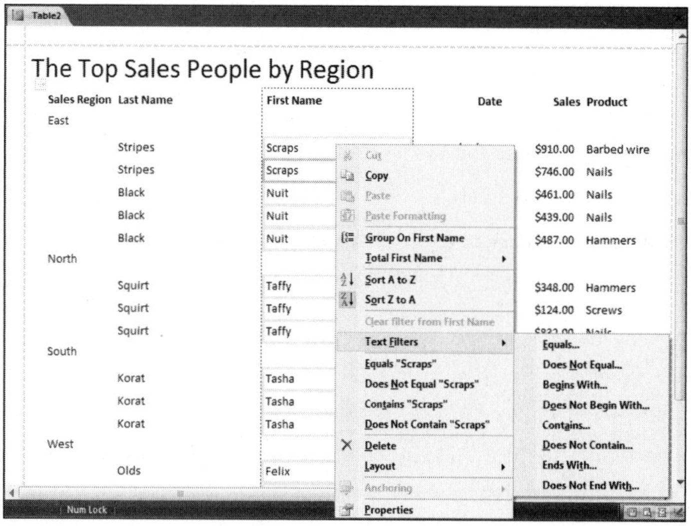

Figure 18-12: The Filters command displays a submenu of different criteria you can choose.

The Top Sales People by Region

Sales Region	Last Name	First Name		Date	Sales	Product
East						
	Stripes		✂ Cut	2/13/2006	$910.00	Barbed wire
	Stripes		📋 **C**opy	1/3/2006	$746.00	Nails
	Black		📋 Paste	2/17/2006	$461.00	Nails
	Black		📋 Paste Formatting	2/4/2006	$439.00	Nails
	Black		Group On Last Name	1/11/2006	$487.00	Hammers
North			Total Last Name ▶	Sum		
	Squirt		↕ Sort A to Z	Average 06	$348.00	Hammers
	Squirt		↕ Sort Z to A	**Count Records** 06	$124.00	Screws
	Squirt		Clear filter from Last Name	**Count Values** 06	$832.00	Nails
South			Text Filters ▶	Max		
	Korat		Equals "Stripes"	Min 06	$645.00	Screws
	Korat		Does Not Equal "Stripes"	Standard Deviation 06	$475.00	Hammers
	Korat		Contains "Stripes"	Variance 06		
			Does Not Contain "Stripes"	1/10/2006	$129.00	Barbed wire
West			✖ Delete			
	Olds		Layout ▶	2/8/2006	$844.00	Nails
			Anchoring ▶			
	Num Lock		📋 Properties			

Figure 18-11: Right-clicking a column displays a pop-up menu for manipulating your data.

Access displays a submenu that displays Count Records or Count Values.

4. Click either Count Records or Count Values.

Access displays the total count in your report.

If you choose the Count Records or Count Values command again, you can hide the total count in your report.

Sorting a field

Access can sort each field in ascending or descending order. *Sorting a field* simply rearranges the data in your report for your convenience. To sort a column (field) in a report, follow these steps:

1. Switch to the Layout view of your report by following Steps 1–3 in the earlier section, "Manipulating the Data in a Report."

2. Right-click in the column (field) that you want to sort.

Access highlights your chosen column and displays a pop-up menu (refer to Figure 18-11).

3 Choose one of the following:

- *Sort A to Z:* Sorts in ascending order
- *Sort Z to A:* Sorts in descending order

Access sorts your chosen data in your report.

Filtering a field

Filtering can tell Access to only display data that meets certain criteria, such as a fixed amount. For example, if you have a report that lists all the sales of products, you could filter your report to show only those products that sold over a fixed amount, such as $1,000.

To filter data in a field, follow these steps:

1. **Switch to the Layout view of your report by following Steps 1–3 in the previous section "Manipulating the Data in a Report."**

2. **Right-click in the column (field) that you want to filter.**

   Access highlights your chosen column and displays a pop-up menu (refer to Figure 18-11).

3. **Click Filters.**

   Depending on the type of data your column contains, the Filter command may appear as Text Filters or Number Filters.

   A submenu appears, as shown in Figure 18-12.

4. **Click a filter criteria, such as Equals or Less Than.**

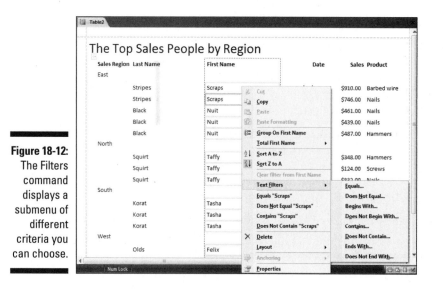

Figure 18-12: The Filters command displays a submenu of different criteria you can choose.

Depending on the criteria you choose, a Custom Filter dialog box appears, as shown in Figure 18-13.

Figure 18-13:
Define your
filter criteria.

Custom Filter

Sales is less than or equal to

OK   Cancel

5. **Type your criteria in the Custom Filter dialog box and then click OK.**

   Access applies your filter to your report.

You can always turn off your filter by clicking the Home tab and then clicking the Toggle Filter icon in the Sort & Filter group.

Editing a Report

After you create a report, you may want to modify it later to expand the space used to display data or eliminate fields altogether.

To edit a report, you must switch to the Design view of your report. After you view the report in Design view, you can modify your report. To switch to the Design view of a report, follow these steps:

1. **Make sure your desired report appears on the screen. (Follow Steps 1–3 in the earlier section, "Viewing and Printing a Report.")**

2. **Click the Home tab.**

3. **Click the downward-pointing arrow underneath the View icon that appears in the Views group.**

   A pull-down menu appears.

4. **Choose Design View.**

   Access displays your report in Design view, as shown in Figure 18-14. At this point, you can move, resize, add, or delete fields on your report. Text that appears in bold are labels that print identifying labeling text, such as First Name or Sales Region. Text that appears in normal type face (not in bold) represents fields that display data when you view your report.

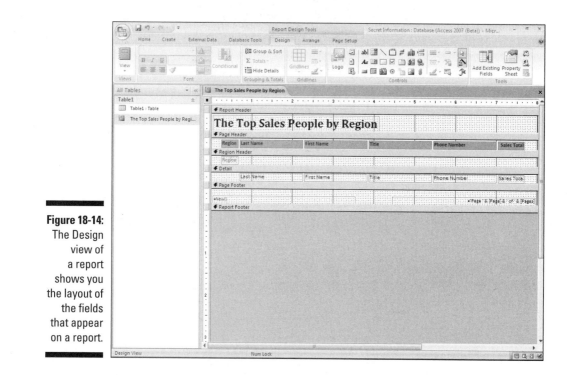

Figure 18-14:
The Design
view of
a report
shows you
the layout of
the fields
that appear
on a report.

Resizing fields

When the Report Wizard creates a report, it doesn't always leave enough room to display your actual data. If a field is too small, Access may display data as a series of x's, such as xxxxx.

If this occurs, resize a field to make it wider. (If your data turns out to be smaller than the field, you may need to shrink the field.) To resize a field, follow these steps:

1. **Display your report in Design view by following Steps 1–4 in the preceding section, "Editing a Report."**

2. **Click the field you want to resize.**

   Access highlights your chosen field and its identifying label, as shown in Figure 18-15.

3. **Move the mouse pointer over the left or right edge of the field until the mouse pointer turns into a two-way pointing arrow.**

4. **Drag the mouse to resize and expand or shrink the field.**

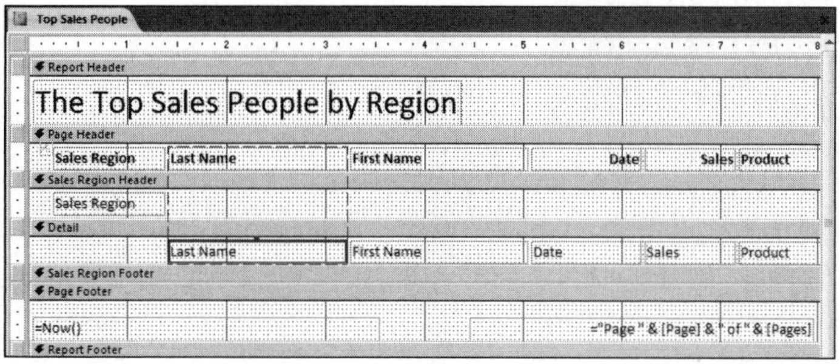

Figure 18-15:
To resize a
field, click
on that field
and then
drag the
side of the
field left
or right.

Top Sales People						

✦ Report Header

The Top Sales People by Region

✦ Page Header

Sales Region	Last Name	First Name	Date	Sales	Product

✦ Sales Region Header

Sales Region

✦ Detail

	Last Name	First Name	Date	Sales	Product

✦ Sales Region Footer

✦ Page Footer

=Now()   ="Page " & [Page] & " of " & [Pages]

✦ Report Footer

5. **Click the downward-pointing arrow under the View icon in the Views group.**

   A pull-down menu appears.

6. **Click Report View.**

   Access displays your report with your modified field size.

Deleting fields

If a report displays data that you no longer want to see, you can delete that field from your report by following these steps:

1. **Display your report in Design view by following Steps 1–4 in the earlier section, "Editing a Report."**

2. **Right-click the field you want to delete.**

   Access highlights your chosen field and its identifying label (refer to Figure 18-15) and displays a pop-up menu.

3. **Click Delete.**

   Access deletes your chosen field.

   You can press Ctrl+Z right away to retrieve any fields you may have deleted accidentally.

4. **Click the downward-pointing arrow under the View icon in the Views group.**

   A pull-down menu appears.

5. **Click Report View.**

   Access displays your report with your modified field size.

Deleting a Report

Eventually, you may find you no longer need a report, so you might as well delete it. To delete a report, follow these steps:

1. **Click the downward-pointing arrow that appears in the left pane.**

   A pull-down menu appears (refer to Figure 18-8).

2. **Click Tables and Related Views.**

   Access displays a list of all your previously saved reports in the left pane.

3. **Click the report you want to delete.**

4. **Click the Home tab.**

5. **Click the Delete icon in the Records group.**

   A dialog box appears, asking whether you really want to delete your report.

   Make sure you really want to delete a report because you won't be able to retrieve it afterwards.

6. **Click Yes (or No).**

Part VII
The Part of Tens

The 5th Wave   By Rich Tennant

"I hate when you bring 'Office' with you on camping trips."

In this part . . .

After spending your valuable time figuring out the many powers and puzzles of Microsoft Office 2007, flip through this part of the book to find out the secret shortcuts and hints that can make any of the programs in Microsoft Office 2007 even easier and more effective for your personal or business use.

Just make sure that your family, coworkers, or boss don't catch you reading this part of the book. They may stop thinking that you're an Office 2007 super-guru and realize you're just an ordinary person relying on a book. (Why not? Many of the best gurus do.)

Then again, why not buy extra copies of this book and give them to your friends, coworkers, and boss so they'll be able to figure out how to use Office 2007 on their own and leave you with enough time to actually do some useful work?

Chapter 19

Ten Tips for Using Office 2007

*M*icrosoft Office is famous for burying tons of useful features that most people never know about, so this chapter is about exposing some of Office 2007's features so you can take advantage of them and make Office 2007 more convenient (and safer) for you to use.

Saving Office 2007 Files

Most people dump their documents inside a folder in the Documents folder, so to make retrieving files easier, you can customize each Office 2007 program to look for files in a specific folder.

In addition to defining a default folder to look for files, you can also define a default file format for your Office 2007 programs. Finally, to protect your data (as much as possible) from inevitable computer crashes and hard disk failures, Office 2007 programs include a special AutoRecover feature, which saves a temporary copy of your file at fixed intervals, such as every ten minutes. That way, if the power goes out, you lose only those changes you made in the last ten minutes and not all your changes.

Access doesn't offer an AutoRecover feature because it automatically saves any changes to your data anyway.

To customize the location, format, and AutoRecover feature of an Office 2007 program, follow these steps:

1. **Load the Office 2007 program you want to customize (such as Word or PowerPoint).**

2. **Click the Office Button.**

   A pull-down menu appears.

3. **Click the Options button.**

   Depending on the program you're using, the Options button may read Word Options or Excel Options. An Options window appears.

4. **Click Save in the left pane.**

   The Options window displays various Save options.

5. **(Optional) Click in the Save Files in This Format list box and choose a file format, such as the 97 – 2003 format to save files that are compatible with previous versions of Office.**

6. **(Optional) Click in the Default File Location text box and type the drive and folder that you want to define as your default folder. (Or click the Browse button and then choose a folder.)**

7. **(Optional) Select the Save AutoRecover Information Every check box, click in the Minutes text box, and type a value or click the up/down arrows to define a value, such as 7 minutes.**

8. **Click OK.**

Password-Protecting Your Files

To prevent prying eyes from peeking at your Word, Excel, or PowerPoint files, you can password-protect them. That way, if someone wants to open, view, or edit your files, she must use your password. If someone doesn't know your password, she won't be able to view — let alone edit — your files.

You can buy programs off the Internet that can crack an Office 2007 password-protected file. For real security, don't rely on Office 2007's password-protection feature.

To password-protect a file, follow these steps:

1. **Load Word, Excel, or PowerPoint.**

2. **Click the Office Button.**

   A pull-down menu appears.

3. **Choose Save As.**

   The Save As dialog box appears.

4. **Click the Tools button.**

   A pull-down menu appears.

5. **Choose General Options.**

   The General Options dialog box appears.

6. **(Optional) Click in the Password to Open text box and type a password.**

   Another dialog box appears and asks you to confirm the password by typing it again.

7. **Type the password again and then click OK.**

8. **(Optional) Click in the Password to Modify text box and type a password.**

   This password can be different than the password you typed in Step 7. Another dialog box appears and asks you to confirm the password by typing it again.

9. **Type the password again and then click OK.**

10. **Click Save.**

You can create a password or remove passwords altogether by repeating the preceding steps and retyping a new password or deleting the password completely.

Guarding Against Macro Viruses and Worms

Macro viruses and *worms* are malicious programs designed to attach themselves to Word, Excel, and PowerPoint files. When an unsuspecting victim opens an infected file, the virus or worm can spread and do something nasty, such as deleting your files or your entire hard disk.

To stop these pests from wrecking your files, get an antivirus program, avoid downloading or accepting any files from unknown people, and turn on Office 2007's built-in macro protection feature, which can disable macros or restrict what macro viruses and worms can do even if they do infect your computer.

To turn on macro protection, follow these steps:

1. **Load Word or PowerPoint.**

2. **Click the Office Button.**

   A pull-down menu appears.

3. **Click Save As.**

   The Save As dialog box appears.

4. **Click the Tools button.**

   A pull-down menu appears.

5. **Click General Options.**

   The General Options dialog box appears.

6. **Click the Macro Security button.**

   The Trust Center dialog box appears with the Macro Settings options displayed.

7. **Select one of the following radio buttons:**

   - *Disable All Macros without Notification:* The safest but most restrictive setting, this prevents any macros (valid or viruses) from running when you open the file.

   - *Disable All Macros with Notification:* This is the default setting and displays a dialog box that lets you turn on macros if you trust that the file isn't infected.

   - *Disable All Macros except Digitally Signed Macros:* Blocks all macros except for the ones "authenticated" (previously defined as "trusted") by the user.

   - *Enable All Macros:* This setting runs all macros, which is the most dangerous setting.

8. **Click OK until you return to the Save As dialog box.**

9. **Click Save.**

Create Your Own Word Keystroke Shortcuts

The more you use Word 2007, the more likely you'll find yourself using certain commands. After a while, choosing these commands through Ribbon tabs may get tedious, so Word gives you the option of defining your own shortcut keystrokes to your favorite commands.

To assign a keystroke shortcut to a command, follow these steps:

1. **Load Word 2007.**

2. **Click the Office Button.**

   A pull-down menu appears.

3. **Click the Word Options button.**

   The Word Options window appears.

4. **Click Customize in the left pane.**

   The Word Options window displays various Customization options.

5. **Click the Customize button.**

   The Customize Keyboard dialog box appears.

6. **Click on a tab name (such as Home or Page Layout) in the Categories box.**

   The Commands box lists all the available commands stored within that tab name.

7. **Click a command in the Commands box.**

   The Current Keys box lists any shortcut keystrokes currently assigned to your chosen command.

8. **Click in the Press New Shortcut Key text box.**

9. **Press a unique keystroke combination, such as Ctrl+F7 or Alt+8.**

10. **Click Assign.**

    Word assigns your keystroke to your chosen command. If the keyboard shortcut you choose is already assigned, Word will alert you.

11. **Click Close.**

    The Word Options window appears again.

12. **Click OK.**

    You can use your keystroke shortcut in any Word documents.

Zooming In (And Out) to Avoid Eyestrain

For many people, Word, Excel, and PowerPoint may display text too tiny to see comfortably. To overcome this problem, you can increase the magnification in Word, Excel, or PowerPoint so that text appears bigger without physically altering the file itself.

Here are three ways to zoom in (or out) the magnification:

- ✔ Drag the Zoom slider that appears in the bottom-right corner.
- ✔ Hold down the Ctrl button and scroll the wheel of your mouse (assuming your mouse has a wheel).
- ✔ Click the View tab and then click the Zoom icon in the Zoom group. When a dialog box appears, click a magnification percentage (such as 125%) or type your own magnification percentage (such as 138%).

Changing the magnification only changes the way your text appears. Zooming in (or out) doesn't physically alter the text itself.

When in Doubt, Right-Click the Mouse

As a shortcut to giving commands to Office 2007, remember this simple guideline: First select, then right-click.

So if you want to change text or a picture, first select it to tell Office 2007 what you want to modify. Then right-click the mouse to display a pop-up menu of the commands. These pop-up menus display a list of only relevant commands for the item you just selected.

Freezing Row and Column Headings in Excel

One problem with creating large spreadsheets in Excel is that your identifying row and column headings may scroll out of sight if you scroll down or to the right of your worksheet.

To prevent this from happening, you can "freeze" a row or column that contains identifying labels. That way, when you scroll through your worksheet, your frozen row or column always remains visible.

To freeze a row or column in an Excel worksheet, follow these steps:

1. **Click the View tab.**

2. **Click the downward-pointing arrow that appears to the right of the Freeze Panes icon in the Window group.**

3. **Click one of the following:**

    • *Freeze panes:* Divides a worksheet into multiple panes

    • *Freeze Top Row:* Always displays the top row no matter how far down you scroll

    • *Freeze First Column:* Always displays the first column no matter how far to the right you scroll.

To unfreeze a row or column, repeat Steps 1–3 but click Unfreeze Panes.

Displaying Slides Out of Order in PowerPoint

When you display a PowerPoint presentation, your slides typically appear in the order that you arranged them, starting with the first slide. If you want to display your slides in a different order in the middle of a presentation, follow these steps:

1. **Load your presentation in PowerPoint and press F5.**

   The first slide of your presentation appears.

2. **Type the number of the slide you want to view and press Enter.**

   If you want to jump to the fifth slide in your presentation, type **5** and press Enter. If you jump to the fifth slide, clicking the mouse or pressing the spacebar next displays the sixth slide, then the seventh, and so on.

Print a list of your slide titles and slide numbers on a sheet of paper so that you know which slide number to type to view a particular slide.

Reduce Spam in Outlook

If you have an e-mail account, you will get *spam,* that unwanted e-mail that clogs millions of inboxes every day with obnoxious offers for mortgage refinancing, low-cost prescription drugs, or celebrity pornography. Unless you actually enjoy deleting these messages manually, you can use Outlook to filter your e-mail for you.

Setting up Outlook's junk e-mail filter

Outlook can either color-code suspected spam or move it to a special junk e-mail folder automatically. Because Outlook looks for keywords in spam, be aware that it will never be 100 percent effective in identifying spam, but it can identify the more blatant spam and save you time from deleting the messages yourself.

To turn on Outlook's spam filter, follow these steps:

1. **Choose Go⇨Mail or press Ctrl+1.**

   Outlook displays the Mail and Inbox panes.

2. **Choose Tools⇨Options.**

   The Options dialog box appears.

3. **Click the Junk E-mail button.**

   The Junk E-mail Options dialog box appears, as shown in Figure 19-1.

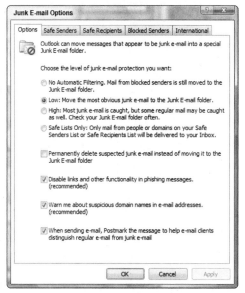

Figure 19-1:
The Junk E-mail Options dialog box lets you define how aggressive you want Outlook's spam filter to work.

4. **Select one of the following radio buttons:**

   - *No Automatic Filtering:* Turns off the Outlook spam filter.

   - *Low:* Identifies and moves most obvious spam to the Junk E-mail folder.

   - *High:* Identifies and moves nearly all spam into the Junk E-mail folder along with some regular e-mail messages, too, so check the Junk E-mail folder periodically to look for valid messages.

5. **Click OK.**

   The Options dialog box appears again.

6. **Click OK.**

Creating a Safe Senders list

A Safe Senders list lets you define all the e-mail addresses you want to accept messages from, and Outlook routes all e-mail from other e-mail addresses directly to your Junk E-mail folder.

The advantage of a Safe Senders list is that it guarantees you will never receive spam. On the down side, though, it also guarantees that if someone tries to contact you whose e-mail address doesn't appear on your Safe Senders list, you will never get that valid message, either.

To create a Safe Senders list, follow Steps 1 through 4 in the preceding section, "Setting up Outlook's junk email filter" to display the Junk E-mail Options dialog box. Then follow these steps:

1. **In the Junk E-mail Options dialog box (refer to Figure 19-1), click the Options tab.**

2. **Select the Safe Lists Only radio button.**

3. **Click the Safe Senders tab.**

   The Safe Sender's tab of the Junk E-mail Options dialog box appears.

4. **(Optional) Select (or clear) the Also Trust E-mail from My Contacts check box.**

   Selecting this check box tells Outlook that if you store someone's e-mail address in your Contacts list, you will also accept e-mail from that person, too.

5. **(Optional) Select (or clear) the Automatically Add People I E-mail to the Safe Senders List check box.**

   This tells Outlook that if you send e-mail to someone, you'll accept his or her messages in return.

6. **(Optional) Click the Add button.**

   The Add Address or Domain dialog box appears.

7. **Type a complete e-mail address. (Or type a domain name — for example, if you trust everyone from Microsoft.com to send you valid e-mail, type @microsoft.com in this dialog box.)**

8. **Click OK.**

9. **Repeat Steps 6–8 for each additional e-mail address or domain you want to add.**

10. **Click OK until all the dialog boxes disappear.**

Creating a Blocked Senders list

If a particular e-mail address persists in sending you spam, you can choose to selectively block that single e-mail address or domain. To create a Blocked Senders list, follow Steps 1 through 4 in the earlier section, "Setting up Outlook's junk email filter" to display the Junk E-mail Options dialog box. Then follow these steps:

1. **In the Junk E-mail Options dialog box (refer to Figure 19-1), select the Safe Lists Only radio button.**

2. **Click the Blocked Senders tab.**

   The Blocked Senders tab of the Junk E-mail Options dialog box appears.

3. **Click the Add button.**

   The Add E-mail Address or Domain dialog box appears (which looks just like the Add Address or Domain dialog box).

4. **Type an e-mail address or domain name and then click OK.**

   The Options dialog box appears again.

5. **Click OK until all the dialog boxes disappear.**

Using Pocket Office

Laptop computers may be light and handy for running Office 2007 on the road, but sometimes you may not want to lug around a laptop computer and its several pounds of dead weight. As an alternative, consider using a Windows Mobile handheld computer instead.

Windows Mobile devices (formerly called Pocket PCs and Windows CE) include miniature versions of Word, Excel, PowerPoint, and Access, which collectively are called *Pocket Office.* These Pocket versions of Office programs don't include all the features of Office 2007, but they will let you view, edit, and save your files so you can take them with you without the weight and bulk of a laptop computer.

If you want the convenience of Office 2007 without the heft of a laptop computer, Windows Mobile and Pocket Office may be for you.

Chapter 20

Ten Keystroke Shortcuts for Office 2007

• •

*O*ne common theme of Office 2007 is that all programs look and work alike. After you get used to using the Ribbon tabs in Word, you'll be able to use the similar Ribbon tabs in Excel and PowerPoint without too much trouble.

Even better, the same keystroke commands work alike in all Office 2007 programs. By memorizing the keystroke shortcuts in this chapter, you'll be able to work faster and more efficiently with Office 2007, no matter which particular program you may be using at the time.

Protecting Yourself with Undo (Ctrl+Z) and Redo (Ctrl+Y)

Many people are terrified of making a mistake using Office 2007, so they wind up never learning any features that could save them time and make their lives much easier. Any time you do anything in Office 2007, from deleting or modifying text to adding a picture or page, you can always immediately reverse — *undo* — your previous command by choosing the Undo command (Ctrl+Z) right away.

Armed with the Undo command, you can experiment freely with different commands. When things don't work the way you thought, press Ctrl+Z and undo your last changes.

If you wind up undoing a change and then suddenly realize you didn't want to undo that change after all, you can redo a command you previously reversed. To redo a command that you had undone, choose the Redo command (Ctrl+Y).

To undo multiple commands, follow these steps:

1. **Click the downward-pointing arrow to the right of the Undo icon on the Quick Access toolbar.**

   A pull-down menu appears of all the latest commands you've chosen.

2. **Highlight one or more commands on the Undo menu and click the last command you want to undo.**

3. **(Optional) If you undo a command and suddenly want to redo it, choose the Redo command by choosing one of the following:**

   • Click the Redo icon on the Quick Access toolbar.

   • Press Ctrl+Y.

You can't undo all commands. If a command cannot be undone, Office 2007 displays a dialog box informing you of this fact to prevent you from wiping out valuable data.

Cut (Ctrl+X), Copy (Ctrl+C), and Paste (Ctrl+V)

Editing any file often means moving or copying data from one place to another. Understandably, three of the most common commands are the Cut, Copy, and Paste commands.

Both the Cut and Copy commands are most often used with the Paste command. However, the Cut command, without the Paste command, is essentially equivalent to deleting selected text or objects.

Using the Cut and Paste commands

The Cut and Paste commands essentially move text or pictures from one location to another, typically within the same file, but also from one file to another file.

To use the Cut command, follow these steps:

1. **Select the text or objects you want to move.**

2. **Choose the Cut command by clicking the Cut icon or pressing Ctrl+X.**

   Office 2007 removes your selected item from your file.

3. **Move the cursor where you want to place the text or objects you selected in Step 1.**

4. **Choose the Paste command by clicking the Paste icon or pressing Ctrl+V.**

    Office 2007 displays the cut items in the location you specified in Step 3.

Using the Copy and Paste commands

The Copy and Paste commands copy text or pictures from one location to another location. To use the Copy command, follow these steps:

1. **Select the text or objects you want to copy.**

2. **Choose the Copy command by clicking the Copy icon or pressing Ctrl+C.**

    Your selected item remains in its original location.

3. **Move the cursor where you want to place the text or objects you selected in Step 1.**

4. **Choose the Paste command by clicking the Paste icon or pressing Ctrl+V.**

    Office 2007 displays the copied items in the location you specified in Step 3.

Using the Paste command with the Office Clipboard

Each time you choose the Cut or Copy command, Office 2007 stores that selected data (text or pictures) on the Office Clipboard, which can hold up to 24 items. After you cut or copy items to the Office Clipboard, you can always retrieve them.

If you turn off your computer or exit Office 2007, any items on the Office Clipboard are lost.

To retrieve a cut or copied item from the Office Clipboard and paste it into a document, follow these steps:

1. **Click the Home tab.**

2. **Click the Clipboard icon in the Clipboard group.**

3. **Move the cursor to where you want to paste an item.**

4. **Click an item displayed on the Office Clipboard.**

    Office 2007 pastes your chosen item in your file.

Saving a File (Ctrl+S)

Never trust that your computer, operating system, or Office 2007 will work when you need it. That's why you should save your file periodically while you're working: If you don't, and the power suddenly goes out, you'll lose all the changes you made to your file since the last time you saved it. If the last time you saved a file was 20 minutes ago, you'll lose all the changes you made in the past 20 minutes.

It's a good idea to save your file periodically, such as after you make a lot of changes to a file. To save a file, choose one of the following:

- ✔ Press Ctrl+S.
- ✔ Click the Save icon on the Quick Access toolbar.

The first time you save a file, Office 2007 asks you for a descriptive name. After you have saved a file at least once, you can choose the Save command, and Office 2007 will save your file without bothering you with a dialog box.

Printing a File (Ctrl+P)

Despite all the promises of a paperless office, more people are printing and using paper than ever before. As a result, one of the most common commands you'll use is the Print command.

To choose the Print command, press Ctrl+P or click the Print icon on the Quick Access toolbar.

Checking Your Spelling (F7)

Before you allow anyone to see your file, run a spell checker first. Just press F7, and Office 2007 diligently checks the spelling of your text. When the spell checker finds a suspicious word, it displays a dialog box, as shown in Figure 20-1, that lets you choose a correct spelling, ignore the currently highlighted word, or store the highlighted word in the Office 2007 dictionary so it won't flag that word as misspelled again.

Spell checkers are handy and useful, but they can be fooled easily. You might spell a word correctly (such as *their*) but use that word incorrectly, such as *You knead two move over their.* Spell-checking won't always recognize grammatical errors, so you still need to proof your file manually just to make sure you don't have any misspelled words in your file.

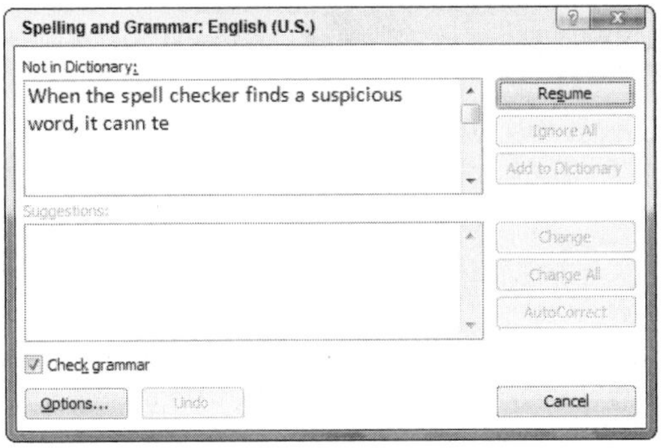

Figure 20-1:
Correct
misspellings
or choose
from a list of
alternative
spellings.

> [Dialog box: Spelling and Grammar: English (U.S.)]
>
> Not in Dictionary:
> When the spell checker finds a suspicious word, it cann te
>
> Resume
> Ignore All
> Add to Dictionary
>
> Suggestions:
>
> Change
> Change All
> AutoCorrect
>
> ☑ Check grammar
>
> Options...   Undo   Cancel

If you don't want Office 2007 to spell-check your entire file, just highlight the text you want to spell-check and then press F7.

Opening a File (Ctrl+O)

Generally, you'll spend more time working with existing files than creating new ones. Here are two shortcuts to open an existing file:

- ✔ Use the Recent Documents pane from the Office Button.
- ✔ Press Ctrl+O.

The first shortcut appears in the Recent Documents pane from the Office Button. Each Office 2007 program keeps track of the last files you opened, so if you want to open one again, you can just click that filename.

To use the Recent Documents pane, follow these steps:

1. **Load an Office 2007 program, such as Word or Excel.**
2. **Click the Office Button.**

   A pull-down menu appears and displays the list of Recent Documents.
3. **Click a filename in the Recent Documents pane.**

   Your chosen file appears, ready for you to view and edit.

A second way to open a file quickly is to press Ctrl+O. This immediately displays an Open dialog box so you can click the file you want to open.

Creating a New File (Ctrl+N)

Each Office 2007 program offers two ways to create a new file:

  ✔ Choose the New command from the Office Button.
  ✔ Press Ctrl+N.

When you choose the New command from the Office Button, Office 2007 displays a New Document dialog box, which lets you create a blank file or a file based on an existing template.

When you press Ctrl+N, Office 2007 immediately creates a blank file without making you wade through any dialog boxes.

If you want to create a new file based on a template, choose the New command from the Office Button. If you want to create a blank file, press Ctrl+N.

Pressing Ctrl+N in Outlook 2007 creates a different item, such as creating a new e-mail message or task, depending on what you're doing with Outlook at the time.

Finding Text (Ctrl+F)

The Find command lets you search for a word or phrase buried somewhere within your file. To use the Find command, follow these steps:

1. **Press Ctrl+F.**

   The Find and Replace dialog box appears, displaying the Find tab.

2. **Click in the Find What text box and type the word or phrase you want to find.**

3. **(Optional) Click the More button to expand the Find and Replace dialog box.**

   The More button expands the Find and Replace dialog box so you can fine-tune your search to make sure you don't wind up finding irrelevant text by mistake.

4. **(Optional) Select one of the following check boxes:**

   • *Match Case:* Use this to find *Bill* but not *bill.*

   • *Find Whole Words Only:* Use this to find *cat* but not words like *catastrophe* or *bobcat.*

   • *Use Wildcards:* Use this to find parts of text, such as all words that being with *fa,* by typing **fa*** in the Find What text box. This would find words such as *fail* and *fattening.* (This option is available only in Word.)

- *Sounds Like:* Use this to find words phonetically, such as searching for *elephant* by typing **elefant** in the Find What text box. (This option is available only in Word.)

- *Find All Word Forms:* Use this to find variations of a word such as *sings, singing,* and *sang.* (This option is available only in Word.)

5. **Click Find Next and repeat this step to continue searching your file.**

6. **Click Cancel when you're done.**

If you select a chunk of text, you can make Office 2007 search within your selected text only, rather than your entire file.

Finding and Replacing Text (Ctrl+H)

The Find and Replace command lets you substitute text throughout a file. You could search and replace a phrase like *Bill Johnson was a loser* with the phrase *Bill Johnson was a failure.*

To use the Find and Replace command, follow these steps:

1. **Press Ctrl+H.**

   The Find and Replace dialog box appears.

2. **Click in the Find What text box and type the text you want to find.**

3. **Click in the Replace With text box and type the text you want to appear instead.**

4. **(Optional) Click the More button and select one or more check boxes, as defined in Step 4 of the preceding section, "Finding Text (Ctrl+F)."**

5. **Click Find Next.**

   Office 2007 finds the first occurrence of the text you typed in Step 2.

6. **Click Replace or Replace All.**

   The Replace command lets you review each word before you replace it to make sure that's what you really want to do. The Replace All command replaces text without giving you a chance to see whether it's correct or not. When using the Replace All command, be aware that Office 2007 may replace words incorrectly. For example, in addition to replacing *Bob* with *Frank,* Office 2007 might also replace all occurrences of *Bobcat* with *Frankcat,* which is probably something you don't want to do.

7. **Click Close when you're done.**

Closing a Window (Ctrl+W)

To close a window, you can either click on that window's Close box or click the Office Button and then click Close. For a faster alternative, just press Ctrl+W and this closes the current window right away.

If you haven't saved the contents of the current window, Office 2007 displays a dialog box asking if you want to save your data before it closes your window.

Index

• A •

.accdb file extension, 18
Access database
  blank database, creating, 314–315
  closing
    database file, 329
    database table, 328
  cursor, moving, 30–31
  database report
    counting records or values in
      database report, 360–361
    deleting, 366
    editing, 363–365
    manipulating data in database report,
      359–363
    previewing, 358–359
    printing, 358–359
    viewing, 357–358
  Datasheet view, 315, 321–327
  Design View, switching to, 363–364
  designing a database, 313–316
  editing, 317–320
  fields
    adding, 317, 325–327
    deleting, 318, 324–325
    deleting fields in database report,
      365
    duplicate field data, creating a query
      that finds, 346–347
    filtering fields in database report,
      362–363
    naming, 317
    resizing fields in database report,
      364–365
    size of field, defining, 318–320
    sorting fields in database report, 361
    type of field, defining, 318–320
  filtering a database
    clearing filters, 339
    criteria for filters, 336–339
    exact match used for a filter,
      334–335
    form, filter defined by, 335–336
    overview, 333–334
  Form view, entering data in, 322
  forms
    creating, 322–323
    editing, 324–327
    editing data in forms, 323–324
    overview, 312
    viewing data in, 323–324
  Layout View, displaying report in,
    359–360
  overview, 311–313
  querying
    crosstab query, creating, 343–346
    deleting queries, 351
    duplicate field data, creating a query
      that finds, 346–347
    overview, 312, 3340
    renaming queries, 350–351
    simple query, creating, 340–343
    unmatched query, creating, 348–349
    viewing queries, 350
  records, 312
  Report Wizard, 353–357
  reports, 311, 312
  retrieval, 311
  saving, 329

Access database *(continued)*
  searching
    filtering a database, 333–339
    overview, 332
    specific record, searching for,
      332–333
  sorting, 339–340
  storage, 311
  tables, 312
  template, creating a database from a,
    316
  typing data into, 321–327
Account Configuration dialog box
  (Outlook), 262
Account Settings dialog box (Outlook),
  266
Add New E-mail Account dialog box
  (Outlook), 263–264
aligning text
  in PowerPoint presentations, 215–216
  in table cell (Word), 103
animated cartoons added to a slide
  (PowerPoint), 235
appointments (Outlook)
  defining recurring appointments,
    305–306
  deleting, 305
  editing, 304
  editing recurring appointments,
    306–307
  new appointment, making a, 301–304
  overview, 301
  printing your appointment schedule,
    307–308
  recurring appointments, 305–307
  setting, 301–307
area chart (Excel), 183
artistic text (Word), 115–118
audio clips added to presentation
  (PowerPoint), 239

audio files added to presentation
  (PowerPoint), 238
auditing formulas (Excel), 175–177
AutoFill (Excel), 130
AutoRecover feature, 369–370
AutoSum command (Excel), 166–167
AVERAGE function (Excel), 164

• *B* •

backgrounds (PowerPoint)
  choosing, 224
  gradient backgrounds, 226–228
  picture backgrounds, 228–229
  solid color backgrounds, 224–226
bar chart (Excel), 183
Bcc list (Outlook), 270
blank database (Access), 314–315
Blocked Senders list (Outlook), 378
bold text (Word), 74
borders
  spreadsheets, 137
  tables (Word), 104–106
browsing Help system, 43–45
built-in styles, formatting cells with
  (Excel), 135
bulleted lists (PowerPoint), 217–218

• *C* •

categories (Outlook)
  color categorizing e-mail messages,
    279–282
  creating, 292–293
  overview, 291
  storing names in, 293
  viewing names by, 294

Cc list (Outlook), 270
CD audio track added to presentation (PowerPoint), 239–240
CD used to package PowerPoint presentations, 257–258
cell
  formatting (Excel), 134–137
  reference (Excel), 159
  Word tables
    borders, deleting, 115
    deleting, 114
    margins, defining, 108–109
    spacing, defining, 109–110
Chart Tools (Excel)
  data source, changing, 189
  deleting a chart, 192
  layout of chart, designing, 191–192
  modifying parts of a chart, 190–191
  overview, 187
  rows and columns, switching, 189–190
  type of chart, changing, 188
charts
  area chart, 183
  bar chart, 183
  Chart Tools, 187–192
  column chart, 183
  creating, 184–185
  data series, 181
  editing, 185–187
  legend, 181
  line chart, 183
  moving
    chart on a worksheet, 185–186
    chart to a new sheet, 186–187
  overview, 181–183
  pie, 183
  resizing, 187
  title, 181
  X-axis, 181
  Y-axis, 181

clearing filters in Access, 339
clickable icons, 25
clip art added to a slide (PowerPoint), 230–231
Close a window (Ctrl+W) command, 386
closing a database file (Access), 329
closing a database table (Access), 328
collapsing headings (Word), 59, 61
collapsing subtitles (PowerPoint), 211–212
color
  categorizing e-mail messages by, 279–282
  coloring all or part of a table in Word, 104
  in spreadsheets, 136–137
  of text, changing, 75–76
column chart (Excel), 183
columns and rows (Excel)
  adding, 146
  deleting, 146
  headings, printing, 155–156
  mouse used to change size of, 144–145
  switching, 189–190
  typing size of, 145
columns
  PowerPoint presentations, 218
  Word
    deleting, 120
    editing, 118–119
    text divided into, 118–120
commands given to Office 2007 with Ribbon, 25–26
contacts (Outlook)
  contact information
    categorizing, 291–294
    printing, 290–291
    searching, 289
    sharing, 294–295

contact information *(continued)*
  storing, 287–288
  viewing, 290–291
  Outlook file, storing information as, 295
  vCards, 295
contextual tabs (Ribbon), 23
contiguous cell ranges, using, 164
converting list items back into text (Word), 79
Copy (Ctrl+C) command, 380–381
copying
  formulas, 163–164
  pasting data, 37–38
COUNT function, 164
count of data in pivot tables, displaying, 201
counting records or values in database report, 360–361
cover page (Word), 92–93
criteria for filters (Access), 336–339
crosstab query (Access), 343–346
Ctrl+C (Copy) command, 380–381
Ctrl+F (Find) command, 384–385
Ctrl+H (Find and Replace) command, 385
Ctrl+N (New) command, 384
Ctrl+O (Open) command, 383
Ctrl+P (Print) command, 382
Ctrl+S (Save) command, 382
Ctrl+V (Paste) command, 380–381
Ctrl+W (Close a window) command, 386
Ctrl+X (Cut) command, 380–381
Ctrl+Y (Redo) command, 379–380
Ctrl+Z (Undo) command, 379–380
cursor
  keyboard used to move, 30–31
  mouse used to move, 29
  speed of, increasing, 30

custom slide show in PowerPoint presentation, 251–252
customization
  lists (Word), 80
  of programs in Office 2007, 26–27
Cut (Ctrl+X) command, 380–381
cutting and pasting data, 36–38

• *D* •

data (Excel)
  data series, 181
  input for spreadsheets, 128–130
  in single cell, editing, 144
  source, 189
  validation, 177–180
database report (Access)
  counting records or values in, 360–361
  deleting, 366
  deleting fields in, 365
  Design View, switching to, 363–364
  editing, 363–365
  filtering a field in, 362–363
  Layout View, displaying report in, 359–360
  manipulating data in, 359–363
  overview, 353
  previewing, 358–359
  printing, 358–359
  Report Wizard, 353–357
  resizing fields in, 364–365
  sorting a field in, 361
  viewing, 357–358
Datasheet view (Access)
  entering data in, 321–327
  overview, 315
decimal numbers, formatting, 134
Deleted Items folder (Outlook), 286

demoting headings (Word), 60
dependent cells, 176–177
Design View (Access), 363–364
designing Access database, 313–316
different slides, creating hyperlinks in
    PowerPoint to, 247–249
.doc file extension, 18
documents (Word)
  Find and Replace command, 66
  Find command, 64–65
  finding text, 64–65
  Full Screen Reading view, using, 57
  Go To command used to navigate, 63–64
  grammar, checking your, 68
  headings
    collapsing, 59, 61
    defining, 59
    demoting, 60
    expanding, 61
    moving, 60–61
    promoting, 60
    rearranging, 59
  keyboard shortcuts, 55
  keyboard used to move cursor in,
    54–55
  mouse scroll wheel used to
    navigate, 63
  mouse used to move cursor in, 53–54
  mouse used to navigate, 62–63
  navigation of, 62–64
  Outline view, using, 58–61
  proofreading, 68
  replacing text, 66
  scroll bar used to navigate, 62–63
  spelling, checking your, 66–67
  switching between views in, 56
  symbols, typing, 69–70
  text, creating, 61
  viewing, 55–61

.docx file extension, 18
double-clicking mouse, 33
downloading and using a template off
    Microsoft Web site, 14–15
drop caps (Word), 115–116
duplicate field data, creating Access
    query that finds, 346–347

• E •

editing
  Access
    data in forms, 323–324
    database report, 363–365
    forms, 324–327
  Access database, 317–320
  charts, 185–187
  columns (Word), 118–119
  data
    adding data by pointing, 29–31
    copying and pasting data, 37–38
    cutting and pasting data, 36–38
    deleting data, 35
    with mouse, 37–38
    with pop-up toolbar, 34–35
    Redo command, 39
    saving files, 29
    selecting data, 31–34
    sharing data between multiple
      programs, 39–42
    Undo command, 38–39
  formulas, 168
  Outlook
    appointments, 304
    e-mail account, 266–267
    recurring appointments, 306–307
    signatures, 278
    tasks, 297

editing *(continued)*
  scenarios, 173
  spreadsheets, 144–148
e-mail. *See also* Outlook
  adding e-mail account, 265–266
  attaching files to messages, 272–274
  categorizing messages, 279–282
  configuring e-mail settings, 261–267
  creating, 267–271
  deleting
    account, 266
    messages, 284–286
  editing account, 266–267
  formatting, 274–278
  forwarding message, 271
  multiple files attached to message,
    272
  new message, creating, 267–269
  Outlook information attached to
    message, 273–274
  permanently deleting, 286
  reading and organizing, 279–284
  replying to message, 269
  retrieving
    file attachment from, 282–284
    previously deleted, 285
  signatures, adding, 275–278
  stored message used to create a new
    message, 270–271
  text, formatting, 274–275
  undeleting, 285
  viewing, 279
enlarging text in Help window, 47
entire table in Word, deleting, 112–113
even pages (Word)
  creating unique footer for, 95
  creating unique header for, 95
exact match used for a filter (Access),
  334–335

Excel
  area chart, 183
  auditing formulas, 175–177
  AutoSum command, 166–167
  bar chart, 183
  cell reference, 159
  Chart Tools
    data source, changing, 189
    deleting a chart, 192
    layout of chart, designing, 191–192
    modifying parts of a chart, 190–191
    overview, 187
    rows and columns, switching, 189–190
    type of chart, changing, 188
  column chart, 183
  columns and rows
    adding, 146
    deleting, 146
    freezing, 374
    mouse used to change size of, 144–145
    switching, 189–190
    typing size of, 145
    unfreezing, 374
  copying formulas, 163–164
  creating
    charts, 184–185
    formulas, 159–164
    pivot tables, 193–195
  cursor, moving, 30–31
  data
    count of data, displaying, 201
    incorrect data in formulas, 175
    input for spreadsheets, 128–130
    missing data in formulas, 175
    series, 181
    in single cell, editing, 144
    source, 189
    validation, 177–180
  dependent cells, 176–177

editing
  charts, 185–187
  formulas, 168
filtering pivot tables, 199–200
functions
  AVERAGE function, 164
  contiguous cell ranges, using, 164
  COUNT function, 164
  MAX function, 164
  MIN function, 164
  noncontiguous cell ranges, using, 164
  overview, 164–166
  recently used functions, list of,
    167–168
  ROUND function, 164
  SQRT function, 164
  SUM function, 164
  using, 164–168
Goal Seeking, 168–170
headings, printing, 155–156
incorrect calculations in formulas, 175
labels in pivot tables, rearranging,
  196–197
legend, 181
line chart, 183
mathematical operators used to create
  formulas, 160
modifying pivot tables, 197–198
moving
  chart on a worksheet, 185–186
  chart to a new sheet, 186–187
operator precedence, 162
parentheses, organizing formulas with,
  162–163
pie chart, 183
pivot tables
  count of data, displaying, 201
  creating, 193–195
  filtering, 199–200
  labels in, rearranging, 196–197

modifying, 197–198
overview, 192–193
precedent cells, 176
printing workbooks
  defining a print area, 152–153
  in Excel, 158
  footer, adding, 151
  gridlines, printing, 152
  header, adding, 151
  margins for printing, defining, 156
  overview, 149
  page breaks, deleting, 154
  page breaks, inserting, 153–154
  with Page Layout view, 150
  paper orientation, 156–157
  paper size, 156–157
  row and column headings, printing,
    155–156
resizing charts, 187
scenarios
  creating, 170–172
  editing, 173
  overview, 170
  viewing, 172
  viewing a scenario summary, 174–175
searching for formulas, 143–144
single cell affecting formulas, 176–177
spreadsheets, 128
title on chart, 181
tracing formulas, 176
X-axis, 181
Y-axis, 181
existing document, creating a Word
  document based on, 89
existing text
  converted to list in PowerPoint
    presentations, 218
  Word
    converted into lists, 79
    creating a table from, 99–102

expanding headings (Word), 61
expanding subtitles (PowerPoint), 211–212
external file hyperlinks (PowerPoint), 247

• F •

fields (Access)
  adding, 317, 325–327
  deleting, 318, 324–325
  deleting fields in database report, 365
  filtering fields in database report, 362–363
  naming, 317
  overview, 312
  resizing fields in database report, 364–365
  size of field, defining, 318–320
  sorting fields in database report, 361
  type of field, defining, 318–320
file attachment (Outlook)
  opening, 283–284
  retrieving, 282–284
file extensions, 18
File menu
  closing a file, 19
  creating
    new file, 12–13
    new file from a template, 13–15
  opening existing file, 15–16
  overview, 12
  saving files, 16–19
Fill color for spreadsheets, 136–137
filtering a database (Access)
  clearing filters, 339
  criteria for filters, 336–339
  exact match used for a filter, 334–335
  field in a database report, 362–363

form, filter defined by, 335–336
overview, 333–334
filtering pivot tables, 199–200
Find and Replace (Ctrl+H) command, 385
Find (Ctrl+F) command, 384–385
finding text in Word documents, 64–65
finishing tasks (Outlook), 299
first page (Word)
  creating unique footer for, 94
  creating unique header for, 94
fonts
  Excel
    color of, 136–137
    formatting, 135–136
  Word
    changing, 72–73
    size, changing, 73–74
footer
  Excel, 151
  Word
    creating, 93–94
    deleting, 95
    even pages, creating unique footer for, 95
    first page, creating unique footer for, 94
    odd pages, creating unique footer for, 95
    overview, 93
    pages to display, defining, 94–95
form, filter defined by (Access), 335–336
Form view (Access), 322
Format Painter (Word), 86
formatting
  e-mail, 274–278
  tables (Word), 102–111
  text in PowerPoint presentations, 214–215

formatting text (Word)
  bold text, 74
  colors, changing, 75–76
  font
    changing, 72–73
    size, changing, 73–74
  Format Painter, using, 86
  highlighting text, 76
  italic text, 74
  justifying text alignment, 76–77
  line spacing, adjusting, 77–78
  lists, creating, 78–81
  overview, 71–72
  removing formatting from text, 89–90
  Ruler, using, 82–84
  showing formatting marks, 84–85
  strikethrough text, 74
  styles, using, 87
  subscripts, 74
  superscripts, 74
  templates, using, 88–89
  text style, changing, 74
  underlined text, 74
forms (Access)
  adding a field, 325–327
  creating, 322–323
  deleting a field, 324–325
  editing, 324–327
  editing data in, 323–324
  overview, 312
  viewing data in, 323–324
formulas
  auditing, 175–177
  cell reference, 159
  copying, 163–164
  creating, 159–164
  dependent cells, 176–177
  editing, 168
  functions, using, 164–168
  Goal Seeking, 168–170

incorrect calculations in, 175
incorrect data in, 175
mathematical operators used to create, 160
missing data in, 175
operator precedence, 162
parentheses, organizing formulas with, 162–163
precedent cells, 176
searching for, 143–144
single cell affecting, 176–177
spreadsheets, 128
tracing, 176
forwarding e-mail message, 271
freezing rows and columns (Excel), 374
F7 (Spellcheck) command, 382–383
Full Screen Reading view (Word), 57
functions (Excel)
  AutoSum command, 166–167
  AVERAGE function, 164
  contiguous cell ranges, using, 164
  COUNT function, 164
  MAX function, 164
  noncontiguous cell ranges, using, 164
  overview, 164–166
  recently used functions, list of, 167–168
  ROUND function, 164
  SQRT function, 164
  SUM function, 164
  using, 164–168

• G •

gallery icons, 25
Go To command (Word), 63–64
Goal Seeking, 168–170
gradient backgrounds (PowerPoint), 226–228

grammar (Word), 68
graphics (PowerPoint)
  clip art added to a slide, 230–231
  deleting, 233
  layering objects, 234
  moving, 233
  overview, 229
  picture files added to a slide, 230
  resizing, 232–233
  rotating, 233
  WordArt, creating, 232
gridlines, printing, 152

• *H* •

handheld device, Office 2007 on, 378
handouts created for PowerPoint
      presentations, 256–257
headers
  Excel, 151
  Word
    creating, 93–94
    deleting, 95
    even pages, creating unique header
      for, 95
    first page, creating unique header
      for, 94
    odd pages, creating unique header
      for, 95
    overview, 93
    pages to display, defining, 94–95
headings (Word)
  collapsing, 59, 61
  defining, 59
  demoting, 60
  expanding, 61
  moving, 60–61
  promoting, 60
  rearranging, 59

Help system
  browsing, 43–45
  enlarging text in Help window, 47
  overview, 43
  printing text in Help window, 47
  resizing Help window, 46–47
  searching in, 45–46
  table of contents, viewing, 48–49
  visible Help window, always
    keeping, 47
hiding slides (PowerPoint)
  overview, 252–253
  in Slide view, 209
highlighting in Word
  tables, highlighting rows and columns
    to create, 96–97
  text, 76
hyperlinks (PowerPoint)
  different slides, creating hyperlinks to,
    247–249
  external file hyperlinks, creating, 247
  overview, 246
  running a program through, 249
  Web page hyperlinks, creating, 246–247

• *I* •

icons
  adding icons, 21–22
  clickable icons, 25
  gallery icons, 25
  list box icons, 25
  Print icon, 20
  Redo icon, 20
  removing icons, 22
  Ribbon, 23–24
  Save icon, 20
  Undo icon, 20–21
  using icons, 20–21

incorrect calculations in formulas, 175
incorrect data in formulas, 175
indentation defined with Ruler
    (Word), 84
indenting list items (Word), 79
Insert tab (Word), 91
Insert Table dialog box (Word), 97–98
italic text (Word), 74

• J •

junk e-mail filter (Outlook), 375–376
justifying text alignment (Word), 76–77

• K •

keyboard
  selecting data with, 33–34
  shortcuts
    documents (Word), 55
    Ribbon, 24
    spreadsheets, 139
  used to move cursor, 30–31
  used to move cursor in documents
    (Word), 54–55
  used to navigate spreadsheets, 138–140
keystroke shortcuts
  Close a window (Ctrl+W) command,
    386
  Copy (Ctrl+C) command, 380–381
  Cut (Ctrl+X) command, 380–381
  Find and Replace (Ctrl+H) command,
    385
  Find (Ctrl+F) command, 384–385
  New (Ctrl+N) command, 384
  Open (Ctrl+O) command, 383
  overview, 372–373

Paste (Ctrl+V) command, 380–381
Print (Ctrl+P) command, 382
Redo (Ctrl+Y) command, 379–380
Save (Ctrl+S) command, 382
Spellcheck (F7) command, 382–383
Undo (Ctrl+Z) command, 379–380

• L •

labels in pivot tables, rearranging,
    196–197
layering objects (PowerPoint), 234
layout of chart (Excel), 191–192
Layout View (Access), 359–360
left and right paragraph margins
    (Word), 83
legend on charts (Excel), 181
line chart (Excel), 183
line spacing
  in PowerPoint presentations, 216–217
  in Word, 77–78
list box icons, 25
lists (Word)
  converting list items back into text, 79
  customizing, 80
  existing text converted into, 79
  indenting list items, 79
  overview, 78–79
  renumbering numbered lists, 80–81
Live Preview (Ribbon), 24–25
loading programs, 10–11

• M •

macro virus protection, 371–372
magnification of text, 373
manipulating data in database report
    (Access), 359–363

margins for printing workbooks, 156
mathematical operators used to create
formulas, 160
MAX function, 164
.mdb file extension, 18
merging cells in tables (Word), 110–111
MIN function, 164
missing data in formulas, 175
mouse
double-clicking, 33
selecting data, 31–33
single-clicking, 33
triple-clicking, 33
used to move cursor, 29
used to navigate spreadsheets, 138
Word
creating tables, 98–99
moving cursor in documents, 53–54
navigating documents, 62–63
using scroll wheel to navigate
documents, 63
movies (PowerPoint)
adding movies to a slide, 235–237
animated cartoons added to a slide,
235
overview, 235
multiple cells, typing data into, 129–130
multiple files attached to message
(Outlook), 272
multiple sections of data selected with
mouse and keyboard, 34
multiple signatures (Outlook), 277

• N •

naming
cells (Excel), 140–141
fields (Access), 317

navigation
documents (Word), 62–64
spreadsheets, 138–141
negative numbers, displaying (Excel),
132–133
new appointment (Outlook), 301–304
New (Ctrl+N) command, 384
new document created from templates
(Word), 88–89
new e-mail message, creating (Outlook),
267–269
new pages (Word), 91–92
new slide created in Slide view
(PowerPoint), 208, 211
noncontiguous cell ranges, using, 164
numbered lists in PowerPoint
presentations, 217–218
numbers in spreadsheets, formatting,
131–134

• O •

odd pages (Word)
creating unique footer for, 95
creating unique header for, 95
Office 2007
AutoRecover feature, 369–370
customizing programs in, 26–27
exiting, 27–28
File menu, 12–19
on handheld device, 378
keystroke shortcuts, 372–373, 379–386
loading programs, 10–11
macro virus protection, 371–372
magnification of text, 373
Office button, 12–19
overview, 9–10
password-protecting your files,
370–371

Quick Access toolbar, 19–23
Ribbon, 23–26
right-clicking the mouse, 374
saving files, 369–370
user interface, 11–26
worms, protection from, 371–372
Office button, 12–19
Office Clipboard
advantages of, 40
deleting items from, 41–42
overview, 40
pasting items off the, 40–41, 381
viewing items on, 40
Open (Ctrl+O) command, 383
opening file attachment (Outlook),
283–284
operator precedence, 162
order of slides in PowerPoint
presentation, 375
organizing tasks (Outlook), 298
other computers, PowerPoint
presentations on, 257–258
Outline view
PowerPoint presentations,
207, 210–212
Word, 58–61
Outlook
Account Settings dialog box, 266
Add New E-mail Account dialog box,
263–264
adding e-mail account, 265–266
appointments
deleting, 305
editing, 304
new appointment, making a, 301–304
printing your appointment schedule,
307–308
recurring appointments, 305–307
setting, 301–307

attaching files to messages, 272–274
Bcc list, 270
Blocked Senders list, 378
categories
color categorizing e-mail messages,
279–282
creating, 292–293
overview, 291
storing names in categories, 293
viewing names by categories, 294
Cc list, 270
configuring e-mail settings, 261–267
contacts
Outlook file, storing information as,
295
printing contact information, 290–291
searching contact information, 289
sharing contact information, 294–295
storing contact information, 287–288
vCards, 295
viewing contact information, 290–291
creating e-mail, 267–271
Deleted Items folder, 286
deleting
e-mail account, 266
e-mail messages, 284–286
editing e-mail account, 266–267
formatting e-mail, 274–278
forwarding e-mail message, 271
junk e-mail filter, 375–376
multiple files attached to message,
272
new e-mail message, creating, 267–269
Outlook information attached to
message, 273–274
overview, 291, 301
reading and organizing e-mail, 279–284
replying to e-mail message, 269
Safe Senders list, 377

Outlook *(continued)*
  signatures
    creating, 275–277
    deleting, 278
    editing, 278
    multiple signatures, 277
    overview, 275
  spam, reducing, 375–378
  stored e-mail message used to create a
    new e-mail message, 270–271
  tasks
    creating, 296–297
    deleting, 299
    editing, 297
    finishing, 299
    organizing, 298
    overview, 295
    viewing, 298

• *P* •

page breaks
  deleting (Excel), 154
  inserting (Excel), 153–154
  inserting (Word), 93
page design (Word)
  adding a cover page, 92–93
  artistic text, creating, 115–118
  columns, dividing text into, 118–120
  deleting a cover page, 92–93
  drop caps, creating, 115–116
  footers, 93–95
  headers, 93–95
  Insert tab, 91
  inserting new pages, 91–92
  overview, 91
  page breaks, inserting, 93
  Page Layout tab, 91

previewing a document before printing,
  120–124
tables
  formatting and coloring, 102–111
  organizing text in, 96–102
WordArt, creating, 116–118
Page Layout tab (Word), 91
Page Layout view (Excel), 150
page size (Word), 120–121
paper orientation
  Excel, 156–157
  Word, 121
paper size (Excel), 156–157
paragraphs in PowerPoint presentations,
  218
parentheses, organizing formulas with,
  162–163
password-protecting your files, 370–371
Paste (Ctrl+V) command, 380–381
pasting items off the Office Clipboard,
  40–41, 381
permanently deleting e-mail, 286
picture backgrounds (PowerPoint),
  228–229
picture files added to a slide
  (PowerPoint), 230
pie charts (Excel), 183
pivot tables (Excel)
  count of data, displaying, 201
  creating, 193–195
  filtering, 199–200
  labels in, rearranging, 196–197
  modifying, 197–198
  overview, 192–193
Pocket Office, 378
pointing, adding data by, 29–31
pop-up toolbar, 34–35
PowerPoint presentations
  adding movies to a slide, 235–237
  animated cartoons added to a slide, 235

audio clips added to presentation, 239
audio files added to presentation, 238
backgrounds
  changing, 224–229
  choosing, 224
  gradient backgrounds, 226–228
  picture backgrounds, 228–229
  solid color backgrounds, 224–226
CD audio track added to presentation,
  239–240
CD used to package, 257–258
creating, 206–212
cursor, moving, 30–31
custom slide show, creating, 251–252
deleting slides in Slide view, 209–210,
  212
graphics
  clip art added to a slide, 230–231
  deleting, 233
  layering objects, 234
  moving, 233
  overview, 229
  picture files added to a slide, 230
  resizing, 232–233
  rotating, 233
  WordArt, creating, 232
handouts, creating, 256–257
hiding slides, 209, 252–253
hyperlinks
  different slides, creating hyperlinks to,
    247–249
  external file hyperlinks, creating, 247
  overview, 246
  running a program through, 249
  Web page hyperlinks, creating, 246–247
movies
  adding movies to a slide, 235–237
  animated cartoons added to a slide,
    235
  overview, 235

new slide created in Slide view,
  208, 211
order of slides in, 375
on other computers, 257–258
Outline view, 207, 208–212
overview, 205
purpose of your presentation, defining,
  205–206
rearranging slides in Slide view, 209, 212
Slide Sorter view, 253–254
Slide view, 207, 208–210
sound
  audio clips added to presentation,
    239
  audio files added to presentation,
    238
  CD audio track added to presentation,
    239–240
  overview, 237–238
spellchecking, 241–242
subtitles, 211–212
switching between views, 210
text
  aligning, 215–216
  bulleted lists, creating, 217–218
  columns, creating, 218
  existing text converted to list, 218
  formatting, 214–215
  line spacing in, adjusting, 216–217
  moving text boxes, 219
  numbered lists, creating, 217–218
  overview, 213
  paragraphs, 218
  resizing text boxes, 219
  rotating text boxes, 220
  text box, typing text in, 213–214
  transitions, 245
text boxes
  moving, 219
  resizing, 219

text boxes *(continued)*
  rotating, 220
  typing text in, 213–214
themes, applying, 221–223
timing, 254–256
transitions
  overview, 242–243
  slide transitions, 243–245
  text transitions, 245
  viewing, 250–256
.ppt file extension, 18
.pptx file extension, 18
precedent cells, 176
previewing a document before printing
    (Word)
  orientation, defining, 121
  overview, 120
  page size, defining, 120–121
  with Print Preview, 122–123
  printing the document, 123–124
previewing database report (Access),
    358–359
print area in workbooks, defining,
    152–153
Print (Ctrl+P) command, 382
Print Preview (Word), 122–123
printing
  database report (Access), 358–359
  Outlook
    contact information, 290–291
    your appointment schedule, 307–308
  text in Help window, 47
  Word document, 123–124
printing workbooks
  defining a print area, 152–153
  in Excel, 158
  footer, adding, 151
  gridlines, printing, 152
  header, adding, 151

margins for printing, defining, 156
overview, 149
page breaks
  deleting, 154
  inserting, 153–154
with Page Layout view, 150
paper orientation, 156–157
paper size, 156–157
row and column headings, printing,
    155–156
promoting headings (Word), 60
proofreading documents (Word), 68
purpose of your PowerPoint
    presentation, defining, 205–206

• *Q* •

querying a database (Access)
  crosstab query, creating, 343–346
  deleting queries, 351
  duplicate field data, creating a query
      that finds, 346–347
  overview, 312, 340
  renaming queries, 350–351
  simple query, creating, 340–343
  unmatched query, creating, 348–349
  viewing queries, 350
Quick Access toolbar
  adding icons, 21–22
  moving, 22
  overview, 19–20
  Print icon, 20
  Redo icon, 20
  removing icons, 22
  Ribbon, minimizing, 22–23
  Save icon, 20
  Undo icon, 20–21
  using icons, 20–21

• R •

reading and organizing e-mail, 279–284
rearranging headings (Word), 59
rearranging slides in Slide view
    (PowerPoint), 209, 212
recently used functions, list of, 167–168
records (Access), 312
recurring appointments (Outlook),
    305–307
Redo (Ctrl+Y) command, 379–380
renaming queries (Access), 350–351
renumbering numbered lists (Word),
    80–81
replacing text (Word), 66
replying to e-mail message, 269
Report Wizard (Access), 353–357
reports (Access), 311, 312
resizing
  charts, 187
  columns and rows (Word), 107–108
  fields in database report (Access),
    364–365
  graphics (PowerPoint), 232–233
  Help window, 46–47
  text boxes in PowerPoint presentations,
    219
retrieval (Access), 311
retrieving a file attachment from e-mail,
    282–284
retrieving previously deleted e-mail, 285
Ribbon
  commands given to Office 2007 with,
    25–26
  contextual tabs, 23
  icons, 23–24
  keyboard shortcuts, 24
  Live Preview, 24–25
  minimizing, 22–23
  overview, 23
  ScreenTips, 23–24
right-clicking the mouse, 374
rotating
  graphics (PowerPoint), 233
  text boxes (PowerPoint), 220
ROUND function, 164
rows and columns
  Excel
    adding, 146
    deleting, 146
    headings, printing, 155–156
    mouse used to change size of, 144–145
    switching, 189–190
    typing size of, 145
  Word, 113
Ruler (Word)
  adjusting left and right paragraph
    margins, 83
  hiding, 82
  indentation defined with, 84
  overview, 82

• S •

Safe Senders list (Outlook), 377
Save (Ctrl+S) command, 382
saving files
  for older versions of Microsoft Office,
    18–19
  overview, 16–17, 29, 369–370
scenarios (Excel)
  creating, 170–172
  editing, 173
  overview, 170
  spreadsheets, 170–175
  viewing, 172
  viewing a scenario summary, 174–175
ScreenTips, 23–24

scroll bar used to navigate documents (Word), 62–63
searching a database (Access)
  filtering a database, 333–339
  overview, 332
  specific record, searching for, 332–333
searching contact information (Outlook), 289
searching in Help system, 45–46
searching spreadsheets, 142–144
selecting all or part of a table (Word), 102–103
selecting data
  with keyboard, 33–34
  with mouse, 31–33
  multiple sections of data selected with mouse and keyboard, 34
  overview, 31
  pictures, selecting, 31–32
  text selection with mouse, 33
setting appointments (Outlook), 301–307
sharing contact information (Outlook), 294–295
sharing data between multiple programs
  with Office Clipboard, 40–42
  overview, 39
showing formatting marks (Word), 84–85
signatures (Outlook)
  creating, 275–277
  deleting, 278
  editing, 278
  multiple signatures, 277
  overview, 275
simple query (Access), 340–343
single cell
  affecting formulas, 176–177
  typing data into, 128–129
single-clicking mouse, 33
size of field (Access), 318–320
Slide Sorter view (PowerPoint), 253–254

slide transitions (PowerPoint), 243–245
Slide view (PowerPoint)
  overview, 207
  used to design presentation, 208–210
solid color backgrounds (PowerPoint), 224–226
sorting
  Access database, 339–340
  field in database report (Access), 361
  tables (Word), 111–112
sound (PowerPoint)
  audio clips added to presentation, 239
  audio files added to presentation, 238
  CD audio track added to presentation, 239–240
  overview, 237–238
spam, reducing, 375–378
specific record, searching for (Access), 332–333
speed of cursor, increasing, 30
Spellcheck (F7) command, 382–383
spellchecking
  documents (Word), 66–67
  PowerPoint presentations, 241–242
splitting cells in tables (Word), 110–111
spreadsheets. *See also* Excel
  adding sheets, 146
  AutoFill, typing in sequences with, 130
  borders, adding, 137
  built-in styles, formatting cells with, 135
  cells, formatting, 134–137
  color, formatting, 136–137
  data in single cell, editing, 144
  decimal numbers, formatting, 134
  deleting data in, 148–149
  deleting sheets, 148
  editing, 144–148
  Fill color, 136–137
  Font color, 136–137

fonts, formatting, 135–136
formulas, 128, 143–144
inputting data, 128–130
keyboard shortcuts, 139
keyboard used to navigate, 138–140
mouse used to navigate, 138
multiple cells, typing data into, 129–130
naming cells, 140–141
navigation of, 138–141
negative numbers, displaying, 132–133
numbers, formatting, 131–134
overview, 127–128
printing workbooks, 149–158
rearranging sheets, 148
renaming sheets, 146–147
rows and columns
  adding, 146
  deleting, 146
  mouse used to change size of, 144–145
  typing size of, 145
scenarios, 170–175
searching, 142–144
single cell, typing data into, 128–129
text
  searching for, 142–143
  style, formatting, 135–136
SQRT function, 164
storage (Access), 311
stored e-mail message used to create a
    new e-mail message (Outlook),
    270–271
storing contact information (Outlook),
    287–288
storing names in categories (Outlook),
    293
strikethrough text (Word), 74
style
  formatting text (Word), 87
  for tables (Word), 106–107
subscripts (Word), 74

subtitles (PowerPoint)
  collapsing, 211–212
  creating, 211
  expanding, 211–212
SUM function, 164
superscripts (Word), 74
switching between views
  in documents (Word), 56
  in PowerPoint presentations, 210
symbols (Word), 69–70

• T •

table of contents in Help system,
    viewing, 48–49
tables
  Access, 312
  Word
    aligning text in table cell, 103
    borders, adding, 104–106
    cell borders, deleting, 115
    cell margins, defining, 108–109
    cell spacing, defining, 109–110
    cells, deleting, 114
    coloring all or part of a table, 104
    creating, 96–102
    deleting, 112–115
    entire table, deleting, 112–113
    existing text, creating a table from,
      99–102
    formatting and coloring, 102–111
    highlighting rows and columns to
      create, 96–97
    Insert Table dialog box used to create,
      97–98
    merging cells, 110–111
    mouse used to create, 98–99
    resizing columns and rows, 107–108
    rows and columns, deleting, 113

Word *(continued)*
  selecting all or part of a table, 102–103
  sorting, 111–112
  splitting cells, 110–111
  style for, choosing, 106–107
  text organized in, 96–102
tasks (Outlook)
  creating, 296–297
  deleting, 299
  editing, 297
  finishing, 299
  organizing, 298
  overview, 295
  viewing, 298
templates
  Access, 316
  downloading and using a template off Microsoft Web site, 14–15
  overview, 13
  using Office 2007 template on your computer, 14
  Word
    existing document, creating a document based on, 89
    new document created from, 88–89
    overview, 88
text
  divided into columns (Word), 118–120
  documents (Word), 61
  formatting for e-mail, 274–275
  organized in tables (Word), 96–102
  searching for (Excel), 142–143
  selection with mouse, 33
  style
    changing (Word), 74
    formatting (Excel), 135–136
text boxes (PowerPoint)
  moving, 219
  resizing, 219
  rotating, 220
  typing text in, 213–214
text in PowerPoint presentations
  aligning, 215–216
  bulleted lists, creating, 217–218
  columns, creating, 218
  existing text converted to list, 218
  formatting, 214–215
  line spacing in, adjusting, 216–217
  moving text boxes, 219
  numbered lists, creating, 217–218
  overview, 213
  paragraphs, 218
  text box
    resizing, 219
    rotating, 220
    typing text in, 213–214
  transitions, 245
themes in PowerPoint presentations, 221–223
timing PowerPoint presentations, 254–256
title charts, 181
tracing formulas, 176
transitions (PowerPoint)
  overview, 242–243
  slide transitions, 243–245
  text transitions, 245
triple-clicking mouse, 33
type of chart, changing (Excel), 188
type of field, defining (Access), 318–320
typing data into Access database, 321–327

• *U* •

undeleting e-mail, 285
underlined text (Word), 74
Undo (Ctrl+Z) command, 379–380

unfreezing rows and columns (Excel), 374
unmatched query, creating (Access), 348–349
user interface, 11–26

• V •

vCards (Outlook), 295
viewing
  Access
    data in forms, 323–324
    database report, 357–358
    queries, 350
  documents (Word), 55–61
  e-mail, 279
  items on Office Clipboard, 40
  Outlook
    contacts, 290–291
    names by categories, 294
    tasks, 298
  PowerPoint presentations, 250–256
  a scenario summary, 174–175
  scenarios, 172
visible Help window, always keeping, 47

• W •

Web page hyperlinks, creating (PowerPoint), 246–247
Word
  adding a cover page, 92–93
  artistic text, creating, 115–118
  bold text, 74
  colors, changing, 75–76
  columns, dividing text into, 118–120
  cursor, moving, 30–31
  deleting a cover page, 92–93

drop caps, creating, 115–116
Find and Replace command, 66
Find command, 64–65
finding text, 64–65
font, changing, 72–73
font size, changing, 73–74
footers
  creating, 93–94
  deleting, 95
  even pages, creating unique footer for, 95
  first page, creating unique footer for, 94
  odd pages, creating unique footer for, 95
Format Painter, using, 86
Full Screen Reading view, using, 57
Go To command used to navigate, 63–64
grammar, checking your, 68
headers
  creating, 93–94
  deleting, 95
  even pages, creating unique header for, 95
  first page, creating unique header for, 94
  odd pages, creating unique header for, 95
headings
  collapsing, 59, 61
  defining, 59
  demoting, 60
  expanding, 61
  moving, 60–61
  promoting, 60
  rearranging, 59
highlighting text, 76
Insert tab, 91
inserting new pages, 91–92

Word *(continued)*
  italic text, 74
  justifying text alignment, 76–77
  keyboard shortcuts, 55
  keyboard used to move cursor in, 54–55
  line spacing, adjusting, 77–78
  lists
    converting list items back into text, 79
    customizing, 80
    existing text converted into, 79
    indenting list items, 79
    overview, 78–79
    renumbering numbered lists, 80–81
  mouse scroll wheel used to navigate, 63
  mouse used to move cursor in, 53–54
  mouse used to navigate, 62–63
  navigation of document, 62–64
  Outline view, using, 58–61
  page breaks, inserting, 93
  Page Layout tab, 91
  previewing a document before printing
    orientation, defining, 121
    overview, 120
    page size, defining, 120–121
    with Print Preview, 122–123
    printing the document, 123–124
  proofreading documents, 68
  removing formatting from text, 89–90
  replacing text, 66
  Ruler
    adjusting left and right paragraph margins, 83
    hiding, 82
    indentation defined with, 84
    overview, 82
  scroll bar used to navigate documents, 62–63
  showing formatting marks, 84–85

  spelling, checking your, 66–67
  strikethrough text, 74
  styles, using, 87
  subscripts, 74
  superscripts, 74
  switching between views in documents, 56
  symbols, typing, 69–70
  tables
    aligning text in table cell, 103
    borders, adding, 104–106
    cell borders, deleting, 115
    cell margins, defining, 108–109
    cell spacing, defining, 109–110
    cells, deleting, 114
    coloring all or part of a table, 104
    creating, 96–102
    deleting, 112–115
    entire table, deleting, 112–113
    existing text, creating a table from, 99–102
    formatting and coloring, 102–111
    highlighting rows and columns to create, 96–97
    Insert Table dialog box used to create, 97–98
    merging cells, 110–111
    mouse used to create, 98–99
    resizing columns and rows, 107–108
    rows and columns, deleting, 113
    selecting all or part of a table, 102–103
    sorting, 111–112
    splitting cells, 110–111
    style for, choosing, 106–107
    text organized in, 96–102
  templates
    existing document, creating a document based on, 89
    new document created from, 88–89
    overview, 88

text
  creating, 61
  style, changing, 74
  underlined text, 74
  viewing documents, 55–61
  WordArt, creating, 116–118
WordArt
  graphics (PowerPoint), 232
  page design (Word), 116–118
worms, protection from, 371–372

• X •

X-axis, 181
.xls file extension, 18
.xlsx file extension, 18

• Y •

Y-axis, 181

BUSINESS, CAREERS & PERSONAL FINANCE

0-7645-9847-3

0-7645-2431-3

Also available:
- Business Plans Kit For Dummies
  0-7645-9794-9
- Economics For Dummies
  0-7645-5726-2
- Grant Writing For Dummies
  0-7645-8416-2
- Home Buying For Dummies
  0-7645-5331-3
- Managing For Dummies
  0-7645-1771-6
- Marketing For Dummies
  0-7645-5600-2

- Personal Finance For Dummies
  0-7645-2590-5*
- Resumes For Dummies
  0-7645-5471-9
- Selling For Dummies
  0-7645-5363-1
- Six Sigma For Dummies
  0-7645-6798-5
- Small Business Kit For Dummies
  0-7645-5984-2
- Starting an eBay Business For Dummies
  0-7645-6924-4
- Your Dream Career For Dummies
  0-7645-9795-7

HOME & BUSINESS COMPUTER BASICS

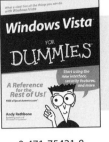

0-470-05432-8

0-471-75421-8

Also available:
- Cleaning Windows Vista For Dummies
  0-471-78293-9
- Excel 2007 For Dummies
  0-470-03737-7
- Mac OS X Tiger For Dummies
  0-7645-7675-5
- MacBook For Dummies
  0-470-04859-X
- Macs For Dummies
  0-470-04849-2
- Office 2007 For Dummies
  0-470-00923-3

- Outlook 2007 For Dummies
  0-470-03830-6
- PCs For Dummies
  0-7645-8958-X
- Salesforce.com For Dummies
  0-470-04893-X
- Upgrading & Fixing Laptops For Dummies
  0-7645-8959-8
- Word 2007 For Dummies
  0-470-03658-3
- Quicken 2007 For Dummies
  0-470-04600-7

FOOD, HOME, GARDEN, HOBBIES, MUSIC & PETS

0-7645-8404-9

0-7645-9904-6

Also available:
- Candy Making For Dummies
  0-7645-9734-5
- Card Games For Dummies
  0-7645-9910-0
- Crocheting For Dummies
  0-7645-4151-X
- Dog Training For Dummies
  0-7645-8418-9
- Healthy Carb Cookbook For Dummies
  0-7645-8476-6
- Home Maintenance For Dummies
  0-7645-5215-5

- Horses For Dummies
  0-7645-9797-3
- Jewelry Making & Beading For Dummies
  0-7645-2571-9
- Orchids For Dummies
  0-7645-6759-4
- Puppies For Dummies
  0-7645-5255-4
- Rock Guitar For Dummies
  0-7645-5356-9
- Sewing For Dummies
  0-7645-6847-7
- Singing For Dummies
  0-7645-2475-5

INTERNET & DIGITAL MEDIA

0-470-04529-9

0-470-04894-8

Also available:
- Blogging For Dummies
  0-471-77084-1
- Digital Photography For Dummies
  0-7645-9802-3
- Digital Photography All-in-One Desk Reference For Dummies
  0-470-03743-1
- Digital SLR Cameras and Photography For Dummies
  0-7645-9803-1
- eBay Business All-in-One Desk Reference For Dummies
  0-7645-8438-3
- HDTV For Dummies
  0-470-09673-X

- Home Entertainment PCs For Dummies
  0-470-05523-5
- MySpace For Dummies
  0-470-09529-6
- Search Engine Optimization For Dummies
  0-471-97998-8
- Skype For Dummies
  0-470-04891-3
- The Internet For Dummies
  0-7645-8996-2
- Wiring Your Digital Home For Dummies
  0-471-91830-X

***** Separate Canadian edition also available**
† Separate U.K. edition also available

Available wherever books are sold. For more information or to order direct: U.S. customers visit www.dummies.com or call 1-877-762-2974.
U.K. customers visit www.wileyeurope.com or call 0800 243407. Canadian customers visit www.wiley.ca or call 1-800-567-4797.

 **WILEY**

SPORTS, FITNESS, PARENTING, RELIGION & SPIRITUALITY

0-471-76871-5

0-7645-7841-3

Also available:
- Catholicism For Dummies
  0-7645-5391-7
- Exercise Balls For Dummies
  0-7645-5623-1
- Fitness For Dummies
  0-7645-7851-0
- Football For Dummies
  0-7645-3936-1
- Judaism For Dummies
  0-7645-5299-6
- Potty Training For Dummies
  0-7645-5417-4
- Buddhism For Dummies
  0-7645-5359-3

- Pregnancy For Dummies
  0-7645-4483-7 †
- Ten Minute Tone-Ups For Dummies
  0-7645-7207-5
- NASCAR For Dummies
  0-7645-7681-X
- Religion For Dummies
  0-7645-5264-3
- Soccer For Dummies
  0-7645-5229-5
- Women in the Bible For Dummies
  0-7645-8475-8

TRAVEL

0-7645-7749-2

0-7645-6945-7

Also available:
- Alaska For Dummies
  0-7645-7746-8
- Cruise Vacations For Dummies
  0-7645-6941-4
- England For Dummies
  0-7645-4276-1
- Europe For Dummies
  0-7645-7529-5
- Germany For Dummies
  0-7645-7823-5
- Hawaii For Dummies
  0-7645-7402-7

- Italy For Dummies
  0-7645-7386-1
- Las Vegas For Dummies
  0-7645-7382-9
- London For Dummies
  0-7645-4277-X
- Paris For Dummies
  0-7645-7630-5
- RV Vacations For Dummies
  0-7645-4442-X
- Walt Disney World & Orlando
  For Dummies
  0-7645-9660-8

GRAPHICS, DESIGN & WEB DEVELOPMENT

0-7645-8815-X

0-7645-9571-7

Also available:
- 3D Game Animation For Dummies
  0-7645-8789-7
- AutoCAD 2006 For Dummies
  0-7645-8925-3
- Building a Web Site For Dummies
  0-7645-7144-3
- Creating Web Pages For Dummies
  0-470-08030-2
- Creating Web Pages All-in-One Desk
  Reference For Dummies
  0-7645-4345-8
- Dreamweaver 8 For Dummies
  0-7645-9649-7

- InDesign CS2 For Dummies
  0-7645-9572-5
- Macromedia Flash 8 For Dummies
  0-7645-9691-8
- Photoshop CS2 and Digital
  Photography For Dummies
  0-7645-9580-6
- Photoshop Elements 4 For Dummies
  0-471-77483-9
- Syndicating Web Sites with RSS Feeds
  For Dummies
  0-7645-8848-6
- Yahoo! SiteBuilder For Dummies
  0-7645-9800-7

NETWORKING, SECURITY, PROGRAMMING & DATABASES

0-7645-7728-X

0-471-74940-0

Also available:
- Access 2007 For Dummies
  0-470-04612-0
- ASP.NET 2 For Dummies
  0-7645-7907-X
- C# 2005 For Dummies
  0-7645-9704-3
- Hacking For Dummies
  0-470-05235-X
- Hacking Wireless Networks
  For Dummies
  0-7645-9730-2
- Java For Dummies
  0-470-08716-1

- Microsoft SQL Server 2005 For Dummies
  0-7645-7755-7
- Networking All-in-One Desk Reference
  For Dummies
  0-7645-9939-9
- Preventing Identity Theft For Dummies
  0-7645-7336-5
- Telecom For Dummies
  0-471-77085-X
- Visual Studio 2005 All-in-One Desk
  Reference For Dummies
  0-7645-9775-2
- XML For Dummies
  0-7645-8845-1